Quiet As It's Kept

SUNY series in Psychoanalysis and Culture
Henry Sussman, editor

Quiet As It's Kept

SHAME, TRAUMA, AND RACE
IN THE NOVELS OF TONI MORRISON

J. Brooks Bouson

STATE UNIVERSITY OF NEW YORK PRESS

Published by
State University of New York Press, Albany

© 2000 State University of New York

Printed in the United States of America

For information, address State University of New York Press,
State University Plaza, Albany, NY, 12246

Production by Cathleen Collins
Marketing by Dana Yanulavich

Library of Congress Cataloging in Publication Data

Bouson, J. Brooks.
    Quiet as it's kept : shame, trauma, and race in the novels of Toni
Morrison / J. Brooks Bouson.
        p.   cm. — (SUNY series in psychoanalysis and culture)
    Includes bibliographical references and index.
    ISBN 0-7914-4423-6 (alk. paper). — ISBN 0-7914-4424-4 (pbk. :
alk. paper)
    1. Morrison, Toni—Knowledge—Psychology.   2. Psychoanalysis and
literature—United States—History—20th century.   3. Women and
literature—United States—History—20th century.   4. Psychological
fiction, American—History and criticism.   5. Afro-American women in
literature.   6. Afro-Americans in literature.   7. Psychic trauma in
literature.   8. Shame in literature.   9. Race in literature.
I. Title.   II. Series.
PS3563.08749Z57   1999
813'.54—dc21   99-16422
                                                             CIP

10   9   8   7   6   5   4   3   2   1

To Members of My Family, Friends of My Mind

Contents

Preface

To Nobel-prize winning author Toni Morrison, "declarations that racism is irrelevant, over or confined to the past are premature fantasies." Describing herself as living in a society in which African Americans have had to "bear the brunt of everybody else's contempt," Morrison uses her art to call attention to the historical and continuing plight of black Americans. "Quiet as it's kept," which is one of Morrison's favorite African-American expressions, is a phrase used by someone who is about to reveal what is presumed to be a secret. Morrison brings to light secrets in her novels—public and collective secrets—as she deals with what has aptly been called the "dirty business" of racism. As Morrison exposes to public view sensitive race matters, she presents jarring depictions of the trauma of slavery and the horrors of racist oppression and black-on-black violence. She also repeatedly, if not obsessively, stages scenes of inter- and intraracial shaming in her fiction as she focuses attention on the damaging impact of white racist practices and learned cultural shame on the collective African-American experience and as she investigates the loaded issues of internalized racism and the color-caste hierarchy in her depictions of the class tensions and divisions within the African-American community.

My aim in the following pages is to offer an in-depth analysis of the painful and shameful race matters that pervade Morrison's novels. To provide a framework for my approach, which draws on recent psychoanalytic and psychiatric investigations of shame and trauma, I begin with an outline of shame and trauma theory and a discussion of the shaping influence of shame and trauma on Morrison's fiction. As I devote the subsequent chapters of this study to a chronological and close reading of Morrison's fiction, I concentrate on Morrison's repetitive but also evolving novelistic representations of shame and trauma. In each chapter, I also analyze the emotional demands Morrison's fiction makes on readers by looking at the lively and often contentious critical conversations her novels have generated. Quiet as it's kept, Morrison's novels force readers into uncomfortable confrontations with the dirty business of racism. Yet while those who have studied shame and trauma often report on the tendency of people to turn away from the shameful and traumatic, Morrison, in her intellectually fascinating but also emotionally disturbing works of art, draws her readers into her fictional worlds, urging them to understand and also to respond viscerally to the painful race matters that she bears witness to in her art.

The fact that academic critics have sometimes admitted that there can be something unsettling, if not discomforting, about the scholarly study of racism points to the difficulty of the work I have undertaken in my investigation of shame, trauma, and race in Morrison's novels. During the time I have spent working on—and struggling with—this project, I have been heartened by those who have expressed an interest in my approach to Morrison's fiction. I want to acknowledge here my gratitude to my colleagues at Loyola University—in particular to Timothy Austin, James Biester, and Suzanne Gossett—and to my undergraduate and graduate students, including Lisa Dresdner, who assisted me in the early stages of my research on this book. Thanks are also due to Loyola University for granting me a research leave during the early stages of my work on this project. I also would like to thank Jean Wyatt for her kind words of encouragement, and I especially want to express my gratitude to Joseph Adamson, whose scholarship on shame and literature helped inspire this work and whose generous words of interest and support urged me on as I researched and wrote this book. Finally, I want to express my heartfelt thanks to James Peltz, the editor at SUNY Press, for his warm and generous support of this project, and to Cathleen Collins, who ably saw this book through production. An earlier version of the chapter on *The Bluest Eye* appeared in *Scenes of Shame: Psychoanalysis, Shame, and Writing*, edited by Joseph Adamson and Hilary Clark (SUNY Press, 1999). I am grateful for permission to reuse this material, which I have revised for this study.

1

"Speaking the Unspeakable"

SHAME, TRAUMA, AND MORRISON'S FICTION

Ann duCille, in her analysis of what she calls "the occult of true black womanhood," expresses concern about the "critical stampede" that has been attracted to black women. "Today there is so much interest in black women that I have begun to think of myself as a kind of sacred text. Not me personally, of course, but me as black woman, the other. Within the modern academy, racial and gender alterity has become a hot commodity that has claimed black women as its principal signifier" (83, 81). "[P]olitically correct, intellectually popular, and commercially precious," the black woman writer is constructed as the exotic, idealized Other, according to duCille (84). Toni Morrison, who published her first novel in 1970 and was awarded the Nobel Prize in Literature a scant twenty-three years later in 1993, has attracted the kind of critical stampede duCille describes. If Morrison was sometimes chastised by early reviewers for not transcending the "limiting classification 'black woman writer,'" among contemporary commentators "it has become almost unimaginable or unspeakable to mention the struggles that marked" Morrison's early career as a novelist (Peterson 462, 461). Now something of a sacred text herself, Morrison has "entered superstardom," becoming known as "*the* American and African American (woman) writer to reckon with" (Peterson 464). And just as Morrison's seven novels—*The Bluest Eye, Sula, Song of Solomon, Tar Baby, Beloved, Jazz,* and *Paradise*—have attracted intense critical scrutiny, so Morrison, herself, has been subjected to the scrutinizing gaze of her many interviewers.

"I see them select or make up details to add to the fixed idea of me they came in the door with—the thing or person they want me to be," Morrison has remarked of the people who have interviewed her over the years (Naylor 215). Portrayed variously by her interviewers, Morrison has been constructed as a romanticized exotic—if not mythic—black artist figure. She has been described as having a magnetic personality and a rich, compelling voice; as a moody and prickly person; and as a warm and amusing individual. One interviewer, who describes Morrison as a "larger than life" woman who has a "powerful way" of fixing people in her gaze and transfixing them with her voice, comments that Morrison "does not so much give an interview as perform one, in a silken voice that can purr like a saxophone or erupt like brass" (Fussell 280). "Morrison's voice recalls the rich sound of our best preachers," writes another. "She is, by turns, warm or wry as she reflects on the wonder of it all. . . . She is sister, teacher, aunt. She speaks with wisdom" (Washington 234). Another interviewer describes how in her conversation Morrison can rapidly "switch from raging about violence in the United States to joyfully skewering the hosts of the trash TV talk shows through which she confesses to channel-surfing late in the afternoon, assuming her work is done" (Schappell 86). Yet another interviewer remarks that Morrison is an enjoyable luncheon companion—"a woman of subversive jokes, gossip and surprising bits of self-revelation (the laureate unwinds to Court TV and soap operas)" (Dreifus 73).

If Morrison often plays to—or skillfully plays—her interviewers, she is, as her descriptions of her writing reveal, a driven woman, a woman who lives intensely within the private world of her writer's imagination and often finds her characters better company than the people who surround her. Writing to her is a "compulsion"; it is like "talking deep" within herself; it is an "extraordinary way of thinking and feeling" (Stepto 24, Tate 169, Watkins 45). An author who writes under a kind of necessity and who has insisted from the beginning of her writing career that art is political (*Black Creation* 3–4), Morrison has viewed part of her cultural and literary task as a writer to bear witness to the plight of black Americans. "[Q]uiet as it's kept much of our business, our existence here, has been grotesque. It really has," she has commented (Jones and Vinson 181). "My people are being devoured" (LeClair 121). One of her central concerns is "how to survive *whole* in a world where we are all of us, in some measure, *victims* of *something*" and "in no position to do a thing about it" (Bakerman 40). Indeed, she deliberately puts her characters "in situations of great duress and pain," and even in "grotesque" situations, in order to "know who they are." Through her "push towards the abyss," as Morrison remarks, she can discover why some people survive and some do not (Jones and Vinson 180–81). Writing provides Morrison with a "safe" place in which she can "think the unthinkable" (Bakerman 39) as she confronts the effects of shame and trauma on the lives of African Americans.

Despite Morrison's unrelenting and unflinching presentation of painful and shameful race matters in her novels, commentators have repeatedly focused on what some have called the magic realism of her novels, or they have placed her fiction in the context of a black feminist aesthetic or black oral tradition, or they have uncovered the black folk or communal values embodied in her work. Just as race matters, according to Morrison, remain unspeakable in American culture—and this despite the unending talk and academic theorizing about race—so race matters remain largely unspoken in the critical conversation that surrounds Morrison's works. Even those critics who have focused their attention on the social-psychological and historical-political concerns voiced in Morrison's fiction have tended to minimize—or even ignore—the sensitive, and at times painful, race matters that pervade and drive Morrison's novelistic narratives.

Insistently, Morrison focuses on inter- and intraracial violence in her fiction, even at the potential cost of alienating, or even unsettling or hurting, some of her readers. But because Morrison's novels are carefully designed and make self-conscious use of folklore and myths, critics have tended to avoid or downplay the violent, even perverse, subject matter of Morrison's novels. Dramatizing the physical and psychological abuse visited on African Americans in white America, Morrison shows that, as some trauma theorists have argued, trauma can result not only from a "single assault" or "discrete event," but also from a "constellation of life's experiences," a "prolonged exposure to danger," or a "continuing pattern of abuse" (Erikson 457). Morrison focuses not only on the collective memories of the trauma of slavery in works like *Beloved*, but also on the horrors of the postbellum years and of racist and urban violence in works like *Song of Solomon* and *Jazz*. She is also intent on portraying the trauma of defective or abusive parenting or relationships and also the black-on-black violence that exists within the African-American community. In Cholly's rape of his daughter, Pecola, in *The Bluest Eye*; in Eva Peace's setting fire to her son, Plum, in *Sula*; in Sethe's slitting her infant daughter's throat in *Beloved*; in Guitar's attempted murder of his friend, Milkman Dead, in *Song of Solomon*; in Joe Trace's hunting down and shooting his young lover, Dorcas, in *Jazz*; and in the Ruby men's massacre of the Convent women in *Paradise*, Morrison dramatizes what one commentator has aptly described as the "oppressor in the next room, or in the same bed, or no farther away than across the street" (D. Johnson 6). Morrison represents the speechless terror of trauma in recurring scenes of dissociated violence—vivid and highly visual scenes in which her characters experience violence from a detached perspective. And she also conveys the haunting and driven quality of traumatic and humiliated memory as she depicts the "rememories"—that is, spontaneous recurrences of the past— that plague her characters. Presenting jarring depictions of child and spousal abuse, incest and infanticide, self-mutilation and self-immolation, suicide and murder, Morrison's novels serve an important cultural function as they reflect and reflect on the incomprehensible violence that pervades the lives of many African Americans in our "catastrophic age," an age in which, it has been argued, trauma may "provide the very link between cultures" (Caruth 11).

Describing herself as living in "a present that wishes both to exploit and deny the pervasiveness of racism" and in a society in which African Americans have had to "bear the brunt of everybody else's contempt" ("Introduction" xiv, Angelo 256), Morrison also focuses attention on the ubiquity and complexity of shame in the African-American experience. Repeatedly, if not obsessively, Morrison stages scenes of shame in her fiction: scenes in which her characters, when they are looked at or treated with contempt by the shaming other, experience the inarticulateness and emotional paralysis of intense shame. Morrison dramatizes the painful sense of exposure that accompanies the single shame event and also the devastating effect of chronic shame on her characters' sense of individual and social identity, describing their self-loathing and self-contempt, their feelings that they are, in some essential way, inferior, flawed, and/or dirty. In *Beloved*, for example, Morrison depicts how Sethe is "dirtied" by slavery and schoolteacher's pseudoscientific racism; in *The Bluest Eye*, how Pecola's parentally transmitted shame is intensified by her inability to meet white standards of beauty in a culture that views black as "ugly"; in *Song of Solomon*, how Milkman Dead is weighed down by the "shit" of inherited family and racial shame; in *Jazz*, how Joe Trace is shamed by the "dirty" and "sloven" Wild, whom he believes to be his "secret mother"; in *Sula*, how Sula, who claims that she likes her "own dirt," hides her abiding sense of shame under a defiant display of shamelessness; and in *Paradise*, how the people of Ruby are shaped by their collective, and humiliating, memory of the Disallowing: the "contemptuous dismissal" of their dark-skinned forebears by light-skinned blacks. Mired in shame, Morrison's novels deal not only with the affects of shame, contempt, and disgust, but also with the feeling traps of shame-shame (being ashamed about shame in an endless, and paralyzing, spiral of feelings) and shame-rage (the inevitable and self-perpetuating sequence of emotions from shame to humiliated fury back to shame).

In novel after novel, as Morrison draws attention to the damaging impact of white racist practices and learned cultural shame on the collective African-American experience, she points to the shaping and shaming power of corrosive racist stereotypes and discursive repertoires in the construction of African-American identities as racially inferior and stigmatized. Investigating the class tensions and divisions within the African-American community, Morrison deals with the sensitive issues of internalized racism and the color-caste hierarchy as she repeatedly brings together dark-skinned, lower-class and light-skinned, middle-class characters, such as Pecola and Geraldine in *The Bluest Eye*, Son and Jadine in *Tar Baby*, and Pilate and

Ruth in *Song of Solomon*, or as she in *Paradise* focuses on the color pre-judice of the dark-skinned people of Ruby toward light-skinned blacks. If as a black writer dealing with race matters Morrison sometimes has found herself struggling with internalized racism as she works with and through a language that promotes, as she has described it, the "dismissive 'othering' of people" (*Playing in the Dark* x), she also deliberately, and with dialogic intent, invokes the shaming race- and class-inflected discourse of dirt and defile-ment, or the shaming language of the racial insult and slur, or shaming racist stereotypes, like that of the sexually promiscuous black woman and the law-less and potentially violent black underclass male. Just as hegemonic dis-course has constructed blackness as a sign of a fundamental and stigmatizing difference, so Morrison, in a classic countershaming strategy, repeatedly constructs whiteness as a sign of pathological difference in her novels. While Morrison is also intent on representing black pride in her novels—such as Milkman's discovery of his "golden" racial heritage in the folk tale of the flying African in *Song of Solomon*, or Violet and Joe Trace's sense of expan-sive black pride and self-ownership as they train-dance their way to black Harlem in *Jazz*, or the pride of the people of Ruby in their utopian all-black town in *Paradise*—she also shows how the humiliated memories and experi-ences that result from living in a racist society reverberate in the lives of her characters.

While in Morrison's novels we find evidence of the desire to bear wit-ness to the shame and trauma that exist in the lives of African Americans, in Morrison's insistent aestheticizing of shame and violence, we also find evi-dence of the reactive desire to cover up or repair the racial wounds she has exposed. Countering the depictions of the white oppressor and the black oppressor in the next room, Morrison's novels also enact a reparative urge in their dramatizations of the potentially healing power of the sense of safety and connection offered by the African-American community and in their antishaming and restitutive fantasies of what Morrison calls the African-American ancestors: that is, "timeless" elder figures who are "benevolent, instructive, and protective" (Morrison, "Rootedness" 343). Morrison, then, seems bent on effecting a cultural cure both through the artistic rendering and narrative reconstruction of the shame and trauma story and also through the fictional invocation of the protective power of the black folk community and the timeless ancestor figures. But the precariousness of that cure is revealed not only by her repeated depictions of the intergenerational trans-mission of victimization and shame but also by her constant restagings of familial and cultural scenes of shame and trauma in each successive novel as she confronts in her fiction the historical legacy of slavery and the persisting conflicts and challenges that continue to haunt African Americans in the race-divided American society where race still matters.

The Impact of Trauma and Shame on the Individual

As Morrison shows that race matters not only in the collective cultural experience of African Americans and in the construction of group identity but also in the experience of the individual, she represents, with almost clinical precision, what has, in recent years, become of interest to psychiatry and psychoanalysis: the impact of shame and trauma on the individual psyche and the family structure. Unlike traditional psychoanalytic inquiries which have tended to ignore the importance of social forces on the construction of group and personal identity,[1] recent investigations of the impact of trauma and shame on the individual as well as sociological inquiries into the ubiquity of shame and pride in daily social interactions can help bring into bold relief the effect of racist practices on African-American identity. A race-cognizant application of shame and trauma theory—which has mainly studied the painful effects of shame and trauma on individuals and families within the dominant white culture—shows that African Americans have been forced to deal not only with individual and/or family shame and trauma but also with cultural shame and racial trauma as they are designated as the racially inferior and stigmatized Other and thus become the targets of white discrimination and violence. An indispensable addition to the analysis of sensitive race matters, psychoanalytic and psychiatric accounts of the impact of shame and trauma on the individual provide an invaluable and necessary starting point for an analysis of Morrison's representations of shame and trauma in her fiction.

Trauma and the Individual

"The ordinary response to atrocities," writes psychiatrist Judith Herman, "is to banish them from consciousness. Certain violations of the social compact are too terrible to utter aloud: this is the meaning of the word *unspeakable*" (*Trauma* 1). Although awareness of horrible events intermittently penetrates public consciousness, it is seldom for very long. Not only do "[d]enial, repression, and dissociation operate on a social as well as an individual level," but the study of trauma itself "has a curious history—one of episodic amnesia" (*Trauma* 2, 7).[2]

Freud—by establishing within psychoanalysis the theory that sexual trauma is a product of fantasy—effectively denied the historical reality of traumatic occurrences, and psychoanalysts who followed the classical Freudian model "sought the determinants of the unconscious meaning" of trauma "in pathogenic fantasies rather than in shattering facts" (Ulman 62). But the shortcomings of the classical psychoanalytic model of trauma have become apparent to recent psychiatric and psychoanalytic investigators like Judith Herman, Bessel van der Kolk, Dori Laub, and Elizabeth Waites who find the source of the dissociated memories that haunt the trauma survivor not in repressed feelings and fantasies but in actual events.

Involving "threats to life or bodily integrity, or a close personal encounter with violence and death," traumatic events confront individuals "with the extremities of helplessness and terror" (Herman, *Trauma* 33). In such threatening situations, the sympathetic nervous system is aroused, causing the endangered person to feel a rush of adrenaline and enter a state of alertness. Traumatic responses occur when both resistance and escape are impossible, overwhelming the individual's self-defense system. Because traumatic events produce "profound and lasting changes in physiological arousal, emotion, cognition, and memory," the traumatized individual "may experience intense emotion but without clear memory of the event, or may remember everything in detail but without emotion" (Herman, *Trauma* 34).

When actual experiences are so overwhelming that they "cannot be integrated into existing mental frameworks," they are "dissociated, later to return intrusively as fragmented sensory or motoric experiences" (van der Kolk and van der Hart 447). Dissociation, rather than repression, is common to the trauma experience. Indeed, "Many trauma survivors report that they automatically are removed from the scene; they look at it from a distance or disappear altogether, leaving other parts of their personality to suffer and store the overwhelming experience" (van der Kolk and van der Hart 437). Paradoxically, situations of extreme and inescapable danger may evoke a state of "detached calm" in which events are still registered in awareness but seem "disconnected from their ordinary meanings." These altered states of consciousness can be viewed as "one of nature's small mercies, a protection against unbearable pain." Not unlike hypnotic trance states, these detached states of consciousness "share the same features of surrender of voluntary action, suspension of initiative and critical judgment, subjective detachment or calm, enhanced perception of imagery, altered sensation, including numbness and analgesia, and distortion of reality, including depersonalization, derealization, and change in the sense of time" (Herman, *Trauma* 42–43).

In the aftermath of traumatic occurrences, explains Herman, individuals find themselves "caught between the extremes of amnesia or of reliving the trauma, between floods of intense, overwhelming feeling and arid states of no feeling at all" (*Trauma* 47). As the intrusive symptoms of reliving the trauma lessen, numbing or constrictive symptoms—feelings of alienation, disconnection, inner deadness—come to predominate (*Trauma* 48–49). Because traumatic experiences become encoded in an abnormal type of memory that spontaneously erupts into consciousness in the form of flashbacks and nightmares, and because even apparently insignificant reminders can provoke these memories, what would otherwise seem a safe environment can end up feeling dangerous to survivors (*Trauma* 37).

While the "social context into which human babies are born relies on the family as a primary buffer against trauma," writes Elizabeth Waites, the "often correct assumption that families protect the best interests of children is so expedient that it often becomes a barrier against recognizing the traumatic potential of families themselves" (69). In abusive families—in which parent-child interactions may mingle protective with brutal behavior or in which punishment may predictably follow indulgence, or in which the sole predictable thing about the abuse is that it is inevitable—traumas that are dangerous, if not life-threatening, are repeatedly inflicted and rarely acknowledged as mistakes (68–69). The disruptive symptoms of post-traumatic stress in children can have a significant impact not only on developing competencies but also on character development, and thus, the attempt to recover from childhood trauma can be made more difficult by the complex ways in which responses to trauma become woven into the structure of the personality (64–65). Because victimization is often vigorously denied by both the perpetrator and the victim, and because victim-blaming is a common individual and even socially institutionalized response, the childhood victim can develop a scapegoat identity or incorporate self-punitive behavior into his or her self-concept (68). Even adult victims who are psychologically healthy prior to an assault commonly suffer disturbances not only in self-regulation but also in self-esteem and self-representation as a result of trauma (104–05).

Survivors of childhood and adult trauma—who feel not only "unsafe in their bodies" but also that their emotions and thinking are "out of control"—are "condemned to a diminished life, tormented by memory and bounded by helplessness and fear" (Herman, *Trauma* 160, 49). Confronting individuals with "the futility of putting up resistance, the impossibility of being able to affect the outcome of events," trauma shatters "assumptions about predictability and mastery" and thus "inflicts a 'narcissistic wound to the fabric of the self'" (van der Kolk, "Foreword" ix). Because a "secure sense of connection with caring people is the foundation of personality development," traumatic events, in calling fundamental human relationships into question, can "shatter the construction of the self that is formed and sustained in relation to others" (Herman, *Trauma* 52, 51). Moreover, trauma can affect autobiographical memory: that is, "the integration of particular events into a coherent, temporally organized, and self-referential pattern." The distortion of autobiographical memory caused by trauma can have subtle or profound effects not only on "self-presentation and self-representation" but also on the "integration of self-experience" into the coherent pattern that is phenomenologically experienced as a "stable personal identity" (Waites 29, 31). Trauma affects not only the individual but also, as studies of those victimized by the Holocaust have shown, victim-survivor populations, and the effects of trauma can be transmitted intergenerationally (see, e.g., Danieli).

Shame and the Individual

Like the study of trauma, the study of shame has, until recent times, been largely neglected. Indeed, it is suggestive that shame, which induces secrecy and a hiding response, is an "only recently rediscovered feeling state" (S. Miller xi). Since 1971, "there has been a rapid increase in the literature on the psychology of shame, thus redressing a long-standing neglect of the subject," writes shame theorist Helen Block Lewis. "Once clinicians' attention is called to shame, it becomes apparent that, although it is easily ignored, shame is ubiquitous" ("Preface" xi).[3]

This neglect of shame, in part, can be attributed to "a prevailing sexist attitude in science, which pays less attention to nurturance than to aggression" and thus "depreciates the shame that inheres in 'loss of love'" (Helen Lewis, "Preface" xi). Because of the Freudian view that attachment is regressive and that women are shame-prone as a result of their need to conceal their "genital deficiency," there is an implicit hierarchy in classical psychoanalytic discourse, which views shame as preoedipal and guilt as oedipal (Helen Lewis, "Role of Shame" 31). To Freudians, guilt was the "more *worthy* affective experience" compared to shame, which was viewed as "the developmentally more primitive affect" (Andrew Morrison, *Shame* 5). Shame, then, until recently, has had a "stigma" attached to it so that "there has been a shame about studying shame in the psychoanalytic and psychotherapeutic fields" (Goldberg x). But with the movement away from the classical Freudian oedipal conflict-guilt model of personality and the intensifying focus on the narcissistically wounded and shame-ridden self—beginning in the 1970s and with increased interest in the 1980s and 1990s—shame has become the subject of psychoanalytic scrutiny, most notably in the work of affect and shame theorists like Silvan Tomkins, Helen Block Lewis, Donald Nathanson, Andrew Morrison, Gershen Kaufman, and Léon Wurmser.

Contrary to Freud, as recent psychoanalytic investigators have shown, "there is no concrete evidence that shame precedes guilt in development"; moreover, shame "exists equally strongly in men and women" (Helen Lewis, "Role of Shame" 31, Andrew Morrison, *Shame* 13). An inherited, physiological response, shame is an innate affect, hardwired in the brain, and there also appears to be a biological, genetic disposition to experience *extreme* forms of shame, which may begin with "a *constitutional* predisposition to overstimulation" (Goldberg 41). Pointing to the biological sources of this painful emotion, shame investigators argue that one can observe a proto or primitive form of shame behavior in infant-parent interactions—manifested in such infant behaviors as shyness, gaze aversion, hiding the face, and stranger anxiety (see, e.g., Nathanson, "Timetable"). One likely reason for the "inarticulateness" of shame is that the "brain is arranged so that key aspects of emotional life . . . can operate largely independent of thought" and thus "emotional input is experienced before cognition" (Goldberg 41). Moreover, the "special affinity" of shame for autonomic reactions, such as blushing, sweating, and increased heart rate, "suggests that it is an emergency response to threatened affectional ties" (Helen Lewis, "Introduction" 16–17).

An intensely painful experience, shame "follows a moment of *exposure*," an uncovering that "reveals aspects of the self of a peculiarly sensitive, intimate, and vulnerable nature" (Nathanson, "Timetable" 4). Shame sufferers feel in some profound way inferior to others—they perceive themselves as deeply flawed and defective or as bad individuals or as failures—and this internalized shame script grows out of early shaming interactions with parents or significant others. Shamed individuals may experience "a brief moment of painful feeling"—a jolt or jab of pain—followed by a compulsive and often repetitive "replaying" of the shaming scene, often in scenarios in which shamed individuals imagine themselves responding to the shaming incident in a more satisfactory way; or they may experience "painful confusion and unwanted physical manifestations," such as blushing and rapid heartbeat, and feel "at a loss for words and also at a loss for thoughts" (Scheff, "Shame-Rage Spiral" 110–11). Shame, then, is a disorganizing experience, and it can leave individuals feeling "overwhelmed" and "small, helpless, and childish." In describing their feelings, shamed individuals often voice common shame fantasies: that they could "'crawl through a hole' or 'sink through the floor' or 'die' with shame" (Helen Lewis, "Introduction" 19). Shame is not only a "quickly spreading and flooding affect," but it also can induce feelings of "shame about shame" (Wurmser, *Mask* 55).

At once an interpersonal and intrapsychic experience, shame derives from the shame sufferer's "vicarious experience of the other's scorn," and, indeed, central to the shame experience is the "self-in-the-eyes-of-the-other" (Helen Lewis, "Introduction" 15). At the core of shame, writes Léon Wurmser, is the "conviction of one's *unlovability*" because of an inherent sense that the self is "weak, dirty, and defective" (*Mask* 92, 93). In the classic shame scenario, in which the "eye is the organ of shame par excellence," the individual feels exposed and humiliated—*looked at* with contempt for being inferior, flawed, or dirty—and thus wants to hide or disappear (Wurmser, "Shame" 67). Fear of visual exposure, as Wurmser explains, leads to the wish to disappear as the person one has shown oneself to be, or to be viewed as different than one is (*Mask* 232). Shame-imbued people may suffer shame vulnerability—that is, "a sensitivity to, and readiness for, shame"—and shame anxiety, which is "evoked by the imminent danger of unexpected exposure, humiliation, and rejection" (Andrew Morrison, *Shame* 14, Wurmser, *Mask* 49).

Experiencing a heightened sense of self-consciousness, shame sufferers may feel inhibited, inferior, incompetent, dirty, defective, scorned and ridiculed by others. Shame, and its related feeling states—chagrin, embarrassment, mortification, lowered self-esteem, disgrace, and humiliation—can lead to withdrawal or avoidant behaviors, which reflect the desire of shamed individuals to conceal or hide themselves in an attempt to protect against feelings of exposure. Other classic defenses against shame function to help shamed individuals recover from painful feelings of exposure and helplessness. For example, "feeling weak may be 'repaired' by arrogance, self-glorification, aggressiveness," and the "powerful, surging" feeling of anger may work to temporarily overcome the "helpless feelings of being disregarded and insignificant" that often accompany shame (Goldberg 69). Many expressions of rage can be understood as attempts "to rid the self of shame," while contempt represents "an attempt to 'relocate' the shame experience from within the self into another person" (Andrew Morrison, *Shame* 14). Other defenses against shame include the defiance of shamelessness—that is, the deliberate flaunting of one's shame—and turning the tables in the attack-other script, in which the shamed individual actively shames and humiliates others (see Wurmser, *Mask* 257–64, Nathanson, *Shame and Pride* 360–73).

Describing the "natural, inevitable sequence from shame into humiliated fury and retaliation and thence into guilt for 'unjust' or 'irrational' rage," Helen Block Lewis has called shame a "feeling trap" ("Introduction" 2). Drawing on Lewis's work, Thomas Scheff and Suzanne Retzinger point to the potentially lethal consequences of the shame-shame or shame-rage feeling traps. A feeling trap, as they explain, "involves a series of loops of shame (being ashamed of being ashamed), which causes further shame, which can continue indefinitely," or it involves a self-perpetuating chain of emotions in which unacknowledged shame leads to anger which, in turn, results in further shame (104–05). Moreover, when an individual has emotional reactions to his or her own emotions and to those of another person, both individuals can become mired in a feeling trap—"a *triple spiral* of shame and rage *between* and *within* interactants," which, in turn, can lead to the emotional impasse of an interminable conflict (126). "Shame-rage spirals may be brief, lasting a matter of minutes, or they can last for hours, days, or a lifetime, as bitter hatred or resentment" (127). Moreover, shame-anger chains, according to Scheff and Retzinger, can endure "longer than a lifetime, since hatred can be transmitted from generation to generation in the form of racial, religious, and national prejudice" (105).

Cultural Shame and the Deference-Emotion System

"Shame is a multidimensional, multilayered experience," observes Gershen Kaufman. "While first of all an *individual* phenomenon experienced in some form and to some degree by every person, shame is equally a *family* phenomenon and a *cultural* phenomenon. It is reproduced within families, and each culture has its own distinct sources as well as targets of shame" (*Shame* 191). While American society "*is* a shame-based culture . . . shame is *hidden*. There is shame about shame and so it remains under strict taboo" (*Shame* 32).

Shame, which is often called the "master emotion" (see, e.g., Scheff, *Bloody Revenge* 53–54), has profound consequences for individuals in their daily interactions with others. Indeed, "Shame and pride seem to be an almost continuous part of human existence not only in crises but also in the slightest of social contacts," according to Thomas Scheff. Cross-cultural investigations of politeness behavior suggest "the universality of shame" in revealing how cultures "provide elaborate means for protecting *face*, that is, protecting against embarrassment and humiliation" (*Bloody Revenge* 51). In daily social interactions, states of shame and pride "almost always depend on the level of deference accorded a person: pride arises from deferential treatment by others ("respect"), and shame from lack of deference ("disrespect"). Gestures that imply respect or disrespect, together with the emotional response they generate, make up the *deference/emotion system*, which exerts a powerful influence on human behavior" (Scheff, Retzinger, Ryan 184–85). Stuart Schneiderman's observation that the "closest approximation" in American history to having "'no face' is being black in America" points to the significance of issues surrounding pride and shame and the deference-emotion system in the social formation of African-American identity (124). In a similar way, shame theorist Andrew Morrison, in his discussion of what he calls "learned cultural shame" over feelings of being different, remarks, "The African American people, often judged by white American society as inferior, have endured the stigma of being different since their history on this continent began. The sense of difference and inferiority imposed by the dominant culture leads to internalization of that judgment by the affected group" (*Culture of Shame* 35).

Race Matters:
Shame, Trauma, and the African-American Experience

Just as individuals who suffer from shame may struggle with the conflicting need to "confess" and "retain" the shameful secret and just as trauma survivors seem driven by "the twin imperatives of truth-telling and secrecy" (Goldberg 169, Herman, *Trauma* 1), so there has been a corresponding cultural impulse to publicly reveal and conceal the humiliations and traumas endured by oppressed groups like African Americans. Even as the process of recovering the silenced black voices in American history and culture goes forward and even as racism and the social construction of African-American identities have become the subject of intense scholarly scrutiny, so there is a corresponding countermovement in the American culture to deny or mini-mize the continuing significance of race and the historical legacy of racism and racist oppression on the cultural memory and collective experience of contemporary black Americans.

Describing the historical traumas suffered by African Americans, black psychiatrist James Comer argues that the trauma of slavery was com-pounded by the fact that children born into slavery were "socialized and developed in ways that defined them as inferior" (154). "Snatch a free man from his own culture, enslave, exclude, degrade and abuse him; and his sense of worth, value and adequacy will be destroyed, reduced or under constant and severe challenge," writes Comer (165).[4] After slavery was abolished, the dominant white culture continued its tactics of physically terrorizing and psychically shaming black Americans. African Americans "found themselves controlled by a government and an economy run by openly racist whites. . . . [U]ntil 1915, more than 90 per cent of the black population lived in the most restrictive and oppressive section of the country, and over 50 per cent of all blacks lived as serfs." And until the 1940s, "[f]raud, theft, economic reprisal and open violence against blacks existed." Between 1882 and 1935, more than 3,000 blacks were lynched and between 1882 and 1955, over 4,700 blacks died in mob action. While the "motives for violence were mixed," the underlying purpose was to maintain white privilege (165–66). In Comer's account, African Americans carry with them collective memories not only of white antagonism and abuse but also of the sound of "contemp-tuous white laughter" in the sight of the tragedy of black life (170).

In a similar way, Cornel West describes the impact of racist violence and racial contempt on the collective historical experience of African Americans. "One of the best ways to instill fear in people is to terrorize them," com-ments West. "Yet this fear is best sustained by convincing them that their bodies are ugly, their intellect is inherently underdeveloped, their culture is less civilized, and their future warrants less concern than that of other peoples. Two hundred and forty-four years of slavery and nearly a century of insti-tutionalized terrorism in the form of segregation, lynchings, and second-class citizenship in America were aimed at precisely this devaluation of black people." Although ultimately this "white supremacist venture was . . . a relative failure," the white endeavor to dehumanize blacks "has left its toll in the psychic scars and personal wounds now inscribed in the souls of black folk" (122–23). Also remarking on the pain of racial wounding, bell hooks discusses the association in the black imagination of whiteness with terror. "All black people in the United States, irrespective of their class status or politics," she writes, "live with the possibility that they will be terrorized by whiteness" (*Killing Rage* 46).

The comments of hooks and West point to the psychic scars and personal wounds suffered by African Americans in the race-divided American society. Historically treated with disrespect—indeed, viewed by the dominant white culture as shamed objects of contempt—African Americans bear the wounds of the intergenerationally transmitted racial shame described in Comer's account of how blacks carry with them the sound of "contemptuous white laughter" and also in W. E. B. Du Bois's well-known turn-of-the-century description of the "double-consciousness" of African Americans, "this sense of always looking at one's self through the eyes of others, of measuring one's soul by the tape of a world that looks on in amused contempt and pity" (9). Du Bois's account of the double-consciousness of African Americans derived from viewing the self through the eyes of contemptuous others recalls Helen Block Lewis's description of the accentuated sense of self-consciousness experienced by the shamed individual. Explaining that the shame experience is "directly about the self, which is the focus of a negative evaluation," Lewis writes, "Because the self is the focus of awareness in shame, 'identity' imagery is usually evoked. At the same time that this identity imagery is registering as one's own experience, there is also vivid imagery of the self in the other's eyes. This creates a 'doubleness of experience,' which is characteristic of shame" ("Shame" 107).

The black Antillean psychiatrist Frantz Fanon provides a vivid account of the shame sufferer's doubleness of experience in his remarks on the black feeling of inferiority that "comes into being through the other" and in his description of the experience of being seen as an object of contempt—as a "Dirty nigger!"—in the eyes of whites (110, 109). Viewed through the shaming gaze of whites, "Negroes are savages, brutes, illiterates" (117). Fanon describes his feeling of being "dissected under white eyes, the only real eyes," and of having his body "given back" to him "sprawled out, distorted" (116, 113). The fact that he wants to hide from the gaze of whites—"I slip into corners, I remain silent, I strive for anonymity, for invisibility"—reveals his reactive desire to defend against feelings of shameful exposure. "Shame. Shame and self-contempt. Nausea. When people like me, they tell me it is in spite of my color. When they dislike me, they point out that it is not because of my color. Either way, I am locked into the infernal circle," writes Fanon as he, in recounting the racist myths that undergird the cultural construction of blackness, reports not only on the experience of being treated as the racially inferior and stigmatized Other but also on the process of the "internalization—or, better, the epidermalization"—of a sense of inferiority (116, 11).

Describing the black shame that arises out of internalized racism—that is, the absorption by African Americans of "negative feelings and attitudes about blackness held by white people"—bell hooks similarly observes that many blacks see themselves as inferior, as "lacking" in comparison to whites and that they overvalue whiteness and "negate the value of blackness" (*Killing Rage* 186, 148, 158). The accounts of Fanon and hooks reveal not only that the "deliberate shaming" of an individual can be used as a "severe punishment" (Helen Lewis, "Introduction" 1–2), but also that shame sufferers, in internalizing the disgust and contempt of the shaming other, can develop a deep sense of self-hatred and self-contempt. Wurmser's description of how basic shame—the inherent sense that the self is weak, defective, and dirty—leads to a deep sense of "pain, hurt, woundedness" (*Mask* 93) provides a compelling description of racial shame: the profound hurt felt by those treated as the racial Other, as shamed objects of contempt. While shamed individuals, as Silvan Tomkins observes, are governed by the "wish not to hear the rasping, tongue-lashing voice of the internalized shamer and condemner," they also may identify with "that not so small voice" (265).

In a white male American culture that is "shame phobic"—for it places value on "achievement, competition, power, and dominance" (Goldberg 78)—African Americans not only have been viewed as objects of contempt, they also have served as containers for white shame.[5] Because white Americans have historically projected their own shame onto blacks, African Americans have been forced to carry a cripplingly heavy burden of shame: their own shame and the projected shame of white America. Gershen Kaufman, in his analysis of the complex interplay of identity, culture, and ideology in intergroup hostilities, such as the historical hostility between whites and blacks in American society, explains how the ideology of group hatred and prejudice is fueled by affects such as shame, disgust, contempt, and rage. Not only is violence targeted at particular groups "shaped by distinct ideologies of superiority and hate," writes Kaufman, but each group enacts its scripted role in the "actions and reactions" played out between various groups. In a culture that devalues those who are different, people belonging to minority groups are viewed with contempt. Indeed, "it is the affect of contempt which partitions the inferior from the superior in any culture or nation. As such, contempt is the principal dynamic fueling prejudice and discrimination" (*Shame* 240–41).

That scholars investigating race have described the study of racism as a "dirty business" or have remarked that it is "virtually impossible to write or say anything on the topic of race that is not in some way objectionable or embarrassing" (Gordon ix, LaCapra 2) points to the profound shame attached to the vexed issues surrounding antiblack racial prejudice and the racial caste system. Commenting on how the "much-heralded stability and continuity of American democracy was predicated upon black oppression and degradation," Cornel West observes that "[w]ithout the presence of black people in America, European-Americans would not be 'white'—they would be only Irish, Italians, Poles, Welsh, and others engaged in class, ethnic, and gender struggles over resources and identity. What made America distinctly American for them was not simply the presence of unprecedented opportunities, but the struggle for seizing these opportunities in a new land in which black slavery and racial caste served as the floor upon which white class, ethnic, and gender struggles could be diffused and diverted. In other words, white poverty could be ignored and whites' paranoia of each other could be overlooked primarily owing to the distinctive American feature: the basic racial divide of black and white peoples" (156–57). Toni Morrison makes a related observation on the experience of immigrants in her analysis of what she calls "race talk," a discursive repertoire that places emphasis on so-called essential racial differences, and that, in constructing African Americans as the deviant and racially inferior Other, is used to provide an ideological rationale for the continuing economic and social oppression of blacks. "[R]ace talk," as Morrison describes it, is an "explicit insertion into everyday life of racial signs and symbols that have no meaning other than pressing African Americans to the lowest level of the racial hierarchy. Popular culture, shaped by film, theater, advertising, the press, television, and literature, is heavily engaged in race talk. It participates freely in this most enduring and efficient rite of passage into American culture: negative appraisals of the native-born black population. Only when the lesson of racial estrangement is learned is assimilation complete. Whatever the lived experience of immigrants with African Americans—pleasant, beneficial, or bruising—the rhetorical experience renders blacks as noncitizens, already discredited outlaws" ("On the Backs of Blacks" 97–98). Describing how race functions as "a metaphor . . . necessary to the construction of Americanness," Morrison writes, "Deep within the word 'American' is its association with race. . . . American means white, and Africanist people struggle to make the term applicable to themselves with ethnicity and hyphen after hyphen after hyphen" (*Playing in the Dark* 47).[6]

Until the black revolution of the 1960s, "To be called 'black' in America meant to live in a state of shame . . . ," remarks shame theorist Donald Nathanson, who views the 1960s expression of the "cultural need to 'shove it to whitey'" as a "shame-reversing" attack-other script (*Shame and Pride* 465). Although the Civil Rights Movement also provided a healthy reversal of black shame by "transforming shame into pride and a sense of relative well-being for many blacks in this country (e.g., 'Black is Beautiful' as a new rallying cry)" (Andrew Morrison, *Shame* 187), racial prejudice and discrimination continue to be significant facts of black American life. "[I]t is time to 'get real' about race and the persistence of racism in America," writes Derrick Bell (5).[7] In the United States where racism is "an integral, permanent, and indestructible component" of American society, African Americans "remain" what they "were in the beginning: a dark and foreign presence, always the designated 'other'" (ix, 10). The "racism that made slavery feasible," in Bell's view, "is far from dead in the last decade of twentieth-century America; and the civil rights gains, so hard won, are being steadily eroded" (ix, 3). For bell hooks, "Confronting the great resurgence of white supremacist organizations and seeing the rhetoric and beliefs of these groups surface as part of accepted discourse in every aspect of daily life in the United States startles, frightens, and is enough to throw one back into silence." hooks describes how "painful" it is to "think long and hard about race and racism in the United States" or to read the information found in Andrew Hacker's 1992 book, *Two Nations*, which reports that many white Americans believe that Africans and African Americans languish "'at a lower evolutionary level than members of other races.'" To hooks, "The anti-black backlash is so fierce it astounds" (*Killing Rage* 3, *Two Nations* 27).

Like bell hooks and Derrick Bell, Morrison has commented on the continuing significance of race in American society. To Morrison, "declarations that racism is irrelevant, over or confined to the past are premature fantasies" ("Official Story" xx). America remains "Star-spangled. Race-strangled" ("On the Backs" 100).[8] Yet while antiblack racism continues to plague African Americans, postmodern theorists have put "race" under erasure.[9] Remarking on the erasure of race in contemporary theory, Morrison observes that "race" remains "a virtually unspeakable thing, as can be seen in the apologies, notes of 'special use' and circumscribed definitions that accompany it—not least of which is my own deference in surrounding it with quotation marks. Suddenly . . . 'race' does not exist." African Americans insisted, for three hundred years, that "'race' was no usefully distinguishing factor in human relationships" only to have "every academic discipline, including theology, history, and natural science" assert that "'race' was *the* determining factor in human development." Then, when black Americans "discovered they had shaped or become a culturally formed race, and that it had specific and revered difference, suddenly they were told there is no such thing as 'race,' biological or cultural, that matters and that genuinely intellectual exchange cannot accommodate it." Morrison counters the theoretical erasure of race by insisting that "there *is* culture and both gender and 'race' inform and are informed by it. Afro-American culture exists. . ." ("Unspeakable Things" 3). Blackness, to Morrison, is a socially constructed category and a social fact in our racialized and race-conscious society. Responding to the description of race as "'both an empty category and one of the most destructive and powerful forms of social categorization,'" Morrison describes "race" as a "powerfully destructive emptiness" ("Introduction" ix).[10]

Anthony Walton, describing his experience as an African American in the 1990s, writes, "I have, for most of my adult life, wondered what, exactly, is the stain we black Americans carry, what is it about our mere presence, our mere existence that can inflame such passion, embroil the nation in such histrionics for so long a time?" (255). In a society in which racial shame remains a social fact and a shaping force in the construction of black identities and in which, in Morrison's words, "blackness is itself a stain, and therefore unstainable" ("Introduction" xviii), it is telling that Morrison, herself, was subjected to a form of public shaming when she received the Nobel prize in literature. Not only did journalists from the United States, Britain, and Europe capitalize on Morrison's race and gender in their stories, as they made use of the opportunity "to 'spice up' their headlines with a variety of eye-catching combinations" of the words "'winner,' 'black,' 'Nobel prize,' 'woman,'" but also "[w]ith amazing cross-cultural consistency, reviewers adopted an apologetic and defensive tone that seemed intended to 'account for' the literary significance of Morrison's fiction by dispelling doubts about its worth, rather than by celebrating its uniqueness" (Fabi 253–54). And Morrison was also dismissed and belittled by some aspiring laureates, who referred to her as an "affirmative action" laureate. "White America demonized black America in the days of Jim Crow. Still true today, though cosmetic changes have disguised some of the uglier aspects of the arrangement," remarks Adam Begley. "Need proof? Think of the way some people try to shrink a rival with the phrase *affirmative action*" (54; see also Reilly).

Trauma, Shame, and Storytelling in Morrison's Novels

Intent on representing painful race matters in her novels, Morrison repeatedly, if not obsessively, stages scenes of inter- and intraracial violence and shaming in her novels. She also uses her fiction to aestheticize—and thus to gain narrative mastery over and artistically repair—the racial shame and trauma she describes. In her commentary on the opening of her first novel, *The Bluest Eye*, Morrison provides insight into her narrative method. She explains that the opening sentence spoken by her child narrator—"*Quiet as it's kept, there were no marigolds in the fall of 1941*"—attracted her because the phrase "Quiet as it's kept" is "conspiratorial" and implies that there is a "secret between us and a secret that is being kept from us." Although the next sentence divulges the shameful secret—"*We thought . . . it was because Pecola was having her father's baby that the marigolds did not grow*"—it also, by foregrounding the flowers, "backgrounds illicit, traumatic, incomprehensible sex coming to its dreaded fruition." The novel's opening, thus, "provides the stroke that announces something more than a secret shared, but a silence broken, a void filled, an unspeakable thing spoken at last" ("Afterword" 212–14).

Morrison seems driven to speak the unspeakable in her fiction. But in foregrounding the flowers and backgrounding the illicit and traumatic, she also defensively aestheticizes the shame and trauma she represents in her novels, and she reminds her readers that violence in fiction is "always verbally mediated" and thus it appears "as something *styled*" (Kowalewski 4). In her constant exposure of shameful and traumatic secrets, Morrison, at times, deliberately evokes the oral quality of gossip through her meandering narrative style and her use of narrative fragments in the progressive and repeated, but constantly interrupted, telling of her characters' stories. But even while Morrison *consciously* affects an improvisational or oral style in her fiction, she also is an author who is caught up in the desire to reveal and conceal, to tell and not tell, which typifies our culture's approach to shame and trauma. Thus readers of Morrison's fiction may come away with the sense of narrative withholding or hesitancy as they follow and piece together a novelistic narrative that circles redundantly around the illicit, traumatic, incomprehensible secret or secrets it represents. If through her use of aesthetic design and fragmented narrative structure Morrison partly defends against the shameful secrets and physical horrors she depicts in her fiction, her description of her imagined reader as a co-conspirator and confidant also reveals that she is intent on involving her readers emotionally in her work.

"Writing and reading," remarks Morrison, "mean being aware of the writer's notions of risk and safety, the serene achievement of, or sweaty fight for, meaning and response-ability" (*Playing in the Dark* xi). An author who makes readers aware of the "response-ability" of her fiction and who demands reader involvement with her texts, Morrison compares the African-American artist to the black preacher who "requires his congregation to speak, to join him in the sermon, to behave in a certain way, to stand up and to weep and to cry and to accede or to change and to modify—to expand on the sermon that is being delivered" (Morrison, "Rootedness" 341). Likening herself to the black preacher and also to the jazz musician, Morrison must, as she describes it, "provide places and spaces so that the reader can participate" (Russell 44). Morrison wants from her readers "a very strong visceral and emotional response as well as a very clear intellectual response" (McKay 147). While Morrison attempts to put her readers "into the position of being naked and quite vulnerable" and to rid them of all "literary" and "social experiences" so she can "engage" them in the novel, she also wants her readers to trust her, for she is "never going to do anything so bad" that her readers "can't handle it" (Ruas 109, Moyers 274). "My writing expects, demands participatory reading," Morrison remarks. "The reader supplies the emotions. . . . He or she can feel something visceral, see something striking. Then we [you, the reader, and I, the author] come together to make this book, to feel this experience." Morrison risks hurting her readers, but she also holds them "in a comfortable place," as she puts it, so they won't be "shattered" (Tate 164).

Demanding participatory reading and having both a cognitive and emotional impact on readers, Morrison's novels exert interactional pressures on readers, who may be held in a comfortable place—through what one commentator calls Morrison's "rational telling of extreme events" (Byerman, "Beyond Realism" 55)—and yet also feel compelled and unsettled, if not emotionally distressed, by what they read.[11] In dramatizing shame, Morrison openly appeals to her readers' active curiosity by positioning them as eaves-droppers and voyeurs—as observers of family or communal secrets—and as receivers of shameful gossip. In her strategic public disclosure of shameful secrets, Morrison also risks shaming her readers, for just as exposed indi-viduals feel shame, so the observers can experience shame if they have "seen too much" or "intruded too deeply into the hidden" (Nathanson, *Many Faces* 65). And if the literary container provides a potentially safe space from which to experience reconstructed stories of shame-laden traumas, Mor-rison's novels are also powerful forms of emotional communication, works, as we shall see in our investigations of critic-reader reactions to Morrison's fiction, that are capable of invoking in readers a range of intensely uncom-fortable feelings and that can also induce readers to respond in affective and collusive ways as they participate in the text's drama. Critic-readers, for example, sometimes report feeling not only afraid or ashamed but also guilty, disgusted, anxious, angry, or even numbed as they read Morrison's novels. In their critical responses to Morrison's works, many commentators also become unwitting participants in the classic shame drama of blame assessment as they attempt to discover who or what is to blame for the plight of Morrison's characters, or they are induced to enact shame- and trauma-specific roles—including those of the advocate or rescuer or the contemp-tuous shamer or hostile judge—as they respond to Morrison's troubled, and troubling, characters.

If the forceful emotional tug and pull of Morrison's novels, with their repeated enactments of shame-shame and shame-rage feeling traps, can unsettle or even vicariously shame and traumatize readers, who become enmeshed in narratives that focus on human brutality and the dis-ease of contemporary culture, readers, as we shall see, often are induced to assume a more comforting role dramatized in Morrison's novels: that of the under-standing witnesses or the supportive community of listeners who help begin the process of healing shame and trauma by responding empathically to the painful stories of Morrison's shame- and trauma-haunted characters.

"Even as intellectuals and politicians posit the declining significance of race, 'racial difference' remains America's preeminent national narrative," writes Ann duCille. Thus, while race may be "an empty category, a slippery concept, a social construction, a trope," it still matters (1). We need to theorize race "not as meaning*less* but as meaning*ful*"—as a site of difference "filled with constructed meanings that are in need of constant decoding and inter-rogation" (58). Morrison, in her own critical writings—most notably in *Playing in the Dark*—is intent on making visible the racist mythologies that "render blacks publicly serviceable instruments of private dread and longing" ("Introduction" xviii). But she also is aware that "for both black and white American writers, in a wholly racialized society, there is no escape from racially inflected language" (*Playing in the Dark* 12–13). As Morrison remarks, "I am a black writer struggling with and through a language that can powerfully evoke and enforce hidden signs of racial superiority, cultural hegemony, and dismissive 'othering' of people and language which are by no means marginal or already and completely known and knowable in my work" (*Playing in the Dark* x–xi). Although Morrison herself sometimes finds it difficult to maneuver around racially inflected language and dis-cursive repertoires, she also is intent on depicting the rich complexities and complicating differences—such as differences in gender, class, education, and culture—that shape African-American identities.

If, quiet as it's kept, much of African-American existence has been grotesque, Morrison is intent on speaking the unspeakable in her novels as she exposes to public view the painful collective and private shame and trauma suffered by black Americans in our race-conscious and wholly racial-ized American society. Although those who have investigated shame and trauma often report on the tendency of people to turn away from the shame-ful and traumatic, Morrison has an uncanny power not only to fascinate but also to draw readers into the fictional worlds she creates. Quiet as it's kept, Morrison's fiction is shame- and trauma-driven, as we shall see in the fol-lowing pages. Yet despite the painful and shameful subject matter of her novels, Morrison, by creating verbally rich and complexly designed fiction, has earned the pride of place among contemporary American novelists as she explores the woundedness of African-American life in an idealized art-form that conveys, but also aesthetically contains and controls, intense feelings of anger, shame, and pain.

2

"The Devastation That Even Casual Racial Contempt Can Cause"

CHRONIC SHAME, TRAUMATIC ABUSE, AND RACIAL SELF-LOATHING IN *THE BLUEST EYE*

Morrison's account of her beginnings as a writer takes on a storylike quality as she tells and retells it in her interviews. She recalls how she "never planned to be a writer." But when in 1965 Morrison, who at the time was an editor for Random House publishers, found herself a divorced woman living in an unfamiliar city, she became depressed and lonely. To occupy herself, she began expanding a short story she had written several years earlier in 1962 for a writing group at Howard University, a story about an African-American girl who wanted blue eyes. "I was in a place where there was nobody I could talk to and have real conversations with. And I think I was also very unhappy. So I wrote then, for that reason," Morrison recalls (Bakerman 30). In writing *The Bluest Eye*, Morrison was also driven by her desire, as she tells it, to write the kind of book that did not exist at the time and the kind of book she wanted to read. For when she began writing, she was "preoccupied with books by black people," but in the works of black male authors like Ralph Ellison and Richard Wright she "missed some intimacy, some direction, some voice" (Ruas 96). Because Morrison found writing her first novel a compelling way to "order" her experience and also an "extraordinary way of thinking and feeling," she determined that it was something she "had absolutely no intention of living without" (Watkins 45). For Morrison, "writing became a way to be coherent in the world. It became necessary and possible for me to sort out the past, and the selection process, being disciplined and guided, was genuine thinking as opposed to simple response or problem-solving" (LeClair 119–20).

Morrison's story of Pecola and her wish for blue eyes grew out of a conversation Morrison remembered having as a girl with one of her elementary school friends, who told Morrison that she knew that God did not exist because her prayers for blue eyes had gone unanswered (Ruas 95). Morrison recalls how she felt "astonished by the desecration" her friend proposed and how she, for the first time, experienced the "shock" of the word "beautiful." Recognizing the implicit "racial self-loathing" in her friend's desire, Morrison, twenty years later, found herself still wondering how her girlhood friend had learned such feelings. "Who told her? Who made her feel that it was better to be a freak than what she was? Who had looked at her and found her so wanting, so small a weight on the beauty scale?" ("Afterword" 209–10).

Morrison began working on *The Bluest Eye*, which was published in 1970, first as a story in 1962 and then as a novel in 1965, a time when there was public focus on the issue of racial beauty. bell hooks, remarking on how the Black Power movement of the 1960s "addressed the issue of internalized racism in relation to beauty," observes that the "black is beautiful" slogan "worked to intervene and alter those racist stereotypes that had always insisted black was ugly, monstrous, undesirable" (*Outlaw Culture* 173, 174). Morrison, who was in part responding to the 1960s black liberation movement in *The Bluest Eye*, recalls that the "reclamation of racial beauty" made her question why racial beauty was not "taken for granted" within the African-American community, why it needed "wide public articulation to exist." Coming to recognize the "damaging internalization of assumptions of immutable inferiority originating in an outside gaze," Morrison, in *The Bluest Eye*, set out to describe "how something as grotesque as the demonization of an entire race could take root inside the most delicate member of society: a child; the most vulnerable member: a female" ("Afterword" 210).

In dramatizing "the devastation that even casual racial contempt can cause" ("Afterword" 210) and in depicting the shame-vulnerability and shame-anxiety of the lower-class Breedloves, Morrison's *The Bluest Eye* explores the chronic shame of being poor and black in white America. Described by Donald Nathanson as a work that provides a "prolonged immersion in the world of shame" (*Shame and Pride* 463), *The Bluest Eye* depicts the damaging impact of the race and class hierarchy on the lives of the "poor and black" Breedloves, who have come to comprehend their designated position in the social order. Having internalized the contempt and loathing directed at them from the shaming gaze of the humiliator—that is, the white culture—the Breedloves believe that they are "relentlessly and aggressively ugly" (38). "It was as though some mysterious all-knowing master had given each one a cloak of ugliness to wear, and they had each accepted it without question. The master had said, 'You are ugly people.' They had looked about themselves and saw nothing to contradict the statement; saw, in fact, support for it leaning at them from every billboard, every movie, every glance. 'Yes,' they had said. 'You are right'" (39). Sander Gilman's analysis of the process of self-stereotyping sheds light on the Breedloves' damaging belief that they are ugly. By projecting negative images onto stigmatized groups, as Gilman explains, the dominant group is assured of its "sense of control, its own power over a group labeled as 'different' and thus inferior." Because individuals incorporate into their self-representation aspects of their understanding of their group identity, those who are labeled as Other or different internalize the stigmatizing stereotypes projected by the dominant culture. This, in turn, leads to a kind of self-stereotyping, to an acceptance of the "projection of the Other" by the dominant group as "*at least an aspect of self-definition*" (*Inscribing the Other* 175, emphasis added). Self-hatred, which has formed the self-awareness of people treated as different "perhaps more than they themselves have been aware," occurs when an outsider group, such as African Americans, accepts as a reality "the mirage of themselves generated by their reference group—that group in society which they see as defining them" (*Jewish Self-Hatred* 1, 2).

The Bluest Eye, in its relentless focus on the self-hatred of the Breedloves, points to the pernicious effects of internalized racism. Accepting as part of their self-definition the shaming qualities whites ascribe to their blackness, the Breedloves see themselves as ugly people, and in what Morrison describes as the "woundability" of Pecola Breedlove ("Afterword" 210), *The Bluest Eye* dramatizes an extreme form of the shame-vulnerability and shame-anxiety suffered by African Americans in white America. Morrison also depicts the intergenerational transmission of shame in her novel, showing how it is passed down from parent to child. And in the response of members of the African-American community, who end up collectively scapegoating Pecola, the novel reveals how humiliated individuals can temporarily rid themselves of their shame by humiliating others. Indeed, the "ugly" Pecola becomes the ultimate carrier of her family's—and her African-American community's—shame.

The Bluest Eye, then, is a complicated shame drama. It also is a trauma narrative, for Pecola, as Morrison has aptly described her, is "a total and complete victim," and she is a victim not only of racial shaming but also of her "crippled and crippling family" (Stepto 17, "Afterword" 210). In a relentless way, *The Bluest Eye* depicts the progressive traumatization of Pecola, who is rejected and physically abused by her mother, sexually abused by her alcoholic and unpredictably violent father, and ultimately scapegoated by members of the community. In her novel, Morrison reveals not only that trauma can result from "a constellation of life's experiences" or a "continuing pattern of abuse," but also that incest is "always, inevitably, destructive to the child" (Erikson 457, Herman, *Father-Daughter Incest* 4). Ultimately, as the closure of *The Bluest Eye* indicates, the "damage done" to Pecola is "total," and she steps "over into madness" (204, 206). Her self damaged beyond repair, Pecola retreats from real life and converses with her alter identity, her only "friend": that is, she ends up living permanently in the dissociated world of the severely traumatized individual.

Aware that the traumatic, shame-laden subject matter of her novel is potentially disturbing to the reader, Morrison, in the opening words of Claudia's narration—*"Quiet as it's kept, there were no marigolds in the fall of 1941"*—entices the reader by invoking the intimate "back fence" world of "illicit gossip." In Morrison's description, the opening phrase—*"Quiet as it's kept"*—is conspiratorial: "'Shh, don't tell anyone else,' and 'No one is allowed to know this.' It is a secret between us and a secret that is being kept from us. . . . In some sense it was precisely what the act of writing the book was: the public exposure of a private confidence." If the publication of the book involved exposure, the writing of *The Bluest Eye* "was the disclosure of secrets, secrets 'we' shared and those withheld from us by ourselves and by the world outside the community." Underlying the conspiratorial whisper was the assumption that the teller of the story was about to impart "privileged information." "The intimacy I was aiming for," Morrison remarks, "the intimacy between the reader and the page, could start up immediately because the secret is being shared, at best, and eavesdropped upon, at the least. Sudden familiarity or instant intimacy seemed crucial to me. I did not want the reader to have time to wonder, 'What do I have to do, to give up, in order to read this? What defense do I need, what distance maintain?'" ("Afterword" 212–13).

By foregrounding the flowers and backgrounding the shameful fact of incest—*"We thought . . . it was because Pecola was having her father's baby that the marigolds did not grow"*—Morrison protects the reader "from a confrontation too soon with the painful details," but also provokes the reader "into a desire to know them." The opening, as she describes it, "provides the stroke that announces something more than a secret shared, but a silence broken, a void filled, an unspeakable thing spoken at last." By "transferring the problem of fathoming" to the readers—"the inner circle of listeners"—the novel justifies the "public exposure of a privacy." If readers enter into the "conspiracy" announced by the opening words, "then the book can be seen to open with its close: a speculation on the disruption of 'nature' as being a social disruption with tragic individual consequences" in which readers, "as part of the population of the text," are "implicated" ("Afterword" 213–14). Moreover, by breaking the narrative "into parts" that have to be "reassembled," Morrison attempts to lead her readers "into an interrogation of themselves for the smashing" of the Pecolas of this world ("Afterword" 211). A powerful form of emotional communication, *The Bluest Eye* has been described as a work that can make readers feel "helpless and afraid" and also "ache for remedy" (Dee 20) or as a work that offers readers "no refuge from Morrison's anger" (Hedin 50) or that uses "obscenity" to shock the readers' "sensibilities" and also urges readers to see the "destructive absurdity" of American life and to recognize that "the real horrors are still loose in the world" (Byerman, "Intense Behaviors" 456–57). And the fact that *The Bluest Eye*, as we shall see, can prompt some readers to participate in the drama of blame assessment or to recognize their own involvement in the smashing of the Pecolas of American society points to the powerful way Morrison works on her readers' emotions.

If Morrison risks vicariously traumatizing her readers in writing about the Breedlove family and Cholly's incestuous rape of Pecola, she also sets up potential shame conflicts in readers as she makes them privy to a shameful family secret. If a mature sense of shame—that is, the recognition that some phenomena should be kept private and shielded from public view—protects the individual in moments of "increased vulnerability," it is also the case that family privacy has served to conceal the fact that the family provides "a dangerous hiding place for family violence and sexual abuse" (Schneider 55, Mason 30). Morrison, in her strategic public exposure of the incest secret, breaks the taboo on looking and thus risks shaming her readers, for just as those who are exposed feel shame, so observers of shaming scenes can feel shame. Indeed, "Shame, by its nature, is contagious. Moreover, just as shame has an intrinsic tendency to encourage hiding, so there is a tendency for the observer of another's shame to turn away from it" (Lewis, *Shame and Guilt* 15–16).

Speaking the unspeakable, Morrison's *The Bluest Eye* is permeated with shame and trauma. But it also uses narrative structure and aesthetic design not only to fascinate and impress readers—and thus to counteract shame—but also to partially defend against the horrors it is assigned to uncover. Describing an early version of the novel, which presented the fragmented narrative of Pecola, the shamed trauma victim, Morrison remarks that *The Bluest Eye* was originally the story of Pecola and her family narrated in the third person "in pieces like a broken mirror." On finding that there was no connection between the reader and the life of Pecola and her parents, Morrison introduced Claudia as an "I"-narrator and thus provided in the narrative someone to "empathize" with Pecola and also to "relieve the grimness" of the narrative (Ruas 97). Yet despite her careful structuring of the novel, there remained a problem in the "central chamber" of the narrative. "The shattered world I built (to complement what is happening to Pecola), its pieces held together by seasons in child-time and commenting at every turn on the incompatible and barren white-family primer, does not in its present form handle effectively the silence at its center: the void that is Pecola's 'unbeing.' It should have had a shape—like the emptiness left by a boom or a cry" ("Afterword" 214–15).

In narratively building a shattered world around the void of Pecola's unbeing in *The Bluest Eye*, Morrison calls attention to the careful design and structure of the novel. But she also, while depicting the incestuous rape of Pecola, partly denies the horrors she sets out to describe. That Morrison chooses to narrate the rape from the father's point of view and that she herself has described the rape as an "awful" thing and yet as "almost irrelevant" (Tate 164) is suggestive, given the fact that "[d]enial, avoidance, and distancing" are common responses to incest (Herman, "Father-Daughter Incest" 182).[1] Thus, the rape scene is the emotional center of the novel and yet it is oddly muted as the narrative proliferates, telling stories—including the tragic and sympathetic stories of Pauline, the complicit mother, and Cholly, the violating father—around the empty center of the text, the "void" of the silenced and backgrounded incest victim.

From the outset of *The Bluest Eye*, readers are aware that part of Morrison's agenda, as she describes the victimization and shaming of Pecola, is to dialogically contest the idealized representation of American life and the white nuclear family found in the Dick-and-Jane primer story:

> Here is the house. It is green and white. It has a red door. It is very pretty. Here is the family. Mother, Father, Dick, and Jane live in the green-and-white house. They are very happy. See Jane. . . . She wants to play. Who will play with Jane? . . . See Mother. Mother is very nice. Mother, will you play with Jane? Mother laughs. . . . See Father. He is big and strong. Father, will you play with Jane? Father is smiling. . . . Here comes a friend. The friend will play with Jane. (3)

Morrison explains that she uses the Dick-and-Jane primer story, with its depiction of a happy white family, "as a frame acknowledging the outer civilization," and then she runs together the words of the primer story— "Hereisthehouseitisgreenandwhite" (4)—because she wants "the primer version broken up and confused" (LeClair 127). Through this broken up and confused discourse—which is found in the opening frame narrative and, as the narrative progresses, is used to head the chapters focusing on Pecola and those who traumatize her—Morrison signals the increasingly fragmented world of the trauma victim. Morrison's stark reversals of the idealized discourse of the Dick-and-Jane primer story also communicate to readers the intense, but highly controlled, feelings of anger that drive the narrative. Thus the chapters of the novel that are headed with the primer descriptions of Jane's idealized green-and-white house and her happy family introduce readers to the decaying storefront dwelling where the ugly Breedloves live; the chapters that begin with primer accounts of the dog and cat tell pointed stories of animal abuse; the chapters headed with primer descriptions of the very nice mother and big and strong father who smiles at his daughter describe the mother's physical and the father's sexual abuse of Pecola; and the chapter headed with the primer passage describing Jane's playful friend relates Pecola's conversation with her only "friend," her dissociated alter self.

In depicting the Breedlove family as a site of violence and in presenting Pecola as a victim of her abusive parents, *The Bluest Eye* invokes shaming racist and class stereotypes that construct the black underclass family as uncivilized and pathological, a pernicious stereotype that had wide public currency in the aftermath of the 1965 Moynihan Report. Made public around the time Morrison was writing *The Bluest Eye*, the Moynihan Report blamed continuing black urban poverty on the breakdown of the African-American family structure, viewing the black family as a "tangle of pathology" and contrasting the "deep-seated structural distortions" of black urban culture against the norm of the dominant white culture (Rainwater 75, 93).[2] *The Bluest Eye*, as it focuses attention on the "anonymous misery" of the Breedloves—whose poverty is "traditional and stultifying" but "not unique" (39, 38)—crystallizes black middle-class anxiety about the black underclass family. Intoning the shaming discourse of dirt and defilement, the narrative describes the Breedloves "[f]estering together in the debris of a realtor's whim" in their storefront dwelling in Lorain, Ohio, where "the joylessness stank, pervading everything" (34, 36). To the extent that homogenizing images of white family normality and black family pathology have historically served to reinforce the essentialist racist construction of white superiority and black inferiority, Morrison's racially and class-inflected—and culturally sedimented—representation of the Breedlove family points to the power and pervasiveness of cultural stereotypes and ideology. But even as the novel repeats the hegemonic view of the black underclass family as a site of "pathology-disorganization" and as a "shattered distortion" of white culture (Morton 128, Berger 413), it also sets out to put a human face on the "anonymous misery" of the Breedloves by telling the life stories of Pecola's parents and revealing that they, too, are victims, people who have been severely damaged by racism. And part of the novel's explicit agenda is to assess the "why" and the "how" of Pecola's plight. Although Claudia, in her opening narration, insists that she takes "*refuge in* how" (6), the narrative is driven by the desire to elucidate the "why" of the Breedloves' story and to indict the cultural—and also family—forces that lead to the destruction of the vulnerable and shame-sensitive Pecola.

While the story of Pecola—who suffers from profound shame-anxiety, feels unlovable and ugly, and thus acts out the defensive withdrawing and hiding behavior characteristic of shame-vulnerable individuals—is at the center of the text, *The Bluest Eye*, through the interconnected experiences of

Pecola and Claudia, enacts a complicated shame drama. Not only does Pecola's characteristic body language fit Donald Nathanson's description of the "purest presentation of the affect shame-humiliation"—in which the eyes are averted and downcast, the head droops, and the shoulders slump (see *Shame and Pride* 134–36)—but Pecola so internalizes white contempt for her blackness that she comes to see her dark skin and African features as markers of a stigmatized racial identity and thus wishes to be invisible or desires to have blue eyes so that others will love and accept her. Unlike Pecola, who is the passive and utterly shamed victim, Claudia, in contrast, gives expression to the anger experienced by the shamed individual, the desire to flail out that signals an attempt to rid the self of shame (see Andrew Morrison, *Shame* 13–14).

Questioning why people look at little white girls and say "Awwwww" but do not look at her that way, Claudia becomes angry when she observes the "eye slide" of black women as they approach white girls on the street, and the "possessive gentleness of their touch" when they handle them (22–23). Whereas Pecola dreams of having blue eyes, Claudia responds with rage when she is given a blue-eyed, yellow-haired, pink-skinned baby doll as a "special" gift. "I had only one desire: to dismember it. To see of what it was made, to discover the dearness, to find the beauty, the desirability that had escaped me, but apparently only me" (20). According to the official culture—the world of adults, shops, magazines, and window signs—girls treasure such dolls, but Claudia defiantly pokes at the doll's glass eyes, breaks off its fingers, and removes its head.[3] "I destroyed white baby dolls," she recalls. "But the dismembering of dolls was not the true horror. The truly horrifying thing was the transference of the same impulses to little white girls. The indifference with which I could have axed them was shaken only by my desire to do so. To discover what eluded me: the secret of the magic they weaved on others" (22).

Claudia's reactive rage is evident in her response not only to interracial but also to intraracial shaming. When the white Rosemary Villanucci rebuffs Claudia and her sister, Frieda, Claudia wants to "poke the arrogance" out of Rosemary's eyes and "make red marks on her white skin" (9). Claudia feels the "familiar violence" rise in her when she witnesses the little white girl, who lives in the house where Pauline Breedlove works as a housekeeper, call Mrs. Breedlove "Polly," even though Pecola herself calls her mother "Mrs. Breedlove" (108). And Claudia's angry reaction to Maureen Peal reveals the force of intraracial shaming within the African-American community. A "high-yellow dream child with long brown hair braided into two lynch ropes that hung down her back" (62), Maureen Peal enchants everyone at the school: the teachers smile at her when they call on her in class; black boys do not trip her in the hallways, and white boys do not stone her; white girls readily accept her as their work partner, and black girls move aside when she wants to use the sink in the girls' washroom. Claudia and Frieda, in an attempt to recover their equilibrium, search for flaws in the much-admired Maureen. They secretly refer to her as "Meringue Pie"; they are pleased when they discover that she has a dog tooth; and they smile when they learn that she was born with six fingers on each hand and had this flaw surgically corrected. When Claudia, who is assigned a locker next to Maureen, thinks of the "unearned haughtiness" in Maureen's eyes, she plots "accidental slammings of locker doors" on Maureen's hand (63). Despite her jealousy, Claudia is "secretly prepared" to be Maureen's friend, and over time is even capable of holding a "sensible conversation" with Maureen without visualizing Maureen falling off a cliff or without "giggling" her way into what she thinks is "a clever insult" (63–64).

Ultimately Maureen pronounces judgment on Pecola, Claudia, and Frieda by insisting that she is "cute" and that the three girls are "[b]lack and ugly." While Claudia and Frieda are temporarily "stunned" by the "weight" of Maureen's shaming remark, they recover themselves enough to reactively and publicly shame Maureen by shouting out the "most powerful" chant in their "arsenal of insults"—"Six-finger-dog-tooth-meringue-pie!" Pecola, in contrast, enacts the classic withdrawing and concealing behavior of the humiliated individual as she folds into herself "like a pleated wing." Pecola's visible pain and shame at the public exposure of her inner sense of defectiveness antagonizes Claudia, who would like to see Pecola assume a defiant antishame posture. "I wanted to open her up, crisp her edges, ram a stick down that hunched and curving spine, force her to stand erect and spit the misery out on the streets. But she held it in where it could lap up into her eyes" (73–74). Yet Claudia also identifies, in part, with Pecola's shame as she sinks under "the wisdom, accuracy, and relevance" of Maureen's taunt. If Maureen is cute, Claudia recognizes, then she is somehow "lesser" and unworthy. Claudia can destroy white dolls, but she is unable to destroy "the honey voices of parents and aunts," or the "obedience" found in the eyes of her contemporaries, or the "slippery light" in the eyes of teachers when they encounter "the Maureen Peals of the world." Despite this, Claudia also recognizes that Maureen Peal is "not the Enemy and not worthy of such intense hatred." Instead, the "*Thing* to fear" is what makes Maureen "beautiful" while denying beauty to Claudia, Frieda, and Pecola (74).

The "Thing" Claudia learns to fear is the white standard of beauty that members of the African-American community have internalized, a standard that favors the "high-yellow" Maureen Peal and denigrates the "black and ugly" Pecola Breedlove. Yet over time Claudia, too, partially internalizes this white standard. The same Claudia who once dismembered white dolls and wanted to axe little white girls becomes ashamed of her own rage: her desire to hurt little white girls and hear their "fascinating cry of pain." When she comes to view her "disinterested violence" as "repulsive"—and she finds it repulsive because it *is* disinterested—her "shame" flounders about "for refuge" and finds a "hiding place" in love. "Thus the conversion from pristine sadism to fabricated hatred, to fraudulent love," remarks Claudia (23). Although Claudia later learns to "worship" Shirley Temple—a popular figure she once responded to with "unsullied hatred"—this change is "adjustment without improvement" (19, 23). Indeed, as *The Bluest Eye* reveals, because the standard of beauty—that is, the idealized version of the black self—is based on whiteness, the Pecolas and Claudias of the world cannot help but feel ashamed. For shame is "a reflection of feelings about the whole self in failure, as inferior in competition or in comparison with others, as inadequate and defective" (Andrew Morrison, *Shame* 12). *The Bluest Eye*, as it highlights the politics of beauty standards and the construction of African-American female identities, shows how dark skin functions as a marker of shame, a sign of a stigmatized racial identity.

If the ultimate "Enemy" that shames and traumatizes African Americans is the racist white society, there are also more immediate and intimate enemies within the African-American community and family. Unlike the dysfunctional Breedloves, the MacTeers—Claudia's family—are presented as a healthy and intact black family. And yet Claudia's recollection of her early years contains troubling descriptions of childhood shaming and physical abuse. "Even now spring for me is shot through with the remembered ache of switchings, and forsythia holds no cheer," she comments. As a child, Claudia learns to associate springtime with a change in the style of whipping, for in place of the "dull pain of a winter strap" or "the firm but honest slap of a hairbrush" is the sting of the new green switches that lasts "long after" the whipping is over (97). Adults, Claudia remarks, "do not talk" to children; instead they "give us directions. They issue orders without providing information. When we trip and fall down they glance at us; if we cut or bruise ourselves, they ask us are we crazy. When we catch colds, they shake their heads in disgust at our lack of consideration. How, they ask us, do you expect anybody to get anything done if you all are sick?" (10). Mrs. MacTeer's response to Claudia's illness mortifies her shame-sensitive daughter. When Claudia becomes ill and vomits on her bed, she feels that her mother views her as an object of disgust, for Mrs. MacTeer talks to the vomit but calls it Claudia's name. "My mother's anger humiliates me; her words chafe my cheeks, and I am crying. I do not know that she is not angry at me, but at my sickness" (11). The adult Claudia, however, also insists that the pain she endured at the hands of her mother was "a productive and fructifying pain" and that the maternal love she experienced was "thick and dark." Claudia recalls that when she was sick as a child, her mother nursed her. "And in the night, when my coughing was dry and tough, feet padded into the room, hands repinned the flannel, readjusted the quilt, and rested a moment on my forehead. So when I think of autumn, I think of somebody with hands who does not want me to die" (12).

Thus, although Claudia is subjected to maternal shaming and although she comes to internalize white contempt for her blackness, she still feels in a deep-rooted way that she is loved and secure. Pecola, in contrast, who feels utterly unlovable and ugly, suffers from an extreme and destructive form of chronic shame-vulnerability and shame-anxiety. In its investigation of the cultural and familial sources of Pecola's profound and crippling shame, *The Bluest Eye* tells the stories of Pecola's parents, revealing how they transmit to their daughter their own "ugliness": that is, their own sense of inferiority and defectiveness.

Pecola's mother, Pauline—whose sense of defectiveness is intensified by her limp—ultimately transfers to her daughter her own "general feeling of separateness and unworthiness" and also her borrowed ideas about beauty, which lead inevitably to "self-contempt" (111, 122). As a young married woman, Pauline goes to the movies, and after she absorbs "in full"—that is, internalizes—the white beauty standards conveyed in Hollywood films, she is "never able . . . to look at a face and not assign it some category in the scale of absolute beauty" (122). Pauline identifies with white movie stars—she even affects a Jean Harlow hairstyle—but then, when she loses a front tooth, she resigns herself *"to just being ugly"* (123). Adding to Pauline's feeling of inferiority is the fact that she is also subjected to intraracial shaming. Pointing to the importance of class and cultural differences in the construction of a stigmatized African-American identity, *The Bluest Eye* describes how Pauline, when she first moves to the North, discovers that northern blacks are *"[n]o better than whites for meanness"* and that they can make her feel *"just as no-count"* as whites (117).

Pauline's feeling that she is "ugly"—that is to say, inferior and defective—is reinforced during the shame drama of Pecola's birth. When Pauline is about to deliver Pecola, she overhears the white doctors at the hospital invoking the discourse of racial degeneration when they refer to black women like her as animallike: *"They deliver right away and with no pain. Just like horses."* When the birth pangs begin, Pauline moans *"something awful"* to let the doctors know that delivering a baby is *"more than a bowel movement."* Shamed by the doctors, who view her as an object of contempt, Pauline unconsciously equates her child with excrement: that is, with something dirty and disgusting. And the fact that Pauline describes her newborn baby as ugly—*"Head full of pretty hair, but Lord she was ugly"*—suggests that from the outset Pauline projects her own sense of ugliness onto her daughter (124–25, 126).

Employing a classic attack-other shame defense, Pauline does express contempt for the white family she works for during her first steady job as a housekeeper, describing them as dirty, which is how poor African Americans are perceived by whites: "*None of them knew so much as how to wipe their behinds. I know, 'cause I did the washing. And couldn't pee proper to save their lives . . . Nasty white folks is about the nastiest things they is*" (119–20). Yet when Pauline works for the well-to-do Fishers, she becomes "what is known as an ideal servant, for such a role filled practically all of her needs" (127). That is, only when Pauline embraces her black shame by assuming the inferior role of the ideal servant at the home of the white Fishers is she able to meet the goals of her ideal self and win the white approbation she desires. In the Fisher household, unlike in her "dingy" storefront dwelling, Pauline finds "beauty, order, cleanliness" (127) and when Pauline acts as the representative of the Fishers, the creditors and service people—who would normally humiliate her—respect her and even find her intimidating. While Pauline dotes on the little white Fisher girl, she neglects and physically abuses Pecola, transferring to her daughter her deep-rooted contempt for her own blackness. Trying to make her daughter respectable, Pauline teaches Pecola "fear" of being a clumsy person, of being like her father, of being unloved by God—that is, "fear" of being inadequate and defective. And she beats into Pecola "a fear of growing up, fear of other people, fear of life" (128).

Like Pauline, Cholly Breedlove transfers his own chronic shame and stigmatized racial identity—his own feelings of humiliation and defeat—to his daughter. Not only is Cholly "[a]bandoned in a junk heap by his mother, [and] rejected for a crap game by his father," but he also is subjected to the racist insults which are "part of the nuisances of life" (160, 153). In a central scene of interracial shaming, Cholly is utterly humiliated when he is forced, during his initial sexual encounter as an adolescent, to perform sexually for two white hunters. The fourteen-year-old Cholly is terrified when he is discovered by two white men carrying long guns while he is "newly but earnestly engaged in eliciting sexual pleasure from a little country girl" (42). When one of the white men, who shines a flashlight on the scene, commands Cholly to "Get on wid it. . . . An' make it good, nigger, make it good," Cholly hates the girl, Darlene, not the white men. While he simulates love-making, he almost wishes that he "could do it—hard, long, and painfully" because he hates Darlene "so much" (148). Remaining paralyzed by his shame afterward, he either obsesses over this episode or feels a "vacancy in his head." Rather than hating the white men, he cultivates his hatred of the girl. "Never did he once consider directing his hatred toward the hunters. Such an emotion would have destroyed him. They were big, white, armed men. He was small, black, helpless. His subconscious knew what his conscious mind did not guess—that hating them would have consumed him, burned him up like a piece of soft coal, leaving only flakes of ash and a question mark of smoke." Thus he despises Darlene because she has witnessed "his failure, his impotence" and because he was unable to protect her (150–51).

Seeking comfort but unwilling to reveal his shame to Blue—an older man the boy Cholly views as a father-surrogate figure—Cholly runs away to find his biological father. Yet when he finally encounters his father, who asks Cholly whose "boy" he is, Cholly does not say "I'm your boy" because that sounds "disrespectful." Cholly is devastated when he is brutally rejected by his belligerent father—"[G]et the fuck outta my face!" he shouts at Cholly in a "vexed and whiny voice" (156). When the traumatically rejected and abandoned Cholly subsequently loses control and soils himself "like a baby," he feels exposed to the humiliating gaze of others. The literally dirtied and helpless Cholly imagines that his father will see him and laugh and, indeed, that everybody will laugh. Fearing shameful visual exposure, the mortified Cholly, in a state of panic, takes flight: "Cholly ran down the street, aware only of silence. People's mouths moved, their feet moved, a car jugged by—but with no sound. . . . His own feet made no sound." Temporarily numbed and disoriented by his shame, Cholly conceals himself under a pier near a river, and he remains "knotted there in fetal position, paralyzed, his fists covering his eyes, for a long time. No sound, no sight. . . . He even forgot his messed-up trousers" (157). Shame, as Wurmser remarks, is the *"affect of contempt* directed against the self—by others or by one's own conscience. Contempt says: 'You should disappear as such a being as you have shown yourself to be—failing, weak, flawed, and dirty. Get out of my sight: Disappear!'" To be exposed as one who fails someone else's or one's own expectations causes shame, and to "disappear into nothing is the punishment for such failure" ("Shame" 67).

As an adolescent, Cholly, who has internalized constructions of black identity as inferior and stigmatized, is deeply traumatized and shamed at the disgraceful exposure of himself as weak and contemptible. As an adult even a "half-remembrance" of the episode with the white hunters, "along with myriad other humiliations, defeats, and emasculations, could stir him into flights of depravity that surprised himself—but only himself" (42–43). In constructing Cholly's oppositionally defined and shameless identity, *The Bluest Eye* invokes the inherited stereotype of the "bad nigger"—the defiant, but also unrestrained and potentially dangerous, male—a stereotype, as we shall see, that Morrison repeats in her representation of other lower-class male characters, including Guitar in *Song of Solomon* and Son in *Tar Baby*. Cholly, who has the "meanest eyes in town" (40), lives in a chronic state of humiliated fury, and he vents his anger on "petty things and weak people" (38), including members of his own family. Cholly defends himself by assuming the defiant posture of the "Dangerously free" man, who is "Free to feel whatever he felt—fear, guilt, shame, love, grief, pity. Free to be tender or violent, to whistle or weep. . . . Free to take a woman's insults, for his body had already conquered hers. Free even to knock her in the head, for he had already cradled that head in his arms." The fact that the dangerously free Cholly has retaliated against white men—Cholly is "free to say, 'No, suh,' and smile, for he had already killed three white men" (159)—reveals that he has attempted to rid himself of his unendurable shame by attacking and destroying those who have shamed him. As Silvan Tomkins observes, "Depending upon the intensity and depth of humiliation, and the feelings of helplessness which grip him, the individual will struggle to express his humiliation, to undo humiliation, to turn the tables on his oppressor and at the extreme to destroy him to recover his power to deal with intolerable humiliation" (296).

A broken, bitter man who flaunts his shame, Cholly ends up as the utterly degraded, and thus socially ostracized, individual when he puts his family outdoors. Repeating the essentialist racist discourse that constructs the lower-class black male as unrestrained and uncivilized, *The Bluest Eye* describes how "that old Dog Breedlove had burned up his house, gone upside his wife's head, and everybody, as a result, was outdoors. Outdoors, we knew, was the real terror of life." While people could drink or gamble themselves outdoors, "to be slack enough to put oneself outdoors, or heart-less enough to put one's own kin outdoors—that was criminal" (16–17). Cholly's defiant displays of shameless behavior—his shamelessness serving as a defense against his deep-rooted shame-anxiety—catapults him "beyond the reaches of human consideration." An object of communal contempt and disgust, Cholly is viewed as a degenerate type: "He had joined the animals; was, indeed, an old dog, a snake, a ratty nigger" (18). Contempt by others, as Wurmser remarks, is a type of aggression that degrades the individual's value by "equating him particularly with a debased, dirty thing—a derided and low animal. . . ." The humiliated person is "shunned," "sent into soli-tude," "discarded from the communality of civilized society" (*Mask* 81, 82).

That contempt is a "'cold' affect," a form of aggression that wants to "eliminate the other being" (Wurmser, *Mask* 81, 80), is evident in the ritual-ized quarrels that occur in the Breedlove marriage. To Pauline, her fights with Cholly give substance to the dull sameness of her life. Wearing the anti-shame mask of Christian respectability, Pauline views herself as an "upright and Christian woman, burdened with a no-count man, whom God wanted her to punish," and she pleads with Jesus to "help her 'strike the bastard down from his pea-knuckle of pride.'" If Pauline's Christian pride and retaliatory fantasies are reaction formations against her deep-seated shame, Cholly's "inarticulate fury," which he vents on his wife, signals his attempt to express and temporarily rid himself of his shame-rage. "Hating her, he could leave himself intact" (42). Constructing the black underclass Breedlove family as a site of violence and pathology, *The Bluest Eye* describes how Pauline and Cholly beat each other "with a darkly brutal formalism." "Tacitly they had agreed not to kill each other. . . . There was only the muted sound of falling things, and flesh on unsurprised flesh" (43).

What Pecola learns from her parents—that like them she is ugly—is confirmed by the hostile gaze and insulting speech of others. Pecola's ugliness makes her "ignored or despised at school, by teachers and classmates alike," and when a girl wants to especially insult a boy, she simply accuses him of "loving" Pecola, a taunt that provokes "peals of laughter from those in earshot" (45, 46). To Geraldine, who teaches her son "the difference between colored people and niggers"—colored people like her are "neat and quiet" while niggers are "dirty and loud" (87)—Pecola is an object of disgust and contempt.

In the deliberately staged encounter between Pecola and Geraldine, *The Bluest Eye* focuses attention on class distinctions and the connection between class and shame within the African-American community. Geraldine is identified by the narrator as one of the "thin brown girls," women who have internalized white, middle-class standards of beauty and behavior, and who, in developing "high morals" and "good manners," have lost their "funkiness," that is, their passion and spontaneity (81, 83). Donning the mask of middle-class respectability perhaps, in part, in an effort to disassociate themselves from the shaming racist and sexist stereotype of the "oversexed-black-Jezebel"—a pervasive stereotype that constructs African-American women not only as connoting sex but also as instigators of sex (Painter, "Hill" 209–10)—the plain brown women walk with their "behind[s] in for fear of a sway too free," and they give their bodies to their husbands "sparingly and partially" (83, 84). To a "clean and quiet" brown girl like Geraldine—a "colored" person of "order, precision, and constancy" (85) who adheres to the cultural norms of self-discipline and self-improvement—lower-class blacks are dirty and disorderly "niggers." Even though "niggers" are easy to identify, "[t]he line between colored and nigger was not always clear; subtle and telltale signs threatened to erode it, and the watch had to be constant" (87).

Defensively positioning herself as racially superior to lower-class blacks, Geraldine shuns Pecola, viewing her dark skin as a sign of her stigmatized racial identity. The narrative, as it directs attention to the class differences among black people, describes Geraldine's prejudice against Pecola, observing the underclass Pecola through Geraldine's middle-class—and shaming—gaze. When Geraldine looks at Pecola—who has a torn and soiled dress with a safety pin holding up the hem, muddy shoes and dirty socks, and matted hair where the plaits sticking out on her head have come undone—she feels that she has "seen this little girl all of her life" (91). Geraldine's revulsion toward poor blacks, whom she sees as the dirty and subhuman Other, reveals her internalization of the essentialist racist construction of black degeneracy. To Geraldine, children like Pecola "were everywhere. They slept six in a bed, all their pee mixing together in the night as they wet their beds. . . . Tin cans and tires blossomed where they lived. They lived on cold black-eyed peas and orange pop. Like flies they hovered; like flies they settled" (92).

In contemporary America where, as Morrison has described it, "blackness is itself a stain" ("Introduction" xviii), racist codes remain pervasive. The middle-class Geraldine, who has internalized the cultural construction of white superiority/purity and black inferiority/impurity, views Pecola through the lens of antiblack racist stereotypes. Sander Gilman's analysis of the phenomenon of group self-hatred sheds light on Geraldine's response to Pecola. The middle-class Geraldine, who as an African American in white America is a member of an outsider group, projects the image of Otherness projected onto her by the dominant white culture onto an extension of herself. Outsiders, as Gilman explains, in taking on the positive qualities ascribed to them as "the potential members of the group in power," transfer the negative qualities ascribed to them as the Other to a "new Other found within the group." But for a member of the outsider group, "it is almost always impossible to create a complete break with the new Other. For even as one distances oneself from this aspect of oneself, there is always the voice of the power group saying, Under the skin you are really like them anyhow" (*Jewish Self-Hatred* 4, 3). Outsiders "see the dominant society seeing them" and "project their anxiety" about being seen as the Other onto members of their own group "as a means of externalizing their own status anxiety" (*Jewish Self-Hatred* 11). In *The Bluest Eye*, Geraldine externalizes her own status anxiety by projecting her fear of being seen as the stigmatized racial Other—as the "dirty" black—onto Pecola. That the "affective roots" of prejudice, as Donald Nathanson remarks, involve "dissmell and disgust" (*Shame* 133) is also apparent in Geraldine's response to Pecola. Linked to the "phenomenology of interpersonal rejection," dissmell is a primitive mechanism by which individuals keep at a distance those people that they perceive as bad-smelling and dirty or that they define as "too awful or too foul to get near" (*Shame* 124; see also 121–33). To be a member of a group perceived as disgusting or dissmelling is to be treated with contempt, a form of anger which declares the other person "worthy only of rejection" and which functions to "instill in the other person a sense of self-dissmell or self-disgust and therefore shame at self-unworthiness" (*Shame* 129). When Geraldine contemptuously pronounces Pecola a "nasty little black bitch" (92), her shaming words reinforce Pecola's fear of exposure and rejection and intensify her feeling that she is ugly, dirty, and defective.

Similarly, in the vacant gaze of the white store owner, Mr. Yacobowski, Pecola senses racial contempt. "He does not see her, because for him there is nothing to see." In his "total absence of human recognition—the glazed separateness"—Pecola senses his distaste. "The distaste must be for her, her blackness. . . . [I]t is the blackness that accounts for, that creates, the vacuum edged with distaste in white eyes" (48–49). After Pecola purchases three Mary Jane candies from Mr. Yacobowski, she attempts to soothe herself. Outside his store, she feels her "inexplicable shame ebb" and takes temporary refuge in anger. "Anger is better. There is a sense of being in anger. A reality and presence. An awareness of worth. It is a lovely surging." But when she recalls Mr. Yacobowski's eyes, her shame "wells up again." Attempting to overcome her inner feelings of defectiveness, she imagines that to eat the Mary Jane candy is to "eat the eyes" of, indeed is to "eat" and to "[b]e," Mary Jane: the blond-haired, blue-eyed white girl pictured on the candy wrapper (50). To incorporate and thus "be"—that is, merge with—the idealized Mary Jane is to be an object of admiration, not contempt, and to turn the shaming or ostracizing gaze of others into a look of approval and acceptance.

In a pivotal episode, which purposefully and with didactic intent brings together the "ugly" black Pecola and the "high-yellow" Maureen Peal, Morrison underscores the role of internalized racism and intraracial shaming in the construction of a stigmatized racial identity. When Claudia, her sister, Frieda, and Maureen Peal notice some commotion in the schoolyard playground and stop to investigate, they discover that a group of black boys is circling Pecola, holding her at bay. "[T]hrilled by the easy power of a majority," the boys "gaily" harass Pecola with an extemporaneous, insulting verse: "Black e mo. Black e mo. Yadaddsleepsnekked." What gives the first insult "its teeth" is their "contempt for their own blackness." Repeating what has been done to them and attempting to rid themselves of their own deeply rooted sense of racial shame and self-loathing, they humiliate Pecola. Their "exquisitely learned self-hatred" and "elaborately designed hopelessness" become expressed in their angry, insulting speech, and they dance a "macabre ballet" around Pecola, "whom, for their own sake, they were prepared to sacrifice to the flaming pit" of their scorn (65). In treating Pecola as the stigmatized racial Other, as the narrative makes clear, the boys express contempt for their own black identity.

Responding passively to her public shaming, the crying Pecola edges around the circle of boys. Although the taunting of the boys stops when an angry Frieda and Claudia intervene, the rescue of Pecola is short-lived, for Maureen Peal then humiliates Pecola by insisting that Pecola has, in fact, seen her own father naked. If Maureen's words suggest that there is already community suspicion about the possibility of sexual abuse in the Breedlove family, Pecola's physical response to Maureen's accusation is also suggestive. Enacting the characteristic hiding or concealing behavior of the shamed individual, "Pecola tucked her head in—a funny, sad, helpless movement. A kind of hunching of the shoulders, pulling in of the neck, as though she wanted to cover her ears" (72). When Maureen subsequently taunts Claudia by calling her "black," Claudia, unlike Pecola who responds passively to Maureen's insults, flails out angrily and defiantly at the humiliator, giving physical expression to Pecola's unexpressed rage. Claudia also takes on the role of the protector-rescuer in this scene. Yet it is telling that when Claudia swings at Maureen, she misses and instead hits Pecola in the face. Despite her enactment of the protector's role, Claudia also shares at some deep level the community impulse to victimize Pecola: that is, to rid herself of her own shame by scapegoating the utterly vulnerable Pecola.

In the plight of Pecola Breedlove, *The Bluest Eye* dramatizes what Wurmser describes as the "theme" of unlovability—"the triad of weakness, defectiveness, and dirtiness" that occurs in the classic shame situation (*Mask* 98). Feeling unloved by her parents and "ugly" in the gaze of others, Pecola defends herself by withdrawing. "Concealed, veiled, eclipsed," she hides behind her "mantle" of ugliness, "peeping out from behind the shroud very seldom, and then only to yearn for the return of her mask" (39). The "goal of hiding as part of the shame affect," as Wurmser explains, is "to prevent further exposure and, with that, further rejection, but it also atones for the exposure that has already occurred" (*Mask* 54). That Pecola, who is terrified by her parents' physical violence, wants to disappear is also suggestive. "If it is appearance (exposure) that is central in shame, disappearance is the logical outcome of shame. . . ," writes Wurmser (*Mask* 81). Indeed, "Shame's aim is disappearance. This may be, most simply, in the form of hiding; . . . most archaically in the form of freezing into complete paralysis and stupor; most frequently, in the form of forgetting parts of one's life and one's self; and at its most differentiated, in the form of changing one's character" (*Mask* 84). Pecola's attempt to bodily disappear also marks the beginning of her experiences of depersonalization: that is, her "estrangement from world and self," which Wurmser describes as symptomatic of shame anxiety (*Mask* 53). Pecola "squeezed her eyes shut. Little parts of her body faded away. . . . Her fingers went, one by one; then her arms disappeared all the way to the elbow. Her feet now. Yes, that was good. The legs all at once. It was hardest above the thighs. She had to be real still and pull. . . . The face was hard, too. Almost done, almost. Only her tight, tight eyes were left" (45).

Pecola, who is unable to make her eyes disappear, spends hours looking at herself in the mirror, attempting to discover "the secret" of her ugliness. And she prays for a miracle—she prays for blue eyes—because she believes that if God grants her blue eyes, she will no longer be ugly, and thus her parents might not "do bad things" in front of her "pretty" blue eyes (45, 46). Because "[l]ove and power are vested in the gaze," writes Wurmser, to "seek forever with the eye and not to find leads to shame." Pecola's wish for blue eyes recalls Wurmser's description of the "magic eye," the use of eye power and looking in an attempt to attract the "beckoning, admiring" gaze of the absent mother and thus undo, "by magic expression, the wound of basic unlovability" (*Mask* 94). In her desire for blue eyes, Pecola also expresses the wish to escape the shaming gaze of the dominant culture, which sees her as the despised and inferior Other. Feeling utterly flawed and dirty, Pecola rejects her stigmatized African-American identity when she imagines that she can cure her ugliness—that is, her shame and basic unlovability—only if she is magically granted the same blue eyes possessed by little white girls.

In the story of Pecola, *The Bluest Eye* depicts not only the wounds caused by inter- and intraracial shaming but also the horrors of father-daughter incest. But although *The Bluest Eye* depicts the shameful family secret of an incestuous rape, it also is caught up in a form of denial. Indeed, Morrison has described the rape as "almost irrelevant," insisting that she wants readers to "*look* at" Cholly and "see his love for his daughter and his powerlessness to help her pain." Cholly's "embrace, the rape," in Morrison's words, "is all the gift he has left" (Tate 164). If Morrison, in writing the novel, found herself thinking the "unthinkable" as she worked out the incest secret that lies buried at the heart of *The Bluest Eye* (Bakerman 39–40), she also ran into difficulties as she felt the need to provoke reader sympathy for Cholly, despite what he does to his daughter.

By insisting that the "pieces of Cholly's life" can be rendered "coherent only in the head of a musician" who can connect together the various fragments of Cholly's life (159), the narrative invites readers to focus on the connection between Cholly's fragmented trauma narrative and his rape of Pecola: that is, to understand Cholly's rape of Pecola, the reader must understand Cholly's traumatic sexual initiation as an adolescent. The fact that Morrison chose to tell the rape from Cholly's point of view and that Morrison's narrative, in part, endorses Cholly—for he is, in Morrison's own description, one of her "salt tasters," a "fearless" and "lawless" character (see Stepto 19–20, Tate 164–65)—suggests the hidden way in which the novel positions readers not only with the humiliated victim but also with the humiliator, the shamed, enraged father who projects his own shame onto his daughter and thus acts as an unwitting agent in the white society's humiliation of the vulnerable Pecola. Although Morrison wants to elicit reader sympathy for Cholly, she also invokes the pernicious—and shaming—racist image of the black man as rapist in this scene. And she risks shaming her readers as she breaks the taboo on looking and positions her readers as voyeurs of the incest scene.

When Cholly sees Pecola—who assumes the permanent posture of the shamed, traumatized individual with her "hunched" back and her head turned to one side "as though crouching from a permanent and unrelieved blow"— he wonders why she looks "so whipped" and why she isn't happy. Feeling accused by the "clear statement of her misery," he wants "to break her neck—but tenderly." "What could a burned-out black man say to the hunched back of his eleven-year-old daughter? If he looked into her face, he would see those haunted, loving eyes. The hauntedness would irritate him—the love would move him to fury. How dare she love him? . . . What was he supposed to do about that? Return it? How?" (161).

Cholly initially responds to the misery of his shamed daughter with anger, and he also sees her as an object of contempt and disgust: "His hatred of her slimed in his stomach and threatened to become vomit." But then, when Pecola scratches the back of her calf with her toe—which is what Pauline did the first time Cholly saw her many years before—the "timid, tucked-in look" of her scratching toe reminds him of the tenderness he once felt toward his wife. Despite the "rigidity of her shocked body, the silence of her stunned throat," he wants "to fuck her—tenderly," and yet the tenderness does "not hold." "His soul seemed to slip down to his guts and fly out into her, and the gigantic thrust he made into her then provoked the only sound she made—a hollow suck of air in the back of her throat. Like the rapid loss of air from a circus balloon." Afterward, Cholly again feels "hatred mixed with tenderness" as he looks at the unconscious body of his daughter lying on the kitchen floor (162–63).

The Bluest Eye presents a disturbing account of Cholly's rape of Pecola and then partially denies what it has described by insisting in the closure that Cholly loved Pecola even though his "touch was fatal," for the "love of a free man is never safe" (206). While some critic-readers of *The Bluest Eye* have remarked on the "raw horror" of the rape scene or have described the rape as a "tremendous and overwhelming act of paternal violence" or have insisted that Cholly's act is "diabolical" (Miner 88, Holloway, "Language" 44, B. Jones 30), others have followed the text's directives by partially denying what Cholly has done or by attempting to exonerate Cholly. Because Cholly has been socially conditioned to view himself as an "object of disgust," he "can do nothing other than objectify Pecola," argues one commentator, and hence Cholly exploits his daughter "because his own exploitation makes it impossible to do otherwise" (Byerman, "Beyond Realism" 59). "At least . . . he wanted to touch his daughter. Pauline Breedlove responds to the rape by beating Pecola, an act not much less brutal than Cholly's," in the view of another commentator (Carmean 24). Although most readers would be unwilling to "forgive Cholly for his crime against his daughter," remarks another commentator, many understand the "why and how" of the rape, which is "a terribly tragic manifestation of a severely skewed upbringing" (Portales 504). If Morrison's treatment of the rape is said to foreground the reader's "awareness of the complexity of judgment and feeling" (Dittmar 139), it is also the case that some critic-readers appear to identify with Cholly's violent act and condemn Pecola. "A profound expression of love, the rape is also an exercise of power and freedom, a protest against an unjust and repressive culture," argues one critic who also claims that while the defeated and ultimately mad Pecola is "someone to be pitied," her "ignorance" and "passivity" merit the reader's "contempt" (Otten, *Crime* 21, 24). Such readers repeat the text by partially denying the horror of Pecola's plight, and they also, in exonerating Cholly and scapegoating Pecola, inadvertently become caught up in the shame drama presented in the text.

If, in the rape scene, Pecola is silenced, earlier she poignantly asked, "[H]ow do you get somebody to love you?" (32). Pecola, who feels that she is unlovable, craves the affection of her father only to be raped by him. The utterly helpless and vulnerable daughter and the embodiment of her father's self-contempt and loathing, the shamed Pecola becomes the target of her father's humiliated fury. He does to her what has been done to him and thus, when he rapes Pecola, he inflicts on her his own feelings of exposure, power-lessness, narcissistic injury, and humiliation. Pecola's fainting depicts not only the somatic reactions that occur in extreme states of shame—which include physiological responses such as "fainting, dizziness, rigidity of all the muscles" (Wurmser, *Mask* 83)—but also the physical and mental paralysis experienced by the trauma victim.

Raped by her father and then severely beaten by her mother, Pecola seeks help from Soaphead Church, a child molester who advertises himself as a spiritualist and psychic reader. When Pecola asks Soaphead Church for blue eyes, he finds her request "the most fantastic and the most logical petition" he has ever received, and he wants the power to help the "ugly little girl asking for beauty" and desiring to "rise up out of the pit of her blackness" (174). In his letter to God, Soaphead insists that he has worked a miracle and given Pecola cobalt blue eyes. "No one else will see her blue eyes. But *she* will," remarks Soaphead (182). And, indeed, Pecola ends up living permanently in the dissociated world of madness where she talks to her alter identity—her "friend"—about her magical blue eyes. The traumatically shamed Pecola believes that others are fascinated with, and envious of, her blue eyes. But she is, in fact, the object of gaze avoidance by her mother, who looks "drop-eyed" at her daughter. As Pecola remarks to her alter "friend," "Ever since I got my blue eyes, she look away from me all of the time. Do you suppose she's jealous too?" Similarly, members of the community look away from the shamed outcast, Pecola, socially ostracizing her with their gaze avoidance. "Everybody's jealous. Every time I look at somebody, they look off" (195). Only in her mad world is Pecola someone special, a black girl with the blue eyes of a white girl.

While Claudia and her sister, Frieda, are initially Pecola's allies despite their "defensive shame"—for they feel "embarrassed for Pecola, hurt for her, and finally . . . sorry for her"—other members of the community, intoning the racist discourse of dirt and defilement, pronounce Cholly a "dirty nigger," and they also insist that the pregnant Pecola carries "some of the blame" for what has happened to her (190, 189). Members of the community, who make Pecola the target of shaming gossip, are "disgusted, amused, shocked, outraged, or even excited" by Pecola's story (190). Expressing their contempt, they remark that Pecola's baby, which is "Bound to be the ugliest thing walking," would be "better off in the ground" (189–90). But when Claudia thinks about the baby that everyone wants dead, she feels "a need for someone to want the black baby to live—just to counteract the universal love of white baby dolls, Shirley Temples, and Maureen Peals" (190). Intent on changing the course of events—and, in effect, breaking the cycle of racial self-loathing expressed in the communal response to the pregnant Pecola— Claudia buries the bicycle money she earned from selling seeds and plants the marigold seeds, hoping that God will be impressed enough with her sacrifice so that he will produce a miracle and save Pecola's baby.

But the baby, which is born premature, dies, and the permanently damaged Pecola is socially ostracized. "She was so sad to see. Grown people looked away; children, those who were not frightened by her, laughed outright." And Claudia, whose marigolds never grow, ends up avoiding Pecola, who spends her days "walking up and down, up and down, her head jerking to the beat of a drummer so distant only she could hear" and who, with her bent elbows and her hands on her shoulders, flails her arms "like a bird in an eternal, grotesquely futile effort to fly" (204). Pecola, who absorbs the "waste" others dump on her, ultimately becomes the community scapegoat as members of the black community project onto her their own self-loathing and self-contempt—their own stain of blackness. "All of us—all who knew her—felt so wholesome after we cleaned ourselves on her. We were so beautiful when we stood astride her ugliness. . . . And she let us, and thereby deserved our contempt. We honed our egos on her, padded our characters with her frailty, and yawned in the fantasy of our strength" (205).

Although it has been claimed that "to read *The Bluest Eye* looking to assign blame" is to "miss the point" (Kuenz 430), critics, again and again, have become caught up in the drama of blame assessment as they have attempted to determine who is responsible for Pecola's plight. Pecola has been described as a character whose "innocence and tragedy" are presented to readers and as "the epitome of the victim in a world that reduces persons to objects and then makes them feel inferior as objects" (Rosenberg, "Seeds" 442, C. Davis 14). But she also has been described as possibly a "participant and not simply victim, victim and at the same moment participant" in the rape, and as a character who is "responsible, in the final analysis, for what happens to her" because she fails to recognize that she must define a life for herself (Gibson 29, Samuels and Hudson-Weems 15). And yet the victimizing father, as we have seen, has often been judged as not fully responsible for his life or actions. Representative of this view is the remark that Cholly, the "victim of earlier, more blatant oppressions," has "struggled throughout his life against a society that treats him, intentionally or not, without compassion or sympathy" and hence, "almost everything that Cholly does, he does as a reaction to forces and pressures around him" (Portales 499, 503). In yet another common reading, blame is displaced from Cholly onto the black community, the white culture, or both. "Pecola seems less a victim of her father than of a whole community, which has allowed itself to become debased by the dominant culture and alienated by adopting its norms" (Göbel 131). Similarly, the black community "must share the blame for Pecola's diminishment," for Pecola has "been made a scapegoat by a neighborhood of people who themselves live their own unnatural lives under the gaze of the dominant culture" (Bjork 53). If Morrison, herself, has been implicitly condemned for writing a novel that is "mired in the pathology of Afro-American experience" (Dittmar 140), the blame and shame are also attached to Morrison's readers. "No one is indicted for Pecola's destruction," remarks one critic, "but then in another way we all are" (Demetrakopoulos, "Bleak Beginnings" 36).

Morrison's "impetus" for writing *The Bluest Eye*, as she recalls, "was to write a book about a kind of person that was never in literature anywhere, never taken seriously by anybody—all those peripheral little girls" (Neustadt 88). As she tells the story of the Pecola in *The Bluest Eye*, Morrison explores the devastation caused by black self-contempt—the sense of the self as racially stained and defective, as "dirty" and "nasty" and "ugly" to use descriptions that recur in the text—but in a carefully shaped narrative that serves to counteract and aestheticize the raw shame and pain the novel exposes. Describing what he calls "gripping art"—creations that exert "a power of fascination, of spellbinding force"—Léon Wurmser finds in such works layers of "woundedness, idealization, and aggression" (*Mask* 293–97). In *The Bluest Eye*, a work that contains layers of woundedness, idealization, and aggression, Morrison exerts the power of fascination as she begins the cultural and literary work that will continue to preoccupy her by exposing the racial wounds and shame-humiliations suffered by black Americans in the race-conscious and race-divided American society.

3

"I Like My Own Dirt"

DISINTERESTED VIOLENCE
AND SHAMELESSNESS IN *SULA*

"Proud? . . . What you talking about? I like my own dirt. . . . I'm not proud," says Sula on her deathbed, intoning the discourse of dirt and defilement associated with black shame and the stigmatized African-American identity (142). If Morrison represents Pecola as the racially shamed and passive victim, she constructs Sula as the seemingly shameless opposite of Pecola. Moving beyond the girlhood stage described in *The Bluest Eye*, Morrison remarks that in *Sula* she wanted to show what the "Claudias and Friedas, those feisty little girls, grow up to be" (Stepto 20), and accordingly one of the focuses in her 1973 novel is on black female sexual expression. Interested in creating a new literary space in the African-American cultural imagination through her oppositional character, Morrison describes Sula as the "New World black woman," explaining that Sula is "experimental" and "sort of an outlaw" and that "she's not going to take it anymore" (Moyers 269).

Because the adult Sula is shameless in her sexuality and because she refuses the expected wife and mother roles, she has sometimes been identified as a feminist heroine. Indeed, it can be argued that part of Morrison's purpose is to use the uninhibited Sula to endorse the late 1960s and early 1970s ideology of sexual liberation and freedom from oppressive social and inner restraints. Yet the second-wave feminist story of women's emancipated sexuality, which was largely told through a white, middle-class perspective, becomes complicated when told through a black perspective, and, thus in Morrison's novel, the drama of gender identity is also race-inflected. If Morrison's character, in her liberated sexuality, is meant to portray a 1970s black feminist character, she also recalls the racist construction of the sexually promiscuous "bad" black girl, the so-called black Jezebel, a shaming stereotype

that Patricia Morton aptly describes as one of the "disfigured images" of
black womanhood that recur in American culture's historical and continuing
"assault" on black womanhood (see 1–13). According to racist mythology,
which constructs black women as the racial and sexual Other, African-
American women are hypersexed and therefore debased. Indeed, "In the
circular logic of segregation, blackness equalled sexuality and sexuality was,
in all senses, *black*," as Diane Roberts observes. "In the hierarchy of purity to
pollution, blackness was dirt" (156). In *Sula*, Morrison evokes but also interrogates these shaming racist constructions through her experimental and
outlaw character. And yet if the lawless and dangerously free Sula is endorsed
by the narrative, she also is cast in the scapegoat role. Not only does Sula
become the carrier of shame and contempt in the Bottom community, she
also, in a classic contempt-disappear scenario, is ushered prematurely out of
the text. This points to the cultural embeddedness of Morrison's representation of her defiant feminist character.

Unlike *The Bluest Eye*, which is an explicit shame drama, *Sula*, at first
glance, appears to shun shame through its shameless characters, Sula and
Shadrack. And yet as Léon Wurmser remarks in his analysis of shamelessness, "if it is shame that is fought against by shamelessness, it is shame
that returns in spectral form" in shameless behavior (*Mask* 262). That
"shameless, feelingless behavior" is a "form of hiding" and that the shameless individual is often "someone who was tragically humiliated and learned
to defend woundedness with a defiant show of strength" (Wurmser, *Mask*
263, Nichols 71) is dramatized in Morrison's novel. While part of Morrison's explicit agenda in *Sula* is to use her two shameless characters, Sula
and Shadrack, to flaunt the shaming racist stereotypes of the black Jezebel
and the degenerate black madman, it is also revealing that both characters,
who can be read as versions of the "bad nigger" folk hero, are presented as
deeply shamed individuals and as social pariahs: both are nihilistic misan-
thropes who are defiant and yet ultimately thwarted and whose dangerous
excesses are subjected to the control and containment of the black community. Not only does this point to the text's inability to totally break free
from hegemonic and shaming constructions of black identity, but it also shows
that internalization—that is, the "profound psychological and social introjec-
tion of negative images and meanings" found in stereotypes—is a "common
and profoundly problematic outcome of stereotyping discourses" (Stepan and
Gilman 89). Thus, although *Sula* is politically invested in reimagining black
cultural identity through its lawless and experimental characters, it also
reveals the insidious and problematic effects of internalized racism and
shaming racist stereotypes on literary discourse.

If in *Sula* Morrison pushes black-white relations to the periphery of her
narrative through her inward focus on the Bottom community and on the

friendship between the conventional Nel and unconventional Sula, she also begins her novel with an account of the insulting "nigger joke" that serves as the originating myth of the Bottom community of Medallion, Ohio. "A joke. A nigger joke. That was the way it got started. Not the town, of course, but that part of town where the Negroes lived, the part they called the Bottom in spite of the fact that it was up in the hills" (4). When a white farmer promises his slave freedom and some "bottom" land if he completes some difficult chores, he tricks the slave into asking for hilly, not valley, land by insisting that hilly "bottom" land is rich and fertile. "[W]hen God looks down, it's the bottom. That's why we call it so. It's the bottom of heaven—best land there is" (5). Using a classic countershaming tactic in describing how the blacks who live in the hills can "literally look down on the white folks" (5), the *Sula* narrator shames the white shamers and uses humor to counteract shame. But the narrator also remarks on the "adult pain" that exists behind the laughter of the Bottom folk, laughter that is "part of the pain" (4). The racial shaming that begins with the "nigger joke" played on the black founder of the Bottom community is perpetuated in the shame-ridden and driven life of an economically emasculated Bottom man like Jude Greene, who lives in a state of chronic resentment because, as he puts it, the black man has a "hard row to hoe" in a world run by white men (103). If whites have traditionally demonized blacks, the Bottom people demonize—and thus shame—whites, seeing them as an "evil" force. To the Bottom people, the "purpose of evil" is "to survive it," and they determine "to survive floods, white people, tuberculosis, famine, and ignorance" (90).

Calling attention to the shame and trauma of African-American life in *Sula*, Morrison describes a world where whites are equated with the uncontrollable and uncontainable evils of life, where black survival may come at the horrible cost of self-mutilation, and where expressions of black rage at the social and economic injustices of life ultimately prove self-destructive. Morrison also evokes the dissociated world of the trauma victim in *Sula* through her enactments of scenes of disinterested violence—jarringly violent but also highly visual scenes that are depicted in a detached and often stylized manner and that recall descriptions of the "sensory and iconic forms of memory" associated with trauma, memories that focus on "fragmentary sensation, on image without context" (Herman, *Trauma* 39, 38). "I thought of *Sula* as a cracked mirror, fragments and pieces we have to see independently and put together," Morrison has suggestively remarked, pointing to the way in which her novel, with its repeated scenes of violence, replicates the disrupted, fragmented trauma narrative (LeClair 127). From the opening description of Shadrack's war trauma through depictions of Sula's and Eva's self-mutilation, Eva's burning of Plum, Chicken Little's drowning, Hannah's fiery death, and the mass drowning deaths of many members of the Bottom community, the novel focuses attention on the unexpected violence of African-American life. Remarking on the chapter that describes the fiery death of Hannah, Morrison explains that the chapter—by starting out with a description of the "second strange thing" and then by recalling the "first strange thing"—warns readers, especially black readers, to "expect something dreadful." But readers can also take comfort in the knowledge that whatever the unknown "strange"—or dreadful—event is, it has already occurred. While she may want to "hold" her readers "in a comfortable place," she also wants them to "know something awful is going to happen," so that when it happens they "won't be shattered" (Tate 163–64).

A novel that plays on the reader's emotions, *Sula*, as Morrison has described it, is also "hermetic and tight," if not "bookish" (Ruas 98) as it, like *The Bluest Eye*, uses narrative form and design to aestheticize violence and also to counteract shame. And *Sula*, like *The Bluest Eye*, demands participatory reading, inviting both a cognitive and visceral response from its audience. In part, Morrison compels reader participation through the "elliptical technique" of her novel (Grant 100). For despite the novel's apparent chronological ordering—in chapters titled by dates beginning in 1919 and ending in 1965—*Sula* "miscues" readers, forcing them to "question" their readings and hold their judgment "in check," and thus, it has been claimed, Morrison forces readers "into the habit of 'new seeing'" by presenting events but withholding their significance until later (McDowell, "Self" 85, 86, Lounsberry 128). To the extent that this narrative technique gives readers the sense that there are narrative gaps or secrets—that is, the feeling that there are things being withheld or concealed—it acts out the hiding and concealing behavior associated with the shame scenario even as it promises, like *The Bluest Eye*, the public exposure of shame- and trauma-laden secrets. And as we shall see, *Sula* is also a work that has provoked critic after critic to become caught up in the enactment of the countershaming and blame-assessment dramas prompted by the narrative.

Structuring the narrative by being strategically placed near the beginning and conclusion of the novel, the descriptions of the madman, Shadrack, focus attention on the systematic traumatization of black American men. The traumatic war experiences of Shadrack, which are described at the outset of the novel, repeat and telescope the historical traumas visited on African-American men in a racist society where black men are sent to fight white wars in Europe only to return home to a climate of pervasive racial oppression. On a day "adangle with shouts and explosions," the young Shadrack, a soldier in France during World War I, finds himself running with his fellow soldiers across a field during his first encounter with the enemy when he unexpectedly sees the face of a nearby soldier "fly off" (7, 8). Before Shadrack can register shock, the rest of the soldier's head disappears under his helmet, leaving the headless body of the soldier to run on, "with energy and grace, ignoring altogether the drip and slide of brain tissue down its back" (8).

That trauma can be both overwhelming and disorganizing and can lead to the feeling that one is unsafe in one's body and that one's emotions and thoughts are out of control (Herman, *Trauma* 160) is dramatized in Shadrack's response to his war experience. Using a narrative gap to signal Shadrack's post-traumatic amnesia, the novel depicts him more than a year later in an American hospital bed. Shadrack is permanently marked by his war experience, his original trauma about exploding body parts now expressed in his fear that "anything could be anywhere" (8) and in his hallucinations about his monstrous, out-of-control hands. When the "weak, hot, frightened" twenty-two-year-old Shadrack is released from the hospital, he does not know "who or what" he is. "[W]ith no past, no language, no tribe, no source, no address book, no comb, no pencil, no clock, no pocket handkerchief, no rug, no bed, no can opener, no faded postcard, no soap, no key, no tobacco pouch, no soiled underwear and nothing nothing nothing to do . . . he was sure of one thing only: the unchecked monstrosity of his hands" (12). Making a veiled allusion to the horrors of slavery in describing how Shadrack has "no past, no language, no tribe," the narrative focuses on the repetition of catastrophic trauma in African-American experience, and Shadrack's disintegration anxiety also anticipates Morrison's later description of Beloved's anxiety about body-self fragmentation. Shadrack, who ends up in jail, is convinced that he is real only when he sees the reflection of his grave face in the water of a toilet bowl. When the "blackness" of his face greets him "with its indisputable presence," he discovers that his hands are "[c]ourteously still," and he subsequently falls into a deep and tranquil sleep, "the first sleep of his new life" (13, 14).

In a twelve-day struggle to "order and focus" his disorganized experience, Shadrack attempts to make "a place for fear" as a way to control it. "He knew the smell of death and was terrified of it, for he could not anticipate it. It was not death or dying that frightened him, but the unexpectedness of both." After he returns to the Bottom, Shadrack institutes National Suicide Day in 1920, for he has come to believe that if one day a year is devoted to death, people will be able to "get it out of the way" and consequently the remainder of the year will be "safe and free" (14). Thus, each January third, Shadrack, with his wild eyes and long matted hair and loud, authoritative voice, walks through the Bottom ringing his cowbell and carrying his hangman's rope as he announces to the people that this is their only opportunity to kill either themselves or each other. Shadrack's Suicide Day ritual, which grows out of a traumatic war experience, is meant as a parody of American patriotic holidays. But it also evokes the horrors of white oppression and points to the insidious effects of internalized racism, for the hangman's rope Shadrack carries recalls the rope of the lyncher even as it prepares, as we shall see, for the black-on-black violence presented in the text in a series of *unexpected* deaths.

Commenting on the pain and shame of being "hated, despised, detested . . . by an entire race," Frantz Fanon describes how the black man is "overdetermined from without" as he is "dissected under white eyes," and how he engages in "a constant effort to run away from his own individuality, to annihilate his own presence" (118, 116, 60). The black man's attitude toward his own race, remarks Fanon, can border on the "pathological" (60). Robbed of his worth and individuality, the black man is told that he is "a brute beast," that he and his people are "like a walking dung-heap," that he has "no use in the world" (98). Morrison's Shadrack, who is presented as the utterly traumatized individual, is also the shamed black man, forced by his war experiences to recognize his own utter helplessness and deficiency. The scene in which Shadrack sees his black face in a toilet bowl, although presented as a comforting moment of racial recognition, is also a parodic, race-inflected rewriting of the myth of Narcissus that draws on the white racist equation between blackness and dirtiness as it represents Shadrack's discovery of his stigmatized racial identity. Even though the narrative seems to endorse Shadrack, enticing readers to make political sense of his shameless, mad behavior, Shadrack also evokes the shaming racist stereotype of the degenerate, pathological black madman.[1] "[D]runk, loud, obscene," Shadrack becomes the "terrible Shad who walked about with his penis out, who peed in front of ladies and girl-children, the only black who could curse white people and get away with it, [and] . . . who shouted and shook in the streets" (15, 61–62). If in his madness the shameless Shadrack articulates the unvoiced defiance and rage of the Bottom men by cursing white people, not only is his behavior ultimately self-destructive, but he also, as we shall see, inadvertently acts as an agent of white oppression when he leads a large number of his own community members to their deaths as they express their collective rage against their white capitalist oppressors.

Like Shadrack, Sula is a misanthrope and shamed social outcast, and she, too, is presented as a textual puzzle. At the beginning of the novel, readers are invited by the narrator to wonder with the members of the Bottom community not only "what Shadrack was all about," but also "what that little girl Sula who grew into a woman in their town was all about" (6). Morrison, herself, as a reader of her own text, seems preoccupied with this question. Morrison has remarked that she wanted readers to "dislike" her character and perhaps to be "fascinated" but also to "feel that thing that the town might feel": that there is "something askew" about Sula (Stepto 16). Morrison also has suggested that to understand Sula one must make sense out of Nel, who is cast as Sula's complement. Unlike Sula, who is "a rule-breaker, a kind of law-breaker, a lawless woman," Nel "knows and believes in" the values and the laws of the community. But Nel pays a price, for she "doesn't know about herself"; Sula, in contrast, "knows all there is to know about herself because she examines herself, she is experimental with herself, she's perfectly willing to think the unthinkable thing" (Stepto 14). Sula and Nel, in Morrison's description, "complement" and "support" each other, and indeed "the two of them together could have made a wonderful single human being" (Parker 62). In deliberately contrasting Nel's middle-class and Sula's lower-class upbringing and family life, Morrison's narrative focuses attention not only on the conjunction of class and race in the construction of African-American identities but also on the class distinctions within the African-American community, concerns that will continue to inform Morrison's fiction.

Although Nel's mother, Helene Wright, is a pillar of middle-class respectability in the Bottom community, she carries with her a deep and inherited sense of shame. The daughter of a Creole whore, Helene was raised in New Orleans "under the dolesome eyes of a multicolored Virgin Mary" by her respectable grandmother, who counseled Helene "to be constantly on guard for any sign of her mother's wild blood" (17). In repudiating her mother's "wild blood" and becoming a proud and utterly respectable middle-class woman, Helene attempts to escape the sexual shame of black women. bell hooks, remarking on the humiliations endured by black women in American society, describes the still common tendency of whites to view black women as sexually loose and thus as not worthy of respect, this shaming stereotype of African-American women being historically rooted in the slavery system in which whites "justified the sexual exploitation of enslaved black women by arguing that they were the initiators of sexual relationships with men" (*Ain't I a Woman* 52). Helene defends against her inherited shame by becoming an "impressive woman" who wins "all social battles with presence and a conviction of the legitimacy of her authority," and she also rises "grandly to the occasion of motherhood" (18). The fact that Helene takes pride in the maternal role recalls hooks's analysis of how many black women tried "to shift the focus of attention away from sexuality by emphasizing their commitment to motherhood." hooks explains that by participating in the "'cult of true womanhood' that reached its peak in early 20th century America," such women "endeavored to prove their value and worth by demonstrating that they were women whose lives were firmly rooted in the family" (*Ain't I a Woman* 70). Undermining the middle-class idealization of motherhood, *Sula* describes Helene as a mother who enjoys "manipulating her daughter" and thus becomes a repressive force in her daughter's life as she calms any "enthusiasms" shown by Nel. Consequently, Nel becomes "obedient and polite" as Helene drives "her daughter's imagination underground" (18).

In the isolated black world of the Bottom community, Helene can maintain her middle-class position and pride. But when she learns that her grandmother is ill, she must venture outside the Bottom and travel by train to New Orleans to be with the dying woman who raised her. Helene is forced to confront her deep-seated shame anxiety when she mistakenly gets onto the white passenger car of the segregated train and is publicly shamed by the white conductor. Treating her as the racial inferior and as a sexual object—as the sexually available black woman—the conductor lets his "eyes travel over the pale yellow" Helene, and then he verbally insults her in front of her daughter by asking, "What you think you doin', gal?" When Helene hears him utter the racially derogatory expression of contempt—"gal"—she feels deeply ashamed. "All the old vulnerabilities, all the old fears of being somehow flawed gathered in her stomach and made her hands tremble" (20). With an "eagerness to please and an apology for living" in her voice, Helene tries to appease the white conductor, insisting that she simply "made a mistake" (20, 21). Despite the contemptuous reply of the conductor—"We don't 'low no mistakes on this train. Now git your butt on in there"— Helene smiles. "Like a street pup that wags its tail at the very doorjamb of the butcher shop he has been kicked away from only moments before, Helene smiled. Smiled dazzlingly and coquettishly at the salmon-colored face of the conductor" (21). In her attempt to mollify the conductor through her coquettish smile, Helene enacts the role she has always shunned: that of the sexually enticing black woman.

When Helene smiles at the white conductor, Nel observes the stricken look of two black soldiers on the train who are eyewitnesses to this scene. Sensing anger and contempt in their frozen gaze—"the muscles of their faces tighten, a movement under the skin from blood to marble"—Nel feels "both pleased and ashamed" when she recognizes that, unlike her father who worships the graceful and beautiful Helene, the soldiers are "bubbling with a hatred for her mother that . . . had been born with the dazzling smile" (21–22). Nel's response to the public humiliation of her mother reveals that she both identifies with her shamed mother (thus Nel feels ashamed) and feels resentment toward her repressive—that is, shaming—mother (thus Nel feels pleased). Nel's fantasy that her mother's dress has come undone, thus exposing Helene's "custard-colored" skin, encodes the shameful visual—and sexual— exposure of her mother Nel has just witnessed. Recognizing that if her "tall, proud" mother is "really custard," then she too may be custard—that is, weak, vulnerable and contemptible—Nel determines to always be on her guard, for she wants to be certain that "no midnight eyes or marbled flesh . . . ever accost her and turn her into jelly" (22).

Readers are text-directed by earlier references to Helene's shame about her mother's "wild blood" to read Nel's encounter in New Orleans with her prostitute grandmother, Rochelle, as a confrontation with the side of her black identity that her middle-class mother has suppressed in her daughter, the side associated with passion and sexuality, but also with racial shame. That affect is contagious—that Rochelle has communicated, through her "tight, tight hug," some of her wildness to Nel—is dramatized in the ten-year-old Nel's sudden rebellious assertion of her own identity after her trip to New Orleans. "'I'm me. I'm not their daughter. I'm not Nel. I'm me. Me.' Each time she said the word *me* there was a gathering in her like power, like joy, like fear" (28). The fact that Nel's discovery of her own oppositional me-ness leads to her friendship with Sula points to the connection between Nel's suppressed "wild blood" and the "wildness" of Sula as Morrison deliberately brings together the middle-class, lighter-skinned Nel and the lower-class, darker-skinned Sula. If part of the text's explicit agenda is to provide a counternarrative to shaming racist stereotypes by romanticizing Sula's spontaneity and lawlessness, the narrative also repeats racist myths— the notion that lower-class blacks are immoral and are all but incapable of self-governance and self-control—in its representation of Sula.

If, in the paired opposites that organize the novel, the orderly, emotionally restrained Wright household is associated with middle-class repression, then the disorderly, and ironically named, Peace household is associated with lower-class spontaneity and passion but also with trauma and violence. Indeed, the text repeats—if not shamelessly flaunts—racist and class stereotypes that associate lower-class African Americans with promiscuity and violence. But Morrison also counteracts, in part, these shaming stereotypes as she simultaneously invokes an opposing set of positively valued images in her representation of the Peace women by constructing Eva as the self-sacrificing mother who goes to great lengths to ensure the economic survival of her children; Hannah as the earthy, natural and sexually liberated woman; and Sula as the heroic nonconformist who defiantly refuses to yield to social conventions. Despite Morrison's conscious antishaming agenda in her presentation of the Peace women, she also makes reader assessment of her characters difficult, as we shall see in our analysis of the conflicting—and conflicted—responses of critic-readers to these characters.

Described as the "creator and sovereign" of an "enormous house" (30) and as a woman who thrives on her hatred for her ineffectual and abandoning husband, BoyBoy, Eva Peace, as some critics have suggested, can be read as a challenge to the black mammy stereotype (see e.g., Bjork 64, Christian 158): the white-created image of the black woman as a submissive and nurturing domestic who not only serves but also loves white people.[2] In her subversion of the black mammy stereotype, however, Morrison plays on yet another stereotype, that of the black matriarch, and Morrison herself has remarked on Eva's "genuine matriarchy" in her comments on this character

(Koenen 78). The notion of the black matriarchy, which had a kind of wide cultural currency around the time the novel was written, was infamously formulated in the 1965 Moynihan Report. In the shaming discourse of the report, a root cause of the "deterioration of the Negro family" and the "tangle of pathology" of black urban life was the black matriarchy, which was said to impose "a crushing burden on the Negro male" (Rainwater 51, 75). As Marianne Hirsch has aptly remarked, "To write the story of the African American family in the wake of the report and the public images it fostered is always to write against the risk either of perpetuating or of appearing to repress this noxious stereotyping" ("Knowing Their Names" 71).

bell hooks, in her analysis of the matriarchy myth, comments that the myth of the black matriarch perpetuates the racist image of black women as "masculinized, domineering, amazonic creatures" (*Ain't I a Woman* 81). Even if it was "readily accepted by black people" (78), the matriarchy myth was a white creation used to discredit black people by describing black women as the aggressive castrators of passive, and emasculated, black men. But although hooks finds the matriarchy myth shaming, she also implicitly recognizes its oppositional, antishaming force, remarking that many black women are "proud to be labeled matriarchs" because the term has "more positive implications" than other stereotypes of black womanhood, such as "mammy, bitch, or slut." Those "who are economically oppressed and victimized by sexism and racism" are encouraged by such a myth to believe that "they exercise some social and political control over their lives" (*Ain't I a Woman* 80, 81). The matriarchy myth, as shame theorists might describe it, expresses the need to counteract passive shame with active—and angry, defiant—mastery. Indeed, at the affective center of the story of Morrison's truculent and fiercely independent matriarch, Eva, are feelings of shame-humiliation and contempt-disgust.

Morrison's novel, despite its at times wry, folksy, and gossipy narrating voice, draws attention to the depredations and humiliations suffered by Eva early in her marriage to BoyBoy. During her five years in a "sad and disgruntled marriage," Eva is repeatedly shamed and victimized, for BoyBoy "did whatever he could that he liked, and he liked womanizing best, drinking second, and abusing Eva third." When BoyBoy abandons Eva, he leaves her destitute and with three young children to feed: the "confused and desperately hungry" Eva has "$1.65, five eggs, three beets and no idea of what or how to feel" (32). In a graphic scene that portrays Eva's poverty but also uses the shaming imagery of the disgusting, dissmelling, and dirty infant, *Sula* describes how Eva uses lard to cure Plum's constipation. Taking her suffering infant son to the outhouse on a cold December night, Eva shoves "the last bit of food she had in the world (besides three beets) up his ass." After the "black hard stools" ricochet onto the frozen ground, Eva wonders what she is doing "down on her haunches with her beloved baby boy warmed by her body in the almost total darkness, her shins and teeth freezing, her nostrils assailed" (34). Intent on provoking a visceral response from her readers in this scene, Morrison also risks disgusting them by drawing on the shame-related "aversion to excreta" and the "fear, disgust, and humiliation associated with defecation" (Nathanson, *Shame and Pride* 175, Schneider 70).

After the outhouse incident, Eva disappears for eighteen months and then returns minus one leg but with a new black purse and enough money to survive on. The narrator—who sometimes provides an insider's account of Peace family secrets but at other times reports on community gossip about the family—omits the trauma narrative of how Eva lost her leg and, instead, provides community speculations about Eva's missing limb. According to one story that circulates in the Bottom, Eva deliberately "stuck" her leg under a train in order to make "them"—that is, the white capitalist society—"pay off." Another story turns the pain and shame of Eva's plight into a "nigger joke." When told that Eva sold her leg to a hospital for $10,000, an incredulous member of the Bottom community asks, "'Nigger gal legs goin' for $10,000 a *piece?*' as though he could understand $10,000 a *pair*—but for *one?*" (31). Like the Bottom townspeople, readers of *Sula* are induced to supplement the text by providing their own interpretive narratives around the omitted story. Following the text's suggestions that Eva sacrificed her leg for the sake of her children, some critic-readers describe Eva, at least in part, in positive terms: as "the embodiment of a black feminist self-determinism"; as a woman whose "gesture of self-mutilation" is done "in the service of survival"; as someone who is "strongly, fiercely, rationally and roughly protective"; and as a person who "converts her very body into a dismembered instrument of defiance" in her desire to "defeat the dreadful course of capitalism's 'joke'" (Bjork 64, Hirsch, *Mother/Daughter Plot* 182, Demetrakopoulos, "*Sula*" 55, Baker 241).

If Eva is portrayed as a fierce matriarch bent on ensuring the survival of her children, she also is an abandoned—and thus shamed—wife. Eva is further humiliated when BoyBoy returns to the Bottom several years later with another woman. Even though BoyBoy appears "a picture of prosperity and good will" (35), Eva is aware of the shame lurking beneath his big city shine. Watching him dance down the steps and strut toward the waiting woman, Eva sees "defeat in the stalk of his neck" and in the "curious tight way" he holds his shoulders (36). When BoyBoy whispers to the woman and she laughs, Eva feels a "liquid trail of hate" flood her chest, and she is filled with "pleasant anticipation" at the thought of hating BoyBoy, an emotion that will protect her from the "routine vulnerabilities" of life and keep her "alive and happy" (36–37). Yet like the humiliated individual who makes a shamefaced withdrawal to protect against further humiliation, Eva begins her retreat to her upper-floor bedroom after BoyBoy's visit. And she becomes an arrogant, contemptuous woman who rids herself of her own shame by shaming others.

When "contempt is turned outward," observes Silvan Tomkins, the contemptuous person, as "the evaluator of others," can enjoy "self-inflation through the deflation of others" and also "self-purification through sullying the selves of others" (266). While the text insists that Eva bequeaths "man-love" to her daughters (41), it also acts out countershaming fantasies of female revenge by presenting Eva as a powerful matriarch who humiliates males. When, for example, Eva looks at the "milky skin and cornsilk hair" of the "beautiful, slight, quiet" man who rents a room from her, she, "out of a mixture of fun and meanness," calls him Tar Baby; and in a dialogic, counter-shaming retort to white racist speech, she further insults Tar Baby by insisting that he is not "half white" as others claim but that he is "all white," for she knows "blood" when she sees it and he doesn't "have none" (39–40). She exercises a similar shaming power when she takes in three boys and names all of them "Dewey" despite their obvious physical differences—one boy is deeply black, one is light-skinned with red hair and freckles, and one is half Mexican with chocolate skin. A "trinity with a plural name," the "surly, and wholly unpredictable" deweys remain "boys in mind" and never grow beyond four feet tall (38, 39, 84): in other words, they become embodiments of the shamed—that is, the feckless, inferior, unsocialized—black male.

Eva's son, Plum, is also presented as an object of contempt, and indeed Plum initially appears in the novel as a dissmelling, dirty infant. Not only is the description of Eva squatting down on her haunches in the outhouse with her constipated son cast as a birthing ritual, but the symbolic equation between Plum and excrement is reinforced later when Hannah asks Eva why she killed the adult Plum. Hannah's question prompts Eva's recollection of the stench of the outhouse on the cold winter night when she opened up the infant Plum's bowels. As Eva explains why she murdered Plum—a soldier in World War I who returned to the Bottom a heroin addict—she describes the difficulty of his birth and how he was trying to return to her womb. An object of shame, the adult Plum was weak, contemptible, dirty. As Eva tells Hannah, "he wanted to crawl back in my womb and well . . . I ain't got the room no more even if he could do it. . . . And he was crawlin' back. Being helpless and thinking baby thoughts and dreaming baby dreams and messing up his pants again and smiling all the time." In a description that risks shaming the voyeuristic reader by violating the taboo against incest, Eva describes how, when she closed her eyes at night, she dreamed that Plum was "crawlin' up the stairs quietlike" and then "creepin' to the bed trying to spread" her legs, trying "to get back up" in her womb. Eva killed Plum, she insists, so that he could "die like a man, not all scrunched up inside" her womb, but "like a man" (71–72).

The actual narration of Eva's murder of Plum—she first douses him with kerosene and then lights a match—occurs earlier in the novel, without Eva's explanation or justification, in a scene intended to misdirect and then jolt readers. That Eva lovingly embraces Plum before killing him recalls the behavior found in abusive parents, who often mingle "protectiveness with brutality" (Waites 69). Following the novel's indirect representation of trauma, the narrative poeticizes the description of Eva's burning of her son, which is mediated through Plum's eyes. "It wound itself—this wet light—all about him, splashing and running into his skin. He opened his eyes and saw what he imagined was the great wing of an eagle pouring a wet lightness over him. Some kind of baptism, some kind of blessing, he thought. Everything is going to be all right, it said. Knowing that it was so he closed his eyes and sank back into the bright hole of sleep" (47). Despite the narrative's insistence that Eva loved Plum, her murder of her son enacts a contempt-disappear scenario as it depicts the annihilating force of parental contempt-disgust. As Léon Wurmser explains, "Contempt says: 'You should disappear as such a being as you have shown yourself to be—failing, weak, flawed, and dirty. . . .' To disappear into nothing is the punishment for such failure" ("Shame" 67). If Morrison partially protects her readers by describing Eva's burning of Plum in an aestheticized and detached way, the account of Plum's death also calls to mind the shameful, horrific experiences of African Americans at the hands of white lynchers, who viewed their black victims, many of whom were burned or "roasted alive" (Harris, *Exorcising Blackness* 7), as objects of contempt: as dirty and worthless human beings.

Because the reader is not "offered easy access" to the scene in which Eva kills Plum (Spillers 46), many critic-readers have become involved in the drama of blame assessment in their varied constructions of this scene. While some critic-readers condemn Eva's murder of her son, describing it as "presumptuous" or remarking that "Eva egoistically eliminates what offends her" (Christian 160, T. Harris, *Fiction* 74), others endorse her act, arguing that Eva's "fully developed humanity" is revealed in this scene or that, as an "agent of death," Eva is acting "primarily out of love" (R. Bell 25, Carmean 35). Just as the text minimizes the horror of what is being described, so some commentators insist that Eva's act is one of "euthanasia," revealing Eva's passionate commitment to "life that has quality" (Demetrakopoulos, *"Sula"* 56–57). Eva's "crime" of burning Plum is even called a "profound act of love" and Plum's death a "victory" because it releases him "from his tortured existence" and allows him "to return to an eternal past" (Otten, *Crime* 43, Montgomery 131–32). The fact that Plum's death is also commonly described as an "act of purgation—a rite of purification" (Samuels and Hudson-Weems 40) suggests that on some level critic-readers may be responding to the shame drama presented in the text. In other words, some critic-readers may find Plum an object of contempt or disgust, recognizing what one commentator refers to as the "threat" posed to Eva and the household by Plum's "degeneration" or what another sees as Eva's "obscenely intimate" relation to her son (Gillespie 37, Hirsch, *Mother/Daughter Plot* 181). Thus, they may experience what one critic describes as "contradictory feelings between shock and relief" (Spillers 47) when Eva sets fire to Plum and he, in a contempt-disappear scenario, vanishes from the text.

Like Plum, Eva's daughter, Hannah, burns to death, and her dramatic textual disappearance also enacts a complicated shame drama. Indirect evidence of this is found in the critical commentary on Hannah, who has been described as a character who "would be considered a slut" in any world other than Morrison's novel, where she embodies the "pleasure principle," and as a character who puts "to rest" the "loose woman" stereotype of black womanhood, for unlike the traditional seductress who makes an effort to be alluring in order to manipulate men, Hannah has a "natural sensuality" and places no demands on the men she is involved with (T. Harris, *Fiction* 75, Christian 157, 159). If, as these critical comments suggest, part of Morrison's aim in her depiction of Hannah is to counteract the shaming racist stereotype of the licentious "bad" black woman by endorsing Hannah's shamelessly open sexual promiscuity, the narrative also repeats the racist discourse that, in suggesting "black people have secret access to intense pleasure, particularly pleasures of the body," inscribes blackness as a "'primitive' sign" and the black body as a sign of sexual pleasure (hooks, *Black Looks* 34).

A woman who "ripple[s] with sex" and who refuses to live without male attention after the death of her husband, Hannah has a series of lovers, most of them the husbands of her neighbors and friends. The sexually enticing Hannah makes men aware of "her behind, her slim ankles, the dew-smooth skin and the incredible length of neck. Then the smile-eyes, the turn of the head—all so welcoming, light and playful" (42). Because Hannah does not make demands on men and treats them as if they are "complete and wonderful" just as they are, they bask in the "Hannah-light" that shines on them. Hannah takes men to the pantry or down into the cellar behind the coal bin but rarely to her bed, because while she will "fuck practically anything," she is "fastidious about whom she slept with" (43). Unlike Helene, who finds Hannah "sooty" and condemns her for her "slackness," and unlike the "good" women of the Bottom who similarly find Hannah "nasty," the *Sula* narrator seems to admire Hannah's "funky elegance of manner" (29, 44, 44–45). Echoing the text's endorsement of Hannah, critic-readers have described her as a "sexually desiring" subject or have admired Hannah for her apparent "womanist stance of simplicity, intimacy, and communal candor" and for her "authenticity of person" (Carmean 36, Bjork 65, Spillers 45). Morrison, herself, as a reader of her novel, has remarked that she feels "more affection" for Hannah than for any other character in the novel (Stepto 15).

Yet despite Morrison's claim of affection for Hannah, her character dies a grisly, fiery death as if she is being bodily punished for her shameless sexuality, and as if her sexualized black body is a site of impurity—a primitive sign of shame that must be exorcised from the text. And like Plum's fiery demise, Hannah's death is linked to the annihilating contempt of her mother, Eva, in yet another textual enactment of the contempt-disappear scenario. "Mamma, did you ever love us?" Hannah asks Eva before she dies. Calling Hannah's question an "evil wonderin'" (67), a contemptuous Eva, in a response replete with shaming rhetoric, insists her mother love is proven by the fact that she kept Plum and Hannah alive when they were children, a time when "[n]iggers was dying like flies." "You settin' here with your healthy-ass self and ax me did I love you? Them big old eyes in your head would a been two holes full of maggots if I hadn't," Eva insists, calling Hannah a "snake-eyed ungrateful hussy." "I stayed alive for you can't you get that through your thick head or what is that between your ears, heifer?" (68–69). When Hannah then asks Eva why she killed Plum, Eva, speaking with "two voices," describes her maternal contempt for her helpless adult son who was trying to return to her womb, yet she insists that she loved Plum, that she held him "[r]eal close" before killing him (71, 72). The day after Hannah asks her question, she dies a fiery death and the fact that Hannah's question precedes her death points to the connection between maternal contempt and violent death in Morrison's novel.

If the description of Hannah's death, like that of Plum's death, is initially aestheticized—for the burning Hannah is described as a "flaming, dancing figure" (76)—the narrative subsequently focuses attention on Hannah's suffering body as it remarks on the look of agony on her face. It also presents Hannah's twitching, seared body as an object of both fascination and disgust by calling attention to the smell of Hannah's "cooked flesh" and the sight of her disfigured body which, even on the way to the hospital, has begun to "bubble and blister" (77). Like the onlookers depicted in the text—the deweys look at Hannah's burned body, "their eyes raked with wonder," while another spectator vomits—readers are meant to be unsettled, if not physically disgusted, by this scene, but are also positioned with the voyeuristic Sula who watches her mother burn to death because she is "interested" (76, 78). Laura Tanner, in her analysis of literary representations of violence, remarks that the victim's body "may be reduced to literary convention or unveiled with agonizing specificity": the victim can emerge as an "object of imaginative manipulation, his or her body simply another text on which the reader inscribes meaning," or the text can push the reader "into a position of discomforting proximity to the victim's vulnerable body" (7, 9, 10). Morrison's staging of violence in this scene recalls Tanner's description of works that exploit "the reader's bodiless status to invite a voyeuristic participation in the scene of violence." Reading, as Tanner explains, "involves a purely imaginary participation in the novel's fictional universe" and thus the reader's "presence in the text . . . is defined by the absence of a body," but such an "absence" can be problematic in literary representations of violence that depend on the "vulnerability of the victim's body" (x, xi). Morrison's narrative, even as it unsettles readers by bringing them into proximity to Hannah's suffering body, also positions readers as voyeurs and invites them to inscribe literary meaning onto Hannah's disfigured body. And Morrison's novel also implicitly raises a concern voiced by bell hooks who, in her reflections on representations of violence in popular black films, worries that black audiences have so internalized racism that they take pleasure in images of black death and destruction (*Black Looks* 7).

The novel's struggle with internalized racism also becomes apparent in its representation of Sula who, as an adult, becomes a combination of "Eva's arrogance and Hannah's self-indulgence" (118) and thus becomes a site in the text of female contempt and shamelessness and also female rage and rebellion. Just as members of the Bottom community wonder what Sula is all about as they watch her grow up, so critic-readers are forced to puzzle out Morrison's character. Constructed as a female rebel but also as an amoral and dangerously free woman, Sula splits under thematic attention so that critics are sometimes ambivalent and more often divided in their perceptions of this character. Thus, in typical responses, Sula has been described as a character that attracts and repels or that readers find both appealing and dreadful, or that readers like or dislike (Bjork 72, Banyina-Horne 28, Holloway, "Response to *Sula*" 77). In critical constructions of the character, Sula has been celebrated as a "visionary" woman whose "glory [is] misperceived as evil"; as a "Promethean artist" and "heroic" woman who transcends racial and sexual stereotypes; and as a character who is the "ambassador of new and liberating perspectives" (Domini 88, V. Middleton 368, 367, Lounsberry 126). But she also has been condemned, sometimes in revealingly shaming descriptions, as a "despicable user" and "immoral" character, and as a selfish and thoughtless individual who "shits on the Bottom community and dies" (T. Harris, *Fiction* 54, 78, Mbalia 42). Described as a character whose position "fluctuates" and thus cannot be "fixed" and as "a moral and psychological enigma" (Bjork 70, Grant 92), Morrison's Sula is designed to puzzle and also emotionally stir readers, who feel compelled to supplement the text as they try to fill in the void at the center of this intriguing, but also troubling, character.

In *Sula*, Morrison brings together her paired characters, Nel and Sula, as she interrogates the purity/pollution, good/bad opposition described by William Grier and Price Cobbs. Pointing to the deep wounds of racism, Grier and Cobbs describe how African Americans are encouraged "to develop disgust and contempt for bad, black . . . behavior" and to see such behavior as sinful, which results in the "pious, white, freshly laundered" African American who is "sans dirt, sans sin" (197). In a strategic maneuver, Morrison has Sula make her appearance in the novel after Nel discovers, during her trip South in 1920, that her proud mother is custard. When the middle-class Nel becomes conscious of the racial and sexual shame which is part of her maternal—and cultural—inheritance, she cultivates the friendship of the lower-class Sula, who responds to social and maternal shaming with displays of contempt, anger, and shamelessness.

Unlike the dark-skinned Sula, who is a "heavy brown," Nel is the "color of wet sandpaper," and thus Nel is just dark enough to escape the physical blows of the "pitch-black truebloods" and the "contempt" of older women who concern themselves with the "bad blood" mixtures of mulattoes. "Had she been any lighter-skinned she would have needed either her mother's protection . . . or a streak of mean to defend herself" (52). But Nel is treated as prey by four Irish boys, who take pleasure in bullying black schoolchildren and who, on one occasion, grab Nel, pushing her from hand to hand until they grow weary of the frightened look on her face. In a dramatic gesture, Sula comes to Nel's aid. Confronting the Irish boys, Sula slashes off the tip of her finger and then says to them, "If I can do that to myself, what you suppose I'll do to you?" (54–55). Not only does this scene show that Sula has internalized the horrible lessons of racist oppression—for she is unable to turn the tables on her attackers and thus her only defense against racial shaming and threatened violence is an act of self-mutilation—but Sula's act also carries with it an explicit warning about her desire to express her humiliated fury and physically retaliate against her white tormentors.

Constrained not only by their racial identity but also by their gender, Sula and Nel, because they are "neither white nor male" and thus "freedom and triumph" are forbidden to them, "set about creating something else to be." Countering the depiction of troubled family relationships with an idealized account of girlhood friendship, the novel describes how Sula and Nel, girls with "distant mothers and incomprehensible fathers," become friends despite their different class backgrounds and upbringings (52). The middle-class Nel seems "stronger and more consistent" than the lower-class Sula, "who could hardly be counted on to sustain any emotion for more than three minutes," and yet the two girls find "relief in each other's personality" (53). In the "safe harbor of each other's company," Nel and Sula can "afford to abandon the ways of other people and concentrate on their own perceptions of things" (55). As the two girls come to share their perceptions, becoming "two throats and one eye" (147), they experience what Silvan Tomkins calls the "intimacy of interocular interaction." Describing how the eyes both receive and send affective messages and thus "express and communicate joy, excitement, fear, distress, anger and shame," Tomkins remarks that the eyes are "critical in mutual affect awareness" (179, 180). Through the eyes, an individual can express an emotion like excitement, "see that this excitement is contagious and responded to in kind by the other, and see that the other is also aware of the excitement in both of them, and aware of their mutual awareness of their mutual excitement" (180). In emphasizing the close bond between Nel and Sula, the narrative focuses on Sula and Nel's interocular intimacy and sharing of affect as they watch "each day as though it were a movie arranged for their amusement," and as they find "in each other's eyes the intimacy they were looking for" (55, 52).

If the narrative uses the idealistic discourse of female friendship in constructing Sula's character—and this discourse is ultimately given interpretive priority in the novel's closing scene, as we shall see—it also represents Sula as a mother-damaged figure, someone who has "no center, no speck around which to grow" (119). The narrative locates the origins of Sula's crippled self in two pivotal and related episodes from her girlhood: a remark made by her mother and the subsequent death of Chicken Little. When Sula overhears her mother say to another woman that she loves but does not like her daughter, Hannah's words are inherently shaming, for a core experience of shame is the sudden exposure of one's basic unacceptability. Hannah's shaming pronouncement bewilders and mortifies Sula, who becomes emotionally paralyzed and numbed. Rather than openly crying, Sula is aware of a "sting in her eye" and only Nel's voice pulls her away from the "dark thoughts" that suddenly take hold of her (57). After Sula hears her mother's remark, she accidentally drowns Chicken Little, for as she is swinging him around, he slips from her hands and then sails out over the river and disappears, sinking into the water. The death of the little boy, which can be read as a displaced enactment of Sula's dark thoughts and feelings, represents the painful and confusing experience of toxic shame. "Debilitating shame is an alienating feeling," writes Carl Goldberg. "It carries the opprobrium that the sufferer is unlovable and should be cast out of human company. The shame-bound person has learned from others and now accuses himself of the 'crime' of being surplus, unwanted, and worthless" (8). The death of Chicken Little also encodes a common response to the sudden exposure of one's shame: the wish to die. Explaining the link between shame and death, Carl Schneider observes how everyday expressions—" 'I was so ashamed, I could have died'; 'I could have sunk into the ground and disappeared'; and 'I was mortified' "—capture this connection, and Schneider also observes that the feeling of "dying in shame" is associated with the "experience of the momentary loss of the self," since shame causes a "disruption of consciousness and loss of control that leads one to appeal, by analogy, to the experience of dying" (78, 79).

"I didn't mean anything. I never meant anything. I stood there watching her burn and was thrilled. I wanted her to keep on jerking like that, to keep on dancing," Sula admits to herself years later as she recalls her voyeuristic enjoyment of her mother's fiery death (147). If Sula's secret pleasure in watching her mother burn to death reveals her desire for revenge against her shaming mother, it also points to her emotional disconnection from the suffering of others as she leads her dangerously free life. "[H]ers was an experimental life—ever since her mother's remarks sent her flying up those stairs, ever since her one major feeling of responsibility had been exorcised on the bank of a river with a closed place in the middle. The first experience taught her there was no other that you could count on; the second that there was no self to count on either" (118–19).

As a girl Sula clings to Nel "as the closest thing to both an other and a self" only to ultimately learn that she and Nel are "not one and the same thing" (119). Despite Nel's deep bond with Sula—the two friends are so close that they find it difficult to distinguish "one's thoughts from the other's" (83)—Nel's relationship with Jude Greene selects her away from her friend. When Nel marries Jude in 1927, Sula disappears, and then, ten years later in 1937, Sula suggestively wades through the "pearly shit" (89) of the robins when she returns to the Bottom. Unlike Nel, who comes to embrace her mother's middle-class values, Sula refuses the conventional roles of wife, mother, and dutiful family member. "I don't want to make somebody else. I want to make myself," the adult Sula says when Eva asks her when she is going to get married and have children (92).

To the adult Nel, the return of her friend initially brings a kind of magic back into her life: it is "like getting the use of an eye back, having a cataract removed"—a description that recalls the interocular intimacy enjoyed by the two friends in girlhood. And yet if "[t]alking to Sula had always been a conversation with herself" (95), Nel's conversation with Sula is edged with contempt for others. Although the text insists that Sula, who has gone to college, knows "lovely college words like *aesthetic* or *rapport*" (105), it focuses on her shaming descriptions of others. When Sula asks Nel how she is and Nel says that she must be "all right" because she "ain't strangled nobody yet," Sula remarks that half the people in the town need to be killed while the rest are a "drawn-out disease" (96). Reminiscing about a "teen-time tale," the two use racist and sexist speech as they repeat a shaming story about John L. and Shirley, recalling how John L., who was "one dumb nigger," tried to stick his penis in Shirley's hip, perhaps because he was sanitary.

"Well. Think about it," remarks Sula. "Suppose Shirley was all splayed out
in front of you? Wouldn't you go for the hipbone instead?" (97). Parodying
the rhetoric of the middle-class good woman like Nel's mother, Helene, Sula
adds, "Neatness counts. You know what cleanliness is next to . . ." (98).
And when Nel's husband, Jude—an economically emasculated man who
expects Nel "to soothe" him and "to shore him up" (83)—offers a "whiney
tale" about a personal insult done to him by whites, he expects his story to
"dovetail into milkwarm commiseration." Instead, Sula intervenes with a
dialogic retort as she answers Jude's shaming story of the emasculated black
male with an account of the racist myth of the hypersexed black male, who
is so loved by whites that not only do white women "think rape" as soon as
they see a black man but white men become so obsessed with the black man's
penis and their desire to "cut off a nigger's privates" that they forget about
their own penises (103).

Not only does Sula's dialogic speech make her a center of verbal energy
in the text, but the narrative, in part, endorses Sula's shaming perceptions of
others. A person who is unable to lie and thus who finds "social conversation . . . impossible," Sula cannot say "Hey, girl, you looking good" when
she sees how the years have "dusted" the bronze of her acquaintances' skin
"with ash" and bent their eyes "into grimy sickles of concern" (121). Insistently, the narrative aligns readers with Sula's contemptuous view of the
Bottom women. "The narrower their lives, the wider their hips. Those with
husbands had folded themselves into starched coffins, their sides bursting
with other people's skinned dreams and bony regrets. Those without men
were like sour-tipped needles featuring one constant empty eye. Those with
men had had the sweetness sucked from their breath by ovens and steam
kettles" (121–22). Sula perceives the Bottom people as objects of contempt,
and she also actively shames them. "In the midst of a pleasant conversation
with someone she might say, 'Why do you chew with your mouth open?' not
because the answer interested her but because she wanted to see the person's
face change rapidly" (119). Living out her days "exploring her own thoughts
and emotions, giving them full reign," Sula becomes an individual who is
"[a]s willing to feel pain as to give pain, to feel pleasure as to give pleasure"
(118).

Ultimately, Sula betrays Nel by having an affair with Nel's husband,
Jude. Positioning readers as voyeurs—as observers of a shameful scene—the
narrative describes how Nel finds Sula and Jude "down on all fours naked . . .
on all fours like . . . dogs" (105). Viewing the sexual behavior of Sula and
Jude as animalistic, the middle-class Nel is not only mortified by what she
sees but also frightened, for Jude's eyes look like the eyes of the soldiers on
the train whose gaze, many years before, turned her mother into custard.
Subsequently abandoned by Jude, Nel suffers from feelings of intense loss:

"her thighs were truly empty and dead too, and it was Sula who had taken the life from them and Jude who smashed her heart and the both of them who left her with no thighs and no heart just her brain raveling away" (110–11). The narrative openly sympathizes with Nel's plight, but it also voices and endorses Sula's contempt for Nel's enactment of the role of the "wronged wife" and for Nel's conventional life, as she comes to belong "to the town and all of its ways" and thus becomes "one of *them*" (120).

While the narrative condemns Nel's conventionality, it praises Sula's rebelliousness, viewing this trait as a potential source of creativity. "Had she paints, or clay, or knew the discipline of the dance, or strings; had she anything to engage her tremendous curiosity and her gift for metaphor, she might have exchanged the restlessness and preoccupation with whim for an activity that provided her with all she yearned for. And like any artist with no art form, she became dangerous" (121). An embodiment of emotional and erotic energy, Sula becomes the site and sign in the text of a "dangerous" primitive blackness and black female shamelessness. But if the text sympathizes with Sula's rebellious wildness and uses her to flaunt, parody, and thus counteract, the debased stereotype of the "bad" black woman, it also associates her with the shaming discourse of dirt and defilement. A primary carrier of the text's rage and contempt, Sula not only is futureless but she also is prematurely ushered out of the text.

To members of the Bottom community, the shameless, contemptuous Sula becomes an object of shame and contempt. When people learn that Sula has put Eva in an old folks home, they call her a "roach"; when they see that she has taken Nel's husband, Jude, and then ditched him for other men, they say she is a "bitch"; when they hear that she has slept with white men— which is "the unforgivable thing," the "dirt that could not ever be washed away"—old women purse their lips in disgust, children look away from Sula "in shame," and young men "fantasize elaborate torture for her" (112–13). In a description that serves as a dialogic retort and countershaming response to white racist rhetoric, the novel describes how the people of the Bottom are filled "with choking disgust" when they imagine the shameful scene of Sula "underneath some white man," for there is "nothing lower she could do, nothing filthier." Insisting that "all unions between white men and black women" are rape and that it is "unthinkable" for a black woman to willingly have sex with a white man, they view integration "with precisely the same venom" as whites (113). Calvin Hernton, in his analysis of the taboo against interracial sex, describes not only how blacks who cross the color line are branded as "'traitors' to the race" but also how some blacks "feel that sex across the color line is 'dirty' and 'perverse'" and become angry at the "very idea of interracial sex" and "nauseous" at the "sight of interracial couples" (xv, xvi, xvi–xvii). Like the interracial couples described by Hernton who are subjected to the "hate stare" for crossing racial barriers (xviii), Sula is similarly looked at in a "stony-eyed" way by the Bottom people, who come to view her as "evil" (113).

Because of Sula's shamelessly experimental life, she becomes the demonized Other to the Bottom community, and because Sula's "hateful" misanthropic gaze communicates her contempt-disgust for others—she is described as looking at others "[l]ike she smellin' you with her eyes and don't like your soap" (117)—she is perceived as someone with a dangerous look: that is, as someone who has the evil eye.[3] As the Bottom people "band together against the devil in their midst," they "protect and love one another" and, in the process, project their own badness onto Sula (117–18, 117). Thus when Teapot's negligent mother thinks that Sula has pushed her son down the stairs, she changes into a model parent by immersing herself in the maternal role, and when Sula sleeps with and then discards the husbands of the Bottom women, the women reactively cherish their men.

The bad black woman, Sula becomes a pariah and a despised woman as members of the community feel disgust for her promiscuous behavior. Coming to Sula's defense, the narrative counters the stereotype of the black Jezebel by providing a poeticized description of Sula's lovemaking. Sula, who initially is attracted to the "sootiness" of sex and likes to think of it as "wicked," comes to find the "cutting edge" in the sexual act: she feels her own power and strength and also profound loneliness and deep sorrow during lovemaking, and afterward, in the moments of "postcoital privateness," she feels authenticated as she meets and joins herself "in matchless harmony" (122, 123). Achieving the "high silence of orgasm" (130) during her sexual encounter with Ajax, Sula fantasizes rubbing Ajax's cheekbone until some of the black flakes off, revealing the gold leaf beneath; scraping away at the gold to find alabaster; tapping away at the alabaster to find fertile loam; and then watering his soil to keep it rich and moist. *"And how much loam will I need to keep my water still?"* Sula wonders. *"And when do the two make mud?"* (131). In her remarks on the lovemaking scene, Morrison points out that she does not use any sexual language in this description, which conceptualizes sex in a childlike, if not primitive, way—as two people playing in the mud (Koenen 76–77). This suggests that part of Morrison's agenda in her depiction of Sula's lovemaking with Ajax as earthy and natural—*"And when do the two make mud?"*—may be to counteract the shaming notion of sex and the sexualized black body as dirty.

When Ajax detects the "scent of the nest" in Sula's sudden domesticity, he leaves (133). The abandoned Sula, who has discovered with Ajax what possession is, finds it difficult to cope with his "stunning absence" (134). In a description that plays on the notion of "losing one's head" in the love relationship and also underlines the precariousness of Sula's selfhood, Sula recalls how, when she was a girl, the heads of her paper dolls came off and how she held her neck stiff because she was afraid that her own head would fall off if she bent it. "I did not hold my head stiff enough when I met him," Sula thinks of her relationship with Ajax, "and so I lost it just like the dolls" (136). But Sula's fantasy that had Ajax stayed she soon "would have torn the flesh from his face" in order to see if she "was right about the gold" also points to the aggression behind her shameless voyeurism. "[N]obody would have understood that kind of curiosity. They would have believed that I wanted to hurt him just like the little boy who fell down the steps and broke his leg and the people think I pushed him just because I looked at it" (136–37). Reassigning meaning to the poetic imagery used to depict Sula's lovemaking with Ajax by associating it with death—"in the hollow of near-sleep she tasted the acridness of gold, left the chill of alabaster and smelled the dark, sweet stench of loam" (137)—Morrison prepares for the closure of Sula's plot. If in describing Sula's demise, Morrison invokes the classic love plot in which the romantic heroine who fails at love consequently dies, she also subverts the romantic formula by having her character "lying at death's door [and] still smart-talking" (142).

When Nel, in the role of the "good woman come to see about a sick person," visits the dying Sula in 1940, she still has the "taste of Jude's exit in her mouth, with the resentment and shame that even yet pressed for release in her stomach" (138). With "[v]irtue" as her "mooring," Nel at first manages to keep her voice "free of the least hint of retribution" (139). "You know you don't have to be proud with me," Nel tells Sula only to be frustrated by the smart-talking of the dying Sula, who insists that she is "not proud" and that she likes her "own dirt" (142). Asked what she has to show for her life, Sula responds, "Show? To who? Girl, I got my mind. And what goes on in it. Which is to say, I got me." And Sula counters romantic love ideology in her refusal to spend her life "keeping a man," remarking that a man "ain't worth more than me" (143). While critic-readers often applaud the defiant individualism of the dying Sula, Nel detects contempt in Sula's words: "You own the world and the rest of us is renting. You ride the pony and we shovel the shit" (144).

As a reader of her own novel, Morrison has remarked that although critics "devoted to the Western heroic tradition—the individual alone and triumphant—see Sula as a survivor," she is nevertheless "lost" in the Bottom community (Koenen 68). The narrative draws on but also problematizes the notion of the self-invented, autonomous, heroic individual in its representation of Sula by presenting her as misanthropic and disconnected from members of her community. "You laying there in that bed without a dime or a friend to your name having done all the dirt you did in this town and you still expect folks to love you?" an exasperated Nel says to Sula. Shamelessly defiant to the end, Sula responds that it will take time but people will love her. "After all the old women have lain with the teen-agers; when all the young girls have slept with their old drunken uncles; after all the black men fuck all the white ones; when all the white women kiss all the black ones . . . ; when Lindbergh sleeps with Bessie Smith and Norma Shearer makes it with Stepin Fetchit . . . then there'll be a little love left over for me" (145–46).

Although Sula, with her transgressive and shaming speech, remains a center of verbal energy in the text, she also is killed off in what can be read as yet another textual staging of the contempt-disappear scenario. Prefaced by a dream of disintegration in which Sula envisions the Clabber Girl Baking Powder lady first beckoning to her and then disintegrating into a white dust that covers her, Sula's death recalls Hannah's and Plum's burning deaths. Not only does Sula awaken from her dream "gagging and overwhelmed with the smell of smoke" but her pain is described as a "liquid pain" and as "a kind of burning" (148). Sula's death is also linked to the watery death of Chicken Little, for she envisions herself curling into the "heavy softness" of water and experiencing the "sleep of water always." As if intent on providing an authorial rescue of Sula, Morrison has the dead Sula think, "[I]t didn't even hurt. Wait'll I tell Nel" (149). Morrison also counteracts her insistent depictions of Sula as misanthropic and contemptuous in this scene by pointing to the primacy of female friendship—a rehabilitative, antishaming gesture that she repeats in the novel's closure.

"How you know? . . . About who was good. . . . I mean maybe it wasn't you. Maybe it was me" (146). Sula's parting words to Nel are often taken as an authorial directive in the drama of blame assessment which Sula's words are meant to provoke. Indeed, the question of who is "good"—the conventional Nel or the unconventional Sula—recurs obsessively in the critical commentary surrounding the novel, and even Morrison, as a reader of her own work, seems preoccupied with this question. Morrison remarks that in *Sula* she "tried to posit a situation where there was a so-called good and a so-called evil people. Nel and Sula are symbolic of this condition. And of course, you can't always tell which is which" (Parker 62). Echoing Morrison's ambivalence, commentators have described Sula as a "cruel and selfish" yet "sympathetic" character, or have reported feeling "disoriented" by the difficulty of deciding which character to feel allegiance to, or have characterized Sula as "a figure of genuine moral ambiguity" (Matza 51, Hoffarth-Zelloe 115, Spillers 29). In another common reading, just as Sula questions Nel about who was good in their last encounter, "so Morrison questions the reader's right to make judgments about any of her characters" (Wagner 199). And yet readers often do pass judgment arguing, for example, that "it is the drab and ordinary Nel rather than the more flamboyant Sula . . . that achieves heroic stature" or conversely that "Sula's claim to verifiable 'goodness' derives from her relative lack of dishonesty in comparison with Nel's hypocritical virtuousness which impels her to visit Sula near the novel's end" (Stein 146, Grant 101). Repeating the novel's discourse of dirt and defilement but using it to shame Nel, one commentator has even argued that the part of Nel that is "exposed" when the adult Sula returns to the Bottom is the "filth" that lies beneath the "Wrights' cleanliness"; in the view of this commentator Morrison's novel is a "joke" in which the "sexually promiscuous" Sula ends up being the heroine while Nel, "a middle-class prig who lives half a life," is the "true villainess" (Ogunyemi 133).

The death of Sula, who has served as the target of and container for the community's angry, resentful feelings, cuts off the Bottom people "from the most magnificent hatred they had ever known" (173). Without Sula's contempt to react against, the Bottom people experience a "falling away" and "dislocation," and thus a "restless irritability" takes hold. Consequently, Teapot's mother beats him again, and similarly other Bottom mothers—women "who had defended their children from Sula's malevolence (or who had defended their positions as mothers from Sula's scorn for the role)"—begin abusing their children. Without Sula's "mockery," the Bottom people's affection for each other wanes, and thus wives uncoddle their husbands, daughters resent taking care of old people, and even the blacks in Medallion who moved there from Canada feel "a loosening of the reactionary compassion for Southern-born blacks Sula had inspired in them" and thus return "to their original claims of superiority" (153–54).

If many of the Bottom people have survived the torments of life—"lost jobs, sick children, rotten potatoes, broken pipes . . . garlic-ridden hunkies, corrupt Catholics, racist Protestants, cowardly Jews"—with an enduring "gentleness of spirit" (150), the death of Sula leads to a public ventilation of black frustration and rage. This occurs in the 1941 National Suicide Day parade, which, as several critics have observed, can be read as a coded reference to the 1960s protest marches and riots (Mbalia 44–45, Reddy 43). Pointing to the political meaning of this carnivalesque scene, the narrative describes Shadrack's pied piper's parade as a "slit in the veil," a "respite from anxiety" and "adult pain," and it also draws a connection between the hope the parade represents and the hope that not only has kept the Bottom people "knee-deep in other people's dirt" and "excited about other people's wars" but also has convinced them that "some magic 'government'" would "lift them up, out and away from that dirt . . . those wars" (160). When Shadrack's parade of strutting and marching people reaches the mouth of the tunnel excavation on the New River Road, the mood of celebration turns to anger. The novel's description of the destructive shame-rage of the Bottom people recalls William Grier and Price Cobbs's remarks on black rage in their 1968 book, *Black Rage*, where they famously warned of the "stored energy" of oppressed African Americans that would be "released in the form of rage—black rage, apocalyptic and final" (210). "[L]ed by the tough, the enraged and the young," the Bottom people want to destroy the tunnel they were not permitted to build, "to kill it all, all of it, to wipe from the face of the earth the work of the thin-armed Virginia boys, the bull-necked Greeks and the knife-faced men who waved the leaf-dead promise" (161–62). In yet another contempt-disappear drama that depicts the annihilating force of white contempt, the narrative represents this venting of retaliatory black rage against the symbol of the contemptuous white capitalist oppressor as self-destructive. This scene also acts out Sula's contempt for the Bottom people expressed in her earlier remark that half of the people of the Bottom community needed "killin'" (96). For while Shadrack stands on the bank ringing his death bell, the tunnel collapses, killing many of the Bottom people in yet another scene of unexpected death.

"Just alike. Both of you. Never was no difference between you," Eva says of Nel and Sula some twenty-four years later in the closing scenes of the novel (169). Accused by Eva of watching Chicken Little drown, Nel recalls her voyeuristic enjoyment of the scene—her shameless looking. Just as Sula was "thrilled" when she watched her mother burn to death, so Nel felt a "joyful stimulation" when she watched Chicken Little fall into the water (147, 170). Pointing to the narrative's preoccupation with shameless looking, these remarks may also be directed, at least in part, toward Morrison's voyeuristic readers who may feel both horrified and stimulated as they respond to the novel's repeated scenes of disinterested violence. Yet if the closure of the novel offers the troubling insight that part of what links Sula and Nel is their shameless pleasure in watching the harming of others, the narrative, rather than elaborating on this realization, focuses instead on the deep girlhood bond between Sula and Nel, showing how Nel's memory of her girlhood friendship with Sula acts as a redemptive force in her life. Suddenly, Nel recognizes that for many years she has been mourning the loss, not of Jude, but of Sula. "And the loss pressed down on her chest and came up into her throat. 'We was girls together,' she said as though explaining something. 'O Lord, Sula,' she cried, 'girl, girl, girlgirlgirl.' It was a fine cry—loud and long—but it had no bottom and it had no top, just circles and circles of sorrow" (174).

By privileging in the closure the idealized discourse of female friendship, Morrison deflects reader attention away from the adult Sula's contempt and anger, and thus, in effect, redeems her character. Evidence of Morrison's power to entice reader involvement in the novel's organizing fantasies is found in the critical conversation surrounding the closure. It has been argued, for example, that after death Sula's dangerous power is "[b]alanced . . . with the loving and stable power of Nel" or that, in the end, Nel merges her self and Sula's self to form "a better, truer" self, or that Sula leads Nel to "self-understanding" (C. Jones 625, Hoffarth-Zelloe 123, Reddy 38). Another commentator, who remarks that she still has to "choke back tears" at the end of the novel, views *Sula* as a work that can potentially rescue its women readers by inviting them to examine their "alliance with other women" (Demetrakopoulos, *"Sula"* 51, 63). Yet another critic insists that Morrison's vision of the "ill-fated friendship" of Nel and Sula urges readers "to be more conscious of and more concerned about the sacrifices of love and human potential exacted by a sexist, racist social order" (Shannon 21).

Aptly described as a novel of "elegant craft and intense emotional power" (R. Bell 24), Morrison's *Sula* uses an elegant narrative design but also plays on the reader's emotions as it enacts complicated shame dramas and depicts jarring scenes of disinterested violence. Through her paired characters, Nel and Sula, Morrison explores issues concerning class and shame within the African-American community as she examines the construction of black femininity, and she also uses the dangerously free and shameless Sula to investigate, if not shamelessly flaunt, the debasing racist stereotype of the socially unrestrained and promiscuous lower-class black female. A novel that uses literary form to contain and also master the contagious, and also potentially toxic, feelings that impel the narrative—feelings of shame-humiliation, contempt-disgust, and rage—*Sula* reveals not only the shame that returns in spectral form in shameless behavior but also the annihilating power of contempt through its repeated stagings of the contempt-disappear scenario.

4

"Can't Nobody Fly with All That Shit"

THE SHAME-PRIDE AXIS AND BLACK MASCULINITY
IN *SONG OF SOLOMON*

Situated in a specific cultural moment, *Song of Solomon*, which was published in 1977, highlights the search for African-American roots. If in *Song of Solomon*, as in *Sula*, Morrison is intent on extending the African-American literary and cultural imagination, she also stages troubling scenes of shame and trauma in *Song of Solomon* as she explores the shame-pride issues surrounding the construction of black masculinity and reflects on the competing and contradictory political ideologies of assimilation and black nationalism. *Song of Solomon* tells the story of Milkman Dead, a member of the black bourgeoisie and a shame-ridden individual who carries with him the "shit" not only of his family's false class pride but also of inherited familial and racial shame. Before the middle-class, urban Milkman can attempt to "fly"—that is, feel healthy family and racial pride—he must learn about the interrelated shame-pride sources of black masculinity through his contact with the black underclass in his Michigan hometown and in the rural South where he learns his true name and thus solves the riddle of his African-American identity. Yet even as *Song of Solomon* seemingly celebrates Milkman's discovery of his African-American "roots" and his "authentic" black identity, it also anticipates a complaint commonly lodged against black identity politics: that the "idea of *the* black experience" covers up "the differences of class and privilege" that divide African Americans (Dean 60–61).

Calling attention to the personal-familial and social-historical forces that shape the formation of African-American identities and also focusing on the social, class, and political tensions within the black community, *Song of Solomon* is addressed, in part, to middle-class African Americans, especially males, who have a kind of amnesia about their cultural history—about the shame and trauma of family histories rooted in slavery—and who, in donning the mask of bourgeois (white-identified) "pride," come to see poor blacks as stigmatized objects of contempt. Like *The Bluest Eye* and *Sula*, *Song of Solomon* deals with the troubling issue of internalized racism as it crystallizes black cultural anxiety about the class and color hierarchies within the African-American community. Morrison deliberately typecasts Milkman Dead as a privileged, middle-class African American only to strip away his mantle of false class pride by putting him in vital contact with the black folk, people like his Aunt Pilate or his poor Southern relations whom he originally sees through the lens of internalized racism as the shameful and inferior Other. If part of the novel's agenda is to show how Milkman Dead is brought to a new and healing sense of racial consciousness as a result of both his association with the black underclass and his discovery of his family's slavery and postslavery "roots," *Song of Solomon* also investigates the link between the shame and trauma of racial oppression and black rage, primarily through the oppositional character of Guitar Bains, a member of the black underclass who is a militant black nationalist and political terrorist. And if the novel intends an "optimistic" ending by depicting Milkman's moment of flight and racial pride, it also undercuts that optimism by suggesting that his leap into the arms of the waiting Guitar is nihilistic and suicidal.

In its investigation of the formation of black masculinity, *Song of Solomon* exposes what shame theorists have referred to as the "collective secret" of pride and shame, the so-called master emotions which, although they serve as continuous monitors of the state of the social bond in the daily lives of individuals, have long been ignored in our culture (Scheff, Retzinger, Ryan 180, Scheff, *Bloody Revenge* 39). The "primary social emotions," pride and shame "have a signal function with respect to the social bond," writes Thomas Scheff. For while "pride generates and signals a secure bond," shame "generates and signals a threatened bond" (*Bloody Revenge* 66, 3).[1] Dependent on the level of respect or deference shown to individuals, pride results from being treated in a deferential or respectful way and shame from a lack of deference or disrespect (Scheff, Retzinger, Ryan 184). Interpersonal and also intrapsychic phenomena, pride and shame states, as Donald Nathanson explains in his description of the shame-pride axis, "form an axis intimately related to the modulation of self-esteem." Pride—"the happy confluence of the affect joy and the experience of personal efficacy"—is "always linked to the emotion shame in reciprocal fashion." Thus, "The search for shame is considerably aided by our understanding of its relationship to pride, both the true healthy pride which accompanies authentic success, and the false pride with which we defend our (denied) fragility" ("Shame/Pride Axis" 186, 204). The false pride that manifests itself as "[i]nsolence and haughtiness," as Scheff similarly observes, "may mask deep-seated feelings of inferiority, i.e., shame" (*Bloody Revenge* 44).

In *Song of Solomon*, Morrison illustrates that shame and pride are at once social emotions, which act as shaping forces in the construction of social and group identity, and intrapsychic phenomena. Part of Morrison's cultural project in *Song of Solomon* is to investigate the social and familial sources of black shame and pride and to distinguish between healthy and false pride. Morrison also explores the issue of class status in the social construction of black identities as she cross-questions the black bourgeoisie's version of African-American manhood. Examining the class divisions within the African-American community, *Song of Solomon* focuses attention on intraracial shaming—the contempt that some middle-class African Americans, like members of the Dead family, feel for poor and lower-class blacks. *Song of Solomon* also deals with the shame and pride issues surrounding skin color, the internalized racism that affords light skin a greater social value than dark skin. In deliberately setting out to confront the vexed issues surrounding color and class, *Song of Solomon* exposes what has been called the "dirty little secret" and "last taboo" of African-American culture, the existence of intraracial color prejudice and discrimination—the so-called color complex—which continues to be an "embarrassing and controversial subject for African Americans" (Russell 3, 2, 1).[2] According to bell hooks, "Those black folks who came of age before Black Power faced the implications of color caste either through devaluation or overvaluation." If being born light meant beginning life "with an advantage recognized by everyone," being born dark meant starting life "handicapped, with a serious disadvantage." The 1960s black liberation movement challenged this notion with its empowering "call to see black as beautiful." But in the late 1970s, around the time *Song of Solomon* was published, the "politics of racial assimilation," which had always operated as a "backlash," not only began to undermine black self-determination but also led, in the 1980s and 1990s, to the "resurgence" of the color-caste hierarchy (*Outlaw Culture* 174, 175, 178).

Song of Solomon acts out an important social mission as it deals with issues that African Americans find painful and embarrassing, such as the slavery origins of black American culture and the persistence of both intraracial color prejudice and class conflict within the African-American community. But because *Song of Solomon* is a densely textured narrative, it succeeds, in part, in concealing or minimizing the racial shame and trauma at its core by inviting critical analysis of its textual patterns and its use of folkloric and mythic sources. While *Song of Solomon* is mired in the excretory discourse of shame, it also, as is characteristic of Morrison's fiction, counteracts shame through its rich literary discourse. Critic-readers thus tend to avoid or minimize the narrative's racist and counterracist rhetoric, including its use of the shaming discourse of dirt and defilement, and discuss, instead, the importance of names and naming in the novel, or Morrison's use of the monomyth of the hero, or her adaptation of the flight motif and its link to both western and African-American mythic sources, or her invocation of black oral culture.[3] Aptly described as a work in which readers "passively . . . absorb the apparently disconnected information provided by the author" at the beginning and then manage to put together the "puzzle" by the end of the novel (Spallino 513), *Song of Solomon*, like the other works we have investigated, enacts the concealments and hesitancies characteristic of shame and trauma discourse. For as Morrison repeatedly feeds her readers, in a piecemeal fashion, tantalizing or horrific details that are gradually elaborated on and/or explained as the narrative unfolds, she partially conceals—in layer after layer of interpretable but disconnected details that must be reconnected by the reader—the painful content of what she is describing. It is also telling that the narrative evokes the comforting world of magic and folklore as it either recounts family stories about or depicts scenes of inter- or intraracial violence. By reactively and defensively associating scenes of trauma with the uncanny and dislocated world of folklore and magic, the narrative diverts reader attention away from its horrific descriptions of violence. Through its insistent mythologizing of African-American roots, *Song of Solomon* effectively transforms the disgrace, degradation, and stigma of slavery and racist oppression into racial pride and the transcendence of suffering, which are represented in the originary figure of Solomon, the heroic flying African. Yet the suicidal flights that begin and end the novel point to the pessimism, even nihilism, at the heart of the narrative. What underlies the at times wry humor of Morrison's novel are the contagious—and potentially overwhelming—affects of fear, shame-humiliation, contempt-disgust, and rage.

That critic-readers often tend to bypass *Song of Solomon's* "tragic realism" and concentrate, instead, on its "magical romance" (see Brenkman 79–80) points to the power of Morrison's richly complex literary discourse to mask or divert attention away from the shame and trauma issues that impel the narrative. Morrison also uses dialogic, parodic discourse to partially shield readers from the troubling subject matter of her novel, and indeed Morrison has described *Song of Solomon* as her "own giggle (in Afro-American terms) of the proto-myth of the journey to manhood" ("Unspeakable Things" 29). The opening scene of the novel, which tells of the aborted, suicidal "flight" of Mr. Smith that presages Milkman's birth, is often read as a deliberately staged dramatization of the birth of the mythic hero. As critics have observed, Milkman's birth is accompanied by the "ritualized celebration" of Pilate's singing and of virgins (i.e., Milkman's sisters) "strewing rose petals as a black Icarus dies" (A. Leslie Harris 72). Yet this opening scene, even as it evokes the hero's birth, is also tinged with shame. With his blue silk wings curved around his chest, Mr. Smith masquerades as the proud hero—the flying African. But he is also an object of ridicule and contempt as he stands on the roof of Mercy Hospital, and thus some of the Southside watchers snigger, a gold-toothed man laughs, and another calls him crazy. While the initial description of Mr. Smith evokes the shaming stereotype of the mad black man, the narrative later explains that Mr. Smith is a member of the terrorist organization, the Seven Days, and thus reveals that the cause of his "madness" is the racist violence perpetrated against African Americans.

Drawing attention away from such issues, the novel indulges in myth-making as it associates Mr. Smith's leap with Milkman's birth the next day in the all-white Mercy Hospital, which, in the covert countershaming and dia-logic speech of the Southside residents, is referred to as No Mercy Hospital since it is a place that, in refusing to treat blacks, has shown "no mercy" toward their physical suffering. "Mr. Smith's blue silk wings must have left their mark, because when the little boy discovered, at four, the same thing Mr. Smith had learned earlier—that only birds and airplanes could fly—he lost all interest in himself" (9). Such authorial directives focus reader attention on the theme of "flight" in the narrative and lead to the unavoidability of critic-reader reactions to and interpretations of this "mythic" drama. Similarly, in telling of Milkman's conception and birth, Morrison deliberately evokes and plays on the mythic story of the hero's origins. Milkman, it is often remarked, "undergoes a 'miraculous' birth" since he is conceived through the magic of Pilate's love potion; he is "nobly born," for he is "descended from American aristocrats, property owners"; and he later "assumes the classic hero's journey of separation, initiation, and return" (Carmean 46). Thus Milkman's birth, his early years, and adult life—including his later journey south in search of gold, which becomes a search for the golden treasure of family origins and racial identity—are patterned after the protomyth of the hero, as critic after critic has remarked. It is typically argued that before Milkman can "ride the air"— that is, transcend "human limitations"—he must "leave his parents' house, encounter dangers and obstacles along the way, endure a journey to the under-world (calling to mind great heroes who have made similar journeys: Aeneas, Odysseus, Tiresias, Dante, Jesus), after which he sees himself clearly and becomes intensely aware of his shortcomings." Consequently, he is able to throw off "the psychic baggage he has been bearing in his soul" and fly (de Weever 133). Yet if many critic-readers, in heroizing Milkman, repeat the narrative's focus on the pride of mythic flight, others become inadvertent players in a shame drama as they devalue Milkman. Morrison's character, for example, has been described as an "anti-classical hero," who exhibits "[w]arped values, inadequate character formation, and self-centeredness," and it also has been argued that Morrison, although she follows the monomyth pattern in the novel, also "shrewdly" mocks Milkman, the "alleged hero" of the narrative, who is presented as an "intolerable egoist" and who does "little" to warrant the "honorific label" of hero (T. Harris, *Fiction* 85, 90, Brenner 117, 118).

That some critics repeat the novel's shaming devaluation of the middle-class Milkman while others counteract shame by focusing on Milkman's ultimate flight points to the shame-pride issues that inform Morrison's representation of Milkman's search for his African-American identity. In order to understand the secret shame that haunts Milkman, who comes to feel like "a garbage pail for the actions and hatreds of other people" (120), the narrative describes Milkman's middle-class upbringing in passages that recall the cozy, backyard world of illicit gossip that Morrison is so fond of evoking in her fiction. In its representation of members of the Dead family, Morrison's novel not only ridicules them for their class pretensions, but also actively humiliates them by insisting on their family pathology and by exposing the shameful family secrets that haunt them.

Intent on locating the familial and cultural sources of black male pride, the narrative initially rejects the false pride of Milkman's maternal grandfather, Dr. Foster, which is based on a mimicry of white supremacist—including antiblack racist—attitudes and behavior. The "most respected" black man in the city while Ruth is growing up, Dr. Foster, for whom Doctor Street is named, is "worshipped" by the black residents. But while members of the black community take pride in the doctor, he does not "give a damn" about them. An assimilated black who occupies a superior class position, the doctor views those below him as objects of contempt. That the doctor refers to lower-class blacks as "cannibals"—thus categorizing them as the degenerate, savage Other—reveals that he has internalized white racist constructions of black inferiority. To the light-skinned doctor, dark skin is a sign of a stigmatizing difference. The doctor's own unacknowledged status anxiety about being categorized as racially stigmatized becomes apparent in his response to his grandchildren. When he delivers his granddaughters, Magdalene and First Corinthians, he is interested only in their skin color, and he would have "disowned" Milkman for his darker skin, according to Macon (71).

In a classic countershaming strategy, the narrative uses Macon's angry, cynical voice to shame the middle-class, light-skinned Dr. Foster. "[T]he pompous donkey found out what it was like to have to be sick and pay another donkey to make you well," remarks Macon, who describes the dying Dr. Foster as an object of contempt and disgust (72). "Couldn't move, holes were forming in his scalp. And he just lay there in that bed where your mother still sleeps and then he died there. Helpless, fat stomach, skinny arms and legs, looking like a white rat" (73). Acting out a classic turning-of-the-tables script, the narrative portrays the proud, socially superior and contemptuous Dr.

Foster as the degenerate, stigmatized Other and interprets his light skin as a mark of his pathological difference.

Just as the narrative rejects the false pride of Dr. Foster, so it rejects the arrogance of Macon Dead. A representative of the upwardly mobile, self-made black capitalist class, Macon, in his "drive for wealth" (28), assumes a white-identified role as he actively exploits poor blacks in the Southside area of town where he is a slum landlord. A character readers love to hate, Macon has been described as the "most hateful" character in the novel, as a "[c]old, objective, and calculating" man, and as an "acquisitive" individual who is "savagely" mocked by Morrison (Coleman, "Beyond the Reach" 154, Samuels and Hudson-Weems 58, Brenner 117). Macon, who is a "colored man of property" by the age of twenty-five, espouses the ethic of materialism: "Own things. And let the things you own own other things. Then you'll own yourself and other people too" (23, 55). In his opportunistic materialism and class elitism, he identifies with the hated white aggressor as he "behaves like a white man, thinks like a white man" (223). Even as the narrative describes Macon's success as a capitalist, it works to undercut his prideful arrogance. "A nigger in business is a terrible thing to see," says the grandmother of Guitar Bains when Macon threatens to evict the Bains family for failure to pay their rent (22). And another tenant of Macon's—Porter, the "wild man in the attic"—uses shaming, racist rhetoric when he angrily refers to Macon as a "baby-dicked baboon" and says to him, "You need killin, you really *need* killin" (28, 26).

A man with a "high behind and an athlete's stride" who "strutted" rather than "walked" (17), Macon attempts to enhance his racial and class status when he marries up by acquiring a trophy wife, the middle-class, light-skinned Ruth. Constructed as a figure of apparent middle-class respect-ability, Ruth is an ultrarefined woman whose life is shaped—and disciplined—by hegemonic ideologies of proper femininity and domesticity. A woman who was "pressed small" by her sterile, isolated, middle-class upbringing, Ruth is a "frail woman content to do tiny things" (124, 64). It is telling that Ruth, a woman ostensibly defined by her social standing and family back-ground, becomes obsessed with the large water mark on her expensive mahogany table, which identifies the place where the bowl of fresh flowers stood on the table during her father's lifetime, flowers that, for her father, represented the touch of elegance that "distinguished his own family from the people among whom they lived" (12). To Ruth, the water mark is a visible reminder of her family pride: it is a "mooring," the "verification" of an "idea" she wants to "keep alive" (13). But the water mark also is the "single flaw on the splendid wood," and it becomes "more pronounced" with the passage of time after it is exposed (11–12). A signifier of the hidden stain on the family honor—the stain of blackness—the water mark represents the family's hidden racial shame. Ruth's obsession with her stained table, then, signals her own status anxiety—her own internalization of a deep sense of familial and racial shame.

As *Song of Solomon*, in an act of textual exposure, brings to light the family pathology that lies behind Ruth's middle-class refinement and the Dead family's bourgeois respectability, it risks being accused, like *The Bluest Eye* and *Sula*, of invoking the corrosive and shaming hegemonic constructions of the black family—in this case the middle-class, not the lower-class, family—as a "tangle of pathology." While Macon marries Ruth to bolster his own class standing, he soon comes to view her as a source of shame and an object of disgust. Early in his marriage, Macon claims that he discovers Ruth in bed with her dead father, "Naked as a yard dog, kissing him. Him dead and white and puffy and skinny, and she had his fingers in her mouth" (73). Although Macon forgets, and even fabricates, some of the details of this scene—and, indeed, Ruth later tells a markedly different version of this event—the "odiousness" remains (17), and some readers may feel vicarious shame-disgust as they are positioned as curious observers of this voyeuristic scene, which hints at Ruth's incestuous, and necrophilic, attachment to her dead father. After Macon witnesses this scene, he becomes suspicious of Ruth. While he knows that his daughters are his own children—for Dr. Foster would not have been concerned about their skin color unless they were fathered by Macon—he begins to read new meaning into the fact that Dr. Foster delivered Ruth's babies. "I'm not saying that they had contact. But there's lots of things a man can do to please a woman, even if he can't fuck. Whether or not, the fact is she was in that bed sucking his fingers, and if she'd do that when he was dead, what'd she do when he was alive?" That contempt can lead to a desire to rid oneself of the despised person is apparent in Macon's angry remark about Ruth. "Nothing to do but kill a woman like that. I swear, many's the day I regret she talked me out of killing her" (74).

Macon's feelings for Ruth lead him to shun her sexually and also to feel disgusted when, after fifteen years of regretting not having a son, he has one "in the most revolting circumstances" (16), for Milkman is conceived when Ruth uses an aphrodisiac prepared by Pilate to lure Macon back to her bed for four days. Whereas Ruth considers Milkman her "single triumph," her "one aggressive act brought to royal completion" (133), Macon sees his son as a source of shame. Although Macon never learns why members of the community call his son "Milkman," he guesses that the name, which sounds "dirty, intimate, and hot," is shameful, and he knows that the name has something to do with his wife and is "like the emotion he always felt when thinking of her, coated with disgust" (15–16). "[I]f the people were calling his son Milkman, and if she was lowering her eyelids and dabbing at the sweat on her top lip when she heard it, there was definitely some filthy connection and it did not matter at all to Macon Dead whether anyone gave him the details or not" (17).

In describing the origins of Milkman's shame-laden nickname, Morrison appeals yet again to her readers' voyeuristic interests while she risks provoking their shame-disgust by positioning them as witnesses to a taboo, oedipally tinged scene. Ruth, who needs "a balm, a gentle touch or nuzzling of some sort" to make her life bearable (13), nurses Milkman until he is old enough to stand up and talk. While Ruth takes secret pleasure in nursing her growing son, Milkman's "secretive eyes" convey his childish sense that there is something "strange and wrong" about this incestuous nursing ritual, which abruptly ends when Ruth is discovered by one of Macon's tenants, Freddie, a notorious gossip (14). Amused at the sight of the lemony-skinned Ruth with her black-skinned son at her breast, Freddie gives Ruth's son his nickname, "Milkman." What the adult Milkman recalls is "Laughter. Somebody he couldn't see, in the room laughing . . . at him and at his mother, and his mother is ashamed. She lowers her eyes and won't look at him. 'Look at me, Mama. Look at me.' But she doesn't and the laughter is loud now. Everybody is laughing" (77). Even as this scene suggests Ruth's desire to baby Milkman—to keep him dependent and treat him as her "velveteened toy" (132)—it also dramatizes a common shame scenario in its account of Milkman's childhood experience of maternal rejection, depicted here in his inability to hold his mother's gaze. Milkman's sense that everybody is laughing at him and his mother conveys not only the maternal transmission of shame but also the global nature of shame: the shame-vulnerable individual's feeling, in the moment of public exposure and ridicule, that his secret shame is visible to all.

Like *Sula*, *Song of Solomon* focuses on the maternal transmission of shame and it also is concerned with the dangers of excessive mothering. But whereas in *Sula* Morrison centers her attention on the woman-centered world of the black matriarchy, in *Song of Solomon* she is concerned—especially in her representation of Macon Dead—with issues surrounding the black patriarchy. bell hooks, in her critique of the black phallocentric view of the patriarchal role—the notion of the "'satisfying manhood'" that "carries with it the phallocentric right of men to dominate women"—remarks on the "chokehold patriarchal masculinity imposes on black men" (*Black Looks* 97, 113). *Song of Solomon* explores the black patriarchy through the figure of the "stern, greedy, unloving" Macon Dead (234). A domestic tyrant who keeps his family "awkward with fear," Macon actively shames his wife and daughters, First Corinthians and Magdalene, who is called Lena. He expresses his hatred for his wife in every word he addresses to her and communicates his disappointment in his daughters, thus "dulling their buttery complexions and choking the lilt out of what should have been girlish voices. Under the frozen heat of his glance they tripped over doorsills and dropped the salt cellar into the yolks of their poached eggs. The way he mangled their grace, wit, and self-esteem was the single excitement of their days. . . . [A]nd his wife, Ruth, began her days stunned into stillness by her husband's contempt and ended them wholly animated by it" (10–11). Macon terrorizes his wife and daughters in private, yet he also indulges in proud public displays of his family. "First he displayed us, then he splayed us," the adult Lena remarks of Macon's treatment of her and her sister. "All our lives were like that: he would parade us like virgins through Babylon, then humiliate us like whores in Babylon" (216).

Macon, who dons the mask of exhibitionistic self-importance and prideful arrogance to defend against his unacknowledged shame, teaches Milkman to fear and respect him. Revolted by the disgusting circumstances in which he has fathered a son, Macon dominates and shames the growing Milkman, "to whom he could speak only if his words held some command or criticism" (28). As an adolescent, Milkman expresses his inherited shame/false pride through his posture and style of walking. Noticing that one of his legs is shorter than the other, Milkman begins to slouch or lean or stand with his hip thrown out. His slouching gait—which depicts the classic shame posture—appears as "an affected walk, the strut of a very young man trying to appear more sophisticated than he was. It bothered him and he acquired movements and habits to disguise what to him was a burning defect. . . . The deformity was mostly in his mind" (62).

Feeling that, because of his leg, he cannot emulate his father, who has no physical imperfection and seems to grow stronger with age, Milkman attempts to fashion an identity in opposition to his father. Setting out to differ from his father as much as he dares, Milkman sports a mustache, shaves a part into his hair, uses tobacco, and gives away his money. But despite his expression of his own individual differences, Milkman, who works for his father as a rent collector, has adopted his father's bourgeois values and ethic of materialism, and he remains enmeshed in his family's pathological system. When the twenty-two-year-old Milkman witnesses what has become a familiar family scene—that of his father hitting his mother—he assaults his father, who "had come to believe, after years of creating respect and fear wherever he put his foot down, after years of being the tallest man in every gathering, that he was impregnable" (67). Milkman, who watches his father crumple before him, experiences contradictory emotions: shame, sorrow, and also the glee of pride. Although this scene is cast as a classic oedipal conflict in which the son triumphs over the father, Milkman also realizes that his action will not change anything between his parents. "[P]erhaps there were some new positions on the chessboard, but the game would go on" (68). Angry when his father tells him "all that shit"

(76) about finding Ruth naked in bed with her dead father and shamed when his father's story leads to the recovery of his repressed memory of being nursed by his mother until he was too old, Milkman comes to feel "like a garbage pail for the actions and hatreds of other people" (120). Mired in the "shit" of family shame, he is caught up in a shame-shame feeling trap.

With oppositional intent, *Song of Solomon* exposes the family secrets of the bourgeois Dead family, uncovering the shame behind the class elitism and false pride of Milkman's parents. Morrison's narrative also deliberately contrasts the false pride of Macon Dead with the natural dignity of Macon's sister, Pilate, who belongs to the black underclass. In its representation of Pilate, the narrative invokes and reverses the pride-shame oppositions associated with class and race—those of high/low, clean/unclean, pure/polluted— as it interrogates the degrading stereotype of the black underclass woman as the low-unclean-polluted Other. Making subversive use of the black cultural stereotype that associates light-skinned women with desirable feminine traits and dark-skinned women with undesirable masculine traits, the novel unfavorably compares the lemony-skinned, fragile, and shame-ridden Ruth with the tall, black Pilate, who is a powerful and proud woman. Thus, in the deliberate contrast between Ruth and Pilate, the narrative works to undermine the color-caste hierarchy, which values light-skinned, middle-class women and devalues those who are dark skinned and lower class. And yet while Pilate is depicted as a woman of natural dignity and black folk pride, she also suffers from a stigmatized identity and becomes the site in the text of middle-class anxieties about the black underclass.

To Macon, who has internalized white constructions of black racial inferiority, Pilate is the stigmatized, racially degenerate Other: marked by the stain of racial and class shame, she is inferior, defective, dirty, dissmelling. After the birth of Milkman, Pilate visits her brother's family only to have Macon eventually tell her to leave his house and not return until she shows some respect for herself. "How far down she had slid. . . ," Macon thinks of Pilate, who has a "sickening smell" and lacks any "interest in or knowledge of decent housekeeping" (20). Pilate, who lives like "poor trash" and is "odd, murky, and worst of all, unkempt," would be a "regular source of embarrassment, if he would allow it. But he would not allow it" (172, 20). "Why can't you dress like a woman?" Macon asks her. "What's that sailor's cap doing on your head? Don't you have stockings? What are you trying to make me look like in this town?" Afraid that her racial and class shame will stigmatize him, he trembles at the thought that his white bankers will discover that he is the brother of the "raggedy bootlegger," who has both an illegitimate daughter, Reba, and granddaughter, Hagar. To Macon, Pilate, Reba, and Hagar are a "collection of lunatics" who make wine and sing in the streets "like common street women" (20). Although he would like to put his bootlegger sister in jail—that is, make use of the dominant society's method of disciplining and controlling the unruly underclass—he is afraid that she might "loudmouth him and make him seem trashy in the eyes of the law—and the banks" (24).

Anything but the common street woman Macon sees in her, Pilate, who is as tall as Macon Dead, looks like "a tall black tree" to Milkman (39): that is, she embodies the natural pride of the black rural folk. Yet while the narrative insists on Pilate's folk pride, it also presents the navelless Pilate as a stigmatized individual. Explaining the link between shame and stigma, Michael Lewis remarks that stigma "is a mark or characteristic that distinguishes a person as being deviant, flawed, limited, spoiled, or generally undesirable." Stigmatization, which is a "public, interpersonal event," prompts a sense of shame and embarrassment: the stigmatized individual is "imperfect" and has a "spoiled identity" (194). Moreover, through the process of "stigma contagion," stigma affects not only the "marked" individual but also those people who associate with the stigmatized person (200). Because Pilate lacks a navel—which others read as a sign of her pathological difference—she is stigmatized and thus shunned by others for fear of stigma contagion. On learning of her defect, "Men frowned, women whispered and shoved their children behind them." During her early life as a wanderer, Pilate takes up with several groups of migrant farmworkers only to have one group ask her to leave when they discover she lacks a navel and another to expel her by leaving her behind. As Pilate comes to realize, "although men fucked armless women, one-legged women, hunchbacks and blind women, drunken women, razor-toting women, midgets, small children, convicts, boys, sheep, dogs, goats, liver, each other, and even certain species of plants, they were terrified of fucking her—a woman with no navel" (148).

That Pilate's lack is associated with female sexuality in this passage calls to mind not only the cultural equation between female genitals and deficiency or lack but also between female sexuality and the fear of stigma contagion evident in the masculinist view of female sexuality as contaminating and defiling. The narrative also uses Pilate's lack of a navel to make a covert political statement by associating Pilate's birth trauma and maternal loss with the black struggle for survival. Macon recalls how Pilate came "struggling out of the womb" after their mother died, how she inched "headfirst out of a still, silent, and indifferent cave of flesh, dragging her own cord and her own afterbirth behind her" (27, 28). In describing Pilate as self-born, *Song of Solomon* constructs her as an honored American type—the self-created individual. Yet it also focuses on Pilate's rebellious shamelessness as it uses this character to dialogically contest the black assimilationist and bourgeois ideology of self-help and self-improvement. Ignoring the pain and powerlessness of the social outcast's situation, the text, instead, insists that when the stigmatized, ostracized Pilate finally takes offense at the way others have treated her, she is liberated and empowered. On recognizing "what her situation in the world was and would probably always be," Pilate discards "every assumption she had learned" and begins "at zero." By focusing on the problem of how she wants to live and what she finds important in life, Pilate reinvents herself, becoming a woman who remains "just barely within the boundaries of the elaborately socialized world of black people." Pilate gives up "all interest in table manners or hygiene," yet she acquires "a deep concern for and about human relationships" (149). In a deliberate strategy to counteract the shame associated with Pilate's stigmatized identity, the narrative, even as it presents Pilate as a shameless individual and a member of the black underclass, also constructs her as a healing figure and insists that she gains a kind of power and freedom as she resists the shame-binding rules of black society. Described as a "natural healer" (150) and as a person who values human—and family—connections above all else, Pilate becomes the site in the text of redemptive folk values.

In its representation of Pilate, *Song of Solomon* deliberately carries out an antishaming agenda as it invokes but also interrogates degrading stereotypes of the black underclass woman. Yet it also insists that Pilate's granddaughter, Hagar—who is "prissy" and hates "dirt and disorganization"—is "embarrassed" by her mother and grandmother (150, 151). Returning to its concern with the issues of class and shame and the color-caste hierarchy in the construction of African-American identities, the narrative describes how Milkman, although he is initially attracted to Hagar, ultimately adopts his family's middle-class values, viewing Hagar as someone who is not of "his own set" (91). Despite Milkman's prolonged affair with Hagar, people do not consider her a "real or legitimate girl friend—not someone he might marry," and indeed Milkman treats her as an object of shame: as a "quasi-secret but permanent fixture in his life" (91, 98). The same Hagar who hates dirt and disorganization is ultimately dismissed by Milkman, who "wouldn't give a pile of swan shit" for her (137).

When Milkman sends Hagar a letter ending their relationship, the "flat-out coldness" of the "thank you" in his letter stuns Hagar, who is sent "spinning into a bright blue place where the air was thin and it was silent all the time . . . and where everything was frozen except for an occasional burst of fire inside her chest that crackled away until she ran out into the streets to find Milkman Dead" (99). The deeply injured Hagar, who is confused and frozen by shame, feels the incipient fire of shame-rage burning within her. After Hagar sees Milkman with his arms around the shoulders of a light-skinned woman—a woman with silky copper-colored hair and gray eyes—she experiences both shame-depression and shame-rage. The lovelorn Hagar becomes "like a restless ghost, finding peace nowhere and in nothing" as she ruminates on her loss: "the mouth Milkman was not kissing, the feet that were not running toward him, the eye that no longer beheld him, the hands that were not touching him" (127). Then her lethargy dissipates and she feels intense rage as the "calculated violence of a shark" grows in her (128).

If Hagar is constructed as a traditional dysphoric romantic heroine—a woman who makes the man the center of her life and thus feels an utter sense of loss and despair when her love relation fails—she also is presented as a potentially violent underclass woman, a precursor of *Jazz's* Violet Trace. Feeling that Milkman is her "home in this world" but unable to win his love, Hagar settles instead "for his fear," and so she begins stalking him, intent on killing him (137, 128). Because she trembles when she is in Milkman's presence, her "knife thrusts and hammer swings and ice-pick jabs" are "clumsy," and thus she is an "inept killer" (129). Milkman's contemptuous remark during Hagar's final attempt on his life when she stands paralyzed, holding a butcher knife in her raised hands—he tells her that her problems will be over if she drives the knife into her "cunt"—devastates Hagar, who has been so "taken over by her anaconda love" that she has "no self left, no fears, no wants, no intelligence that was her own" (130, 137).

"You think because he doesn't love you that you are worthless," Guitar says to Hagar. "If he throws you out, then you are garbage. . . . He can't value you more than you value yourself" (305–06). While Guitar finds Hagar a "[p]retty little black-skinned woman" (306), Hagar, recalling *The Bluest Eye's* Pecola, sees herself as black and ugly. Viewing herself through the shaming eyes of Milkman, Hagar, who is languishing in bed, determines to "fix" herself when she looks at herself in the tiny compact mirror Pilate gives her. "No wonder. . . . Look at how I look. I look awful. No wonder he didn't want me. I look terrible. . . . Ohhh. I smell too. . . . I need a bath. A long one. . . . Oh, Lord, my head. Look at that. . . . I look like a ground hog. Where's the comb?" (308–09). Hagar attempts to refashion herself by purchasing new clothes and makeup. But her efforts at self-improvement and self-transformation are doomed to failure because the dark-skinned Hagar cannot possibly compete in Milkman's bourgeois world, which favors lighter-skinned women. Focusing attention on the homogenizing power of mass cultural images in shaping identity, the narrative describes Hagar's failed attempt to conform to cultural norms. Hagar dresses herself up "in the white-with-a-band-of-color skirt and matching bolero, the Maidenform brassiere, the Fruit of the Loom panties, the no color hose, the Playtex garter belt and the Joyce con brios," and she rubs "mango tango on her cheeks" and puts "jungle red" on her lips and "baby clear sky light" on her eyelids. But when Hagar presents herself to Pilate and Reba and sees herself reflected in their shaming gaze, she recognizes what she was unable to see in the mirror: "the wet ripped hose, the soiled white dress, the sticky, lumpy face powder, the streaked rouge, and the wild wet shoals of hair" (314). Hagar, who has always hated dirt and disorganization, recognizes her social distance from Milkman as she perceives herself as a sad spectacle: as the dirty black underclass woman. Having internalized hegemonic beauty standards, which link skin color and hair texture to class status and construct dark-skinned women as the racially inferior and stigmatized Other, Hagar feels unworthy, dirty, spoiled, undesirable. Milkman "hates" her hair, she insists, and he "loves" silky, penny-colored hair[4] and lemon-colored skin, a thin nose, and gray-blue eyes (315–16). When the shame-haunted Hagar dies, her death is as much an expression of her desire to do away with her spoiled, racially stained identity as it is of her lovesickness.

Racial and class shame also govern the love relationship between Porter and Milkman's sister, Corinthians, a "[h]igh toned and high yellow" woman. According to the standard black middle-class narrative, the college-educated Corinthians, who had been taught how to be "an enlightened mother and wife," should have been able "to contribute to the civilization—or in her case, the civilizing—of her community," and she should have been "a prize for a professional man of color." But despite her education and class privileges, she remains unmarried, for such men prefer wives unlike the "elegant" Corinthians, who is accustomed to black middle-class life and thus lacks the necessary "ambition," "hunger," and "hustle" such men look for in a wife (188). The granddaughter of the distinguished Dr. Foster, the forty-four-year-old Corinthians ends up working as the maid of a white woman, the State Poet Laureate, and she becomes romantically involved with the Southside yardman, Porter. The narrative deliberately brings together the elegant Corinthians and Porter, individuals who occupy opposing sites in the black social hierarchy, as it examines the issue of class and shame in the construction of African-American identities, and it also, in its initial description of Porter, reproduces the culturally embedded stereotype of the impulsive and potentially violent black underclass male by portraying him as the "wild man in the attic" (28). When Porter makes his initial dramatic appearance in the novel, he is a "crazy drunk" man perched in an attic window with a gun, who demands from the Southside onlookers "somebody to fuck" and who pulls out his penis and urinates in a high arc over the heads of the women onlookers, thus acting out the shaming invective, "piss on you" (24–25).[5] Porter's words to the crowd—he shouts that he loves the Southside people and would die and kill for them—are explained much later when readers learn that the "cowering, screaming, threatening, urinating" Porter is a member of the Seven Days terrorist organization, a group that plans and carries out black-on-white revenge killings (26).

Corinthians and Porter, who ride the same city bus, start talking to each other after Porter gives Corinthians a friendship greeting card. When they begin their romantic relationship, Corinthians not only is ashamed of Porter but she also hates him for the shame she feels. Initially refusing Porter's invitation to visit his room, she explains that her "strict" father does not want his daughters "to mix with . . . people": that is, with Southside underclass blacks like Porter (195). Porter's accusation that she is a "doll baby" and not a "grown-up woman" shames and angers Corinthians, who feels that she has been unfavorably compared to the "only people she knew for certain she was superior to": the fat, promiscuous, illiterate women on the bus. "They'd love to have a greeting card dropped in their lap," Corinthians says to Porter. "But oh, I forgot. You couldn't do that, could you, because they wouldn't be able to read it. . . . They wouldn't know mediocrity if it punched them right in their fat faces. They'd laugh and slap their fat thighs and take you right on into their kitchens. Right up on the breakfast table" (196). In dramatizing Corinthians's status anxiety, this scene also illustrates the co-construction of social identities, revealing how the construction of the lower-class Other—as sexually loose and uncivilized—functions to consolidate black middle-class identity.

If Corinthians's contemptuous, middle-class voice brings into the text the intraracist discourse of the black bourgeoisie, the narrative also acts out a kind of shaming revenge on Corinthians, who is subsequently reduced to clinging to the hood of Porter's car in a panic, lest he leave her behind. A man "who rented a tiny room from her father, who ate with a knife and did not even own a pair of dress shoes," Porter is the kind of man Corinthians's parents had kept her from "because such a man was known to beat his woman, betray her, shame her, and leave her." But after having sex with Porter, Corinthians feels, in place of the "vanity" of false class pride, a new sense of "self-esteem," and thus she is "grateful" to Porter (201). Sending out contradictory messages, the narrative presents Porter as a gentle lover and potential rescuer of Corinthians but also as a killer. And even as it seems intent on humanizing Porter and thus counteracting the initial shaming and racist representation of him as a "wild man in the attic," it also reminds readers that he is the "same Henry Porter" who had "screamed, wept, waved a shotgun, and urinated over the heads of the women in the yard" (28, 199).

In a similar way, *Song of Solomon* sends out contradictory messages in its presentation of the underclass Guitar, who is initially described as the person who can "liberate" Milkman (36) and yet who ultimately tries to kill Milkman. "Wanna fly, you got to give up the shit that weighs you down," Guitar tells Milkman when they see a white peacock that can fly "no better than a chicken" because of its jewelry-like tail. "All that jewelry weighs it down. Like vanity. Can't nobody fly with all that shit," Guitar insists (179). Milkman, who is weighed down by "shit"—that is, the vanity of false class pride—is also capable of treating others like "shit" as he attempts to defend against the "shit" of inherited racial and family shame. Indeed, Lena accuses Milkman of "peeing" on his mother and sisters all of his life—that is, treating them in a contemptuous way—and he has similarly shown contempt for Hagar, a person he sees as worth less than "a pile of swan shit" (214–15, 137). Although Guitar offers Milkman potentially liberating advice when he insists "Can't nobody fly with all that shit," the narrative also registers uneasiness about Guitar, who comes to embody black middle-class fears about the potentially destructive shame-rage of the violent black underclass male.

"If things ever got tough, you'd melt. You're not a serious person, Milkman," Guitar remarks at one point (104). Unlike Milkman, who is bored by talk of "insults, violence, and oppression" (107), Guitar becomes consumed by racial politics. Bringing in Guitar's oppositional voice, *Song of Solomon* examines the construction of conflicting black political identities, contrasting the middle-class assimilationist Milkman and the lower-class black nationalist, Guitar. For someone like Guitar, to live in a racist society that persecutes and stigmatizes poor black people is to live in a state of chronic shame-rage. The site of black rage and revenge in the text, Guitar has been contrastingly described as a character that Morrison "purposefully makes . . . fascinating" because she does not want his "solution of violence to be easily dismissed" and as a "vindictive racist" who "gets Morrison's scorn" (Atlas, "Darker Side" 6, Brenner 117).

In explaining the personal and social forces that shape the construction of Guitar's political identity as a militant black nationalist and member of the Seven Days terrorist organization, the narrative presents Guitar as an individual who has been deeply scarred and traumatized by his childhood loss of his father. Guitar is unable to eat sweets, which make him vomit and think of dead people and white people, because when his father got sliced in half in a sawmill, his father's white boss gave Guitar and his brother and two sisters some sweet candy his wife had made especially for them, and also Guitar's mother bought candy for the children with part of the forty dollars the white sawmill owner gave her in lieu of an insurance settlement. In linking Guitar's aversion to candy to his aversion to white people, the narrative sends out the covert and countershaming message that white people make Guitar vomit: that is, they disgust him. A basic emotion originating in the rejection of bad-tasting, offensive food, disgust has evolved into "a wide range of emotion completely unrelated to food" and can signal the desire to "spit out with violence" or reject the other (Nathanson, *Shame and Pride* 127, 128). "Like anger and contempt, disgust can be a moral reaction to other people, implying that their actions or character have violated normative standards. . . . [A]s disgust becomes elaborated, it becomes a more general feeling of revulsion, even to sociomoral violations, and it begins to shade into anger" (Rozin 588).

At the emotional core of Guitar's aversive antiwhite racism is what affect theorists refer to as the "hostility triad" of disgust, contempt, and anger (see Rozin 589). With dialogic intent, the text sets out to countershame white racists, who construct African Americans as mad, savage, and degenerate people, by constructing whites as a mad, depraved people who viciously kill blacks. "There are no innocent white people," Guitar tells Milkman, "because every one of them is a potential nigger-killer, if not an actual one. You think Hitler surprised them? You think just because they went to war they thought he was a freak? Hitler's the most natural white man in the world. He killed Jews and Gypsies because he didn't have us. Can you see those Klansmen shocked by him? No, you can't" (155). Using the white racist discourse of difference and pathology to define whiteness, Guitar construes whites as an "unnatural" race: as a morally degenerate, violent, and uncivilized people who kill "for fun." "[I]f Kennedy got drunk and bored and was sitting around a potbellied stove in Mississippi, he might join a lynching party just for the hell of it. Under those circumstances his unnaturalness would surface" (156). Similarly, had Roosevelt found himself in a small Alabama town, "he'd have done it too." Constructing whites as a monolithic or generalized Other, Guitar insists that all whites, under the right circumstances, would kill blacks. Moreover, whites know that they are depraved, for their "writers and artists have been saying it for years. . . . They call it tragedy. In the movies they call it adventure. It's just depravity that they try to make glorious, natural. But it ain't." Invoking the shaming discourse of racial biology to define whiteness, Guitar explains that the "disease" whites have is "in their blood, in the structure of their chromosomes" (157).[6]

If Guitar's antiwhite racist discourse is meant, in part, to underscore the social constructedness of essentializing and pathologizing discourses of racial difference, the narrative also warns of the potentially lethal consequences of racist stereotypes and us-them thinking in describing Guitar's membership in the Seven Days, a terrorist organization that carries out revenge killings against whites. In a classic attack-other revenge script—a script that combines power, rage, and contempt scripts—members of the Seven Days assume a secret killing power over their white oppressors.[7] The Seven Days society, as Guitar explains, executes whites. "[W]hen a Negro child, Negro woman, or Negro man is killed by whites and nothing is done about it by *their* law and *their* courts, this society selects a similar victim at random, and they execute him or her in a similar manner if they can. If the Negro was hanged, they hang; if a Negro was burnt, they burn; raped and murdered, they rape and murder" (154–55). While the members of the Seven Days enact a compulsive repetition of shame and trauma scenarios, they also, through their secret acts of revenge, assume power over whites by taking on the role of the violent perpetrator. By identifying with the white aggressor and thus reversing the (white) perpetrator and (black) victim roles, members of the Seven Days attempt not only to discharge collective black shame-based rage onto whites but also to exorcise collective black trauma by relocating feelings of humiliation, terror, and vulnerability in white victims. Through a reversal of the balance of power, they secretly act out the desire to disempower and traumatize whites, instilling in them the feelings of utter powerlessness experienced by black victims of white violence. Thus, they stigmatize their white victims before killing them, for "human-induced" victimization is not only "humiliating" but it also sullies and tarnishes the victim who is rendered utterly helpless (Janoff-Bulman 80).

Claiming that he is reasonable when he kills whites—for he does not kill out of anger or for amusement or to gain power or money—Guitar explains that he participates in revenge killings because he loves black people and because he wants the black-white ratio to remain static. While the "earth is soggy with black people's blood" and white people cannot be cured of their depravity, the Seven Days is nevertheless "trying to make a world where one day white people will think before they lynch" (158, 160). If *Song of Solomon* at first glance appears to reinforce the stereotype of the pathological, violent black man in its description of the Seven Days, the narrative also actively reprojects the shame associated with this derogatory stereotype onto whites. It does this by revealing that Guitar and his cohorts are driven mad by the violent acts they commit and that their behavior is an imitation of the racist violence perpetrated by whites against African Americans. And even as *Song of Solomon* uses Guitar to express black rage and to enact a revenge fantasy, it also voices black middle-class concerns about Guitar's violent behavior. While Milkman is secretly attracted to Guitar's killing behavior—"Did you do it yet?" Milkman wonders. "How did it feel? Were you afraid? Did it change you? And if I do it, will it change me too?" (176)—he also calls Guitar's behavior crazy and warns that killing can become habitual. "If you do it enough, you can do it to anybody. . . . You can off anybody you don't like. You can off me" (161), Milkman remarks to Guitar, his words preparing for the final sections of the novel which describe how Guitar hunts down Milkman, intent on killing him.

If Part I of *Song of Solomon*, in showing that Milkman is weighed down by the "shit" of inherited racial shame, ends in an emotional impasse, Part II attempts to work through Milkman's shame-shame feeling trap by describing how he comes to take pride in his family roots. Thus, according to the standard, text-directed reading of *Song of Solomon*, when Milkman goes on his journey to Danville and Shalimar in search of Pilate's buried gold, he discovers, instead, the real golden treasure of his family roots. But what such readings tend to bypass are the shame and pain associated with Milkman's discovery. In using folk tale and magic and following the pattern of the hero's purposeful quest as it describes Milkman's journey south, *Song of Solomon* also deflects attention away from the trauma and violence that have threatened to interrupt—if not disrupt and fragment—the narrative from the beginning, not only in the story of Guitar but also in the family story of the Deads. What lies behind the dark comedy of manners and grotesqueries of Morrison's interwoven and layered narratives about the Dead family is an originary trauma narrative, which tells of the family's slavery and postslavery beginnings in a world of racist oppression and violence.

Milkman first begins to learn about his family history from Pilate, a woman reputed to be a conjure woman who has "the power to step out of her skin, set a bush afire from fifty yards, and turn a man into a ripe rutabaga" (94). Even as the narrative associates Pilate with magic and female power, it also depicts her as a victim of trauma. Not only is the navelless Pilate's stigma a sign of her birth trauma and maternal loss, but Pilate also has never recovered from the traumatic loss of her father. The first time Milkman meets Pilate, she tells him the story of her father's murder, describing how he was killed in front of his two children, the sixteen-year-old Macon and the twelve-year-old Pilate. "They blew him five feet up into the air. He was sitting on his fence waiting for 'em, and they snuck up from behind and blew him five feet into the air" (40). When asked for specific information about her father's murder, Pilate responds in a vague way, remarking that she doesn't know "who" killed him or "why" and that "where" it happened was "[o]ff a fence" and "when" was "[t]he year they shot them Irish people down in the streets. Was a good year for guns and gravediggers, I know that" (42). If the description of Pilate communing with the ghost of her dead father serves to reinforce the idea that she is a conjure woman, it also suggests that she—and by extension the collective black folk she represents—is trauma-haunted.

Macon's account of his father's death repeats and elaborates on Pilate's fragmented memory of this traumatic and formative event. When Milkman asks Macon how he was treated by his father when he was a boy, Macon suddenly recalls the "numbness that had settled on him when he saw the man he loved and admired fall off the fence" and how "something wild ran through him when he watched the body twitching in the dirt" (50–51). An emancipated slave, Macon's father spent sixteen years making his farm, Lincoln's Heaven, profitable only to have it forcibly taken from him by whites, who tricked the illiterate farmer into signing over his property to them when he made his mark on a deed to the property. "White people did love their dogs," Macon recalls in a passage that focuses on the shame of being treated as less valuable than an animal. "Kill a nigger and comb their hair at the same time. But I've seen grown white men cry about their dogs" (52). Preserving Pilate's voice as one relaying healing folk wisdom and community values, the narrative uses Macon's elaboration of Pilate's story to bring into focus what her account omits: the shame and rage suffered by victims of white supremacist persecution and violence.

When Milkman begins his journey in search of Pilate's gold, he seemingly undergoes a corrective emotional experience as he escapes from his "real life," where he is constrained by "other people's nightmares" and where everybody wants his "living life" (220, 222). At Reverend Cooper's house in Danville, Pennsylvania, Milkman discovers a newfound family and racial pride in having *"people,"* that is, family links (229). There he is visited by a series of old men who speak with "awe and affection" of his grandfather and remember "both Macon Deads as extraordinary men." To them, Milkman's father and grandfather embody black male pride. They recall Milkman's father, their contemporary, as a strong and energetic boy who "outran, outplowed, outshot, outpicked, outrode them all" (234). And Milkman's grandfather, "the tall, magnificent Macon Dead," was "the farmer they wanted to be, the clever irrigator, the peach-tree grower, the hog slaughterer, the wild-turkey roaster, the man who could plow forty in no time flat and sang like an angel while he did it." His farm, Lincoln's Heaven, "spoke to them like a sermon. 'You see?' the farm said to them. 'See? See what you can do? Never mind you can't tell one letter from another, never mind you born a slave, never mind you lose your name, never mind your daddy dead, never mind nothing. Here, this here, is what a man can do if he puts his mind to it and his back in it. Stop sniveling,' it said. 'Stop picking around the edges of the world'" (235). Attempting to revive their dying dream—"[b]ut they shot the top of his head off and ate his fine Georgia peaches" (235)—Milkman begins to tell the old men stories about his father. "He bragged a little and they came alive. How many houses his father owned (they grinned); the new car every two years (they laughed); and when he told them how his father tried to buy the Erie Lackawanna (it sounded better that way), they hooted with joy. That's him! That's Old Macon Dead's boy, all right!" (236).

"I knew one day you would come back," the witchlike Circe says to Milkman, mistaking him for his father when he finds his way to the ruined mansion of the Butlers, the white people who murdered his grandfather (240). The woman who once worked for the Butlers and who hid Milkman's father and Pilate from the Butlers after the murder of their father, Circe is an embodiment of black folk memory and survival. A study in contrasts, Circe has dainty habits but wild, dirty hair and torn filthy clothes, and she has a wizened face and toothless mouth yet the cultivated voice of a twenty-year-old. In a deliberate parody of the traditional white representation of the loyal black servant, Morrison describes how Circe, who has outlived the Butlers, has remained in the decaying Butler mansion taking care of their dogs. "You loved those white folks that much?" Milkman asks Circe (246) only to learn that what truly motivates her is the desire for revenge, the wish to turn the tables by returning white contempt with black countercontempt.

Contempt, which combines the affect of anger with dissmell, underlies white prejudice against blacks, as shame theorists have observed. The "facial scene in contempt is the sneer, which is a learned transformation of dissmell," Gershen Kaufman writes, drawing on the observations of Silvan Tomkins. "By combining anger with dissmell, contempt functions as a signal and motive to others . . . of either negative evaluation or feelings of rejection. The face pulls away in dissmell from the offending, 'bad-smelling' other. . . ." The contemptuous individual "feels elevated" and looks down on others, who are "deemed inferior, beneath one's dignity" (*Psychology of Shame* 40, 41). But contempt also breeds contempt and can lead, as it does in the case of Circe, to a desire to retaliate.

In a displaced drama, Circe acts out a revenge script that signals her long-thwarted wish to humiliate her former, and now dead, humiliators by overseeing the transformation of their mansion—a symbol of white pride and greed—into a dirty, dissmelling place. "Everything in this world they lived for will crumble and rot," Circe tells Milkman (247). Once a beautiful mansion, the Butler home is now "[d]ark, ruined, evil" and permeated with a "hairy animal smell, ripe, rife, suffocating" (238, 239). Acting out her long-suppressed shame-rage against Mrs. Butler—a woman who committed suicide so she would not have to live the way Circe did—Circe turns the dogs loose in the bedroom of her dead employer. "Her walls didn't have wallpaper. No. Silk brocade that took some Belgian women six years to make. She loved it—oh, how much she loved it. Took thirty Weimaraners one day to rip it off the walls. If I thought the stink wouldn't strangle you, I'd show it to you," Circe says to Milkman (247–48). Acting as an agent of black revenge, Circe, as Reverend Cooper tells Milkman, has evened up things. For Circe symbolically dirties—that is, shames—the once powerful and superior white family, representatives of the prejudiced white culture that has historically shamed blacks by treating them as dirty and dissmelling objects of contempt.

When Milkman's search for Pilate's gold at Hunters Cave proves futile, he goes to Shalimar, Virginia, believing that Pilate took the gold there. Because Milkman was "the object of hero worship" in Danville, he is unprepared for his reception in Shalimar where he is "damned near killed" (270) when he unwittingly insults the men he encounters by treating them as inferiors, thus reminding them of their allotted place in American society. "He hadn't found them fit enough or good enough to want to know their names, and believed himself too good to tell them his. They looked at his skin and saw it was as black as theirs, but they knew he had the heart of the white men who came to pick them up in the trucks when they needed anonymous, faceless laborers" (266). Feeling their own manhood insulted—

for Milkman's middle-class monied manner reminds them that they don't
have any crops of their own to harvest and that they depend on women and
children for their food—they insult Milkman's manhood, engaging in a
version of the ritualized insult game, the dozens. When one of the men asks
if it is true that Northerners wear their pants tight because their "pricks" are
"[w]ee, wee little," Milkman replies:

> "I wouldn't know. . . . I never spent much time smacking my
> lips over another man's dick." Everybody smiled, including Milk-
> man. It was about to begin.
> "What about his ass hole? Ever smack your lips over that?"
> "Once," said Milkman. "When a little young nigger made me
> mad and I had to jam a Coke bottle up his ass."
> "What'd you use a bottle for? Your cock wouldn't fill it?"
> "It did. After I took the Coke bottle out. Filled his mouth
> too."
> "Prefer mouth, do you?"
> "If it's big enough, and ugly enough, and belongs to a ignor-
> ant motherfucker who is about to get the livin shit whipped out of
> him." (267)

Described as a "cruel game" in which words are "weapons aimed at the
destruction of another man's honor and pride" and in which "opponents try
to bring each other to the point of initiating physical combat," the dozens
game uses taunts—including "[a]ccusations of cowardice, homosexuality, or
stupidity"—to humiliate the opponent. Because this verbal game often takes
place before a group, losing can be "devastating," for the "loser may be seen
as ineffectual, or even worse, effeminate" (Majors and Billson 97, 93, 92,
97).[8] In its staging of the dozens game, *Song of Solomon* dramatizes the link
between shaming insults and violence by showing how the "name-calling
toilet contest" between Milkman and the Shalimar men (269) leads to a fight
between a knife-wielding local man and Milkman, who defends himself with
a broken bottle. Afterward an enraged Milkman thinks that if "he'd had a
weapon, he would have slaughtered everybody in sight," and, echoing the
class elitism and internalized racism of his father and grandfather, he
contemptuously dismisses the men, viewing them as "black Neanderthals"
and "savages" (269, 270, 276).

Milkman assumes, when the older men invite him to go on a night hunt,
that they plan to "test him, match and beat him" (269). Finding himself in
the woods at night with a "mean bunch of black folk," Milkman feels he has
not done anything to "deserve their contempt." In a conscious attempt to
rehabilitate Milkman's character, the narrative describes his sudden questioning of his middle-class—and narcissistic—sense of entitlement. "He didn't

deserve. . . . It sounded old. *Deserve.* Old and tired and beaten to death. Deserve. Now it seemed to him that he was always saying or thinking that he didn't deserve some bad luck, or some bad treatment from others. He'd told Guitar that he didn't 'deserve' his family's dependence, hatred, or whatever. That he didn't even 'deserve' to hear all the misery and mutual accusations his parents unloaded on him. Nor did he 'deserve' Hagar's vengeance" (276). As Milkman recognizes that he has selfishly refused to be responsible for the pain of others or to share their unhappiness, he feels "his self—the cocoon that was 'personality' "—give way. Alone in the dark in the woods where there is nothing to aid him—"not his money, his car, his father's reputation, his suit, or his shoes"—Milkman is stripped of his false class pride (277).

And yet, ironically enough, just as Milkman feels a "sudden rush of affection" for other people and believes he really understands his friend, Guitar, who has been "maimed" and "scarred" by his past (278), Guitar attempts to kill Milkman, and almost succeeds. "Your Day has come," Guitar tells Milkman as he fastens a wire around Milkman's throat (279) only to be scared off by the close sound of the baying dogs, who have treed a bobcat. Later, during the ritualized skinning of the bobcat, Milkman recalls Guitar's words: *"Everybody wants a black man's life. . . . Not his dead life; I mean his living life. . . . It's the condition our condition is in"* (281–82). That Guitar is associated with the predatory bobcat—for Guitar is described as a "natural-born hunter," as someone who has catlike movements and who can see like a cat with his "phosphorous" eyes (85, 118)—points to the narrative's embeddedness in hegemonic discourse. In describing Guitar as an instinctual, animallike killer, the narrative evokes the race- and class-coded stereotype of the lower-class black male as a potentially dangerous predator. Adding to the complexity of this scene, the bobcat (hunter) also signifies the traumatized black male (the hunted), who is preyed on by white society or by lynch mobs who want the life of a black man or who, like Milkman, is the victim of black-on-black violence. Indeed, during the skinning of the bobcat, just before Milkman pulls out the animal's heart, he recalls Guitar's earlier explanation that he engages in revenge killings because he loves black people, words that come back to haunt Milkman after his friend has attempted to kill him: *"It is about love. What else but love? Can't I love what I criticize?"* (282; see 223).

If, as it is sometimes claimed, the bobcat hunt is consciously patterned after an Africanized, tribal hunting ritual in which the initiate, Milkman, comes into his black manhood—and, indeed, Milkman is suggestively rewarded with the heart of the bobcat—the narrative also deliberately undercuts Milkman's moment of manly pride by interjecting into this scene a peacock, which was established earlier in the text as a signifier of false male pride (283; see

179). The narrative also sends out mixed messages in its description of Milk-man's discovery of his true family name as he decodes the children's song—the song of Solomon—which is the original version of Pilate's blues song. Milkman is initially elated when he learns that his grandfather, Macon Dead, was Jake, the son of the flying African—Solomon—who left his wife and twenty-one children and flew back to Africa. "That motherfucker could fly! Could fly! . . . He could fly his own self! . . . He just took off; got fed up. *All the way up! . . .* No more shit! He flew, baby" (328). But to fly away is also, the narrative insists, to place individual needs above the family, and, by extension, the community. "Who'd he leave behind?" Sweet asks Milkman. "Everybody! He left everybody down on the ground and he sailed on off like a black eagle. 'O-o-o-o-o-o Solomon done fly, Solomon done gone/Solomon cut across the sky, Solomon gone home!'" (328–29). The "Song of Solomon" is, at once, a song of male pride and shame, for as Morrison herself has remarked, "The fathers may soar, they may triumph, they may leave, but the children know who they are; they remember, *half in glory and half in accu-sation*" (Watkins 46, emphasis added). Thus flying—the proud and glorious moment of escape from the "shit" of racial shame—is also associated with the blaming, shaming accusations of those left behind. In a similar way, as Milkman takes pride in his family name, the narrative also reminds readers of the painful, shameful racist legacy of African-American names, names that people got "from yearnings, gestures, flaws, events, mistakes, weaknesses. Names that bore witness. Macon Dead . . . Pilate, Reba, Hagar, Magdalene, First Corinthians, Milkman, Guitar . . . Cock-a-Doodle-Doo, Cool Breeze, Muddy Waters, Pinetop, Jelly Roll, Fats, Leadbelly, Bo Diddley . . . Shine, Staggerlee, Jim the Devil, Fuck-Up and *Dat* Nigger" (330).

The text's hesitancies and ambivalences—which originate in its painful emotional content—are given final expression in the closing scenes. "Perhaps that's what all human relationships boiled down to: Would you save my life? or would you take it?" Milkman thinks when he realizes that a "deranged" Guitar is after him (331, 330). In an uncanny repetition of family trauma, the trauma-haunted Pilate is killed by Guitar after she buries her father's remains on Solomon's Leap. Pilate's final words are healing. "I wish I'd a knowed more people. I would of loved 'em all," she tells Milkman. "If I'd a knowed more, I would a loved more" (336). Constructed as an ancestor figure in this scene—as an embodiment of folk wisdom and natural pride—Pilate can fly without leaving the ground. And yet the killing of Pilate—the character designated by the narrative as a natural healer—suggests the text's inability to heal the deep emotional wounds that result from collective black shame and trauma.

"'You want my life? . . . You need it? Here.' Without wiping away the tears, taking a deep breath, or even bending his knees—he leaped. As fleet and bright as a lodestar he wheeled toward Guitar and it did not matter which one of them would give up his ghost in the killing arms of his brother. For now he knew what Shalimar knew: If you surrendered to the air, you could *ride* it" (337). Despite the positive rhetoric of the closure, which depicts Milkman's heroic flight and his manly confrontation with the murderous Guitar, Milkman's leap can also be read as a suicidal and nihilistic gesture: an enactment of Milkman's wish to disappear and thus escape the "shit" of his chronic shame. Moreover, the fact that Milkman's search for his African-American roots ends in a traumatic assault sends out the covert message that the middle-class African-American male cannot truly understand his racial heritage without experiencing, firsthand, what trauma specialists have referred to as the "black hole" of trauma (van der Kolk, "Foreword" ix). But the narrative, as we can see in the critical conversation surrounding the closure, also generates a powerful—and text-directed—wish to see Milkman rescued and to turn shame into pride. By deliberately withholding information—the reader does not know if Milkman will live or die—the closure poses a crisis of interpretation and compels reader involvement in concluding what remains inconclusive and in completing the emotional work the text began in its exploration of black male shame and pride.

Presenting a cognitive puzzle at the end, Morrison compels readers to think and she also involves them emotionally in the text's shame-pride drama. Some critics, in insisting on Milkman's failure at the end, read an implicit shame drama in the closure. According to this view, Milkman's flight is "destined to be either suicidal or murderous," and "however changed by his experiences," he "plunges, in darkness, to the earth" (Bowman 13). While Morrison's prose is celebratory, writes another critic, behind the "seemingly upbeat ending of her novel lies Morrison's disdain for Milkman," and when he leaps "into Guitar's arms and certain death," his action is irresponsible, for he avoids "doing something meaningful in life, preferring the sumptuous illusion that he will ride the air" (Brenner 119). But although the narrative seems unable to transform, in any permanent way, shame into pride, most critic-readers follow the text's directives and interpret the closure as a heroic gesture and thus an affirmation of black pride and achievement. Such commentators assert that Milkman's final gesture "affirms his relation to Solomon and Pilate" and as a "'lodestar' setting his own course, he meets them in their mythic and elemental flight," or they argue that Milkman, in his final flight, is able to "transcend death" and "embrace the life of humanity" (Carmean 61, O'Shaughnessy 125). Since Milkman "has achieved . . . connectedness" to his African-American community, "it does not matter whether Milkman survives his encounter with Guitar," writes one commentator (Duvall, "Doe Hunting" 111). And yet another asserts, "The novel does not end with a cliff-hanger; the final battle is both a confrontation and a confirmation, marking Milkman's emergence as a champion who understands and will defend his world," and whether or not Milkman dies, his "joyful acceptance of the burden of his past transforms his leap toward Guitar into a triumphant flight" (A. Leslie Harris 71, 76).

That most critic-readers enact an antishaming gesture as they turn shame into pride suggests that *Song of Solomon* generates in some readers the wish to rescue the character and also to avoid the painful content of the novel by reading it primarily as an ultimately triumphant "heroic" quest. Because shame is a contagious emotion and, indeed, people are ashamed of shame, critic-readers may feel at once riveted to the text, which appeals to readers' voyeuristic interests, but also want to avert their gaze—that is, avoid or bypass the shameful content of the novel. The novel itself, while shaming the bourgeois Dead family, also bypasses shame by de-emphasizing the shameful legacy of slavery that haunts African Americans in its suggestion that the real gold Milkman seeks is the *golden* legacy of his racial heritage. Indeed, the myth of the Flying African encapsulates the fantasy-wish to escape or bypass the "shit" of racial oppression and shame and also the desire to convert shame into pride.

There may be something golden in the survival of the slaves and of family stories about one's black family roots in slavery, but slavery also constitutes a shameful and largely secret legacy in the African-American cultural memory. In *Song of Solomon*, Morrison focuses on intraracial shaming, the color-caste hierarchy, and black-on-black violence as she depicts the effects of shame and trauma on the lives of African Americans and on the construction of African-American cultural and political identities. While Morrison, in *Song of Solomon*, is also invested in extending the black cultural imagination and memory by looking back to African-American "roots" in slavery, she will carry out the emotional and cultural work of fully confronting the catastrophic and painful issue of slavery later, in *Beloved*. There she will bear witness to the horrors of slavery and racist oppression, which "dirtied" the selves of the slaves, as she attempts to aesthetically confront and begin to heal the deep and abiding wounds inflicted on black Americans in our race-divided American culture.

5

"Defecating Over a Whole People"

THE POLITICS OF SHAME AND
THE FAILURE OF LOVE IN *TAR BABY*

" [W]hat is the problem between a pair of lovers who really love one another but are culturally different?" Morrison remarks of *Tar Baby*. "What is the battle about? Culture? Class?" (Moyers 270). Described by Morrison as a "very contemporary love story" that deals with class problems (Russell 44), *Tar Baby*, like *Song of Solomon*, focuses on issues of racial shame and pride as it presents the ultimately failed love relationship between Son and Jadine. Part of Morrison's avowed purpose is to illuminate the "cultural illness" that underlies the lovers' conflict in *Tar Baby* (McKay 147). "Racism hurts in a very personal way," as Morrison comments. "Because of it, people do all sorts of things in their personal lives and love relationships based on differences in values and class and education and their conception of what it means to be Black in this society" (Wilson 135).

In *Tar Baby*, which like *Song of Solomon* is located in a specific cultural moment, Morrison investigates the crisis-of-identity within the African-American community as she examines what it means to be a black in the post–Civil Rights period in which the idea of black solidarity has been challenged by a recognition of the differences in values and class and education that divide African Americans. Morrison's "least popular" novel (Carmean 62), *Tar Baby* is a willfully disturbing work in which Morrison openly invokes racist stereotypes and makes extensive use of the shaming discourse of dirt and defilement and insulting, contemptuous racist speech as she probes divisive race and class issues. Continuing and expanding on the cultural and literary work of her earlier novels, Morrison explores in *Tar Baby* the complex ways in which race, class, and gender are inflected in the African-American experience as she illuminates the complicated processes of constructing black identities. As Morrison exposes to public view the class tensions within the black community, placing particular stress on the black bourgeoisie's prejudice against lower-class blacks, she points to the damaging impact of inherited and internalized racist stereotypes and discourses on African-American identities and the black cultural imagination.

Morrison, in her discussion of *Tar Baby*, remarks that she makes deliberate use of the Tar Baby folk tale in the novel, "dusting off the myth, looking closely at it to see what it might conceal" (LeClair 122). Although the Tar Baby folk story[1] points to a shameful racial legacy—and even the term, "tar baby," has come down as a racial slur—Morrison, in a characteristic antishaming maneuver, also locates a positive African message in this story. In her original conception of the novel, Morrison saw part of her novelistic project as a reprocessing of the Tar Baby story, which she first heard as a child. The story, as she recalls, "bothered" her "madly," if not "terrified" her, for she found the description of the white man creating the Tar Baby to trap the rabbit, who got "stuck and more stuck," to be "really quite monstrous" (Ruas 102). As she worked on the novel, Morrison viewed the Tar Baby tale as a "love story" in which a black woman is the tar baby and a black man the rabbit, and she wondered how a black woman who had enjoyed "all the benefits of what the white Western world has to offer" would relate to the black man who came "out of the briar patch" (Watkins 47, Ruas 102). During the process of reworking this story, she also kept in mind the racial shame attached to the term "Tar Baby," which, as she comments, is "a racial slur, like 'nigger,'" and is "also a name . . . that white people call black children, black girls" (Ruas 102, LeClair 122). Morrison's characteristic antishaming impulse is indicated in her description of the possible racial pride that underlies this "monstrous" story and racial epithet. When she discovered that there is a tar woman in African mythology, as she recalls, she began thinking about tar. "At one time, a tar pit was a holy place, at least an important place, because tar was used to build things. It came naturally out of the earth; it held together things like Moses' little boat and the pyramids. For me, the tar baby came to mean the black woman who can hold things together" (LeClair 122).

As Morrison dusts off the myth of the Tar Baby in her intentionally discomfiting novel, she addresses, often in blunt, shame-eliciting speech, issues of racial identity and class warfare within the black community. In *Tar Baby* not only is the black elitist Jadine identified as the white-constructed tar baby used to trap Son, the representative black underclass man of the folk, but Jadine also lacks the positive qualities Morrison associates with tar: both the maternal, nurturing qualities that act as a social "glue," and also the "tar" of blackness that comes from being in touch with one's African-American roots. Because Jadine's identity is white-constructed, she must become aware of her black roots and identity, and one of Son's primary functions is to serve as Jadine's guide in her search for her "authentic" cultural identity. But if part of *Tar Baby*'s cultural agenda is to celebrate black American folk roots and the maternal, nurturing tarlike qualities of black women, the narrative also expresses, through the character and voice of Jadine, the black bourgeoisie's ambivalence about blackness. Jadine associates blackness with the proud and noble African woman in yellow, but she also links it not only to the terrifying swamp women—and to the swamp tar that stains, blackens, and engulfs—but also to the night women with their grotesque sagging bodies. Thus while Morrison's novel sets out to consciously celebrate the tarlike quality of black women and the "authentic" black folk, it also uses Jadine's middle-class voice and perspective to express deep anxieties about the "tar" of blackness—that is, the black racial identity that stains and stigmatizes.

Identifying Son with the black rural folk culture and Jadine with the Euro-American urban white culture, *Tar Baby* invokes and contests dominant representations with their polarizing binarisms of black/white, nature/culture, primitive/civilized, polluted/pure. Part of the text's antishaming agenda is to reverse the white hierarchical value system by celebrating Son's African (black, nature-identified, primitive) qualities. Yet the narrative also expresses persisting ambivalences and hesitancies in its presentation of Son, who remains off-stage, hidden in the text as it were, for the first third of the novel, and who, when he initially erupts into the narrative, is constructed as the racial Other, as the shamed object of contempt. As seen through the shaming gaze of both the black and white characters in the Valerian Street household, Son is the sexual savage, the dangerous primitive, and the dirty, dissmelling underclass man. While the text's aim is to repeat these shaming racist and class stereotypes in order to counteract them, and while Jadine's initial fears of sexual—and racial—contamination dissipate when Son washes away his dirt and becomes stunningly attractive, the narrative continues to use Jadine's black elitist perspective to register uneasiness about Son and the black underclass rural folk culture he represents. Through the dialogic exchanges between the underclass Son and elitist Jadine, who become lovers but fail to permanently bridge the class-education-social divide between them, Morrison points to the cultural ailment that comes out of the deep legacy of racial shame and the color-caste hierarchy. Indicating the permanence of the cultural and emotional separation between the lovers, the novel closes without resolving the lovers' dilemma; instead, Jadine returns to her adopted European culture and Son enters the mythic folk culture. Failing to heal the racial wounds it opens, *Tar Baby* is unable to complete the emotional labor it begins and thus it ends in an emotional impasse. Just as the narrative is unable to overcome the cultural barriers between Son and Jadine, so critic-readers remain split in their perceptions of these characters. While some critic-readers come to Jadine's defense against Son, others act as Son's advo-cate. In other words, the shame drama of blame assessment, as we shall see, is a central feature of the critical discourse that surrounds this novel.

Dialogically contesting the traditional Western story that pits the heroic white man against the forces of nature, *Tar Baby* is invested in articulating an anticapitalist and anti-imperialist message as it describes how men like Valerian Street—who functions in the text as a representative of the white Euro-American invaders in the Caribbean—have, in their attempt to tame and control nature, ruined it. Delegitimizing the authoritative cultural nar-rative that normalizes the exercise of white power and economic interests in places like the Caribbean, *Tar Baby* describes how white men have folded the earth "where there had been no fold" and hollowed it "where there had been no hollow," forcing the river into "unknown turf" so that it began to run "every which way" (9). And when the men cut down the trees to build houses in the hills, the rain changed, "abusing the river even more." In an angry, shaming indictment of the Euro-American desecration of nature, *Tar Baby* describes how Nature itself is defiled and shamed by the white invaders. "Poor insulted, brokenhearted river. Poor demented stream. Now it sat in one place like a grandmother and became a swamp the Haitians called Sein de Vieilles. And witch's tit it was: a shriveled fogbound oval seeping with a thick black substance that even mosquitoes could not live near" (10). As the white invaders use their power to defile nature, so too they degrade the native Caribbean culture. Whites "had not the dignity of wild animals who did not eat where they defecated but they could defecate over a whole people and come there to live and defecate some more by tearing up the land and that is why they loved property so, because they had killed it soiled it defecated on it and they loved more than anything the places where they shit." Whites would "fight and kill to own the cesspools they made, and although they called it architecture it was in fact elaborately built toilets, decorated toilets, toilets surrounded with and by business and enterprise in order to have something to do in between defecations since waste was the order of the day and the ordering principle of the universe" (203).

Tar Baby, through its scandalized, oppositional discourse about the white defecators, challenges the dominant cultural narrative and memory. In constructing whiteness as a sign of racial contamination and pathological difference, *Tar Baby* also employs a classic countershaming tactic as it inverts the white racist construction of blacks as unclean and the self-degrading black construction that "a nigger ain't shit."[2] Drawing on essentialist racist dis-course by equating whiteness with defilement and degradation, the narrative actively reprojects onto whites the shame they have long projected onto blacks so that one of the coded messages in the novel is that "a white ain't shit." Yet despite this strategy, *Tar Baby*, like the other Morrison works we have examined, presents its black characters as shame-ridden and shame-driven. Moreover, both Son and Thérèse—who, like Son, is associated with the black folk ethos and who also serves as Son's guide into the world of myth and legend—become sites of racial shame and rage in the text.

If the originating story of whites in the island world is that of the pathological white defecators and destroyers, the originating story of the black islanders is that of the black victims of white imperialism who, some three hundred years before, escaped slavery when they were marooned on the island. In telling the story of the marooned slaves, the narrative oscillates between expressions of pride and shame. When the French ship containing slaves and horses sank, as Gideon tells Son, the slaves, who went blind when they saw Dominique, eventually found their way to shore along with some horses from the ship. Those who were only partially blinded were "rescued" by the French, the term "rescue" used ironically here to refer to their return to slavery. Those who were totally blind, in contrast, hid on the island, ultimately becoming the legendary blind horsemen who continue to ride through the hills of the Isle des Chevaliers. Like the tale of the flying African used in *Song of Solomon*, this story can be read as an uplifting diasporan tale of racial pride, since it describes an escape from slavery and entry into the glorious world of myth and legend. But the narrative also dialogically contests its own mythic discourse. Gideon, who recounts this story, calls it a "fishermen's tale," and when he describes how the horsemen sleep with the swamp women—"Just before a storm you can hear them screwing way over here. Sounds like thunder"—he bursts into "derisive laughter." Moreover, he speculates that the blindness of the people descended from the marooned slaves is a symptom of second-degree syphilis (152–53).

A telling example of the emotional and intellectual ambivalences that pervade the text, the mythic story of the escaped, marooned slaves expresses, at one and the same time, cultural pride and shame. In a similar way, the text sends out mixed signals in its depiction of Thérèse. Because the nearly blind Thérèse, a descendent of the marooned slaves, plays a pivotal role in Son's story—she initially associates Son with the legendary horsemen who haunt the island and, at the end, urges him to reject Jadine and join the horsemen—and because Thérèse, who has "magic breasts" (108), is associated with the tarlike nurturing and folk qualities that Jadine lacks, critic-readers have typically focused on Thérèse's mythic or maternal qualities. She has been variously characterized as Son's "benevolent maternal sponsor"; as the "wise woman guardian of folk traditions and the intermediary between humankind and nature"; and as a "visionary" character and "ancestral figure" (Erickson 26, T. Harris, *Fiction* 147, Paquet 508, 513). Although Thérèse does assume such roles in the novel's mythic drama, she also is a site of black underclass shame and anger, and thus she serves an important and largely neglected function in *Tar Baby*'s presentation of the class positions and divisions among its black characters.

Providing a provocative and unsettling analysis of the class tensions and resentments that underlie black intraracial and intercultural relationships, *Tar Baby* exposes the complicated contempt scripts—the unending cycles of contempt and countercontempt—that drive the interactions between the black American couple, Sydney and Ondine, and the black islanders, Thérèse and Gideon. Despite their implicitly shameful position as servants of the Streets, Sydney and Ondine occupy a hierarchal, socially superior class position in the island's black culture. As the perfect butler, Sydney is self-effacing with the Streets: "One hardly knew if he left the room or stood in some shadowy corner of it" (74). But he also is a proud man, "one of those industrious Philadelphia Negroes—the proudest people in the race" (61). Ondine, similarly, is a proud and hard-working woman, and before Son's disruptive arrival, she is satisfied with her life, finding herself in "beautiful surroundings which included her own territory where she alone governed" (96). "[H]ow she could reign from a sitting position," Jadine thinks of Ondine (90). Similarly, Sydney sees Ondine as regal, "her heavy white braids sitting on her head like a royal diadem" (97).

A proud couple, Sydney and Ondine consolidate their black American middle-class identity by inferiorizing the black islanders and treating them with contempt. Viewing the islanders who work for them as faceless natives and replaceable laborers, Sydney and Ondine refer to Gideon as "Yardman" and Thérèse as "Mary." Although Thérèse—who "doesn't like the Americans for meanness . . . because they a little snooty sometimes"—is repeatedly dismissed by Sydney and Ondine, Gideon always brings her back, telling them "it's a brand-new woman" (153). While "Mary" looks "a little different" each time Gideon brings her, they refer to her as Mary "because all the baptized black women on the island had Mary among their names" (40). To Thérèse, who tries to avoid the gaze of the "malevolent"—that is, shaming—Americans, Ondine's white braids are like two silver machetes crossed on her head that "glitter and clang" when she flies into a rage with Thérèse for talking when she is supposed to be working (41, 104).

Responding to the open contempt of the black Americans with her own private countercontempt, Thérèse is a woman of "complex and passionate" hatreds who refuses to speak to the black Americans and "never even to acknowledge the presence of the white Americans in her world" (110–11). Insulted and treated as an inferior by the black members of the Street household, who do not even bother to learn her name, Thérèse, in turn, insults the American blacks behind their backs. When talking to Gideon, Thérèse refers to Ondine as "machete-hair"; to Sydney, the proper black

butler, as "bow-tie"; and to Jadine, the successful career woman and assimilated black elitist, as the "chippy," the "fast-ass," the "bitch," and the "cow"
(108, 107, 112). The story that Thérèse makes up about the black inhabitants
of the Street household after Son's arrival is also telling. In her "romance," as
Gideon calls it (111), she imagines that Son is one of the legendary horsemen
from the island hills who has come for Jadine or that he is Jadine's French
boyfriend, but "machete-hair she don't like it. Tried to keep them apart. But
it didn't work. He find her, swim the whole ocean big, till he find her, eh?
Make machete-hair too mad. Now she tell her bow-tie husband. . . . Bow-tie
get mad very. 'Cause he lives near machete-hair's thumb . . ." (108). That
Thérèse's story pointedly ignores the white actors in the Street household
drama, just as white storytellers have long marginalized or neglected blacks in
their stories, is made explicit in Gideon's observation that Thérèse's story does
not take into account what the "white bosses" are "thinking about it all"
(111). Just as white storytellers, in an implicitly shaming gesture, have traditionally denied black subjectivity, so Thérèse, in her counternarrative, denies
white subjectivity. Recognizing that, indeed, she has "forgotten the white
Americans," Thérèse realizes that she cannot "imagine" them or see how they
would "fit into the story" because she has always assumed that whites feel
"nothing at all" (111, 112).

Although Thérèse cannot imagine whites in her story about Son and
Jadine, white characters, even though marginalized in *Tar Baby*, serve important functions in the narrative. One of the text's aims is to disrupt the class-
and race-stratified world of the seventy-year-old Valerian Street and, in effect,
to dethrone the white master. The narrative also subverts the myth of idealized
white motherhood by divulging that the nearly fifty-year-old Margaret secretly
abused her son, Michael, when he was a child. Cross-questioning the construction of Valerian and Margaret as "decent people" (68)—that is, as benevolent
and humane—the narrative actively shames these characters, who become
textual sites of cultural and familial pathology.

In telling the story of Valerian, *Tar Baby* challenges the hegemonic construction of white decency and also ridicules—and thus undermines the
authority of—the proud white patriarch and colonizer, who has built his
impressive retirement home high in the hills on the Isle des Chevaliers and
who enjoys directing the lives of the people in his "plantation" world (219),
as Son views it. While Valerian sees himself as decent—for he has "done the
better thing whenever he had a choice and sometimes when he did not," and
"his politics were always rational and often humane" (54)—the narrative
describes his controlling behavior toward others, including his wife, showing
him to be a man who expects other people to follow his orders. The narrative also deliberately mocks Valerian—the representative white capitalist
who is named for a Roman emperor and who inherits his family's candy

business—by referring to him as the "Candy King" and by calling the red-and-white gumdrop candy the family names after him "faggot" candy (31, 51). And in the account of Valerian's initial response to Margaret's beauty, *Tar Baby* both uses and undercuts romantic discourse. Although Valerian worships female beauty—"something inside him" kneels down when he first sees Margaret (16)—he also views beautiful women as objects for male consumption. This is made explicit in the description of how the Candy King Valerian falls in love with Margaret, "the Principal Beauty of Maine" (11). When he first sees the rosy-cheeked Margaret on a parade float dressed in a red velvet coat and waving an ermine muff to the crowd, he is attracted to her because she is red and white like the Valerian candy.

The marital relationship of Valerian and Margaret, like that of other husband-wife relationships depicted in Morrison's fiction, becomes bound by shame and resentment. Valerian, while initially worshiping the beautiful Margaret, ultimately treats her as the object of his withering contempt. "You are too stupid to live. . . . Idiot. I married an idiot!" he says to Margaret during one of their frequent quarrels. When she retorts in kind, saying that she married "an old fool," Valerian replies, "Of course you did. Who else but an old fool would marry a high school dropout off the back of a truck!" (70). Jadine, who is an eyewitness to some of their quarrels, insists that Valerian and Margaret are "decent people." Yet she also recognizes that they deliberately bait each other, and she apprehends "flecks of menace" in their arguments. "Bits of blood, tufts of hair seemed to stick on those worn claws," as she imagines it (68).

Just as *Tar Baby* dethrones the white patriarch, so too it unmasks and undermines white motherhood in its representation of Margaret. "[T]he predominant image of the mother in white Western society is of the ever-bountiful, ever-giving, self-sacrificing mother," write Donna Bassin, Margaret Honey, and Meryle Kaplan in their discussion of representations of motherhood. Such a mother "lovingly anticipates and meets the child's every need. She is substantial and plentiful; she is not destroyed or overwhelmed by the demands of her child. Instead she finds fulfillment and satisfaction in caring for her offspring. This is the mother who 'loves to let herself be the baby's whole world'" (2–3). *Tar Baby* contradicts this idealized, sentimentalized image of the mother by portraying Margaret, who appears innocent with her "blue-if-it's-a-boy blue eyes" (64), as a secret child abuser.

Following Morrison's typical pattern of narrative withholding—which she uses both to tell the shame and trauma story and to evoke the gossiper's tantalizing method of slowly divulging shameful secrets—*Tar Baby* chronicles the history of Margaret, describing her loneliness and isolation in her marriage but remaining silent about her destructive response to her unhappy situation until much later in the narrative. If early in the novel Margaret tells herself that she is not anything like those mothers in the *National Enquirer*—a comment that functions in the narrative not unlike the forewarning hints dropped by the gossiper—ultimately the narrative reveals Margaret's kinship with such unnatural women. For what the young Margaret does to fill up the ensuing emptiness of her life, as readers learn during the famous Christmas dinner scene, is abuse her son, Michael, by sticking pins in him and burning him with cigarettes. The abuse starts on one of the long, tedious days when there is nothing to fill the time. The first time she hurts him, it is an accident, but then hurting him becomes "the thing to look forward to, to resist, to succumb to, to plan, to be horrified by, to forget, because out of the doing of it came the reason." Countering the hegemonic myth of the utterly patient, self-sacrificing mother who exudes unconditional love, *Tar Baby* describes how Margaret is "outraged by that infant needfulness. There were times when she absolutely had to limit its *being there;* stop its implicit and explicit demand for her best and constant self. . . . [W]hen she felt hostage to that massive insolence, that stupid trust, she could not help piercing it" (236). That Margaret's action also grows out of her unexpressed rage toward her husband is revealed in Ondine's observation that Margaret "didn't stick pins in her baby. She stuck em in his baby. Her baby she loved" (279).

"[Y]ou felt good hating me, didn't you? I could be the mean white lady and you could be the good colored one," Margaret later remarks to Ondine who years before comforted the abused Michael but also kept the secret of Margaret's mistreatment of her son (240). Countering the white myth that the black family is a tangle of pathology, *Tar Baby* depicts the culturally idealized white family as pathological as it describes Margaret as a secret abuser. Valerian is devastated when he realizes that Margaret "had loved the bloodying of her own baby. Had loved it dearly. . . . Nothing serious, though. No throwing across the room, or out of the window. No scalding, no fist work. Just a delicious pin-stab in sweet creamy flesh. That was her word, 'delicious.' 'I knew it was wrong, knew it was bad. But something about it was delicious too,'" she tells him (231). A woman who took secret pleasure in hurting her son, Margaret is "not natural" (36): that is, she is perverse, cruel, inhuman. Anything but the morally pure white woman celebrated by Euro-American culture, she is dirtied, and she has "a lot of cleaning up to do" with her son, who has been dirtied—that is, shamed—by the maternal abuse he suffered as a child (192). As Margaret tells Valerian when he asks why Michael never told him about the abuse, "He was probably too ashamed. . . . I think he is still ashamed" (238).

After belatedly learning of Margaret's abuse of their son, Valerian calls her "disgusting" and "monstrous" (238), but he also feels culpable. Forced to review his past, he recognizes that he was a detached, largely absent father who knew nothing about his growing son and chose not to understand the message his son was sending him as he sat under the sink humming a lonely song after his mother had abused him. Valerian, who initially sees himself as a decent man, ultimately recognizes that he is guilty of "the crime of inno-cence" (242). "Was there anything so loathsome as a willfully innocent man? Hardly. An innocent man is a sin before God. Inhuman and therefore unworthy. No man should live without absorbing the sins of his kind, the foul air of his innocence . . ." (243). In describing Valerian as "loathsome," "unworthy," and dirtied (the "foul air of his innocence") and in identifying Valerian with the white defecators who defile and destroy the natural island world and its culture, the narrative enacts not only a contempt script, by actively humiliating the white humiliator, but also a blaming script. Moreover, in accusing Valerian of being guilty of the crime of innocence for not taking the trouble to learn about the abuse of his own son, *Tar Baby* also indirectly accuses "innocent" whites for their willful ignorance of the persecution of black people.

If the narrative seems to exonerate Margaret, despite her admission that she took pleasure in her sadistic behavior, it punishes and shames Valerian, who suffers an utter loss of physical power and control after he learns of Michael's abuse. Undergoing a rapid physical decline, Valerian becomes dependent and helpless, and thus ends up under the control of his wife and servants. In contrast, Margaret, who appears to be a vacuous empty-headed woman, takes on substance. She becomes "real," not "like a piece of Valerian candy, but like a person on a bus, already formed, fleshed, thick with a life" that does not belong to Valerian (239). After her exposure, which brings "the wonderful relief of public humiliation, the solid security of the pillory," Margaret grows "stronger" while Valerian wastes away, "filed to nothing by grief" (235, 237).

Acting out a countershaming agenda, *Tar Baby* is intent on dislodging the idea of white decency and cultural innocence. Yet even as it constructs whiteness as a sign of pathology in its presentation of Valerian and Margaret Street, *Tar Baby* remains mired in black shame. In describing how members of the Street household respond to Son, *Tar Baby* provides a scathing exposé of the complicated contempt scripts that underlie the inter- and intraracial relationships in Valerian's plantation world. The stigmatized outsider who is categorized as socially inferior and whose dark skin and smell are markers of his pathological difference, Son is initially subjected to the contemptuous gaze of others, who see Son not as an individual but as an embodiment of derogatory racist stereotypes about the black underclass male: that such men are thieves and are potentially violent beast-rapists. With oppositional intent, *Tar Baby* uses corrosive and inflammatory racist discourse to initially con-struct Son as the racial Other—as a dissmelling, dirty, and disgusting object. That the "affective roots of prejudice *always* involve dissmell and disgust"

(Nathanson, *Shame and Pride* 133) is made apparent in the complex shame drama that surrounds Son, a character who comes to function in the text as a kind of literary container for the shaming constructions of Otherness used to represent the black underclass male.

Margaret's initial response to Son reflects standard white racist attitudes about black Americans: that they are, to quote Calvin Hernton, "sexually dirty, vulgar, beastly" and thus are "threats to white racial purity" (xiii). To Margaret the "filthy" Son is an object of disgust, "literally a nigger in the woodpile" (85, 83). After she finds him lurking in her closet, she thinks of her closet "as a toilet . . . where something rotten had been and still was." Hernton's observation that racial hatred is "sexualized hatred" (xiii) is reflected in Margaret's concern that Son was "[i]n her things. Actually in her things. Probably jerking off. Black sperm was sticking in clots to her French jeans or down in the toe of her Anne Klein shoes. Didn't men sometimes jerk off in women's shoes? She'd have the whole closetful cleaned. Or better still, she'd throw them all out and buy everything new—from scratch" (86). Pointing to the black bourgeoisie's internalization of white racist assumptions and binary us-them thinking, *Tar Baby* describes how Sydney and Ondine similarly categorize Son as the degenerate and dangerous Other: as a "stinking ignorant swamp nigger," a "wild-eyed pervert," and a "crazy hobo" (100, 101). "If that nigger wants to steal something or kill somebody you think he's going to skip us, just 'cause we don't own it?" Sydney says at one point, referring to Son as a "wife-raper" (99). Jadine, similarly, views Son as a "raggedy black man" hiding in Margaret's closet "with rape, theft or murder on his mind" (91).

Son's sudden intrusion into the Street household, thus, brings to light the destructive class and racial tensions that mar and tar black relationships. When Sydney and Ondine initially look at Son "with faces as black as his but smug," Valerian finds their manner "Uncle Tom-ish," and he feels "[d]is-appointment nudging contempt" at the outrage they exhibit "in defending property and personnel that did not belong to them from a black man who was one of their own" (144, 145). Like Sydney, Ondine is upset when she realizes that they have to wait on Son, who is invited to remain as Valerian's guest. "If he'd been a white bum in Mrs. Street's closet," Ondine comes to realize, "well, she would have felt different. . . . The man upstairs wasn't a Negro—meaning one of them. . . . And even if he didn't steal, he was nasty and ignorant and they would have to serve him anyway, if Mr. Street wanted it. Clean his tub, change his bed linen, bring his breakfast to his bed if he wanted it, collect his underwear (Jesus), call him sir . . ." (102). Unlike Thérèse and Gideon who take pride in Son when he later visits their home, parading him through the streets of their town "like a king" (149), Sydney and Ondine shame Son, consolidating their socially superior, middle-class identity by inferiorizing the lower-class Son. "I am a Phil-a-delphia Negro mentioned in the book of the very same name," Sydney says to Son.[3] "My people owned drugstores and taught school while yours were still cutting their faces open so as to be able to tell one of you from the other" (163). Just as Sydney and Ondine view Son as an object of contempt, so Son perceives the proud couple as contemptible, as little more than docile slaves. He is "less than sympathetic to Ondine's plight because she had acted too shuffle-footed—keeping her white lady's secret 'lak it wuz hern' and loving her white lady's baby 'lak it wuz hern, too.' And much less sympathetic to Sydney because in thirty years he had not split Valerian's skull. Eighty percent of both Sydney's and Ondine's conversation was the caprice and habits of their master" (226). In a similar way, Son returns Jadine's contempt for him with his own countercontempt, seeing her as the "Gatekeeper, advance bitch, house-bitch, welfare office torpedo, corporate cunt, tar baby side-of-the-road whore trap" (219–20).

That the image of the hypermasculinized black male rapist frames black masculinity "as the bestial excess of an overly phallic primitivity" (Wiegman 96) is reflected in *Tar Baby*'s depiction of Jadine's initial response to Son. Like the other characters, the haut-bourgeois Jadine initially views the lower-class, dark-skinned Son, who burrows in his plate "like an animal, grunting in monosyllables" (94), as a disgusting, dissmelling, animalistic man. Drawing attention to Son's "animal smell," the narrative describes how Son, before being discovered, slipped into Jadine's room at night, attempting to influence her by manipulating her dreams. Fearful that his odor would awaken Jadine, Son "fought hard against the animal smell and fought hard to regulate his breathing to hers, but the animal smell got worse . . . so he barely had time to breathe into her the smell of tar and its shiny consistency before he crept away hoping that she would break wind or believe she had so the animal smell would not alarm her or disturb the dream he had placed there" (120). When Jadine puts on her expensive sealskin coat and looks at herself in a full-length mirror in her bedroom only to be struck by an odor, she discovers that Son is standing behind her. To Jadine, Son's long and unkempt hair looks "overpowering—physically overpowering, like bundles of long whips or lashes that could grab her and beat her to jelly. And would. Wild, aggressive, vicious hair that needed to be put in jail. Uncivilized, reform-school hair. Mau Mau, Attica, chain-gang hair" (113). Jadine constructs Son as the racially stigmatized Other, perceiving his dark skin, hair texture, and smell as markers of his racial—and biological—difference.

Anything but a romantic sexual encounter, Jadine and Son's initial meeting alone is willfully presented as a shame-rage drama. Son, after admiring Jadine's fashion photographs, subsequently insults her by asking her how much "[d]ick" or "pussy" she "had to suck" to make money as a model and gain a role in a film (120). Shamed and angered by his remark, Jadine retaliates by hitting him, and he, in turn, grabs her and holds her from behind. "You smell," Jadine tells Son. "You smell worse than anything I have ever smelled in my life." When Son threatens to throw her out the window, she calls him an "ape." "You rape me and they'll feed you to the alligators. Count on it, nigger. You good as dead right now." Son's retort— "Why you little white girls always think somebody's trying to rape you?"— further antagonizes Jadine, who accuses Son of "pulling that black-woman-white-woman shit" on her and of trying to tell her "what a black woman is or ought to be." Responding to Son's assertion that he, indeed, can tell her what a black woman is, Jadine again resorts to racist insults, calling him an "ugly barefoot baboon." "I know you're an animal because I smell you," she tells him (121).

Jadine and Son's relationship, then, begins mired in feelings of shame and shame-rage. Jadine, who feels sexually—and racially—contaminated by her physical contact with the dirty and dissmelling Son, wants to "clean him off her" after their encounter (122). "God, what a nasty motherfucker. Really nasty. Stink nasty. Maybe that was it. His smell," she thinks of Son. But she also recognizes that Son has "jangled something in her that was so repulsive, so awful, and he had managed to make her feel that the thing that repelled her was not in him, but in her. That was why she was ashamed. He was the one who smelled. Rife, ripe. But she was the one he wanted to smell. Like an animal. Treating her like another animal and both of them must have looked just like it in that room" (123). As Jadine begins to recognize in herself a quality of difference marking Son—namely, his smell—she is troubled by Son's words that there is something in her "to be smelled," something that he has "discovered" and "smelled" and that cannot be disguised by her sealskin coat or expensive jewelry (125).

Accentuating the interplay of sexual longing and loathing in Jadine's response to Son, *Tar Baby* crystallizes black middle-class anxieties about female sexual desire. It also reveals the potentially damaging impact of internalized racism on the construction of black femininity as it repeats culturally embedded, shame-eliciting racist stereotypes of black female sexuality as animalistic. Jadine feels "authentic loathing" for Son—that is to say, she sees him an object of contempt—and she senses that she is in "strange waters," for she has not seen a black man like Son in ten years (126). That Jadine is also sexually attracted to Son is made clear in voyeuristic, masturbatory scenes in which Jadine lies naked on her sealskin coat and brushes her nipples across its "dark luxury," or in which she sinks into the "blackness" of the coat and licks its fur (91, 112). The narrative interprets these scenes when Son subsequently shames Jadine by telling her that he smells something in her—her animalistic sexuality—which cannot be disguised by the coat. In a similar way, the narrative conveys Jadine's attraction to Son through repeated references to her attempt to hold on to the leashes of the "small dark dogs galloping on silver feet" (94; see also 113, 115, 116, 158, 159). And yet the poeticized image of silver-footed galloping dogs is associated with Jadine's core memory of a female dog in heat, which provides a troubling depiction of the sexual act as animalistic. Jadine recalls how, when she was growing up in Baltimore, she saw a female dog in heat being sniffed and then mounted by a male dog that "smelled her ass and stuck his penis in, humping and jerking and grinding away while she stood there . . . and other dogs too, waiting, circling until the engaged dog was through." Thus at age twelve, Jadine determined "never to be broken in the hands of any man. . . . And anybody who wanted nice from this little colored girl would have to get it with pliers and chloroform, because Never. . . . It smoothed out a little as she grew older. The pugnacious lips became a seductive pout—eyes more heated than scary. But beneath the easy manners was a claw always ready to rein in the dogs, because Never" (123–24). Jadine's sexual attraction to Son, as the text reveals, revives her fear not only of male sexual aggression but also of her own sexual—and racial—humiliation.

After Jadine's initial encounters with Son, she wonders what kind of "white people's" game Valerian is playing, for instead of defending Margaret or becoming upset, he invites Son to dinner and to stay as a house guest as if he does not know "the difference between one Black and another" (125). If *Tar Baby* presents a shame drama as it exploits the racist myth of the black-beast rapist, it also acts out a countershaming agenda by reconfiguring the derogatory image of the black rapist, following Black Power's oppositional, political use of this racist stereotype to construct a disempowered white and empowered black masculine identity. The Black Power movement, as Robyn Wiegman remarks, "marshaled the fear-induced imagery of black men as violent and potent to assert to white culture a bold and resistant political production, one that appropriated the fear that underwrote the mythology of the black rapist in order to recast the passive resistance school of civil rights reform." Moreover, in the process of asserting black masculinity, Black Power raised "the specter of a *white* masculine feminization" (107). *Tar Baby* represents this power struggle in the Christmas day dinner scene in which Valerian angrily orders Son to leave the house only to have Son refuse. Not only does the novel deliberately contrast the youthful Son's phallic power with the aging Valerian's physical powerlessness, but by the end of the novel Valerian is presented as utterly helpless—that is, as shamed—for he is reduced to a dependent, babylike condition.

"Your first yalla?" Gideon says to Son of Jadine. "Look out. It's hard for them not to be white people. Hard, I'm telling you. Most never make it" (155). Using romantic discourse to describe Son's worship of Jadine's "yalla" beauty, *Tar Baby* recounts how Son, before he is discovered in the Street house, spends his nights in Jadine's room, "gratified beyond belief" to be in the company of the beautiful sleeping Jadine (138). In a similar way, Son is awestruck by the fashion photographs of Jadine, which show Jadine, with her mink-colored eyes and open, wet lips, in the stylized pose of the sexually alluring woman. Suggestive evidence of the pervasiveness of culturally mediated stereotypes is found in *Tar Baby*'s coded representation of the dark-skinned Son as hypermasculine and the light-skinned Jadine as ultra-feminine. As bell hooks has observed, because dark skin is "stereotypically coded in the racist, sexist, or colonized imagination as masculine," a man's power "is enhanced by dark looks" whereas a woman's "dark looks diminish her femininity" (*Outlaw Culture* 180). Discussing how "the most intimate of relationships are still governed by the politics of color and race," Kathy Russell, Midge Wilson, and Ronald Hall observe that "most Black men prefer their women to be 'light, bright, and sometimes White.'" Moreover, beautiful light-skinned women—who are sometimes referred to as "Black American princesses"—are often viewed as trophies by black men (107, 111). Adding to the complexity of such relationships is the connection between light and white skin. Explanations of the racial and psychological dynamics of interracial sexual unions—that possessing an ideal (white) beauty gives the black man a feeling of power or that the black male's desire for a white woman stems from the desire to degrade (i.e., shame) the woman and, by extension, turn the tables on the white oppressor (Grier and Cobbs 91)—may also shed light on the complex power and shame dynamics of the relationship between Son and Jadine in *Tar Baby*. But while Morrison's novel expresses Jadine's initial fear of being degraded by her relationship with the dissmelling Son, it also acts out an antishaming agenda by associating Son with the African-American rural folk culture that Jadine has lost touch with and needs to recognize if she is to discover repressed aspects of her "authentic" racial identity.

Emphasizing Jadine's affiliation with Euro-American urban and high culture, *Tar Baby* depicts Jadine as a student of art history, an expert on cloisonné, and a graduate of the Sorbonne. Traveling in the "fast lane," Jadine has worked as a fashion model and had a role in a film, and she identifies with other haut-bourgeois blacks who are interested, like her, in "making it" (117, 126). Jadine recalls how, years before when she was a college student, she was questioned about her life by the Streets' son, Michael, who claimed that Jadine was abandoning her African-American history and people. But she knew, as she tells Valerian, that the life she was leaving was not "all grits and natural grace," as Michael thought (74). Although at the time she felt the need to apologize for preferring "Ave Maria" to gospel music, she comes to openly assert her belief in the superiority of European art. "Picasso *is* better than an

Itumba mask," she tells her patron, Valerian. "The fact that he [Picasso] was intrigued by them is proof of *his* genius, not the mask-makers'" (74).

Because part of the text's mission is to undermine Jadine's elitist attitudes and put her in vital contact with her African-American roots, *Tar Baby*, with didactic intent, shames the proud and successful Jadine. On one of the best days of her life—the day the "intelligent and lucky" Jadine learns that her photograph has been selected for the cover of *Elle* magazine and that she has passed her oral exams in art history—Jadine's pride is suddenly shaken. While shopping in a Paris grocery store for a celebratory dinner, Jadine sees a tall, dark-skinned African woman, whose skin is "like tar" against her long canary-yellow dress. Jadine recognizes that the woman has "too much hip, too much bust" under her yellow dress, and yet she, like the other people in the store, is "transfixed." Depicting the woman in yellow as a timeless, mythic figure, *Tar Baby* conveys the power and pride of the African woman, who walks down the aisle "as though her many-colored sandals were pressing gold tracks on the floor" and who has something in her eyes "so powerful it had burnt away the eyelashes" (45). Readers are text-directed to interpret Jadine's encounter with the African woman, which is presented as an eruption of the dreamlike experience into waking reality, as a confrontation with unacknowledged—or repressed—aspects of her racial and gender identity. Indeed, the stylized description of the woman carrying aloft three white eggs in the tar-black fingers of her right hand openly invites a symbolic reading, the three eggs being typically read as a signifier of the fertility and maternity Jadine has eschewed.

But Jadine's encounter with the woman in yellow is also presented as a classic shame drama. As the awestruck Jadine stares at the African wo-man—"that woman's woman—that mother/sister/she; that unphotograph-able beauty"—the woman turns her head, looks directly at Jadine, and spits (46). In this governing scene of shame, Jadine feels that she has been judged and found unworthy by the woman in yellow. Thus the African woman's expression of contempt-disgust undermines Jadine's feeling of success. Not only is Jadine "derailed" by the woman's "insulting gesture," but the woman also makes Jadine feel "[l]onely and inauthentic" (47, 48). After this encounter, Jadine comes to question whether her white European lover, Ryk, wants to marry her or any black woman who looks, talks, and acts like her. Aware that she is being encouraged to perform an identity—that of the exotic and erotic racial Other—Jadine wonders what will happen when her white lover discovers that she hates ear hoops and does not have to straighten her hair and that she sometimes wants to "get out" of her "skin" and "be only the person inside—not American—not black" but only herself (48).

If the middle-class Jadine's desire to "get out" of her skin reveals her self-consciousness about her black identity, her relationship with Son is con-sciously staged by the narrative to put her in vital contact with her black cultural roots. Associated with nature and with Africa, Son is described as having a "woodsy" voice and "[s]paces, mountains, [and] savannas" in his forehead and eyes (181, 158). By insisting on Son's "authentic" African and folk-heroic qualities, the narrative counteracts its earlier shame-ridden descriptions of Son as the uncivilized and unclean Other. But it also, in part, undercuts its antishaming agenda by invoking yet another problematic stereotype in constructing Son: that of the lawless "bad nigger," a folk character that has long fascinated Morrison and that is reflected in some of her other male characters, such as *The Bluest Eye*'s Cholly and *Song of Solomon*'s Guitar.

A "[p]ropertyless, homeless" and solitary man, Son is an individual "without human rites: unbaptized, uncircumcised, minus puberty rites or the formal rites of manhood" (166, 165–66). Son belongs to "that great underclass of undocumented men," the "international legion of day laborers and musclemen, gamblers, sidewalk merchants, migrants, unlicensed crewmen on ships with volatile cargo, part-time mercenaries, full-time gigolos, or curbside musicians." "Anarchic, wandering," such men are distinguished from other men by "their refusal to equate work with life and an inability to stay anywhere for long." While some are "Huck Finns" and "Nigger Jims," others are "Calibans, Staggerlees, and John Henrys" (166). *Tar Baby* deliberately constructs Son as an amalgam of classic oppositional types—as the Nigger Jim wandering man and the Staggerlee and John Henry "bad nigger" folk hero.[4] And yet if the classic "bad nigger" character is heroized for his defiant masculinity and resistance to hegemonic culture, this figure also represents a corrosive form of self-stereotyping, an internalization of antiblack racist images of the lower-class black male as irresponsible and prone to violence. Getting caught up in the same kind of shame-pride dialectic that occurs in *Song of Solomon*'s representation of black masculinity, *Tar Baby*, even as it presents Son as a lawless, wandering man, also uses Jadine's middle-class voice to contest Son's heroic folk voice.

With dialogic intent, *Tar Baby* focuses on the cultural differences that govern the relationship between Jadine and Son, highlighting the shame-pride dynamics of their initial encounters. When Son speaks with a kind of folk pride about his "original dime"—"The one San Francisco gave me for cleaning a tub of sheepshead. . . . Nothing I ever earned since was like that dime. . . . That was the best money in the world and the only real money I ever had"—Jadine shames him by calling him "lazy," and she tells him to "stop making excuses about not having anything. Not even your original dime. It's not romantic. And it's not being free. It's dumb. You think you're above it, above money, the rat race and all that. But you're not above it, you're just without it. It's a prison, poverty is" (169, 170, 171). When Son, who jumped bail after getting into "some trouble with the law," tells Jadine that he is on the run because he refused "their punishment" and instead wanted his "own," she deflates his folk-heroic masculine pride with her withering contempt, calling him "a baby. A big country baby" (171, 172). "I hate killers. . . . All killers. Babies. They don't understand anything but they want everybody to understand them," Jadine says to Son when he tells her that he has killed someone, her words openly scornful of what she thinks is his fake remorse. Son's remark that killing someone "takes no nerve, no nerves at all," and that he "went too far"—for although he "meant the killing," he did not mean "the death"—provokes another shaming retort from Jadine. "Temper, temper, temper," she mockingly chants (175). Son's subsequent explanation that he killed a woman is met with yet another stinging rejoinder. "'I should have known. That's all you could think of to do with your life? Kill a woman? . . . What did she do? Cheat on you?' She said it ugly. Cheat. Like 'Take away your candy?'" (176). Jadine's disgust turns to fear when Son tells her what happened: that when he caught his wife in bed with a thirteen-year-old boy, he drove his car through the house, thus causing the explosion that killed his wife. Basking in Jadine's fear, which makes him feel "protective and violent at the same time," Son tells Jadine that he will not kill her because he loves her. Jadine, who senses the threat of violence in his remark, once again deflates his masculine ego with her look of disgust and her insulting words. "People don't say things like that. Nobody says that. Where do you think we are, in some jungle? Why would you say you're not going to kill me?" (177). Son's explanation—that he was not trying to scare but to comfort her—emphasizes the deep divide between these embattled characters.

That Son's touch both excites and endangers is suggested in the displaced drama that marks the beginning of their physical relationship. When Son tells Jadine that he senses she is frightened of him because she tucked in her legs and then asks if he can touch her foot, she complies with his request. Afterward, she can still feel where his forefinger had touched the arch of her naked foot. Aware that Son expects to become her lover, Jadine is rehearsing the reasons why she is not going to have sex with him when she sinks up to her knees in the staining tar of the island swamp, a "shriveled fogbound oval seeping with a thick black substance" and emitting a "funny jungle-rot smell" (10, 181). If tar is Son's element—for earlier Son tried to breathe into Jadine the smell of tar and he passed through the tarry island swamp when he first arrived on the island—tar, to Jadine, is something that dirties, stains, and endangers.

Deliberately disrupting the novel's realistic surface, *Tar Baby* evokes the world of myth in its description of Jadine's swamp experience. In a coded drama that invites a psychosymbolic reading and anticipates Jadine's lovemaking with Son, the narrative describes how Jadine clings to a tree that sways as if it wants to dance with her as she sinks into the tar pit. "Don't sweat or you'll lose your partner, the tree. Cleave together like lovers. Press together like man and wife. Cling to your partner, hang on to him and never let him go. . . . Sway when he sways and shiver with him too. . . . Love him and trust him with your life because you are up to your kneecaps in rot" (182–83). Adding to the complexity of this scene, Jadine's attempt to extricate herself from the engulfing "rot" of the tar pit is linked to her wish to escape the mythic swamp women, who, like the tar-black African woman in yellow holding aloft three eggs, are text-identified as embodiments of the nurturing, female qualities that Morrison associates with the positive meaning of tar in the Tar Baby folk tale. The island swamp women, who look down from the trees, are at first delighted to see Jadine, thinking that she is a runaway who has been returned to them. But when they discover that Jadine is struggling to free herself from the tar and thus to get away from them, they become "arrogant—mindful as they were of their value, their exceptional femaleness; knowing as they did that the first world of the world had been built with their sacred properties; that they alone could hold together the stones of pyramids and the rushes of Moses's crib; knowing their steady consistency, their pace of glaciers, their permanent embrace, they wondered at the girl's desperate struggle down below to be free, to be something other than they were" (183). Morrison's antishaming agenda is apparent in this passage as she transforms the racial shame associated with tar—tar as a signifier of the stain or dirt of blackness—into racial pride by stressing the "sacred properties" and "exceptional femaleness" of the tarlike swamp women.

Part of *Tar Baby*'s open agenda, then, is to counter the shaming racist discourse found in the realistic narrative surface, with its focus on inter- and intraracial class conflict, by privileging the embedded mythic narrative, which celebrates the body- and nature-identified black primitivism associated with Son, the woman in yellow, and the tarlike swamp women. Yet if the novel's mythic discourse is presented as a repository of racial truth and natural pride, it also inscribes the white-constructed and shaming myth of an earthy and natural—and intellectually and culturally inferior—black primitivism. Perhaps this is why *Tar Baby* undercuts, at least in part, its own romantic primitivism by elaborating on Jadine's fears of entrapment and contamination as she sinks into the "tar" not only of blackness but also of black womanhood.

After her swamp experience, Jadine wants to remove the "black stuff," the "shit," from her skin, just as before she wanted to "clean" Son "off her" after he touched her (184, 122). Associating Son's touch with the staining tar, the narrative describes how, after Jadine bathes, her clean feet are "peachy soft again as though they had never been touched and never themselves had touched the ground." But the narrative also affirms Jadine's growing attraction to Son as she competes with Margaret for rape. "He doesn't want you, Margaret," Jadine thinks, responding to Margaret's alarm that Son hid in her closet because he wanted to rape her. "He wants me. He's crazy and beautiful and black and poor and beautiful and he killed a woman but he doesn't want you. He wants me and I have the fingerprint to prove it" (186). Sending out mixed messages, *Tar Baby* insists that Jadine's relationship with Son puts her in touch with her "essential" blackness and femaleness—that is, her tarlike qualities—and yet tar, to Jadine, not only sullies but also threatens to entrap. For Jadine to become mired in the tar of her black female identity is to be caught up in a shame-shame feeling trap.

"[U]ntil you know about me, you don't know nothing about yourself," Son tells Jadine (264). During the idyllic stage of their love affair—"[t]hey were the last lovers in New York City"—the first in the world"—Jadine feels "unorphaned" by Son, who cherishes and safeguards her, giving her "a brand-new childhood," and they enjoy a kind of prolonged postcoital intimacy during the early months of their relationship (229). In depicting the love relationship between Son and Jadine, *Tar Baby* seems intent on interposing in the crisis of African-American identity represented by Jadine's assimilation into Euro-American culture by endorsing the idea of an "authentic" black folk identity and of racial bonding based on a shared racial identity. Yet ultimately, just as the love relationship between Son and Jadine fails, so the narrative comes to refuse cultural prescriptions of what *the* "authentic" black experience or black identity should be.

Separated by class and social fault lines, Jadine and Son are constructed as paired opposites. To the cosmopolitan Jadine, New York City is home. "[I]f ever there was a black woman's town, New York was it. . . . Snapping whips behind the tellers' windows, kicking ass at Con Edison offices, barking orders in the record companies, hospitals, public schools. . . . They jacked up meetings in boardrooms, turned out luncheons, energized parties, redefined fashion . . . and turned an entire telephone company into such a diamond-head of hostility the company paid you for not talking to their operators. The manifesto was simple: 'Talk shit. Take none'" (222). To Son, in contrast, New York is a place where the black girls cry, the men walk through the streets on tiptoe, and the old people are in kennels. When Son tries to watch American television, he is unnerved by "the black people in whiteface playing black people in blackface" (216). In New York, Son feels estranged, as if he is confronting an entirely new race of black people. "If those were the black folks he was carrying around in his heart all those years, who on earth was he?" Son wonders (216–17).

In a similar way, Jadine is unable to share Son's perceptions of Eloe, Florida, the all-black town where he was raised. During his homeless years of wandering, Son has used Eloe to "people his dreams, and anchor his floating days" (294). To Son, Eloe is a simple, welcoming, homey place "of yellow houses with white doors which women opened wide and called out, 'Come on in here, you honey you'" (6). Unlike Son, who finds his black roots in Eloe, Jadine views the community and its values as "Paleolithic" (257). When she visits the all-black town with Son, Jadine is "shunted off" with other women and children while the men group together, and she is forced to sleep away from Son, in his Aunt Rosa's house, making her feel that she is "stuck . . . with a pack of Neanderthals who think sex is dirty or strange" (246, 257). Just as Jadine feels contempt for the rural folk she meets, so she, in turn, is shamed by them. Son's friend, Soldier, insults Jadine with his sexist speech, telling her not only that Son's dead wife, Cheyenne, had the "best pussy in Florida, the absolute best," but also that Son "thinks with his dick" when he is with women (254, 255). Jadine is also shamed by Son's Aunt Rosa who, on discovering that Jadine is sleeping in the nude, gives Jadine a slip to sleep in. "No man had made her feel that naked, that unclothed. Leerers, lovers, doctors, artists—none of them had made her feel exposed. More than exposed. Obscene" (253).

Jadine's sense of shameful exposure culminates in her terrifying vision of the night women, which occurs in the suffocatingly small, dark, and air-less room at Rosa's house. Attempting to "outdo Cheyenne and surpass her legendary gifts" during her lovemaking with Son (257), Jadine is suddenly aware that the room is crowded with women: with Cheyenne, Rosa, Thérèse, Son's dead mother, Ondine, Soldier's wife, her own dead mother, and the woman in yellow. As the women watch Jadine, they shame her not only with their gaze but also with their shame-eliciting gestures. For the women hold out both their breasts to Jadine as they look at her, and the woman in yellow does something even more appalling when she shows Jadine her three eggs. As in the descriptions of Jadine's encounter with the woman in yellow and the island swamp women, the surreal and fantastic are used to frame this scene and to accentuate the essentialist message that Jadine is confronting suppressed aspects of her identity: that is, the female-nurturing and maternal parts.

But even as the narrative directs readers to determine that Jadine is shamed because she has denied her essential femaleness, it also, in part, sub-verts this message by presenting the night women as a shameful, if not gro-tesque, spectacle and as embodiments of a stigmatizing difference. "The women had looked awful to her: onion heels, pot-bellies, hair surrendered to rags and braids. And the breasts they thrust at her like weapons were soft, loose bags closed at the tip with a brunette eye. Then the slithery black arm of the woman in yellow, stretching twelve feet, fifteen, toward her and the fingers that fingered eggs" (261–62). Jadine feels "hurt" by her vision, some of the hurt coming from "the frontal sorrow of being publicly humiliated"

by people she "had loved or thought kindly toward." Most of her hurt, however, is a result of her dread, for the night women not only look "superior
over their sagging breasts and folded stomachs," but they also seem "in agree-
ment with each other about her." Jadine imagines that the night women are
"all out to get her, tie her, bind her. Grab the person she had worked hard to
become and choke it off with their soft loose tits" (262). In conjuring up the
emotionally potent and shame-laden image of the engulfing, persecutory, and
body-identified primal mother, *Tar Baby* partially undercuts the positive message that associates tar with the sacred, tarlike qualities of female nurturing.
Jadine's fantasy, which is given narrative force by the viscerally powerful
feelings and fears it taps into, depicts the process of identifying with—and
thus becoming part of—the night women as a suffocating merger experience
and a terrifying loss of body-self control. Thus Jadine shuns the night women
(m)others, and yet she also feels judged and shamed by them. Caught in a
shame quagmire, Jadine is ashamed of her femaleness and also ashamed of
being ashamed. Adding to the complexity of this scene, Jadine's shame-dread
of the night women—who are also representatives of the stigmatized black
underclass woman, for they are potbellied women with "hair surrendered to
rags and braids"—reflects her status anxiety and her need to distance herself
from and disidentify with those who embody what she fears she will discover
in herself: the tarlike stigma or stain of blackness.

Morrison reports that while she was writing *Tar Baby*, she was "eager"
for Son and Jadine "to make it" and to "get married," but they "didn't,"
because "each had to learn something else . . . before that could happen"
(Moyers 270). As Son and Jadine begin to clash over their cultural differences,
each tries to rescue the other. Jadine attempts to rescue Son from the night
women, the "mamas who had seduced him and were trying to lay claim to
her," while Son wants to rescue Jadine from Valerian and the "plantation"
world he represents (262, 219). But as class warfare erupts between Son and
Jadine and each deliberately shames the other, they become caught up in a
shame-rage feeling trap.

Pointing to the contradictions and complexities inherent in the construction of group racial identity, *Tar Baby* contrasts Jadine's assimilationist
to Son's black separatist beliefs and values. When Jadine acts as Valerian's
advocate, arguing that he paid for her education when he was not *"required"*
to, Son responds that Valerian's "debt is big" and cannot ever be repaid.
"That was toilet paper, Jadine. He *should* have wiped his ass after he shit all
over your uncle and aunt. He *was* required to; he still is" (263). Jadine's
assertion that she was being educated while Son was driving his car into his
wife's bed and hiding from the law—"Stop loving your ignorance—it isn't
lovable," she tells him—leads to Son's rejoinder that whatever Jadine "learned
in those colleges" that didn't include him "ain't shit" (264). Accusing her both

of being complicit with the white oppressor and of racial infidelity, Son tells Jadine to go and marry her white European lover and have his children. "Then you can do exactly what you bitches have always done: take care of white folks' children" (269). In yet another stinging indictment of Jadine's Euro-Americanized ways, Son derides her by describing how the white farmer (i.e., Valerian), who has "this bullshit bullshit bullshit farm," constructs the tar baby (Jadine) to trap the rabbit (Son) (270). As Son verbally humiliates Jadine with his pointed retelling of the Tar Baby story, he acts out his shame-rage at her sexual and racial betrayal by sexually forcing himself on her in this scene, which has been described as a "hidden rape" because it is constructed in such a way as to "deny the reader's awareness" of Son's sexual violence (Duvall, "Descent" 333). "I can't let you hurt me again," Jadine tells Son afterward. "You stay in that medieval slave basket if you want to. You will stay there by yourself. Don't ask me to do it with you" (271). Taking a dime out of her wallet, she tells Son, "Now you know where it came from, your original dime: some black woman like me fucked a white man for it and then *gave* it to Frisco who made you work your ass off for it. That's your original dime." When Jadine throws the dime onto the floor and orders Son to pick it up, he is embarrassed when he notices that she is naked below the waist. "He had produced that nakedness and having soiled it, it shamed him" (272). That their quarrels not only dissolve into bitter recriminations but also involve physical and sexual violence points to the destructive shame and shame-rage feelings that drive them apart.

In describing the failure of the romantic relation between Son and Jadine, *Tar Baby* cross-questions what Ann duCille has referred to as the "myth" that the "shared racial alterity" of black men and women—their "common American experience of slavery, institutionalized racism, and discrimination"—makes them "okay with each other" (64). *Tar Baby*, as it describes the cultural rift between Son and Jadine, also points to the complex negotiations of gender and class as well as racial and group identifications in the production of African-American identities. In a passage that openly thematizes the text but also refuses to close the political debate between the assimilationist Jadine and the separatist Son or to take sides in the class and gender warfare between them, *Tar Baby* insists that each wants to rescue the other. "She thought she was rescuing him from the night women who wanted him for themselves, wanted him feeling superior in a cradle, deferring to him; wanted her to settle for wifely competence when she could be almighty, to settle for fertility rather than originality, nurturing instead of building. He thought he was rescuing her from Valerian, meaning *them*, the aliens, the people who in a mere three hundred years had killed a world millions of years old." While Son has "a past," Jadine has "a future," and they both believe that they bear "the culture to save the race" in their hands. "Mama-spoiled black man, will you mature with me? Culture-bearing black woman, whose culture are you bearing?" (269).

As is typical of Morrison's fiction, readers are invited to supplement the text, to insert themselves into and even take sides in the cultural conflict staged in *Tar Baby*. While critics writing on the novel repeatedly comment on the problematic nature of the characters and the cultural and political identities they represent, they also frequently amass evidence for and/or against each character. Arguing the case against Jadine, for example, critics characterize her as "a hard-driving, selfish, materialistic Black woman with no strong connections to other people and to the folk past"; as a character readers find it "easy to be unsympathetic" toward since she is "a black woman who turns her back on family, denies her heritage, [and] profanes her love relationship"; and as a "jaded child" readers "cannot forgive" for her sterility, a person who abandons the "African ethos" and who is "no Black woman, and ultimately, no woman" (Coleman, "Quest" 68, T. Harris, *Fiction* 128, Holloway, "African Values" 121, 118, 122). Yet despite claims that the novel "makes its view of Jadine clear by its constant satiric viewing of her" or that Morrison treats her character "with contempt" (Hawthorne 104, Reckley 136), other critic-readers come to Jadine's defense. Thus the same character who is condemned as an "*anti*-Madonna" or as an embodiment of the "disease of disconnection" (Reyes, "Ancient Properties" 21, Traylor 146) is defended as a heroine who, although "uncentered in the traditional sense of what it means to be a woman," is also "very much about the business of shaping her own identity" (Paquet 512). "[S]urely a nonmaternal Jadine is more attractive and laudable than the swamp women who, in all their 'exceptional femaleness,' would gladly watch Jade sink in the slime," argues one commentator who sees Jadine as "questing for and creating self" (Lepow 374). Another commentator, who finds herself "defensive of Jadine's position" as she responds to critical condemnation of the character, remarks, interestingly enough, that there is "more sympathy" for the plight of black men than black women in the African-American culture, and also that black women carry "blame and shame for the Black man's plight" (Demetrakopoulos, "Morrison's Creation" 131, 135).

In a similar way, critics are split in their perceptions of Son. Like Jadine, Son has been the subject of critical blame. He has been described as an "ambiguous" character, for he is a criminal and a hero, a healer but also potentially destructive; as a character connected to the "devouring aspect" of the maternal, to forces that "can mutilate, blind, [and] stop human individuation as surely as white colleges can castrate the natural and instinctual in the human"; as a representative of the "dangerous forces that would seek to dominate" Jadine and to "define her as body"; and as someone who sees whites defecating on the world and yet is "just as willing to defecate on Jadine, to dirty her and therefore control her" (Otten, *Crime* 69–70, Demetrako-poulos, "Morrison's Creation" 135, Everson 72, T. Harris, *Fiction* 123). But critics also have commented that the novel tries to win reader "approval" of Son (Erickson 24). One commentator writes that although Son is "the most socially unredeemable of the characters in the novel (he has killed a wife, is undereducated, is incapable of making a future in America, and has invaded and menaced a household), he is the most sympathetically treated character in the novel" (Hawthorne 104). Another remarks that while Jadine's "appraisal" of Son has "some truth," readers' "sentiments . . . are most likely with Son, a sensitive, warm man who possesses definite folk values and qualities" (Coleman, "Quest" 65). Acting as Son's advocate, critic-readers have described him as an "embodiment of the folk"; as "an idealist, a romantic child-man" who "carries within his bones the collective ancestral values of his race"; as "Africa's son/Son, the bearer of its culture and values, its black Messiah come to save Jadine from the street/Streets of Babylon"; and as a "Christ-like figure . . . who saves his people, the revolutionary who politically educates his people, the son, everyone's son . . . devoid of selfish individualism and conscious of himself as an African" (Paquet 509, Reckley 134, Samuels and Hudson-Weems 85, Mbalia 76).

Just as Morrison invites reader participation in assessing her characters, she also, as is her wont, ends *Tar Baby* in a way that is calculated to enforce reader participation and provoke interminable critical discussion and debate. Responding to the comment that the closure of *Tar Baby* is open-ended, Morrison remarks, "It's a very classic, peasant story. Peasant stories don't pass any judgments. The village participates in the story and makes it whatever it is." Although she "tried" and "wished" for a happy ending to her novel, what she found "vital" was the exploration of the cultural battle between the two characters (Judith Wilson 132, 134). Morrison, who is unable to resolve the cultural tensions that underlie the class conflict and black crisis-of-identity represented in the novel, sends Jadine back to Europe and Son into the mythic world of the black folk culture.

When Jadine leaves Son, she is glad to be away from his "original-dime ways, his white-folks-black-folks primitivism. How could she make a life with a cultural throwback, she asked herself, and answered No way" (275). Jadine, who relishes her aloneness, rejects hegemonic ideologies of proper femininity and domesticity, and she refuses Ondine's wish that she assume the dutiful-daughter role in her relationship with Ondine and Sydney. "There are other ways to be a woman. . . . I don't want to be . . . like you," Jadine tells her aunt (281–82). At the end, Jadine determines to return to Paris "and begin at Go. Let loose the dogs, tangle with the woman in yellow—with her and with all the night women who had *looked* at her. . . . No more dreams of safety. No more. Perhaps that was the thing—the thing Ondine was saying.

A grown woman did not need safety or its dreams. She *was* the safety she longed for" (290). Jadine's future-looking quest is likened to the activity of the soldier ants: "Bearing, hunting, eating, fighting, burying. No time for dreaming. . ." (291). The narrative constructs Jadine as a proud and power-ful figure in these passages, but also insists that she will find it "very hard to forget the man who fucked like a star" (292). And it uses the maternal and folk voice of Thérèse to shame Jadine. "Forget her," Thérèse tells Son. "There is nothing in her parts for you. She has forgotten her ancient properties" (305).

The narrative's closing descriptions of Son also send out mixed shame-pride messages. When Son examines the photographs taken by Jadine in Eloe, he tries to "find in them what it was that used to comfort him so, used to reside with him, in him like royalty in his veins" (294). Instead, everything looks "miserable in the photographs, sad, poor and even poor-spirited," and the people look "stupid, backwoodsy, dumb, dead" (295, 273). Yet if the narrative thus suggests that Son's folk pride is undercut by shame, it also, in a calculated antishaming maneuver, attempts to redeem his utopian folk vision in the end. Son, who seems stuck to the tar-baby, Jadine, is given a choice by Thérèse, who urges him to free himself from Jadine and join the blind horsemen who are waiting for him. Taking on the role of the rabbit who escapes into the briar patch—his home turf—Son first crawls on the rocks, then he stands and walks "steadier, now steadier," and, finally, he runs. "Lickety-split. Lickety-split. Looking neither to the left nor to the right. Lickety-split. Lickety-split. Lickety-lickety-lickety-split" (306). Rather than resolving the shame-shame and shame-rage feeling traps dramatized in the narrative, the closure depicts Son's retreat from society with its shaming categories of difference and his entry into an idealized world of black primi-tivism. By placing the hyperembodied, hypermasculinized Son in a mythic, and purely literary, space, the closure, in effect, acts out the desire to escape the cultural dilemma posed by Son's troubling difference.

Morrison's aim in *Tar Baby* is to explore but not resolve the cultural conflict that divides her characters, yet as a reader of her own novel she has become involved in the drama of blame assessment. She has, for example, described Jadine as a "very modern" woman who is "interested in fulfilling herself" (Koenen 82). "No Black woman should apologize for being edu-cated or anything else," she insists. "The problem is not paying attention to the ancient properties—which for me means the ability to be 'the ship' *and* 'the safe harbor'" (Judith Wilson 135). Remarking on Son's dilemma, Morrison says he has a choice either to "join the twentieth century as a kind of half-person like Jadine" or to "abandon it" (Ruas 106). But she also com-ments that if Son decides not to join the twentieth century, he "may identify totally and exclusively with the past, which is a kind of death, because it means you have no future." Son and Jadine's situation "is literally a cul-de-sac," according to Morrison (Ruas 112).

If Morrison leaves readers "as confused" about Son as they are about Jadine (Coleman, "Quest" 70), critic-readers often act out the narrative inducement to provide closure or clarity to Morrison's inconclusive narrative. For example, one commentator, who says that readers of the novel "are left uncertain about the attitude Morrison intends us to take toward Jadine," nevertheless offers a "hopeful" interpretation of Jadine's decision to return to Europe, arguing not only that this signals Jadine's "decision to become herself—a subject, rather than an object," but also that Jadine has not rejected her entire heritage but "only those aspects that seem confining rather than liberating" (Everson 76, 77). Another critic similarly argues that at the end Son moves toward "the source of his entrapment," while Jadine, in contrast, is "newly aware of the many choices open to her" and thus "shows potential for continued development and eventual self-redemption" (Lepow 375, 376). While some critics question Son's outcome, wondering, for example, whether Thérèse is leading him "into an awakening" or "to his death" (Reyes, "Politics" 200), others argue that Son is "triumphant" at the end or that he is transformed into "a legendary male" (Mobley, *Folk Roots* 166, Erickson 27). Still others question how Son, if he is "enmeshed . . . in a world of the primal and of wholesome folk tradition," can "function as a modern, twentieth-century man" (Coleman, "Quest" 71). Getting caught up in the shame-and-blame drama generated by the text, some commentators claim that Son is "trapped by a woman who sucks him dry" but is "too full of his own past to be emptied by Jadine," or conversely that at the end Son is entrapped while Jadine shows potential for "self-redemption" (Holloway, "African Values" 125, Lepow 375–76). It has also been argued that Son "irrevocably damages and changes Jadine as she does him" so that "the two characters cancel each other out in what may be one of the darkest endings of all Morrison's works" (Demetrakopoulos, "Morrison's Creation" 135).

Like the other Morrison novels we have investigated, *Tar Baby* invites reader participation in the drama presented in the text. *Tar Baby*, as is evident in the critical conversation surrounding the novel, also urges readers to think about the cultural conflict—and lovers' impasse—presented in the novel and provokes an impassioned response from readers. Just as *Tar Baby* ends in an emotional impasse, for it is unable to resolve the shame dilemma it presents, critic-readers similarly get stuck in the "tar-baby" of a critical and emotional impasse as they participate in the shame-and-blame drama presented in the narrative. Morrison, as we have observed, acts out an anti-shaming agenda not only as she dusts off the tar baby folk story and locates a positive African message in the tale, but also as she sets out to celebrate the tarlike, nurturing qualities of the black folk and black female culture. Yet it is telling not only that *Tar Baby* is unable to resolve the realistic dilemma presented in the narrative and overcome the cultural division that separates the lovers, but also that the narrative continues to express, especially through the black bourgeois voice of Jadine, persisting uneasiness about Son, the underclass male, and also about the rural folk culture he represents. Thus, like *Song of Solomon*, *Tar Baby* is a divided novel as it associates black cultural identity with both shame and pride.

Highlighting both gender and intraracial class conflict in *Tar Baby*, Morrison reveals the potentially destructive impact of racial shame on the construction African-American identities. In her next novel, *Beloved*, Morrison continues her investigation of the social production of a stigmatized racial identity as she engages in the cultural work of recovering African-American roots in slavery. In showing in *Beloved* how African Americans were "dirtied"—that is, shamed and traumatized—by slavery, Morrison dares to look more directly at the historical sources of racial shame and at the pernicious effects of internalized racism as she attempts to heal the painful and abiding wounds inflicted on black Americans by the dominant white culture.

6

"Whites Might Dirty Her All Right, but Not Her Best Thing"

THE DIRTIED AND TRAUMATIZED SELF OF SLAVERY IN *BELOVED*

Continuing the cultural and literary labor of her earlier novels in *Beloved*, Morrison shows just how much race has mattered historically to African Americans as she explores the cultural "roots" of black Americans in slavery. As Morrison examines the white supremacist ideology and essentialist discursive repertoires that defined the African-American slave as the racial Other—as biologically inferior, morally degenerate, and animalistic—she focuses attention on the formative and "dirtying" power of racist representations. She also dramatizes the social and political consequences of racist thinking and practices in *Beloved*, describing not only the humiliations and traumas the slaves were forced to endure at the hands of their white oppressors but also the insidious effects of internalized racism—that is, socially produced feelings of self-contempt and self-hatred—on the construction of African-American identities.

Because of the shameful and traumatic subject matter of *Beloved*, Morrison thought that the novel would be the "least read" of her works. The subject of slavery, as she puts it, is something "black people don't want to remember, white people won't want to remember. . . . [I]t's national amnesia" (Angelo 257). Describing her own "terrible reluctance about dwelling on" the slave era, she recalls how the amount of time involved—three hundred years—"began to drown" her. "Three hundred years—think about that. Now, that's not a war, that's generation after generation." To the slaveholders, the slaves were "expendable," had the "status of good horses" and the "advantage of reproducing without cost" (Angelo 256–57). Imagining the "torturous restraining devices" that slaves sometimes had to endure while working—such as the bit in the mouth, which clamped the tongue to the jaw, or the face mask worn while cutting cane to ensure that the slaves would not eat the cane—Morrison comments that "humiliation was the key to what the experience was like" (Angelo 257–58). While the slave was humiliated and dishonored, the Southern slave master, as Orlando Patterson has observed, had an "excessively developed sense of honor and pride" and, indeed, the slave owner derived his honor "directly from the degradation of his slave" (95). In a similar way, shame theorist Donald Nathanson describes the shame-pride dynamics of the master-slave relationship. Remarking on how the slaves were "kept under control by terror mediated by whips, chains, forced concubinage, lynching, ritual murder, castration, branding, and public humiliations of unimaginable variety," Nathanson observes that slavery "afforded every southern Caucasian the opportunity to be far more powerful than every African." Under a system of white racist domination, white shame "could always be mitigated by an *attack other* action taken against" blacks. "To be called 'black' in America meant to live in a state of shame; negritude implied helpless submission to overwhelming force" (*Shame and Pride* 464–65).

Morrison, who views the literary text as an important site for the production of African-American culture and the extension of the African-American cultural memory, is driven by the desire to remember the horror and humiliation of slavery in *Beloved*. But she also wants to remember slavery "in a manner in which the memory is not destructive," and she has a writer's sense of responsibility for the "unburied, or at least unceremoniously buried" slaves (Darling 248, Naylor 209). Morrison understands why the ex-slaves did not dwell on slavery. Yet in "rushing away from slavery," African Americans also "rushed away from the slaves because it was painful to dwell there, and they may have abandoned some responsibilities in so doing" (Darling 247). Believing that the slaveholders would have won if the slave experience had been beyond her writer's imagination and novelistic powers, Morrison is determined to take back the "authority" and "power" by telling the story of the forgotten slaves (Caldwell 245).

"[N]o slave society in the history of the world wrote more—or more thoughtfully—about its own enslavement," Morrison remarks in her discussion of American slave narratives ("Site" 109). But she also observes that nineteenth-century popular taste "discouraged the writers from dwelling too long or too carefully on the more sordid details of their experience," and, moreover, the writers of slave narratives could not offend the white reader "by being too angry, or by showing too much outrage, or by calling the reader names" ("Site" 109, 106). Avoiding the "violent" or "scatological" or "excessive" incident, such writers took refuge in the literary conventions

of their age by resorting to phrases like, "'But let us drop a veil over these proceedings too terrible to relate'" ("Site" 109, 110). In so doing, they partially
covered over the shame and trauma suffered by the victims of slavery. Part of
Morrison's task in *Beloved* is to "rip that veil drawn over 'proceedings too
terrible to relate'" ("Site" 110). In her re-imagining of traditional modes of
representation, she also is determined, as she has commented, to "find and
expose a truth about the interior life of people who didn't write it" and to
"properly, artistically" bury them ("Site" 113, Naylor 209).

Through the portrayal of her slave mother character, Sethe, Morrison
attempts to expose a truth about the interior life of the historical figure,
Margaret Garner. A slave who escaped from Kentucky to Cincinnati, Ohio,
Margaret Garner attempted to kill all four of her children when her slave
owner found her, and she actually succeeded in killing one child, an infant
daughter. Morrison has commented that she deliberately avoided doing
extensive research on the Margaret Garner case—a case she first became
interested in while editing *The Black Book*,[1] which was published in 1974—
because she "wanted to invent" Margaret Garner's life and "be accessible to
anything the characters had to say about it" (Darling 248). "[W]hat struck
me," Morrison recalls, was that when Margaret Garner was interviewed
after killing one of her children, she "was not a mad-dog killer. She was very
calm. All she said was, 'They will not live like that'. . . . [S]he decided to kill
them and kill herself. That was noble. She was saying, 'I'm a human being.
These are my children'" (Moyers 272). In using the historical account of
Margaret Garner as the beginning point for her story of Sethe—who wants
to kill her children to protect them from the system of slavery which dirties,
that is, shames, African Americans—Morrison is intent on investigating not
only the collective memories of the physical traumas the slaves endured but
also the internalized and abiding psychic wounds caused by racial shaming
in a white supremacist system of differentiation that imprisons African
Americans in what Robyn Wiegman has aptly described as the "prisonhouse
of epidermal inferiority" (11).

Posing the question of why Morrison chose to base her novel on the
Margaret Garner story of infanticide, one commentator suggests that Morrison is intent on producing in her readers the experience "of scandal, of
shock." By centering her novel on infanticide, "an event still with the power
to shock an audience blunted by pervasive representations of violence,
Morrison is able to capture the horrific contradiction of the slave mother"
(Keenan 70). Through the Margaret Garner story, Morrison exposes the
shameful treatment of African-American slave mothers who, according to
the racist constructions of nineteenth-century apologists for slavery, were
"more primitive" than white women, and were "not 'civilized'—not really
'attached' to their children" (Wolff 107). Margaret Garner's murder of her

child, which provided pro-slavery forces with a shameful example of African savagery, became a *cause célèbre* of the abolitionists, who publicly pronounced Garner's act to be noble and constructed her as the heroic mother.[2] As Morrison retells the Margaret Garner story through her slave mother character, Sethe, she reinvestigates the shame-pride issues surrounding the Garner case. In Morrison's description, Sethe makes the "unheard-of claim" for a slave that she is the mother of her children, but in her "excess of maternal feeling," she "almost steps over into what she was terrified of being regarded as, which is an animal" (Darling 252). The fact that critic-readers, as we shall see, are repeatedly drawn into the acts of judging and sometimes of justifying the infanticide—which is presented as an example of excessive mother love that is, at once, brutal and protective, shameful and heroic—reveals the power of Morrison's narrative to involve readers in the shame-and-blame drama that it stages.

Whereas in *Song of Solomon* Morrison explores the golden legacy of Milkman's racial heritage, which leads back to his slavery roots, in *Beloved*, in contrast, she reveals why the ex-slaves tried to rush away from slavery and the slaves as she describes how the ex-slave Sethe, who lives near Cincinnati in 1873–1874, remains haunted by memories of her slave experiences at the ironically named Kentucky plantation, Sweet Home. In 1855, after the death of her supposedly enlightened and good slave master, Garner, and her mistreatment and humiliation at the hands of Garner's successor, schoolteacher, Sethe makes her difficult flight to freedom only to be tracked down by schoolteacher one month later, leading to the infanticide and to Sethe's subsequent haunting by the ghost of her dead baby daughter. As Morrison insistently dramatizes the pain and shame endured by Sethe, she depicts the nightmarish world inhabited by victims of trauma, using the device of the ghost to convey the power of trauma to possess and trap its victims. "To be traumatized is precisely to be possessed by an image or event," remarks Cathy Caruth in her description of the "haunting power" of trauma ("Introduction" 3). Because traumatic experiences are too overwhelming to be "integrated into existing mental frameworks," they are "dissociated, later to return intrusively as fragmented sensory or motoric experiences" (van der Kolk, "Intrusive Past" 447). Victims of trauma suffer from both intrusive symptoms, in which they experience an unbidden reliving of the trauma, as well as the numbing symptoms of disconnection and inner deadness. Trapped in what has been called the "black hole" of trauma (van der Kolk, "Foreword" ix), they are unable to control their thoughts and emotions, and they lose a normal sense of predictability and safety.

That there remains at the center of the trauma survivor, as Dori Laub has remarked, "a danger, a nightmare, a fragility, a woundedness that defies all healing" (73) is dramatized in the plight of Morrison's ex-slave, Sethe, who experiences the haunting power of trauma. "Some things go. Pass on. Some things just stay," Sethe explains to her daughter, Denver. "I used to think it was my rememory. You know. Some things you forget. Other things you never do. But it's not. Places, places are still there. If a house burns down, it's gone, but the place—the picture of it—stays, and not just in my rememory, but out there, in the world. . . . The picture is still there and what's more, if you go there—you who never was there—if you go there and stand in the place where it was, it will happen again; it will be there for you, waiting for you" (35–36). Sethe's account of her "rememory"—that is, her uncontrolled remembering and reliving of emotionally painful experiences—recalls descriptions of a visual form of memory that trauma investigators refer to as traumatic memory. "[E]ncoded in the form of vivid sensations and images," traumatic memory "lack[s] verbal narrative and context." What gives traumatic memory its "heightened reality" is the "intense focus on fragmentary sensation, on image without context" (Herman, *Trauma* 38). Because traumatic memories, unlike normal or so-called narrative memories, are not readily incorporated into existing mental categories and schemes, victims of trauma find it difficult to assimilate and articulate what has happened to them. Caught in the grip of an "unspeakable secret," traumatized individuals, as Judith Herman writes, are driven by the desire to "deny horrible events" and to "proclaim them aloud," and indeed the fact that victims "often tell their stories in a highly emotional, contradictory, and fragmented manner which undermines their credibility . . . thereby serves the twin imperatives of truth-telling and secrecy" (*Trauma* 1).

As Morrison focuses on the physical oppression and also the shame-humiliation suffered by the slaves, she underscores the link between trauma and shame in *Beloved*, showing that, as trauma investigators have concluded, the deliberate and sadistic infliction of injury can induce unbearable and chronic feelings of shame. Judith Herman, for example, discusses how victims of repeated trauma, such as those held in captivity, may suffer from a "contaminated identity" and be preoccupied with "shame, self-loathing, and a sense of failure" (*Trauma* 94). Ronnie Janoff-Bulman similarly remarks that "human-induced victimizations are . . . characterized as humiliating," since the victims, who are "overpowered by another, a malevolent perpetrator," feel not only "helpless" but also "sullied and tarnished in the process" (80). The lethal impact of shame has also been commented on by Lawrence Langer in his studies of Holocaust victims. The fact that some survivors of the Holocaust have insisted that the humiliations they suffered in the concentration camps were "often worse than death" points to the toxicity of what Langer calls "humiliated memory," an "intense form of uncompensating recall" that reanimates the "governing impotence of the worst moments" of a debilitating past (77, 83–84).

Plagued by intrusive memories, trapped in a fragmented world of repetition, Morrison's ex-slave character, Sethe, is driven by the need to reveal and conceal as she struggles to both remember and not remember, to say and not say the painful secrets of her slavery past. While Sethe feels that she must keep the past "at bay" (42), she remains haunted by her traumatic and humiliated rememories. For "her brain was not interested in the future. Loaded with the past and hungry for more, it left her no room to imagine, let alone plan for, the next day" (70). Deliberately using a fragmented and repetitive narrative structure to convey the disrupted, obsessive world of the trauma victim, Morrison circles around and around the shameful secrets that haunt her character: Sethe's paralyzing and dirtying memories of the physical and psychic assaults on her humanity she suffered as a slave, memories that are too awful to speak of directly and can only be told incrementally, in bits and pieces. In *Beloved*, Morrison also dramatizes the inherent difficulty of the trauma testimony. As Cathy Caruth has remarked, the fact that "in trauma the greatest confrontation with reality may also occur as an absolute numbing to it" leads to the paradox of trauma: that its "overwhelming immediacy . . . produces its belated uncertainty" ("Introduction" 5). Thus, there is a "crisis of truth" in the trauma testimony, for traumatized individuals carry "an impossible history within them, or they become themselves the symptom of a history that they cannot entirely possess" ("Introduction" 5, 4).

In describing the impossible history Sethe carries within her, Morrison bears witness to the affronts of slavery in *Beloved*, using the ghost to keep alive the reader's sense of the incomprehensibility of the slave experience. But the haunting also serves to distract the reader as the narrative unfolds. "The fully realized presence of the haunting," writes Morrison, "is both a major incumbent of the narrative and sleight of hand. One of its purposes is to keep the reader preoccupied with the nature of the incredible spirit world while being supplied a controlled diet of the incredible political world" ("Unspeakable Things" 32). The fact that the novel has been characterized as "a highly poetic haunting" (Ferguson 113) indicates Morrison's ability to aestheticize, at least in part, what she describes, and Morrison also invites readers to piece together the narrative's "broken chronology of events" (Jessee 209), a process repeated over and over in the critical conversation surrounding the novel. While Morrison uses her novelistic art to gain some aesthetic mastery over—and thus to afford readers some protection from—the horrors she depicts, she also involves readers emotionally in the text's drama. Because Morrison is exposing the shame and degradation suffered by the slaves, and because shame is a contagious affect, *Beloved*, like Morrison's other novels, risks generating shame conflicts in readers. Evidence of this is found in the suspicion voiced by one critic that there is "a kind of voyeuristic enterprise at work" in *Beloved*, that the reader "read[s] on to see if Morrison's imagination will overstep the bounds of good taste" by providing "some of the specifics of the atrocities of whites' inhumanity to blacks during slavery" (T. Harris, *Fiction* 171). Critic-readers of *Beloved* also have remarked on the "chill horror" of the infanticide, or have said that they feel "intimately" and "personally" threatened as they read the novel, or have claimed that reading *Beloved* is a "physical experience" for those readers "who are naturally squeamish about violence and brutality, and who suffer some physical discomfort as a result of reading about them"—descriptions that provide suggestive evidence of the novel's ability to unsettle readers (Rodrigues, "Telling" 159, Atlas, "Toni" 52, T. Harris, *Fiction* 172). Moreover, *Beloved*, as we shall see, also prompts readers to assume text-directed advocacy or rescuer roles by acting, for example, as Sethe's advocate or by supplementing the rescue fantasy staged in the closing scenes of the novel, which depict the exorcism of the ghost and the possible healing of Denver and Sethe.

It is revealing that Morrison herself enacts a rescue-cure of Margaret Garner through her story of Sethe, for as Morrison has admitted, her novelistic "invention" is "much, much happier" than what actually happened to Margaret Garner, who was tried not for the infanticide but for the "*real* crime, which was running away," and who was subsequently returned to slavery (Darling 251). Just as Morrison enacts an authorial rescue of Margaret Garner, so she attempts to work toward a cultural cure in *Beloved* as she examines the painful and secret legacy of slavery and focuses attention on the pernicious effects of internalized racist assumptions about black inferiority on the construction of African-American identities. Continuing the emotional work begun in her earlier novels, which, like *Beloved*, provide enactments of shame-shame and shame-rage feeling traps, Morrison explores in *Beloved* the painful—and intergenerationally transmitted and internalized— wounds caused by racist oppression, and she works to counteract shame and trauma by establishing an affective and cognitive connection with the lost victims of slavery and by depicting, and in places poetizing, the inner lives of the slaves. Also making a strategic use of a countershaming tactic we have observed Morrison deploy to great effect in her other novels, *Beloved* actively shames the white shamer. There is "no bad luck in the world but whitepeople," says Baby Suggs, her words exemplary of the way the novel points the finger of blame and shame at the white oppressors who have traumatized and dirtied blacks (104).

That Sethe kills her infant daughter to prevent her from being defined as racially inferior and animalistic—and thus from being dirtied—underscores the historical shaming of African slave women that Morrison is intent on exposing in *Beloved*. Tracing the historical and cultural origins of the essentialist racist discourse that constructed the African woman as animallike, Patricia Collins notes how "[b]iological notions of race and gender prevalent in the early nineteenth century which fostered the animalistic icon of Black female sexuality were joined by the appearance of a racist biology incorporating the concept of degeneracy." There were also critical economic factors at work in treating blacks as animals, for animals could be "economically exploited, worked, sold, killed, and consumed," treatment that slave women became "susceptible to" (171). The "externally defined, controlling image of the breeder woman" created during slavery also served white economic interests. "By claiming that Black women were able to produce children as easily as animals, this objectification of Black women as the Other provided justification for interference in the reproductive rights of enslaved Africans. Slaveowners wanted enslaved Africans to 'breed' because every slave child born represented a valuable unit of property, another unit of labor, and, if female, the prospects for more slaves" (76).

While nineteenth-century Southern society exalted white motherhood, slave women, in the words of Angela Davis, were "not mothers at all." Because they were "classified as 'breeders' as opposed to 'mothers,' their infant children could be sold away from them like calves from cows" (7). The African slave woman, who was subjected to an "institutionalized pattern of rape" under the slavery system (Davis 23), also became associated with illicit sexuality, giving rise to the shaming stereotype of the black Jezebel. The "controlling image" of the Jezebel, explains Collins, "originated under slavery when Black women were portrayed as . . . 'sexually aggressive wet nurses.'" By relegating black women to the sexually aggressive category, the Jezebel image provided "a powerful rationale for the widespread sexual assaults by white men typically reported by Black slave women." Moreover, "If Black slave women could be portrayed as having excessive sexual appetites, then increased fertility should be the expected outcome. By suppressing the nurturing that African-American women might give their own children which would strengthen Black family networks, and by forcing Black women to work in the field or 'wet nurse' white children, slaveowners effectively tied the controlling images of Jezebel and Mammy to the economic exploitation inherent in the institution of slavery" (77).

In examining in *Beloved* the economic and sexual exploitation of slave women and the shaming racist constructions of slave women as hyperembodied and hypersexualized, Morrison reflects the recent endeavors in the developing scholarly study of black women's history to challenge the "old image" of the slave woman as "collaborator with white oppression" and to show that the slave woman was "doubly oppressed in that both her productive and reproductive capacities were used and abused" (Morton 144). The female slave, as Barbara Omolade aptly puts it, was a "fragmented commodity," whose "back and muscle were pressed into field labor," whose "hands were demanded to nurse and nurture the white man and his family as domestic servant," whose "vagina, used for his sexual pleasure, was the gateway to the womb, which was his place of capital investment" (354). In *Beloved*, the doubly oppressed Baby Suggs, whose years as a slave "busted her legs, back, head, eyes, hands, kidneys, womb and tongue," is forced to have eight children by six fathers (87). What Baby Suggs calls the "nastiness of life" is the shock she feels on discovering that "nobody stopped playing checkers just because the pieces included her children." Out of all her children, her son, Halle, is the one Baby is allowed to keep the longest—twenty years. Halle is given to Baby "to make up for *hearing* that her two girls, neither of whom had their adult teeth, were sold and gone and she had not been able to wave goodbye. To make up for coupling with a straw boss for four months in exchange for keeping her third child, a boy, with her—only to have him traded for lumber in the spring of the next year and to find herself pregnant by the man who promised not to and did. That child she could not love and the rest she would not" (23). In focusing on the doubly oppressed slave woman and slavery's disruption of the mother-child bond, *Beloved* also dramatizes that the slave woman's "resistance tactics" to "forced miscegenation" included infanticide, as recent historians have pointed out (Morton 144).[3] Ella, for example, who spends her puberty in a house where she is "shared" by a father and son, whom she calls "the lowest yet," delivers but refuses to nurse the "hairy white thing, fathered by 'the lowest yet,'" and thus the infant lives only five days (256, 258–59). Similarly, Sethe's mother—who is hanged when Sethe is a child—is raped many times by members of the white crew on the slave ship that brings her to America. Resisting her sexual exploitation, she throws away the child from the crew and also the other children fathered by other whites, keeping only Sethe, who is fathered by the black man she willingly put her arms around.

Affectively and cognitively invested in ripping the veil historically drawn over proceedings too terrible to relate in *Beloved*, Morrison details the oppression of slave women as she tells the story of Sethe, who learns of the shaming power of the white definers: their power to define her as less than human. When the "iron-eyed" and proud Sethe first comes to Sweet Home as a thirteen-year-old, she is left alone by the men, allowed to "choose" one of them "in spite of the fact that each one would have beaten the others to mush to have her" (10). "Only my wool shawl kept me from looking like a haint peddling," Sethe remarks, describing the wedding dress she patches together from stolen fabric when she "marries" Halle, Baby Suggs's son. "I wasn't but fourteen years old, so I reckon that's why I was so proud of myself" (59). Yet even as *Beloved* describes Sethe's youthful pride, it also shows that she is implicitly shamed, objectified as the racial and sexual Other—as the animalistic breeder woman. "[M]inus women, fucking cows, dreaming of rape," the Sweet Home men wait for Sethe to select one of them (11). When

Sethe and Halle have sex in the cornfield—Halle wanting "privacy" for Sethe but, instead, getting "public display"—the Sweet Home men, "erect as dogs," watch the corn stalks "dance at noon." To Paul D, the "jump . . . from a calf to a girl wasn't all that mighty," nor was it the "leap Halle believed it would be" (26–27). Although Sethe has the "amazing luck of six whole years of marriage" to a man who fathers every one of her children, after the death of Garner and the arrival of schoolteacher, she learns of her value and function as a breeder slave woman, as "property that reproduced itself without cost" (23, 228).

"It was a book about us but we didn't know that right away," Sethe remarks as she recalls how schoolteacher asked the Sweet Home slaves questions and then wrote down what they said in his notebook with the ink Sethe mixed for him (37). Schoolteacher, despite his "pretty manners" and "soft" talking and apparent gentleness (36–37), is a cruel racist. A practitioner of the nineteenth-century pseudoscience of race, which included the systematic measurements of facial angles, head shapes, and brain sizes (see Stepan, "Race" 43, 45–47), schoolteacher is bent, as he makes his "scientific" inquiries, on documenting the racial inferiority of the Sweet Home slaves. At first Sethe is not concerned about schoolteacher's measuring string. "Schoolteacher'd wrap that string all over my head, 'cross my nose, around my behind. Number my teeth. I thought he was a fool," she recalls (191). Describing the biosocial investigation of racial difference in the nineteenth century, which was given "political urgency" by the abolitionist movement, Nancy Stepan notes how the "scientific" study of race served to "elevate hitherto unconsciously held analogies"—such as the long-standing comparison of blacks to apes—into "self-conscious theory" ("Race" 43, 42). A theory that codified the shaming of blacks and white contempt for the "lower" races, the study of racial differences functioned to give so-called scientific confirmation of the superiority (pride) of the higher and civilized white race and the inferiority (shame) of the lower and degenerate black race.[4]

Sethe, who initially thinks that schoolteacher is a fool, is humiliated on discovering the purpose of schoolteacher's measurements and observations when she overhears him instructing his pupils on how to scientifically describe her as a member of a lower race by listing her human traits on one side of the page and her animal traits on the other. In the essentialist racist discourse of schoolteacher, Sethe is constructed as animalistic: that is, as fundamentally and biologically different from white people. That the contempt of another has the power to degrade the individual's "value as a person" by equating the individual "with a debased, dirty thing—a derided and low animal"—and that the purpose of contempt is to instill in the individual a sense of "self-disgust and therefore shame at self-unworthiness" (Wurmser, *Mask* 81, Nathanson, *Shame and Pride* 129) is illustrated in this scene. The contemptuous racist discourse of schoolteacher engenders feelings of self-contempt in Sethe, who feels dirtied when she is suddenly exposed to the magnitude of schoolteacher's disgust for her race. The fact that this humiliating moment of exposure continues to haunt Sethe years later—that, indeed, she becomes caught up in a feeling trap of shame as she continues to replay this scene in her mind—reveals the depth of the shame she feels on learning of her designated role as the contemptible and debased racial inferior. Following her inscription into schoolteacher's shaming discourse on essential racial differences, Sethe feels blameworthy, believing that she has somehow collaborated with schoolteacher. "I made the ink. . . . He couldn't have done it if I hadn't made the ink," she later tells Paul D (271).

Despite her proud demeanor, the "quiet, queenly" (12) Sethe is a woman tormented by humiliated memories not only of how schoolteacher defined her as animallike but also of how his nephews treated her like an animal. Before Sethe, who is pregnant with Denver, is able to escape from Sweet Home, she has her milk stolen by schoolteacher's nephews. When Sethe learns from Paul D that her husband, Halle, watched this degrading spectacle and was consequently driven mad by what he had witnessed, her "rebellious" and "greedy" brain takes in this "hateful picture," adding it to her painful memory of this central shame event. "I am full God damn it of two boys with mossy teeth, one sucking on my breast the other holding me down, their book-reading teacher watching and writing it up. . . . Add my husband to it, watching, above me in the loft . . . looking down on what I couldn't look at at all. . . . There is also my husband squatting by the churn smearing the butter as well as its clabber all over his face because the milk they took is on his mind" (70). Objectified as the racial and sexual Other, Sethe is treated like a sexually aggressive wet nurse and mammy when schoolteacher's nephews sexually assault her in the barn, nursing from her breasts and stealing her milk. She also is treated like an animal, milked as if she were "the cow, no, the goat, back behind the stable because it was too nasty to stay in with the horses" (200). Afterward, she is beaten like an animal by schoolteacher's nephews for telling Mrs. Garner what has happened to her. Following schoolteacher's orders, the two boys dig a hole in the ground to protect the developing foetus—which is considered to be the property of the white slave owner—and then they brutally beat Sethe on her back with cowhide.[5] "Felt like I was split in two. . . . Bit a piece of my tongue off when they opened my back. It was hanging by a shred. I didn't mean to. Clamped down on it, it come right off. I thought, Good God, I'm going to eat myself up" (202).

Escaping Sweet Home alone, the pregnant and traumatized Sethe gives birth to Denver on the "bloody side of the Ohio River" with the help of Amy Denver, a shamed white girl, the "raggediest-looking trash you ever saw" (31,

31–32). When Amy, who claims she is "good at sick things" (82), treats Sethe's injured back, she describes the pattern made by the seeping and pus-filled wounds as a chokecherry tree—a description that serves to aestheticize the shame and trauma of Sethe's situation. "It's a tree," Amy tells Sethe. "See, here's the trunk—it's red and split wide open, full of sap, and this here's the parting for the branches. You got a mighty lot of branches. Leaves, too, look like, and dern if these ain't blossoms. Tiny little cherry blossoms, just as white. Your back got a whole tree on it. In bloom" (79). Years later, when Paul D and Sethe are reunited at Sethe's haunted house, Paul D lovingly touches the "sculpture" of Sethe's scarred back, which is "like the decorative work of an ironsmith too passionate for display" (17). And yet after Paul D and Sethe make love, he thinks of "the wrought-iron maze he had explored" as a "revolting clump of scars" (21)—this change in Paul D's perception exemplary of the way the narrative alternates between providing an explicit and revolting depiction of slavery's atrocities and aestheticizing what it describes. Sethe's scarred back is a visible reminder of her traumatic abuse, both her physical violation and her psychic wounds, and it also concretizes her marked identity as the racially and stigmatized Other. The fact that even Paul D comes to react with revulsion to Sethe's scarred back points to the way that victims of extreme trauma and humiliation may be viewed by others as tainted and damaged. Thus, Paul D, even though he identifies with and honors Sethe's suffering, also perceives her, on some level, as an object of shame and disgust.

Despite the fact that Sethe is shamed when she is objectified as the sexualized breeder woman and the Jezebel-Mammy, that is, as the sexually aggressive wet nurse, she continues to identify herself primarily as a mother, taking deep pride in her fiercely protective mother love. Indeed, Sethe registers her resistance to the white slave-owner culture through her mothering and her desire to nurse her own children. "I had milk," Sethe recalls. "I was pregnant with Denver but I had milk for my baby girl. I hadn't stopped nursing her when I sent her on ahead. . . . Anybody could smell me long before he saw me. And when he saw me he'd see the drops of it on the front of my dress. . . . All I knew was I had to get my milk to my baby girl. Nobody was going to nurse her like me" (16). Also proud of her escape from Sweet Home, Sethe tells Paul D, "I did it. I got us all out. Without Halle too. Up till then it was the only thing I ever did on my own. Decided. And it came off right, like it was supposed to." Recalling her expansive feeling of pride, she remarks, "I was big, Paul D, and deep and wide and when I stretched out my arms all my children could get in between. I was *that* wide" (162). Commenting on how individuals evaluate their actions against the "yardstick" of the shame-pride axis, Donald Nathanson explains that while shame is associated with "incompetence, failure, or inadequacy," pride stems from the pleasure felt "in a moment of competence." The individual's "precarious sense of self" is balanced between shame and pride, between the "hoped-for *personal best*" and the "terribly feared *personal worst* that . . . will trigger an avalanche of deadly shame" (*Shame and Pride* 20). Whereas there is a "wish to conceal" shame, there is a "tendency to broadcast" pride. But it is also the case that "in adult life pride is viewed with suspicion." Because it is associated with "vanity, foolishness, weakness, indeed becoming almost a synonym for narcissism, adult pride is dangerously close to the very shame that is supposed to be its opposite" ("Shame/Pride Axis" 184, 188). Just how dangerously close pride is to shame is revealed in the shame-pride drama that unfolds after Sethe's successful escape from Sweet Home and her arrival at Baby Suggs's home on the outskirts of Cincinnati.

At 124 Bluestone Road with Baby Suggs, who was bought out of slavery by her son, Halle, Sethe enjoys twenty-eight days before "the Misery," which is Stamp Paid's term for Sethe's "rough response" to the Fugitive Slave Act of 1850 (171). Sethe has twenty-eight days of happy family and community life, of "having women friends, a mother-in-law, and all her children together; of being part of a neighborhood; of, in fact, having neighbors at all to call her own" (173). When Baby Suggs bathes Sethe's injured body in sections, she attempts to begin the healing of Sethe, who was treated like a fragmented commodity as a slave and dirtied by schoolteacher. Despite the fact that as a slave Baby Suggs lived in fear that a white man would knock her to the ground in front of her children—that is, treat her as an object of contempt and publicly humiliate her—she is a generous woman with a big heart. A lay preacher, Baby Suggs is presented as the healing and wise ancestor figure familiar to readers of Morrison's fiction. In her sermons, Baby Suggs exhorts the ex-slaves to replace shame with pride, to love their black flesh, flesh that is despised by the white man. "Love it hard," she insists. "Yonder they do not love your flesh. They despise it. They don't love your eyes; they'd just as soon pick em out. No more do they love the skin on your back. Yonder they flay it. And O my people they do not love your hands. Those they only use, tie, bind, chop off and leave empty. Love your hands! Love them. . . . More than your life-holding womb and your life-giving private parts, hear me now, love your heart. For this is the prize" (88–89).

When Sethe arrives "all mashed up and split open, but with another grandchild in her arms," Baby Suggs feels the "idea of a whoop" move "closer to the front of her brain," but because she does not know what has happened to Halle, she lets "the whoop lie—not wishing to hurt his chances by thanking God too soon" (135). But some twenty days later when Baby Suggs decides to share with some of her neighbors the blackberry pies she has made from the two full buckets of blackberries given to her by Stamp Paid, this simple gesture of sharing grows into a feast for ninety people after

Sethe provides some chickens and Stamp Paid some catfish and perch. "124 shook with their voices far into the night. Ninety people who ate so well, and laughed so much, it made them angry" (136). Focusing attention on the class tensions and divisions within the black community—a concern that recurs in all of Morrison's fiction—the narrative describes how Baby Suggs's generous gesture stirs smoldering feelings of class resentment and envy among the ex-slaves, who wonder where Baby Suggs gets "it all," and why "she and hers" are "always the center of things." Baby Suggs's neighbors are also angry about the privileges that they assume Baby Suggs has enjoyed in her life. "Loaves and fishes were His powers—they did not belong to an ex-slave who had probably never carried one hundred pounds to the scale, or picked okra with a baby on her back. Who had never been lashed by a ten-year-old whiteboy as God knows they had. Who had not even escaped slavery—had, in fact, been *bought out* of it by a doting son and *driven* to the Ohio River in a wagon . . . and rented a house with *two* floors *and* a well from the Bodwins—the white brother and sister who gave . . . clothes, goods and gear for runaways because they hated slavery worse than they hated slaves" (137).

When members of the community begin to voice their class grievances, they whisper to each other about "fat rats, doom and uncalled-for pride" (137). "Pride, well, that bothers em a bit," as Stamp Paid later tells Paul D. "They can get messy when they think somebody's too proud. . ." (232). Baby Suggs's neighbors accuse her of pride because they perceive her as elevating herself above others and thus viewing them with contempt. They respond to her assumed contempt—which activates their own deep-seated feelings of shame—with countercontempt. "Contempt, a blend of dissmell and anger, is the communicator of and is experienced as rejection," explains Gershen Kaufman. "The object of contempt . . . is found offensive, something to be repudiated" (*Psychology of Shame* 108). Baby Suggs, who becomes an object of the community's contempt, smells the "scent" of her neighbors' "disapproval," which is "heavy in the air," and senses their "free-floating repulsion" because she has "overstepped, given too much, offended them by excess" (137, 138).

Because of community resentment toward the bountiful Baby Suggs, nobody warns Sethe and Baby Suggs of the approach of four white men with the "righteous Look every Negro learned to recognize along with his ma'am's tit," the look that "telegraphed and announced the faggot, the whip, the fist, the lie, long before it went public" (157). In part deflecting reader attention away from the horror of the central scene that is about to unfold—the infanticide—by focusing on biblical signs and portents, the narrative describes how Baby Suggs senses, far behind the odor of disapproval emanating from the community, a "dark and coming thing": that is, a portent of the death brought by the apocalyptic "four horsemen" (139, 148). *Beloved*'s portrayal of the white men in this passage recalls bell hooks's description of "representations of whiteness in the black imagination" as "terrorizing." The association of whiteness with "the terrible, the terrifying, the terrorizing," hooks explains, "emerges as a response to the traumatic pain and anguish that remains a consequence of white racist domination, a psychic state that informs and shapes the way black folks 'see' whiteness" (*Killing Rage* 37, 39, 37–38).

In a maneuver meant to be jarring, *Beloved* locates readers within the shaming perspective of the racist white onlookers—those with the contemptuous "look"—as it provides the first detailed account of the infanticide. Since it is quiet at the house on 124 Bluestone Road, the four whites—schoolteacher, one of his nephews, a slave catcher, and the sheriff—think that they are too late. Aware that fugitive slaves sometimes "do disbelievable things," like grabbing at the mouth of a rifle or throwing themselves at the person holding the rifle, they act cautiously. "Unlike a snake or a bear, a dead nigger could not be skinned for profit and was not worth his own dead weight in coin" (148). In the woodshed they find "a nigger woman holding a blood-soaked child to her chest with one hand" and swinging another infant by its heels toward the wall with the other hand while two bleeding boys lie at her feet. "Right off it was clear, to schoolteacher especially, that there was nothing there to claim." Viewed through the shaming gaze of schoolteacher, Sethe, who has "at least ten breeding years left," is worthless property. She has "gone wild" because she was mishandled by nephew, "who'd overbeat her and made her cut and run" (149). In the racist discourse of schoolteacher and the other white onlookers, Sethe is constructed as the racial Other, the uncivilized, violent primitive. Sethe's action is explained as an example of degenerate African behavior, a reversion to animal savagery. "Suppose you beat the hounds past that point thataway. Never again could you trust them. . . . You'd be feeding them maybe . . . and the animal would revert—bite your hand clean off" (149–50). Sethe's act gives "testimony to the results of a little so-called freedom imposed on people who needed every care and guidance in the world to keep them from the cannibal life they preferred" (151).

"I stopped him. . . . I took and put my babies where they'd be safe," Sethe tells Paul D when he belatedly learns about the infanticide and looks to her for an explanation of why she killed her "crawling already" baby daughter (164, 159). Sethe spins around the room, circling Paul D the way she is "circling the subject," and thus he catches "only pieces" of what she says (161). "Circling, circling . . . instead of getting to the point"—which is the way victims of extreme trauma and shame tell their stories—Sethe knows that the "circle" she is making around the subject will "remain one," that she cannot "close in, pin it down for anybody who had to ask. If they didn't get it right off—she could never explain" (162, 163). The truth, to Sethe, is simple. When she saw the approaching horsemen and recognized school-teacher's hat, she tried to make her children safe. "She just flew. Collected every bit of life she had made, all the parts of her that were precious and fine and beautiful, and carried, pushed, dragged them through the veil, out, away, over there where no one could hurt them. Over there. Outside this place, where they would be safe" (163).

When Sethe commits her act of rough love by slitting the throat of her child with a handsaw, as the circling narrative ultimately discloses, she attempts to protect her children from being dirtied by whites. Her act grows out of her awareness "That anybody white could take your whole self for anything that came to mind. Not just work, kill, or maim you, but dirty you. Dirty you so bad you couldn't like yourself anymore. Dirty you so bad you forgot who you were and couldn't think it up." Sethe wants to protect her children from being victimized by the destructive, dehumanizing forces of slavery and from succumbing to the defining and dirtying power of racist discourse, which constructs white identity as racially and biologically pure and black identity as impure or dirty. "The best thing she was, was her children. Whites might dirty *her* all right, but not her best thing, her beau-tiful, magical best thing—the part of her that was clean. . . . And no one, nobody on this earth, would list her daughter's characteristics on the animal side of the paper" (251).

Not only is Sethe determined to prevent her children from taking on their prescribed social role as the biologically inferior and racially stigma-tized Other, but she also, in attempting to keep her child—the part of her that is clean—from being dirtied, acts to defend against or undo *her own* shame and recover the pride of an idealized self-image. But to Paul D, Sethe, who talks about "safety with a handsaw," does not know "where the world stopped and she began" (164). He tells her that her love is "too thick" and that what she did was "wrong" (164, 165). Insisting that there must have been some other way, he humiliates her in the same way that schoolteacher did. Revealing his own internalization of schoolteacher's racist thinking, Paul D compares Sethe to an animal. "You got two feet, Sethe, not four," he tells her, only to later realize how quickly he "had moved from his shame to hers" (165). "Too thick, he said. My love was too thick. What he know about it?" Sethe subsequently says to herself as she justifies her act. "Who in the world is he willing to die for? Would he give his privates to a stranger in return for a carving?" (203), she asks herself, referring to yet another dirtying act she committed: her shameful, Jezebel-like "rutting" (5) with a white stonemason so she could have the word "Beloved" carved on the headstone of her murdered daughter.

Pointing to the narrative's own uncertainties and ambivalences in presenting the infanticide, Sethe's "rough choice" in killing Beloved, a decision that Baby Suggs cannot "approve or condemn" (180), is represented as an act of fierce mother love and resistance to slavery, but also as a brutal act. Sethe tries but is unable to explain to Beloved "what it took to drag the teeth of that saw under the little chin; to feel the baby blood pump like oil in her hands; to hold her face so her head would stay on; to squeeze her so she could absorb, still, the death spasms that shot through that adored body, plump and sweet with life" (251). Repeating a pattern we have observed in other depictions of parental violence in Morrison's novels—such as Cholly's rape of Pecola in *The Bluest Eye* or Eva's murder of Plum in *Sula*—the infanticide mirrors a behavior often found in abusive parents: the mingling of protective with brutal behavior. The infanticide is also explained as an act of revenge against schoolteacher—as Sethe's determination to "outhurt the hurter" (234), that is, to turn the tables by wounding the wounding schoolteacher—and as an expression of "rage" that is "prideful, misdirected" (256). Because Sethe's violent act thus reveals her hidden identification with the sadistic white persecutor, Beloved's scarred neck—the mark made by the handsaw Sethe used to slit her daughter's throat—signifies not only the shaming mark or stigma of slavery but also the maternal and intergenerational transmission of black shame and trauma.

That the infanticide is an act designed to force readers to participate in the shame-and-blame drama staged in the text is evident in the critical commentary on the novel. Despite the claim that the narrative "withholds judgment on Sethe's act and persuades the reader to do the same, presenting the infanticide as the ultimate contradiction of mothering under slavery," for many critic-readers "[j]udging Sethe's action in all its stark extremity is in fact the crux of *Beloved*" (Wyatt 476, Schmudde 123). The infanticide is typically described as "gory," as "crazed and horrifying," and as "morally reprehensible and monstrous" (B. Bell 10, Liscio 38, Otten, *Crime* 86). But it also is commonly argued that readers cannot "easily condemn" Sethe's act even when they "clearly do not condone it." Locked "into participation" by the moral questions raised by the novel, readers are encouraged to ask themselves, "Is Sethe right to kill Beloved? . . . Are some conditions of life worse than death?" (T. Harris, *Fiction* 171).

Acting as Sethe's advocate and carrying out the text's antishaming agenda, many, if not most, critic-readers construct the infanticide as a desperate but heroic act of mother love. In a typical reading, the infanticide, "as impossible as that may be to absorb . . . is a maternal act of . . . preservation: Sethe wants to make sure her baby will be *safe* from the dehumanization of slavery" (Hirsch, "Maternity" 104). As Sethe "creates a counternarrative" to the slave-master's narrative of her animality and wildness, in another positive reading of the infanticide, "a story of inhumanity has been overwritten as a story of higher humanity" (Henderson 79–80). But while many commentators interpret the infanticide as an act of mother love, others become actively involved in the text's shame script when they describe it as an act of "mis-love" or refer to it as Sethe's "dirty secret" (Rhodes 89, 90). The fact that Paul D and the black community turn against Sethe is often cited as evidence of her blameworthiness. Critic-readers have also questioned whether Sethe's act reflects the behavior of the white slave master. "[W]as that act of love crossing the boundary into the acts of hate that were committed by the owners of the slaves' bodies?" asks one commentator (Askeland 798). Arguing that Sethe's wish to be "self-defined as mother-owner of her children is a form of obsessive possession," another critic characterizes Sethe's "maternal protection" as "unlawful possession" (McKinstry 267, 268).

If the infanticide is at once a protective and brutal act that grows out of Sethe's intense shame (her feelings of dirtiness) and shame-rage (her desire to "outhurt the hurter"), to members of the black community like Ella, Sethe's crime is "staggering" while her "pride outstripped even that" (256). The black people gathered outside 124 Bluestone are shocked by the "clarity" of Sethe's "knife-clean" profile as the sheriff takes her away. "Was her head a bit too high? Her back a little too straight? Probably. Otherwise the singing would have begun at once. . . . Some cape of sound would have quickly been wrapped around her, like arms to hold and steady her on the way" (152). Because of her apparent pride and defiant individualism, Sethe does not enjoy the benefits of group solidarity. Members of the community do not come to the aid of Sethe, who tries "to do it all alone with her nose in the air" (254). Shame begets shame as Sethe's desperate act to protect her children from being dirtied leads to the public shaming of members of her family, who become ostracized by the black community. After the infanticide a brokenhearted and exhausted Baby Suggs takes to her bed. At the time Stamp Paid thinks that shame is what drives Baby Suggs to her bed, but later he thinks that her fatigue resulted from the cumulative impact of her years of suffering. Baby Suggs, who "devoted her freed life to harmony," is buried amidst "a regular dance of pride, fear, condemnation and spite," and the townspeople long to see Sethe "come on difficult times," for Sethe's "outrageous claims, her self-sufficiency," seem to demand it (171).

Thus Sethe's twenty-eight days of happiness are followed by eighteen years of "disapproval and a solitary life" (173). When Sethe retreats to 124 Bluestone Road after she is released from jail, she defensively withdraws to a walled off and presumably safe place. But the isolated and secretive world she enters affords her little protection against her painful past. That Sethe remains psychically numbed by her slavery past is revealed in the fact that her scarred back, a visible reminder of her persecution as a slave, has no feeling. While

Sethe works hard to forget her past, she suffers from rememories, that is, spontaneous recurrences of her traumatic and humiliating past. In describing Sethe's delimited life, a life plagued by haunting rememories that become literalized in the ghost, *Beloved* presents what Judith Herman calls the "dialectic of trauma," the oscillation of "opposing psychological states"— those of intrusion and constriction—which is "perhaps the most characteristic feature of the post-traumatic syndromes." In the aftermath of a traumatic experience, the individual "finds herself caught between the extremes of amnesia or of reliving the trauma, between floods of intense, overwhelming feeling and arid states of no feeling at all, between irritable, impulsive action and complete inhibition of action" (*Trauma* 47). Because "the trauma repeatedly interrupts," Herman explains, the traumatized individual is unable to resume "the normal course" of her life, and "even normally safe environments may come to feel dangerous, for the survivor can never be assured that she will not encounter some reminder of the trauma" (*Trauma* 37). Moreover, because the "instability produced by these periodic alternations further exacerbates the traumatized person's sense of unpredictability and helplessness," the dialectic of trauma is "potentially self-perpetuating" (*Trauma* 47).

Caught up in the dialectic of trauma, Sethe lives a constricted, diminished life as she attempts to avoid reminders of and forget the emotional distress of her past and reassert some semblance of control over her inner life. But the past returns to haunt Sethe in the form of the ghost of her dead daughter. The unpredictable intrusions of the ghost aptly convey not only the trauma victim's experience of intrusive memory—an "abnormal form of memory, which breaks spontaneously into consciousness"—but also the "involuntariness," the "driven, tenacious" and "'daemonic' quality" of traumatic reenactments in intrusive phenomena (Herman, *Trauma* 37, 41). Because the ghostly Beloved gives expression to the powerful and dysphoric affects arising out of the shame and trauma of slavery—feelings of shame, disgust, rage, dread, and sorrow— the house haunted by Beloved is "full of strong feeling" and is like "[a] person that wept, sighed, trembled and fell into fits" (39, 29).

Persecuted by the emotionally volatile ghost of her dead daughter, Sethe lives in a house that commits insults against and feels "lively spite" for its inhabitants, a house "[f]ull of a baby's venom" and "palsied by the baby's fury at having its throat cut" (3, 5). The ghostly presence of Beloved expresses the humiliated fury of the trauma victim and also the despair. When Paul D initially walks into the house and through "a pool of red and undulating light"—the red pool an insistent and spontaneous rememory of the baby's spilled blood—he feels a "wave of grief" soak him so completely that he wants to cry (8, 9). Paul D's emotional response to the ghostly presence, which provides a potent description of vicarious traumatization and the contagion of affect, recalls the experience sometimes reported by those who deal with trauma victims, that of being "'engulfed by anguish' or 'sinking into despair'" (Herman, *Trauma* 144). A repository of strong feelings and also a place haunted by the past, the house at 124 Bluestone Road represents the secretive, emotionally unpredictable and dangerous inner world of the shame and trauma victim. If a house is usually considered to be a place of safety and control, Sethe's haunted house, like the psychic world inhabited by the trauma victim, is an unsafe world where there is a loss of controllability. Plagued by the ghost, other members of the family come to experience not only the hypervigilance and hyperarousal symptoms of the trauma victim but also the emotional depletion as the ghost tires and wears out family members.

When Paul D finds his way to Sethe's trauma- and shame-haunted house, Sethe thinks that perhaps she will be able to "feel the hurt her back ought to" and to "remember things" because Paul D, the "last of the Sweet Home men," is there "to catch her if she sank" (18). Although Paul D seemingly ousts the ghostly presence from 124 Bluestone Road, the past is not so easily gotten rid of, and thus Beloved, the embodiment of the ghost and the rememoried past, comes to life. A "greedy ghost" that "needed a lot of love" (209), Beloved returns from the dead as a physically traumatized and emotionally abandoned child in an adult body. With her expressionless and empty eyes, her failed memory, and her disintegration anxiety—she fears that she will "fly apart" and end up "in pieces" (133)—Beloved recalls descriptions of abused children, who have "expressionless" faces, who often develop "dissociative virtuosity" as they "hide their memories in complex amnesias," and who sometimes suffer from "annihilation panic," fear of the disintegration of the self (Herman, *Trauma* 100, 102, 108). In describing Beloved's vast neediness, the novel also points to the awful emotional costs of slavery's disruption of the mother-child bond and the slave mother's forced abandonment of her children. "The helplessness of the searching eye and of the cry for love is the helplessness of feeling doomed to unlovability," as Léon Wurmser writes in his description of "basic shame" as the wound of feeling unloved and unlovable. "To be unlovable means not to see a responsive eye and not to hear a responding voice, no matter how much they are sought" (*Mask* 97). Suffering from the basic shame and pain of unlovability, Beloved, as the abandoned and abused-murdered child, is desperately needy for her mother's responsive eye and voice.

Sethe "is the one I need," Beloved tells Denver. "You can go but she is the one I have to have" (76). From the outset, Beloved can not "take her eyes off Sethe," who is "licked, tasted, eaten by Beloved's eyes." Sethe is "flattered by Beloved's open, quiet devotion" at first. "Like a familiar," Beloved hovers near Sethe, staying in the same room where Sethe is unless she is told to leave, and waiting for Sethe to return each day from work (57). When Beloved touches Sethe, her touch, though "no heavier than a feather," is "loaded . . . with desire," and the "longing" in her eyes is "bottomless" (58). Beloved's hunger for maternal love is expressed in her craving for sweets. "It was as though sweet things were what she was born for" (55). What lies behind Beloved's "petlike adoration" (64) are unspoken demands for Sethe's undivided attention. On overhearing the lovemaking of Sethe and Paul D, Beloved feels like crying, which is preferable to the anger she feels when Sethe does or thinks anything that excludes her. Upset at Sethe's "willingness to pay attention to other things"—particularly Paul D—Beloved moves Paul D out of the house, "[i]mperceptibly, downright reasonably," so that it seems as if he is doing it himself (100, 114).

Greedy to hear Sethe's voice, Beloved prompts Sethe to tell stories about the past, and Sethe complies, for she discovers that storytelling is a way to "feed" Beloved. Although before Sethe found that every reference to her "unspeakable" past life caused her pain, she begins to take "an unexpected pleasure" in talking about the past (58). Similarly, as Denver tells Beloved the story of her own birth, she sees and feels it "through Beloved," whose interest prompts Denver to give "blood to the scraps her mother and grandmother had told her—and a heartbeat" (78). Yet while Beloved's hunger for stories helps Sethe recall and talk about her painful past, it also brings with it the recovery of unspeakable secrets. That the revelation of shameful secrets can lead to regressive disorganization (Skolnick 229) is dramatized in Sethe's growing distress as she finds herself obsessing on and literally being taken over by the past. The danger of rememory is illustrated in the scene in which Sethe finds herself being strangled as she reflects on Paul D's trauma-inducing story about how Halle's face was smeared with butter and his own face was jammed with iron. When Denver later accuses Beloved of making Sethe choke, Beloved claims that Sethe was choked by the "circle of iron" (101)—that is, the iron collar used to restrain the slaves. If Sethe's frightening experience is the repetition of a collective trauma, it also is the repetition of a family trauma. For Sethe's near-strangulation, as she helplessly claws at invisible hands and thrashes her feet in the air, is a rememory of the murder of the baby who died by having its throat slit. In this rememory, however, the victimized baby/reincarnated ghost turns the tables and exacts revenge by victimizing Sethe.

"She reminds me of something. Something, look like, I'm supposed to remember," Paul D says of Beloved (234). To Denver, Beloved is her dead sister and at times she is "more" (266). Presented as a textual puzzle to be solved by the reader, Beloved is Sethe's murdered and magically resurrected daughter, but she is also more. If the representation of Beloved as a ghost suggests that Morrison is deliberately playing on the social constructionist notion that race is an empty category, Beloved is also an excessive character that mobilizes and accumulates meaning after meaning as the narrative unfolds, becoming identified not only with Sethe's shameful and painful rememories but also with the collective and disremembered shame and trauma of the slave experience.

Beloved, who "disremember[s] everything" (118), initially reminds Paul D of the displaced, dazed wanderers he saw traveling the roads after the end of the Civil War. Beloved also represents the sexually abused slave woman. Both Sethe and Stamp Paid think that perhaps Beloved has escaped from the clutches of a whiteman-rapist, and Beloved, herself, describes her sexual abuse by white men, who called her "beloved in the dark and bitch in the light" (241). Moreover, when Beloved induces Paul D to have sex with her, he sees her as a promiscuous Jezebel, as a "lowdown something" who has "fixed" him, and he couples with her "in the midst of repulsion and personal shame" (127, 264). Embodying the sexual shame of the slave woman, Beloved becomes a kind of literary container for the shaming stereotypes used by hegemonic culture to define the racial and sexual Otherness of black female identity. She also comes to represent the collective suffering and shame-rage of the "black and angry dead" (198) as well as the psychic woundedness of those who survived the Middle Passage and were victimized by slavery. A powerful presence and yet an empty void, Beloved objectifies the fragmented selfhood of the traumatized victim of slavery, who is aware of "the desolated center where the self that was no self made its home" (140). Moreover, the fact that Beloved comes back as an incarnated ghost conveys not only the peculiar dissociative quality—the depersonalization and derealization—of extreme trauma but also the haunting quality of traumatic and humiliated memory.

After Paul D leaves 124 Bluestone Road, Sethe and her two daughters enter, for a brief period of time, a joy-filled world free of shame and trauma. "She ain't even mad with me," Sethe ironically thinks of Beloved (182) when things initially click into place and she identifies Beloved as her dead but magically resurrected daughter. Sethe, who cannot hear the voices that surround her house "like a noose," shuns the outer world, finding "all there is and all there needs to be" at 124 Bluestone Road (183). She feels she does not have to rememory or say anything because Beloved knows it all and knows that Sethe would never have left her. Because her dead girl has returned home, Sethe can "look at things again" (201). In a section that Morrison has described as "a kind of threnody" in which Sethe and her daughters "exchange thoughts like a dialogue, or a three-way conversation, but unspoken" (Darling 249), the narrative depicts the closed-off world of mother-daughter intimacy and melding identities:

> Beloved
> You are my sister
> You are my daughter
> You are my face; you are me
> I have found you again; you have come back to me
> You are my Beloved
> You are mine
> You are mine
> You are mine (216).

Yet, as is characteristic of Morrison's fiction, the joy and safety of this mother-daughter world of blissful intimacy and merging identities are illusory. For the interior voices of the women, with their "unspeakable thoughts, unspoken" (199), are mixed in with other voices that, nooselike, ring the house. Stamp Paid hears from the road the loud "pack of haunts" (170) that plague 124 Bluestone Road: the "conflagration of hasty voices—loud, urgent, all speaking at once"; the "mumbling of the black and angry dead"; and the "roaring" noise made by the "people of the broken necks, of fire-cooked blood" (172, 198, 181).

Morrison, in describing Beloved's function in the novel, has commented that Beloved, at one and the same time, represents Sethe's resurrected daughter and she also is a survivor from a "true, factual slave ship," who speaks "the language, a traumatized language, of her own experience" (Darling 247). That Beloved's traumatized speech—her song—is presented in fragments that readers must carefully reconstruct points to the incipient textual breakdown at this moment of historical recollection and narrative rememory of the collective experience of the Middle Passage. Through the iconic, sensory word-pictures of her monologue, Beloved tells how she and her mother were captured in Africa by white men, "men without skin," and then placed, like human cattle, in a crowded, filthy slave ship where people were forced to crouch in their own excrement and vomit. Locked in traumatic, dissociated memory, the experience remains fixed, frozen in time:

> All of it is now   it is always now   there will never be a time
> when I am not crouching and watching others who are crouching
> too   I am always crouching   the man on my face is dead. . . .
> we are all trying to leave our bodies behind   the man on my face
> has done it (210).

The slave ship was a hellish place of mass suffering and death where the dead remained next to the living for prolonged periods of time, where the men without skin pushed the "hill of dead people" into the sea (211), and where some captive Africans, like Beloved's mother, who did not like the iron circle around her neck, committed suicide by jumping into the sea. In describing the torments of the slave ships in the traumatized language of Beloved's monologue, the narrative also presents a puzzling, even poetic, text that readers must decode, and thus provides a kind of cognitive-literary shield to protect readers from the abject shame and horror of what is being described. This fragmented narration also enforces reader participation in the careful reconstruction of the trauma- and shame-ridden narrative of the Middle Passage.

Initially, the blissful merging of Sethe and her daughters appears to be healing, a way for Sethe to overcome her traumatic and humiliated rememories. But while Sethe thinks that she can lay down her burdened past and live in peace, she instead becomes involved in a deadly battle for survival. Thus the happy time during which Sethe and her two daughters play together is followed by "furious arguments, the poker slammed up against the wall . . . shouting and crying," which eventually give way to quiet exhaustion as Sethe, Denver, and Beloved become "locked in a love that wore everybody out" (239, 243).

"It was as though her mother had lost her mind . . . ," Denver thinks of Sethe, who becomes entangled in a deadly emotional impasse with Beloved. Attempting to undo the past, Sethe aspires to satisfy the insatiable Beloved, who cannot get enough of anything—"lullabies, new stitches, the bottom of the cake bowl, the top of the milk"—and who, after Sethe runs out of things to give her daughter, invents "desire" (240). Then, when the mood changes and the arguments begin, Beloved complains and Sethe apologizes. The more Beloved takes—"[t]he best chair, the biggest piece, the prettiest plate"—the more Sethe tries to justify the past by describing how much she had endured for the sake of her children. "None of which made the impression it was supposed to. Beloved accused her of leaving her behind. Of not being nice to her, not smiling at her. She said they were the same, had the same face, how could she have left her?" (241). Arriving at a "doomsday truce," the two reenact the infanticide. "Sometimes she [Beloved] screamed, 'Rain! Rain!' and clawed her throat until rubies of blood opened there, made brighter by her midnight skin. Then Sethe shouted, 'No!' and knocked over chairs to get to her and wipe the jewels away" (250). In a repeated drama, Sethe tries to make amends for the handsaw and Beloved makes her pay for what she has done. During the times Beloved becomes quiet and withdrawn, Sethe stirs her up again by "muttering some justification, some bit of clarifying information," forcing Denver to recognize that Sethe does not "really want forgiveness given," but instead wants it "refused" (252).

Sethe, who has been overtaken by the past and caught in an interminable feeling trap, begins to waste away. Denver feels ashamed when she sees Sethe serving Beloved and is deeply pained when she watches her mother, as they run low on food, go without. Over time, Sethe, who gives in to Beloved's incessant demands, becomes depleted, diminished, while Beloved grows fat: "The bigger Beloved got, the smaller Sethe became. . . . Beloved ate up her life, took it, swelled up with it, grew taller on it. And the older woman yielded it up without a murmur" (250).

Describing her creation of the Beloved character, Morrison remarks, "I got to a point where in asking myself who could judge Sethe adequately, since I couldn't, and nobody else that knew her could, really, I felt the only person who could judge her would be the daughter she killed. And from there Beloved inserted herself into the text . . ." (Darling 248). As the judge of Sethe's act, Beloved becomes an actor in the shame-and-blame drama that propels the narrative. Because the victimized daughter comes to victimize her mother, many critic-readers, in turn, judge Beloved in their focus on the novel's depiction of the mother-child relationship. While Beloved has been described as a character who "gives by taking" (Fields 160), she also has often been characterized as a "possessive, demanding tyrant" who becomes "mean-spirited and exploits her mother's pain" (Horvitz 160, 161); as a "demonic" character who is "inhumanly vengeful" and "parasitic" (T. Harris, *Fiction* 153, 158); and as a "succubus" and as "vampirelike" (Demetrakopoulos, "Maternal Bonds" 56, Stave 61; see also Barnett).

Whereas Beloved is often condemned as the destructive and vengeful daughter who represents an enslaving past, Denver, in contrast, is applauded as "the redemptive figure" in the text who "represents the future," or as the "daughter of hope," or the "agent" of the family's "recuperation and regeneration" (Bowers 69, Rushdy 578, Sale 48). Yet while it is Denver's role to ultimately protect the mother she both loves and fears, her story also illustrates that trauma and shame are contagious and can be transmitted from parent to child. Denver, who as an infant swallowed Beloved's blood along with her mother's milk, becomes a stigmatized individual. When Denver is seven, she has almost a year of schooling with Lady Jones, who "did what whitepeople thought unnecessary if not illegal: crowded her little parlor with the colored children who had time for and interest in book learning" (102). Although shunned by the other children because of her spoiled identity, Denver is not aware of the fact that her classmates are avoiding her until Nelson Lord questions her about Sethe's imprisonment for murder. "Didn't your mother get locked away for murder?" he asks Denver. "Wasn't you in there with her when she went?" (104). When Denver then questions Sethe about the infanticide, she goes deaf rather than hear her mother's answer, and she does not experience the return of her hearing until two years later when she hears the sound made by the baby ghost as it crawls up the stairs.

Denver, who lives a constricted and secretive life, keeps watch for the baby ghost and withdraws from everything else. Seeking refuge in her hidden boxwood bower, where she is "closed off from the hurt of the hurt world," she teaches herself "to take pride in the condemnation" that members of the black community place on members of her family (28, 37). While Denver feels safe in the company of the ghost, she views white people as a terrifying and terrorizing evil force and is fearful of the larger world outside 124 Bluestone Road, a place inhabited by schoolteacher and the white men who invaded Baby Suggs's yard. Afraid of the evil that comes from the outside world, and afraid that there may be "something else terrible enough" to make her mother kill again, Denver never leaves the house and watches over the yard "so it can't happen again and my mother won't have to kill me too" (205). Denver, who lives in fear of her mother, rememories the trauma of Beloved's murder: "She cut my head off every night. . . . Her pretty eyes looking at me like I was a stranger" (206).

When Beloved returns from the dead, the lonely Denver bonds with her and wants to protect her from Sethe. Beloved's attentive gaze, unlike the critical, shaming gaze of outsiders, feeds Denver. "It was lovely. Not to be stared at, not seen, but being pulled into view by the interested, uncritical eyes of the other" (118). But with Beloved, Denver also experiences painful rememories—rememories of Beloved's death, of her own fears of self-dissolution, and of the trauma experienced by those on the slave ships. In the cold house with Beloved, Denver feels an overwhelming sense of loss when she discovers that Beloved has disappeared. "If she stumbles, she is not aware of it because she does not know where her body stops, which part of her is an arm, a foot or a knee. She feels like an ice cake torn away from the solid surface of the stream, floating on darkness, thick and crashing against the edges of things around it. Breakable, meltable and cold" (122–23). Experiencing a temporary loss of self, "crying because she has no self," Denver feels "her thickness thinning, dissolving into nothing" (123). Denver's dissociative and annihilatory experience, in turn, mirrors Beloved's disintegration anxieties. When Beloved loses a back tooth, she fears that she is beginning the process of bodily fragmentation—"Next would be her arm, her hand, a toe. Pieces of her would drop maybe one at a time, maybe all at once. Or . . . she would fly apart"—and she dreams that she is either exploding or being swallowed (133).

The vicariously shamed and traumatized Denver at first chooses Beloved over Sethe. But over time, as Denver watches Sethe waste away and realizes that her mother might die, she recognizes that she must ask for help from the community. Afraid of the outside world—"Where words could be spoken that would close your ears shut" and where "there were whitepeople and how could you tell about them?" (243, 244)—a shamefaced and frightened Denver at first walks down the road with lowered head and averted gaze, afraid to look up for fear of encountering white men. Wanting to seek help from someone "who wouldn't shame her on learning that her mother sat around like a rag doll, broke down, finally" (243), Denver eventually finds her way to the home of Lady Jones. That Denver receives assistance from Lady Jones and ultimately from members of the black community, who first provide gifts of food to the starving family and then neighborly support, is suggestive, pointing as it does to the shame-pride script that has governed Sethe's relationship with the community. If many years before Baby Suggs's excessive feast offended people, now the starving family is fed by the black community. "In any case, the personal pride, the arrogant claim staked out at 124 seemed . . . to have run its course" (249).

Enacting a rescue fantasy and illustrating the potentially healing communality of those who have survived a common traumatic experience, *Beloved* describes how thirty women from the community gather at 124 Bluestone Road and drive out the ghost with their cathartic and wordless shout-song. That this holler is driven by collective memories of trauma and shame is revealed in the description of how Ella, who leads the women, recognizes her affinity to Sethe. As Ella recalls being raped by a white man and his son, "the lowest yet," she understands Sethe's rage in the shed many years before, and while Sethe's "crime was staggering and her pride outstripped even that," Ella does not "like the idea of past errors taking possession of the present" (256). When Ella recalls the child fathered by "the lowest yet" which she let die, the thought of "that pup coming back to whip her too set her jaw working, and then Ella hollered" (258–59). As Ella shouts out—her holler recalling the shame-rage heard in the voices of the angry ancestors that encircle 124—she is joined by the others. "They stopped praying and took a step back to the beginning. In the beginning there were no words. In the beginning was the sound, and they all knew what that sound sounded like" (259). As the women search for "the right combination, the key, the code, the sound that broke the back of words," the noise of their voices breaks over Sethe, who trembles "like the baptized in its wash" (261). Sethe, who has been dirtied by schoolteacher's words—his racist discourse—is baptized by the women's shout-song, which breaks "the back of words." And yet, despite the religious and healing import of this description, and despite the soaring lyricism of this passage, which inscribes the transformation of black suffering and rage into aestheticized, literary speech, Sethe's subsequent action—her attack on Bodwin—reveals the continuation of the shame-rage drama enacted in the narrative.

Sethe's act is presented as a kind of vivid textual rememory of slavery and the infanticide. But in this reenactment of the infanticide, Sethe, rather than killing her own daughter, acts to protect her child and to kill the white perpetrator. Mistaking Bodwin for schoolteacher, Sethe is prevented from attacking Bodwin with an ice pick by Denver and by the crowd of women who, in a description evocative of the pile of dead people on the slave ship, "make a hill. A hill of black people, falling" (262). An abolitionist, Bodwin helped Sethe. Not only did the Society Bodwin belonged to manage to "turn infanticide and the cry of savagery around" (260) and thus use Sethe's case to further the abolitionist cause, but Bodwin also was largely responsible for keeping Sethe from the gallows. And yet Bodwin, a man who "hated slavery worse than [he] hated slaves," unthinkingly displays in his house a Sambo figurine coin holder that depicts an African-American boy—with a thrown-back head, bulging eyes, and gaping mouth—kneeling on a pedestal that says "At Yo Service" (137, 255). Despite Bodwin's liberal humanist and abolitionist politics, the racial iconography of the blatantly racist and shaming Sambo figurine speaks volumes about Bodwin's view of the power-imbalanced relationship between blacks and whites, representing as it does the inferior position of blacks in the social and racial order.[6] The narrative also pointedly associates the abolitionist Bodwin with the white slave traders and slave masters by describing how Beloved sees him as the man "with a whip in his hand, the man without skin" (262).

Because Sethe, in this replay of the infanticide, attacks what she believes is the white perpetrator, this scene is often construed by critics as a thera-peutic and self-healing reenactment of the original trauma of the infanticide in which the past is revised or reversed. It has been argued, for example, that Sethe, by directing "her fury at the white source of her agonized condition," leaves behind the past; or that Sethe reenacts and works through the " 'primal scene' " of the infanticide; or that she is purged of her "haunted memory" (Finney 35, Henderson 81, Duvall, "Authentic" 95). But even though the exorcism of the ghost does suggest that Sethe is delivered from her haunted past, some commentators question whether there is redemption in Sethe's attempted murder of Bodwin, which, in signaling Sethe's willingness "to kill again," reveals "the potential for new cataclysms," or they feel that while the novel's conclusion appears to offer an "ambiguous" escape from "a hopeless repetition of action and memory," the "weight of the past" may also imply "a tragic frame for history" (Pesch 402, Scruggs 126). "Events in the United States today make it difficult to agree with readers who claim that the exor-cism of Beloved represents a successful working through of America's racial traumas," writes another critic, who argues that "such optimistic interpre-tations of *Beloved* participate in the repressions and denials of trauma that the novel opposes" (Berger 415).

That Sethe's attack on Bodwin, which can be read as redemptive, is also an act of revenge points to the unresolved interracial conflict and shame-rage feelings that shape *Beloved*'s presentation of black-white relations. "Those white things have taken all I had or dreamed . . . and broke my heartstrings too. There is no bad luck in the world but whitefolks," says the brokenhearted Baby Suggs—the novel's voice of healing and ancestral wisdom—after the infanticide (89). Baby Suggs, who feels "mocked and rebuked by the bloodspill in her backyard" (177), ultimately becomes worn out by her dealings with whites. Like the numbed and paralyzed trauma victim, she retires to her bed where she thinks about the colors of things, a covert reference to the problem of skin color that continues to plague African Americans within the black-white binary of American society. Stamp Paid, too, becomes worn out by white people. "Eighteen seventy-four and white-folks were still on the loose. Whole towns wiped clean of Negroes; eighty-seven lynchings in one year alone in Kentucky; four colored schools burned to the ground; grown men whipped like children; children whipped like adults; black women raped by the crew; property taken, necks broken. He smelled skin, skin and hot blood." When he finds a red ribbon knotted around some woolly hair and still clinging to a piece of scalp, a shocked and horrified Stamp Paid asks, "What *are* these people? You tell me, Jesus. What *are* they?" (180). In constructing whiteness as a terrorizing force and in repeating the racist discourse of purification and pollution by describing the white "cleansing" of towns, these passages also carry out a countershaming agenda by graphically describing the savage and brutal—and shamefully perverse—behavior of whites. Sethe, who once believed that she could "discriminate among" whites, telling the good from the bad, comes to feel that all "news about whitefolks" is "rot" as she recalls how white people buttered Halle's face, made Paul D eat iron, and hanged her own mother (188). In saying that news about whites is "rot," Sethe, by extension, is saying that whites, who have dirtied her, are full of "rot," that is, are dissmelling and dirty objects of contempt and disgust.

Beloved uses a similar countershaming maneuver to describe the "jungle" that whites have planted in blacks as it constructs whiteness and violence as mutually informing categories and locates the source of black shame in white-projected constructions of blackness. "Whitepeople believed that whatever the manners, under every dark skin was a jungle. Swift unnavigable waters, swinging screaming baboons, sleeping snakes, red gums ready for their sweet white blood," thinks Stamp Paid. Using themselves up in their attempt to persuade whites of their gentle and loving nature and their cleverness, blacks grow inside them a "tangled" jungle. "But it wasn't the jungle blacks brought with them to this place from the other (livable) place. It was the jungle white-folks planted in them." When this spreading jungle invades the whites who made it, it makes them "bloody, silly, worse than even they wanted to be, so scared were they of the jungle they had made. The screaming baboon lived under their own white skin; the red gums were their own" (198–99). In reprojecting shaming racist stereotypes of the animalistic, savage African Other back onto its white source and thus recoding whiteness as violence, the narrative works to actively counteract racist ideology and discourse.

The novel's closing scene acts out the desire for rescue and reparation as it gestures toward healing, yet it also points to the haunting, enslaving power of traumatic and humiliated memory. While the description of Beloved as a "beautiful," "[t]hunderblack and glistening" woman standing on "long straight legs" (261) is an image of African pride and power, Beloved, at the same time, evokes the shaming stereotypes of the black woman as the primitive and demonic Other, for the onlookers see Beloved as a "devil-child" or as a naked, pregnant woman "with fish for hair" who runs through the woods (261, 267)—this image of Beloved as a pregnant woman running through the woods recalling the pregnant Sethe's escape from Sweet Home and also anticipating *Jazz*'s description of Wild. And the final dramatic image of Beloved's disappearance—"the girl who waited to be loved and cry shame" explodes and disappears, erupting "into her separate parts" (274; also 263)—recalls earlier descriptions not only of the self-fragmentation of the trauma victim but also of the slave woman as a fragmented commodity. If this description of Beloved's disappearance also suggests that Morrison is playing on the idea that race is an empty category, Morrison, as we shall see, will continue to explore the shame and trauma issues that govern her representation of Beloved in her next novel *Jazz*, in which she, as it were, provides a literary revival of Beloved in the haunting character of Wild.

In its closing scenes, *Beloved* offers a fictive rescue to its characters and holds out hope for the next generation, embodied in Denver. "I'm proud of her. She turning out fine. Fine," Stamp Paid says of the once shamefaced and traumatized Denver (266). When Paul D returns to Sethe, who, like Baby Suggs, has retired to her deathbed, he vows to care for her and to bathe her the way Baby Suggs once did in a symbolic attempt to cleanse the dirtied Sethe. Yet even as the narrative acts out a rescue fantasy in this scene, it conveys lingering doubts by having Sethe ask Paul D if he will count her feet, a reference to his insulting remark that she had two feet and not four. The fact that Sethe wonders whether the parts will hold if Paul D washes her in sections also reveals her continuing fear of self-fragmentation. When Paul D tells Sethe that she is her "best thing," her response—"Me? Me?" (273)—at once suggests the potential for healing and yet also leaves open the question of whether Sethe can ever truly recover from her memories and feelings about her traumatic, shame-ridden past.

Reflecting the text's split perceptions, critics vary in their constructions of the novel's closing rescue scenes: the communal exorcism of Beloved and the reunion of Sethe and Paul D. In a personal response to the novel, one commentator discusses her struggle with the novel's "potentially positive ending." Initially wondering if the "brutalized" Sethe could "find the energy to create from her experiences a healthy family and a viable future," she describes how she came to "accept the possibility of a positive future for

Sethe" in the closure (Atlas, "Toni" 52, 53, 54). Other commentators act out and supplement the novel's rescue fantasy in their insistence that the novel's closure reveals a "therapeutic alternative" to the psychic damage of slavery by depicting "the cooperative self-healing of a community of survivors" or in their claim that at the end Sethe, with the help of Paul D, "has come to the point where she can reclaim her life and love life again" (FitzGerald 685, Carmean 92). But although some commentators feel that readers are "given to hope" that the characters can achieve their "loving claim" or that the novel closes "on a gently forward-looking note," other critic-readers observe that while the novel is "ultimately hopeful about the possibility of community," it also shows that "the past can never be completely escaped," or they remark that "while Sethe is reunited with the black community, Morrison does not offer a reconciliation with white society or an encompassing, pluralistic 'American' society" (Askeland 802, Levy 119, Booker 311, Woidat 542).

The concluding section of the novel also sends out mixed signals and compels readers to explain the text. Beloved, as a representative of the "[d]isremembered and unaccounted for," is "quickly and deliberately" forgotten "like a bad dream," for remembering her seems "unwise" (274). "This is not a story to pass on," the narrative insists (275). Yet, as critics have repeatedly remarked, this authorial injunction is profoundly ironic, given the fact that in *Beloved* Morrison has "passed on" the story of slavery and told of the forgotten "beloveds" unrecorded in history but living and lingering in the collective racial memory. Thus, "This is not a story to pass on" has been taken to mean that Beloved is not a story to "pass by" or "pass over" or that it is "not a story to die" but one to be "passed on" (Krumholz 407, Holloway, "*Beloved*" 517).

And, indeed, *Beloved* is a work that is *passed on*—told and retold in the vast and proliferating critical conversation that surrounds it. Part of the haunting power of the novel derives from the enigmatic character of Beloved. In a representative expression of bewilderment, one commentator writes, "The question 'Who the hell is Beloved?' must haunt every reader of the novel, just as it hounds the characters. . . . Of course Morrison, like any mystery writer, wants us to wonder, and to try to figure it out. But the challenge of decoding and interpreting this spirit is severe . . ." (Broad 190). Although typically identified as Sethe's dead child and also as a survivor of a slave ship, Beloved is also described by critics as a "complex" character who cannot "be pinned down . . . in a final, materially defining sense"; as an elusive character who "dissolves into multiple fragments"; or as a character who is "progressively attenuated, subjected to a form of systematic dispersal" (Carmean 85, Phelan 711, Novak 212). A difficult-to-categorize character, Beloved also has the power to trouble and haunt readers who, in the words of one critic, take on "slavery's haunt" as their "own." In forcing readers "to face the historical past as a living and vindictive presence," *Beloved* "comes to represent the repressed memories of slavery, both for the characters and for the readers" (Krumholz 397, 400).

If *Beloved*'s haunting power stems, in part, from the cognitive puzzles Morrison presents to her readers, it also derives from the visceral immediacy of the novel, which has been described as "a hair-raiser" and as a work that immerses readers in its "spooky world" (Atwood 143, Osagie 426). "I am in Beloved and Beloved is in me," writes one critic, describing his personal response to the novel. "For days I live at 124. . . . The days are intense, difficult, exhausting, rewarding. I reach to understand" (Phelan 709). Again and again commentators make mention of the affective force of the novel as they remark on how the readers' "desire to know more is joined with a concomitant dread of knowing"; or as they describe *Beloved* as a "far from harmless" novel that arouses painful feelings; or as they comment that it is a work that "victimizes" readers, pushing them "into a situation in which they have to grope for meaning, where they are being displaced repeatedly, where they enter spheres of knowledge and experience completely alien to them" (Jessee 203, Bowers 74, Pesch 403). And the fact that critics have remarked that Morrison's novel requires white readers "to occupy the position of the other in all of its abjection" or have asserted that white male readers read the novel "under siege" because they belong to the culture "responsible" for the genocide described in the novel points to the ability of *Beloved* to urge or even compel reader participation in the shame-and-blame drama that it enacts (Travis 186, Todd 43, 49).

Intent on memorializing and honoring the lives of the dishonored, disremembered slaves and properly, artistically burying them, Morrison attempts to transform the shame and pain of slavery into artistic pride in *Beloved*. A novel that has achieved a place of honor in the American literary canon, *Beloved* also is a shame- and trauma-saturated work in which Morrison bears witness to the horrors of slavery and rips the veil drawn over proceedings too terrible to relate. Morrison, who views the literary text as an important site for the production—and potential healing—of African-American culture, speaks the unspeakable in *Beloved* as she dares to penetrate to the dark and disremembered sources of the humiliated and traumatic memories and feelings that continue to haunt the African-American cultural imagination, like a lingering bad dream, in our race-conscious and race-divided American society.

7

"The Dirty, Get-on-Down Music"

CITY PRIDE, SHAME, AND VIOLENCE IN *JAZZ*

In *Jazz* Morrison continues her fictional reconstruction of the African-American historical and cultural legacy, which she began in *Beloved*'s examination of the shame and trauma of slavery, by highlighting the Jazz-age city world of the 1920s. Conceived as the second part of a trilogy that begins with *Beloved* and concludes with Morrison's next novel, *Paradise*, *Jazz* focuses attention on the newfound sense of pride and self-ownership enjoyed by African Americans when they migrated from the South and train-danced their way, like Joe and Violet Trace, to the exuberant, but also dangerous, world of the northern city. Remarking that the black migration from the rural south to northern cities was a "major event in the cultural history" of the United States, Morrison observes that when the ex-slaves moved into the city, they were "running away from something that was constricting and killing them and dispossessing them over and over and over again." Thus, to such migrants, the city "must have seemed so exciting and wonderful, so much the place to be" (Schappell 112). Morrison sets *Jazz* in New York's black Harlem, which she has described as "the closest thing in American life as well as literature to a Black city, and a mecca for generations of Blacks" ("City Limits" 38).[1] Part of Morrison's cultural and artistic agenda in *Jazz* is to communicate what the city "meant" to the second- and third-generation ex-slaves, and in *Jazz*, as in *Beloved*, she also is "concerned with personal life. How did people love one another? What did they think was free?" (Schappell 112).

Elaborating on *Beloved*'s definition of freedom as not needing "permission for desire" (162), *Jazz* explores the exercise of choice in love, a concern Morrison finds expressed in the music of the age. "It's as though the whole tragedy of choosing somebody, risking love, risking emotion, risking sensuality, and then losing it all didn't matter, since it was their choice," she remarks. The music of the jazz age "reinforced the idea of love as a space where one could negotiate freedom," and to people who had been slaves as children or whose parents had been slaves, jazz and the blues also represented the claiming of their "own bodies" and the "ownership" of their "own emotions" (Schappell 113). Yet while Morrison's novel conveys a sense of black pride, hope, and excitement, it also looks back to the unspeakable horrors depicted in *Beloved*, showing how the humiliated and traumatic memories of the white persecution that occurred after the Civil War reverberate in the lives of the characters. During Reconstruction, as Morrison has remarked in her discussion of the early historical context of the novel, there was a "huge backlash" as blacks began to prosper. "Blacks were attacked by white people, including the business community, because they were making a lot of money, were self-sufficient, and were on land that other people wanted. Then the lynchings began to increase. . . . Of course the huge repression of black people prompted many of them to move to places like New York, Chicago, and Detroit—the big industrial centers where there was safety in numbers and where they could make a good life" (Carabi 40). While part of Morrison's aim in *Jazz* is to focus on the black migrants' newfound feelings of self-ownership and freedom, she also represents her characters as driven and determined, in large part, by their troubled pasts as she depicts the unexpected violence of black city life and tells the story of a love relationship gone terribly awry. And *Jazz*, like the other novels we have investigated, gives verbal expression to feelings not only of pride but also of shame and rage as it describes the damaging impact of internalized racism on the construction of African-American identities. The novel's split perceptions are reflected in the term *jazz*, which, as Morrison has remarked, she chose not only because it sums up the "joie de vivre" of 1920s black culture—the "moment when black culture . . . began to alter the whole country"—but also because it "has implications of sex, violence, and chaos," which she also "wanted in the book" (Carabi 41).

The opening passage of the novel, which is designed to jolt readers and provoke their curiosity, describes how the fifty-year-old Joe Trace's "deep-down, spooky" love for the eighteen-year-old Dorcas "made him so sad and happy he shot her just to keep the feeling going," and how Joe's wife, Violet, disrupted the funeral of Dorcas when she attempted to cut the face of the dead girl (3). Commenting on how she put the entire plot of *Jazz* on the first page, Morrison explains that this seemed a "suitable technique" since she viewed the novel's plot focusing on "the threesome" of Violet, Joe, and Dorcas "as the melody of the piece, and it is fine to follow a melody—to feel the satisfaction of recognizing a melody whenever the narrator returns to it." The "real art of the enterprise" for her was "bumping up against that melody time and again, seeing it from another point of view, seeing it afresh each time, playing it back and forth." The "jazz-like structure," Morrison remarks, "wasn't a secondary thing" but was "the raison d'être of the book"; moreover, the "trial and error" process used by the narrator to reveal the plot was "as important and exciting" to her "as telling the story" (Schappell 110). In *Jazz* she "wanted to convey the sense that a musician conveys—that he has more but he's not gonna give it to you. It's an exercise in restraint, a holding back—not because it's not there, or because one had exhausted it, but because of the riches, and because it can be done again" (Schappell 111).

The opening words of *Jazz*—"Sth, I know that woman" (3)—evoke the back-fence world of illicit gossip that so fascinates Morrison. Deliberately using a gossipy, and sometimes intrusive and self-reflexive, narrator in *Jazz*—described by Morrison as the "voice" of the book "talking" to the reader (Carabi 41–42)—Morrison conveys what she has called the "village quality" that Harlem once held for black people ("City Limits" 38). Abruptly, the opening of *Jazz* outlines the facts of Dorcas's murder, and then the narrative, in typical Morrison fashion, slowly circles around this central event as it looks into the shame- and trauma-ridden pasts of the characters and tells the interconnected stories of Joe, Violet, and Dorcas and also the related stories of Alice and Felice. In a jazzlike performance, Morrison's narrative reveals and withholds in the process of telling and then retelling the stories of the characters. This narrative strategy, which Morrison self-consciously uses to provide an improvisational and oral quality to her carefully structured novel, also enacts the withholding and avoidance pattern characteristic of shame and trauma narratives in their exposure of painful secrets.

If Joe is a neighborly and kind man, he also is associated with the lawlessness of the defiant "bad nigger," an oppositional character, as we have seen, that recurs in Morrison's fictional representation of lower-class black masculinity and that, even as it constructs a black folk-heroic figure, also evokes the inter- and intraracist stereotype of the lower-class black male as prone to criminal acts of violence. Remarking on the pride and satisfaction of Thursday men—men who exhibit a "conquering stride in the street" and "command the center of the sidewalk" on Thursdays when they enjoy their "outlaw love" (50, 49)—the narrator describes how male pride inevitably turns to shame-anger, which is what ultimately happens to Joe Trace. In a textual rehearsal of Joe's murder of Dorcas, the narrator comments that the expansive sexual pride and satisfaction of Thursday men "doesn't last of course, and twenty-four hours later they are frightened again and restoring themselves with any helplessness within reach. So the weekends, destined to disappoint, are strident, sullen, sprinkled with bruises and dots of blood" (50). In his affair with Dorcas, which leads to her eventual murder, the middle-aged Joe Trace thinks he is "free to do something wild." Instead, he is "bound to the track," which "pulls him like a needle through the groove of a Bluebird record. Round and round about the town. That's the way the City spins you. Makes you do what it wants, go where the laid-out roads say to. All the while letting you think you're free . . ." (120).

In the city, people have to know "[w]hen to love something and when to quit" or they, like Joe, "can end up out of control or controlled by some outside thing" (9). Insisting on the music's seductive, but also dangerous, pull on people, *Jazz* blames Dorcas's plight, in part, on the "Come and do wrong" music (67). In Morrison's novel, jazz music is ambivalently constructed as a sign of the transgressive and improvisational, on the one hand, and the lawless and out-of-control, on the other. Just as Joe's "outlaw" (49) and thus bluesy love ends in violence, Violet's behavior at Dorcas's funeral is inspired by the desire to "do something bluesy, something hep" (114) and by her imitation of a standard blues scenario in which the woman fights for her man, and she, too, evokes the intra- and interracist stereotype of the lower-class black as potentially irrational and violent. In placing Joe's murder of Dorcas and Violet's violation of the corpse at the center of her novel and suggesting that the nonvolitional behavior of Violet, Joe, and Dorcas is blues-inspired, Morrison runs the risk of being accused of reinforcing the racial coding of violence found in dominant representations of black urban culture as a site of lawlessness, crime, and social decay. But Morrison also investigates the reasons for her characters' behavior, showing that her memory-haunted characters are driven to repeat—that they are caught up in the repetition of their traumatic pasts.

As is typical of Morrison's fiction, the narrative interruptions and recurrences in *Jazz* evoke the disrupted narrative pattern found in the recollection of traumatic and humiliated memories. In a jazzlike way Morrison also replays and plays on themes and characters from her earlier work in *Jazz*, which reads, in part, like a textual reprise or rememory of her earlier works. Through the cryptic character of Wild, who comes to represent the stigmatized racial and sexual Otherness of black female identity, *Jazz* extends and makes an intertextual commentary on the story of the ghostly Beloved. Morrison signals the Beloved-Wild connection—something she has made mention of in her public remarks on the novel (Carabi 43)—by depicting Wild as a naked pregnant girl running in the woods, which is the reader's final image of Beloved. Moreover, aspects of Wild/Beloved, as we shall see, are also repeated in the character of Dorcas. Through the inset story of Golden Gray, the apparent white male who is, in fact, black-fathered and who has a dramatic encounter with Wild, Morrison not only continues her investigation of the stigma of black identity, she also portrays what she, in her critical writing, has called the Africanist presence in white culture and literature. Morrison's use of this character also looks back to *The Bluest Eye*, for Golden Gray, the blond boy who has come to inhabit Violet's mind as a false identity, recalls Pecola's internalization of a blond-haired white identity. Repeating Morrison's deliberate pairing of conventional, middle-class characters and unconventional, lower-class characters, such as *Sula*'s Nel and Sula or *Song of Solomon*'s Ruth and Pilate, *Jazz* continues Morrison's investigation of issues of class and shame within the African-American community through its representation of Alice and Violet as paired opposites. And central to *Jazz* is Morrison's ongoing novelistic investigation of the effects of trauma and shame on the construction of African-American identities, for in *Jazz*, as in her other works, Morrison lays stress on the psychic damage caused not only by family trauma—in particular, maternal abandonment or rejection—but also by inter- and intraracial shaming and violence.

In an implicit intertextual contrast to *Beloved*'s shame drama, *Jazz* describes the expansive pride and power felt by the black migrants living in Harlem in the 1920s. To move from the rural South to the city North, *Jazz* suggests, is seemingly to move to a new position on the shame-pride axis. Yet while *Jazz*'s depiction of city pride derives in part from Morrison's attempt to convey how the black migrants felt about the city, it also recalls *Beloved*'s account of the conspiracy of silence surrounding the trauma of slavery, the desire of the ex-slaves and the generations after them to consciously "forget" the past. When the black migrants, who are "running from want and violence," come to the city, they fall in love with it. "There, in a city, they are not so much new as themselves: their stronger, riskier selves" (33). The city exerts a kind of "fascination, permanent and out of control," that "seizes children, young girls, men of every description, mothers, brides, and barfly women, and if they have their way and get to the City, they feel more like themselves, more like the people they always believed they were. Nothing can pry them away from that . . ." (35). To the *Jazz* narrator, "A city like this one makes me dream tall and feel in on things. Hep. . . . When I look over strips of green grass lining the river, at church steeples and into the cream-and-copper halls of apartment buildings, I'm strong." In 1926 when "all the wars are over and there will never be another one," people are "happy about that." Miming the optimistic mood and jazzy-bluesy voice of the postwar 1920s, the *Jazz* narrator remarks that the "bad stuff" and "sad stuff" of history, the "things-nobody-could-help stuff," is over. "Forget that. History is over, you all, and everything's ahead at last" (7).

If the city is a locus of black pride, hope, and power, it also is a place of black shame and fear. *Jazz* describes, for example, how Dorcas's father dies in the East St. Louis riots, in which two hundred blacks are killed. Even though Dorcas's father is not involved in the riots and has no weapons and does not confront anyone on the street, he nevertheless becomes a target of mob violence. After he is pulled off a streetcar and "stomped to death,"

Dorcas's mother burns to death when her house is torched (57). *Jazz* makes overt references to the catastrophic traumas suffered by blacks as a result of white racist terrorism, and it also describes the racial harassment experienced by blacks in the city. Alice Manfred, who becomes acutely aware of the social geography of New York City, learns that to travel out of Harlem is to become the potential target of white harassment and humiliation. When Alice ventures onto Fifth Avenue, a place racially coded as off-limits to African Americans, she is hypervisible to whites, who treat her like a black Jezebel or as someone who is tainted and dirty. "That was where whitemen leaned out of motor cars with folded dollar bills peeping from their palms. It was where salesmen touched her and only her as though she were part of the goods they had condescended to sell her; it was the tissue required if the management was generous enough to let you try on a blouse (but no hat) in a store. It was where she, a woman of fifty and independent means, had no surname. Where women who spoke English said, 'Don't sit there, honey, you never know what they have'" (54). When Alice takes charge of her niece, the orphaned Dorcas, she instructs her about the value and necessity of being deaf and blind "in the company of whitewomen who spoke English and those who did not, as well as in the presence of their children" (54–55). Alice also teaches Dorcas "how to crawl along the walls of buildings, disappear into doorways, cut across corners in choked traffic—how to do anything, move anywhere to avoid a whiteboy over the age of eleven" (55).

Alice, who has been subjected to racial harassment, has been afraid "for a long time—first she was frightened of Illinois, then of Springfield, Massachusetts, then Eleventh Avenue, Third Avenue, Park Avenue. Recently she had begun to feel safe nowhere south of 110th Street, and Fifth Avenue was for her the most fearful of all" (54). After the murder of Dorcas, Alice's feelings of city danger are intensified as she comes to fear black-on-black violence. To the middle-class Alice, who has internalized racist assumptions fostered by hegemonic culture, Joe and Violet Trace embody not only lower-class lawlessness but also black shame and violence. Alice sees Joe and Violet as the "embarrassing" and "dangerous" kind of black people she had trained Dorcas to avoid: people Alice associates with vice and flashy clothes—red dresses and yellow shoes—and "race music to urge them on" (79). Alice, who recalls earlier Morrison middle-class characters, like *The Bluest Eye*'s Geraldine or *Song of Solomon*'s Ruth Dead or *Tar Baby*'s Ondine, shuns the "dirty, get-on-down" jazz music of the age, which she associates with the unlicensed sexuality and violence of lower-class-black city life (58).[2] When Joe Trace—who initially seems to be a "nice, neighborly, everybody-knows-him man" (73)—proves to be a murderer, Alice feels "truly unsafe because the brutalizing men and their brutal women were not just out there, they were in her block, her house." Alice reads newspapers differently after Dorcas's death, seeing in them a record of urban violence against women: "a paper laid bare the bones of some broken woman. Man kills wife. Eight accused of rape dismissed. Woman and girl victims of. Woman commits suicide. White attackers indicted. Five women caught. Woman says man beat. In jealous rage man" (74).

If *Jazz*, in part, reproduces the culturally entrenched representation of lower-class blacks as potentially dangerous and violent by placing the crime of murder perpetrated by a man in a jealous rage at the thematic and emotional center of the text, it also works to minimize and aestheticize the criminal act it depicts by presenting the murder as a kind of blues-inspired spectacle or performance. Obsessively circling around the murder, the narrative, even as it exposes the secrets of the central characters—all of whom are represented as both victims and aggressors—also seems engaged in an attempt to gloss over the violence of Dorcas's death. As it explains why Joe killed Dorcas and why Violet attempted to mutilate the corpse, *Jazz* traces the histories of the murder victim, Dorcas, and the victimizers, Violet and Joe Trace, but it also presents Dorcas as an aggressor and Joe and Violet as victims. The fact that the *Jazz* narrator is ultimately identified as the imaginative source of the shame-rage that pervades the text, as we shall see, also seems designed to obscure the violence at the heart of the novel. Countering the 1920s progressive and optimistic view of history—that the "bad" and "sad" stuff of history is over—*Jazz*, like *Beloved*, focuses attention on the traumatic and humiliated memories that are part of the black cultural memory as it places the early family histories of the characters against the larger backdrop of the pervasive white racist violence and oppression that existed in the postbellum rural South and the cities of the North.

"Mama. Mama? Is this where you got to and couldn't do it no more?" wonders the fifty-year-old Violet, a "bootblack" dark and "pick thin" woman with "slicked back" hair (110, 206). Despite her strong and masculine appearance, Violet is a woman whose "public craziness" reveals her lack of a "foundation," that is, a coherent and stable sense of self (22, 23). If Violet is initially presented as a textual puzzle, *Jazz*, in reconstructing Violet's history, explains her "crazy" behavior, showing it to be symptomatic of her troubled family past. "[T]he children of suicides are hard to please and quick to believe no one loves them because they are not really here," the *Jazz* narrator remarks of Violet at the outset of the novel (4). When Violet, in her middle years, begins to exhibit the "private cracks" in her foundationless life (22), she, in essence, is memorializing the death of her mother, Rose Dear, who committed suicide by jumping into a well when Violet was a girl.

Violet, who determines never to be like her mother, recalls Rose Dear's paralyzed response to the repossession of the family's goods and property. In a scene of abject humiliation, Rose Dear is treated contemptuously, like a tainted object, when the white men, after removing the plow and scythe and mule and sow, come into the house and take the table out from under Rose Dear, who sits with an empty white china cup in her hand. The men tip her out of the chair "the way you get the cat off the seat if you don't want to touch it or pick it up in your arms. You tip it forward and it lands on the floor. No harm done if it's a cat because it has four legs. But a person, a woman, might fall forward and just stay there a minute looking at the cup, stronger than she is, unbroken at least and lying a bit beyond her hand. Just out of reach" (98). Despite the comforting presence of Rose's mother, True Belle—the "chuckling, competent" woman who comes to take care of the family and who stitches by firelight and gardens and harvests during the day—Rose Dear commits suicide four years after True Belle's arrival by jumping down a well. The *Jazz* narrator's speculations on the cause of Rose Dear's suicide—the "final thing" that she was unable to "endure or repeat"— points to the daily humiliations and catastrophic traumas suffered by African Americans in the postbellum South. "Had the last washing split the shirtwaist so bad it could not take another mend and changed its name to rag? Perhaps word had reached her about the four-day hangings in Rocky Mount. . . . Or had it been the news of the young tenor in the choir mutilated and tied to a log, his grandmother refusing to give up his waste-filled trousers, washing them over and over although the stain had disappeared at the third rinse. . . . Or was it that chair they tipped her out of? Did she fall on the floor and lie there deciding right then that she would do it. Someday?" In *Jazz*, as in other Morrison novels, the search for family and cultural roots involves the recovery of painful and shaming memories of racial domination and white supremacist terrorism: memories, like Rose Dear's, of "mewing hurt or over-board rage" (101).

Continuing *Beloved*'s examination of the legacy of slavery and racist oppression, *Jazz* slowly exposes toxic family secrets as it reveals the familial and cultural origins of Violet's troubled selfhood. Like Violet, Joe remains troubled by his past, and he too is a mother-haunted person. When told as a child that his real parents "disappeared without a trace," Joe thinks that he is the "trace" his parents disappeared without, and thus when he discovers in school that he needs a surname, he calls himself "Joseph Trace" (124). While Joe never solves the mystery of his parentage, vigilant readers of Morrison's novels can surmise Joe's family roots. As Morrison has remarked, "Wild is a kind of Beloved. . . . You see a pregnant black woman naked at the end of *Beloved*," and "at the same time . . . in the Golden Gray section of *Jazz*, there is a crazy woman out in the woods." Thus, Wild "could be Sethe's daughter, Beloved," who may be either a ghost or a real person who has been impregnated by Paul D and who "runs away, ending up in Virginia, which is right next to Ohio" (Carabi 43). This suggests that the Beloved who disappears so that "[b]y and by all trace is gone" (*Beloved* 275) is Joe's wildwoman mother, who similarly disappears "without a trace," and thus Joe is the son of Beloved and Paul D.

To Joe, the local crazy woman—Wild—is at first an object of fear, and then, as he grows older, little more than a joke. "[S]he ain't prey," says Hunters Hunter when Joe and another boy jokingly speculate on what it would take to kill Wild. When Hunter looks directly at Joe and says that Wild "is *somebody's* mother and *somebody* ought to take care," Joe begins to wrestle with the idea that Wild is his mother (175). Even as he tries to convince himself that he has misconstrued Hunter's remarks, Joe becomes obsessed with Wild, and he is alternately ashamed or angry at the thought that he has a madwoman for a mother.

Joe's ensuing quest for Wild is presented as a shame drama. During his first search, he ends up near the opening of Wild's cave, where he is aware of a disgusting odor that combines the smells of honey and shit. When Joe returns to Wild's cave a second time after the dispossession, he finds no sign of her in the cave but thinks that he hears her breathing in the hibiscus bushes growing nearby when he sights the birds that mark her presence: red-winged blackbirds. Begging for some sign from her, pleading that she show him her hand, he suddenly feels deeply ashamed as he paws around "in the dirt for a not just crazy but also dirty woman who happened to be his secret mother. . . . Leaving traces of her sloven unhousebroken self all over the county. Shaming him . . ." (178). A woman who is so "brain-blasted" that she does not do "what the meanest sow managed: nurse what she birthed," Wild is an "indecent speechless lurking insanity" (179). Using a discursive repertoire of derogatory racist stereotypes to construct Wild in this scene, *Jazz* depicts Joe's mother as a shamed object of contempt: an embodiment of racial, biological, and sexual otherness. Primitive and uncivilized, Wild is a dirty, degenerate, animalistic creature. In *Jazz*, as in other Morrison novels we have investigated, the search for family roots and the slave legacy leads to a painful confrontation with racial shame. And yet Joe desperately wants some sign of recognition from his mother, some acknowledgment that he is her son. "Maybe she did it. Maybe those were her fingers moving like that in the bush . . . maybe he missed the sign that would have been some combination of shame and pleasure, at least, and not the inside nothing he traveled with from then on . . ." (37).

Despite the adult Joe's claim that he has been "a new Negro"[3] all his life (129), he remains a mother- and shame-haunted person, and like Violet, who lacks a solid foundation, he similarly knows what the "inside nothing" of self is like. In tracing Joe's repeated creations of new social identities—like the American self-made and new man, the "new Negro" Joe repeatedly re-creates himself—*Jazz* chronicles, in part, the social history of African Americans from the 1870s to the 1920s, focusing attention on the racist and economic oppression that they confronted and that shaped their identities. As the middle-aged Joe reviews his life, he marks the emergence of the first version of himself by his self-naming—calling himself Trace—and the emergence of his second self by his relationship with Hunters Hunter, who trains him to be a man—a hunter—so he can be independent and provide food for himself no matter what happens. Joe changes for the third time in 1893 when his home-town, Vienna, Virginia, is burned to the ground, the "fire doing fast what white sheets took too long to finish: canceling every deed; vacating each and every field; emptying us out of our places so fast we went running from one part of the county to another—or nowhere" (126). It is against this background of trauma and dispossession that Joe and Violet meet, and Violet not only claims ownership of Joe, but in order to win him she becomes a "powerfully strong young woman who could handle mules, bale hay and chop wood as good as any man. . . . [T]he palms of her hands and the soles of her feet grew shields no gloves or shoes could match. All for Joe Trace . . . who was willing" (105–06).

After Joe and Violet marry, they struggle to survive in the post-Reconstruction South. Working as sharecroppers on the worst land in the county, the two spend years of extra labor paying off their debt. In 1901, Joe changes for a third time when Booker T. Washington has a chicken sandwich with the President at the White House. Emboldened, Joe buys some land, foolishly believing that whites will allow him to keep it. "They ran us off," he recalls, "with two slips of paper I never saw nor signed" (126). Joe's fourth change occurs in 1906 when he and Violet move to the city where, at first, they struggle to survive, Violet going into service and Joe taking on various menial jobs. When they leave behind the stench of Mulberry Street and Little Africa and the rats on West Fifty-third Street and move uptown, Joe changes for a fifth time. Ultimately, Joe ends up doing hotel work and selling Cleopatra beauty products on the side while Violet works as a hair-dresser,[4] and they move to Lenox Avenue, where the buildings are like castles but where they also must fight the light-skinned renters who try to keep them from moving in. Joe becomes brand-new for the sixth time when he is almost killed during the 1917 riots by some white men, who hit him on the head with a pipe, and he becomes the seventh Joe in 1919 when he proudly marches down the street with the black troops who fought in the First World War.

As a "new Negro," Joe experiences moments of pride in the city world of Harlem, but he also, like Violet, remains haunted by his shame-ridden past. Despite the fact that Joe and Violet Trace—Morrison's representative migrant couple—happily train-dance into the city as migrants and despite the measurable economic gains they make after they leave the rural South and move to the city, nearly twenty years later, the middle-aged Joe and Violet are still together but are scarcely talking to each other and by 1925 Violet has begun to sleep with a doll in her arms.

As a middle-aged woman, Violet, who was once a "snappy, determined girl and a hardworking young woman, with the snatch-gossip tongue of a beautician," begins to exhibit her "private cracks" (23, 22). "I call them cracks," explains the *Jazz* narrator, "because that is what they were. Not openings or breaks, but dark fissures in the globe light of the day" (22). Experiencing the dissociative state of altered consciousness called "depersonalization"—in which individuals report feeling a sense of unreality about the self or that the real self is distanced or that they are observing the self from the outside (Steinberg 62)—Violet visualizes well-lit scenes in which daily food or work tasks are being done but she is not the one doing them. Lacking a solid inner foundation, Violet sometimes "stumbles" onto the "cracks" in her consciousness—like the time she sits down in the middle of the street or the occasions she feels the "anything-at-all begin in her mouth" as her "renegade tongue" speaks words "connected only to themselves" (23, 24, 23). Violet, who also experiences the co-consciousness that sometimes occurs in dissociative states (see Waites 124), comes to wonder "who on earth that other Violet" is who walks around the city "in her skin" and looks out "through her eyes" but sees "other things" (89). Invoking the racially coded dominant discourse of pathology, the narrative constructs Violet as an irrational and a potentially dangerous woman. While Violet has forgotten that the knife is in the parrot's cage, the other Violet—*that* Violet—retrieves the knife and knows where Dorcas's funeral is being held and when to arrive. It is not Violet but *that* Violet who aims the knife at the dead Dorcas's arrogant face, and who, animallike, is carried kicking and growling out of the funeral home; it is *that* Violet who feels rage and resentment as she imagines Joe's tenderness to the high-yellow Dorcas, the heifer who took what belonged to Violet; it is *that* Violet who is strong and powerful and who, instead of feeling shame and disgust at what she did at Dorcas's funeral, feels proud of the fact that she tried to kill a dead girl.

"[Q]uiet as it's kept," Violet did try to steal the baby even if there is "no way to prove it," reports the *Jazz* narrator (17), describing one of Violet's more notorious acts of public craziness: the kind of behavior that makes Violet the target of the shaming gaze and gossip of the neighborhood people. When Violet walks off with a baby that she has agreed to watch for a few minutes, she is accused of stealing the child. At the time, she loudly protests her innocence to the crowd of people gathered on the street, and many years later she still views the kidnapping accusation as "an outrage to her character." Despite Violet's denials, the memory of "the light . . . that had skipped through her veins" when she held the light-skinned child occasionally comes back to her, and she sometimes imagines "a brightness that could be carried in her arms" and "[d]istributed, if need be, into places dark as the bottom of a well" (22).

In the child-stealing episode, as the narrative ultimately explains, the childless Violet, who has had three miscarriages, expresses her intense "mother-hunger," a longing that becomes "heavier than sex: a panting, unmanageable craving." Violet's mother-hunger drives her to buy a doll, which she hides under the bed and takes out in secret or sleeps with in her arms, and it also leads to her "deep-dreaming" imaginings about her last miscarried child, whom she envisions as a daughter. "Who would she favor?" Violet wonders. "What would her speaking voice sound like?" (108). When Violet—who imagines herself feeding, singing with, and dressing the hair of her fantasized daughter—wakes up from her deep-dreaming, Joe has shot Dorcas, a girl who is young enough to be Violet's daughter, the very daughter whose hair Violet had "dressed to kill." In a self-conscious, if not parodic, invocation of psychoanalytic discourse, the narrative makes explicit the oedipal dynamics of the rivalrous triangular relationship between Violet, Dorcas, and Joe in which Dorcas (the daughter) becomes the rival of Violet (the mother) for the affections of Joe (the father). As Violet sorts through her conflicted feelings about Dorcas, she wonders, "Who lay there asleep in that coffin? . . . The scheming bitch who had not considered Violet's feelings one tiniest bit, who came into a life, took what she wanted and damn the consequences? Or mama's dumpling girl? Was she the woman who took the man, or the daughter who fled her womb?" (109). To Violet, who places a photograph of the dead Dorcas on the fireplace mantle in her parlor, the memory of the dead girl "is a sickness in the house—everywhere and nowhere" (28).

The yearned-for daughter, Dorcas also is the light-skinned rival who steals the husband of the dark-skinned Violet, and indeed Violet thinks that perhaps part of what attracted Joe to Dorcas was the girl's hair and skin color. Yet even as Violet finds herself losing the grief-stricken Joe to the dead girl, she begins to wonder if she, too, is falling in love with Dorcas. "When she isn't trying to humiliate Joe, she is admiring the dead girl's hair; when she isn't cursing Joe with brand-new cuss words, she is having whispered conversations with the corpse in her head . . ." (15). Focusing attention on the loaded issue of skin color, *Jazz* reveals that Violet, who reports that she is "having trouble" with her head (80), has internalized a white identity as an idealized version of self. Like *The Bluest Eye*'s Pecola, Violet has a blond child living inside her mind. As Violet comes to recognize, she "messed up" her life because she "[f]orgot" it was hers. Instead of accepting her black identity, she wished she were "White. Light," an impulse Violet traces to her grandmother's stories about Golden Gray, the golden-skinned, blond child True Belle once cared for. "He was a boy, but I thought of him as a girl sometimes, as a brother, sometimes as a boyfriend. He lived inside my mind. Quiet as a mole" (208). If Violet's attempted kidnapping of the baby with a "honey-sweet, butter-colored face" (19) and her fantasy that the dead Dorcas might be her daughter are symptomatic of the middle-aged woman's intense mother-hunger, they also express Violet's desire to appropriate a white identity. Moreover, the fact that Violet keeps a parrot, which has a "green and blond head" and repeatedly tells her "Love you," enacts, even as it parodies, Violet's need for white approbation (93). Violet's ultimate recognition of her need to kill the blond child inhabiting her mind—that is, to rid herself of this white introject—so that she can discover her own me-ness not only revisits and rewrites Pecola's story in *The Bluest Eye* but also casts light on Violet's symbolic "killing" of the dead Dorcas.

Creating the sense, even as it exposes secrets, of withholding information from readers, *Jazz* looks to the past to explain the present. In the inset and delayed story of Golden Gray, which is a deliberately designed imitation of a nineteenth-century American romance tale, *Jazz* deals with hurtful issues concerning African-American identity. Initially presented as a linear quest story until the elusive Wild erupts onto the scene, the Golden Gray story reads, in part, as a fictionalization of Morrison's theoretical discussions about the Africanist presence in white-authored American literature. But as is typical of Morrison's work, the Golden Gray story also uses mythic and literary containers to master and distance its disturbing racial—and emotional—content.

In *Playing in the Dark*, Morrison analyzes the cultural and literary construction of what she calls "American Africanism." Arguing that "the imaginative and historical terrain upon which early American writers journeyed is in large measure shaped by the presence of the racial other," Morrison insists that "the Africanist presence informs in compelling and inescapable ways the texture of American literature. It is a dark and abiding presence, there for the literary imagination as both a visible and an invisible mediating force" (46). In the construction of American identity, American is equated with white while the Africanist presence is constructed as "decidedly not American, decidedly other" (48). A white "projection of the not-me" onto blacks, American Africanism is "a fabricated brew of darkness, otherness, alarm, and desire that is uniquely American" (38). Pointing to the shame-pride issues that undergird the construction of American Africanism, Morrison writes, "Africanism is the vehicle by which the American self knows itself as not enslaved, but free; not repulsive, but desirable; not helpless, but licensed and powerful . . . ; not a blind accident of evolution, but a progressive fulfillment of destiny" (52). Thus, "Africanism is inextricable from the definition of Americanness . . ." (65). In the Golden Gray story, Morrison, in part, presents a parody of nineteenth-century novelistic discourse of the New World white male, the gentleman who is "backgrounded by savagery," as she describes it in *Playing in the Dark* (44). And in the character of Wild, a revival and revisioning of Beloved, she depicts the "dark, abiding, signing Africanist presence" (5) in American literature and also illustrates the inherent shaming involved in the racial othering of black Americans.

Called "Golden" because of his "radiantly golden" skin and "sunlight" colored hair (139), Golden Gray is the son of Hunters Hunter, who remains unaware of the fact he has fathered a son by the white Vera Louise Gray. Ostracized by her parents when they discover that she is pregnant by a black man, Vera Louise and her slave, True Belle, leave Virginia and begin a new life in Baltimore. Thrilled by the baby's golden color, Vera Louise, rather than placing her son in the Catholic Foundling Hospital "where whitegirls deposited their mortification" (148), decides to raise him herself, and so she tells other people that he is an orphan she has taken in. "[G]iven a fussy spoiling by Vera Louise and complete indulgence by True Belle" (140), Golden Gray is brought up as a privileged white male, and by age eighteen, he has become the perfect gentleman. On learning that his father is a "black-skinned nigger," he shows a "cavalierlike courage" as he sets out to find his father (143, 142–43). Typecasting Golden Gray as a nineteenth-century gentleman-hero, the *Jazz* narrator pictures him riding in a two-seated, open carriage drawn by a fine black horse and bringing with him a large truck, which is crammed with beautiful shirts, linens, and silver toiletries. Unlike Milkman Dead's quest for the "golden" legacy of his racial and cultural heritage, the goal of Golden Gray's quest is "to insult not his father but his race," and, if he is "lucky," to kill his father (143).

What Morrison finds implicit in traditional nineteenth-century American literature she makes explicit in her story of Golden Gray's encounter with the "dark" and "abiding" presence of American Africanism in the "decidedly other" figure of Wild, who literally erupts onto the scene and into the narrative. In a continuation of the story of the haunting figure of Beloved, Morrison deliberately associates Wild with Beloved. Beloved-like, Wild laughs a "low sweet babygirl laugh" when she haunts the cane fields—her attraction to cane pointing to her Beloved-like affinity for sweet things (37). More significantly, when Golden Gray encounters Wild, she is a young, naked, berry-black, and pregnant woman who is mud-covered and has leaves in her hair—a description that is meant to recall the conclusion of *Beloved*, which recounts how the naked Beloved, who is pregnant with Paul D's child, disappears into the woods (see Carabi 43). Reinforcing the Wild-Beloved connection, Golden Gray initially thinks that what he has seen is "not a real woman but a 'vision'" (144). Moreover, the traumatized Wild's terror at the sight of Golden Gray—a white-appearing man who wears a hat and travels in a horse-drawn carriage—brings to mind Beloved's fear of white men and, in an intertextual repetition of a trauma, it replays Beloved's response, just before her disappearance, to the sight of Bodwin/schoolteacher. This scene, in a more general way, also recalls the recurring representations in Morrison's fiction of whiteness as a terrorizing or terrifying force.

Viewed through Golden Gray's shaming gaze, Wild is a dirty and repulsive object and someone who provokes a feeling of nausea: that is, a disgust response. Constructing Wild's black skin as a marker of her racial-biological difference, Golden Gray perceives her as the stigmatized and biologically impure Other. When he leans down to examine Wild—who has knocked herself unconscious in her frantic attempt to run away from him—he holds his breath "against infection or odor or something. Something that might touch or penetrate him" (144). But because he is uneasy with the picture of himself leaving the unconscious and pregnant Wild behind, he gathers her up in his arms and takes her in his carriage to his father's house, amused at the idea of meeting his "nigger" father while carrying "an armful of black, liquid female" (145). Golden Gray feels that the "Black and nothing" Wild will serve as a "proper protection against and anodyne to" what he believes his father, and thus himself, to be (149). Yet even as Golden Gray perceives Wild as the unrestrained and uncivilized Other, there is also a part of him that wants to "wallow in" her leafy hair and "unfathomable" black skin (150). Thinking that the exposed Wild will, Beloved-like, "explode in his arms, or worse, that he will, in hers," Golden Gray finds everything about her "violent," and yet he also finds himself attracted to the "savage" black girl (153, 155).

"[T]he subject of the dream is the dreamer," Morrison writes in *Playing in the Dark*, describing how the fabricated Africanist persona provides an "astonishing revelation" of white fears and desires: "of longing, of terror, of perplexity, of shame, of magnanimity" (17). If American "coherence" is organized "through a distancing Africanism"—a "fabricated brew of darkness, otherness, alarm, and desire" (8, 38)—Morrison, through the staged encounter between Golden Gray and Wild, is intent on exposing the projective processes at work in the cultural construction of the new white American male. And by showing how the black-fathered Golden Gray finds himself sexually attracted to Wild and her unfathomable black skin despite his initial attempts to preserve the coherence of his white identity by keeping Wild distanced and contained, *Jazz* subverts and also rewrites the classic script of nineteenth-century American literature. Moreover, by focusing on Golden Gray's mixed racial origins, the narrative questions the social logic of received racial categories. As Valerie Smith has observed in her discussion of narratives of racial passing, which feature characters who are legally black but pass as white, "The light-skinned black body . . . both invokes and transgresses the boundaries between the races. . . . It indicates a contradiction between appearance and 'essential' racial identity within a system of racial distinctions based upon differences presumed to be visible" (45).

If in the preface to *Playing in the Dark* Morrison remarks that her "vulnerability" as a writer would be in "vilifying whiteness rather than reifying it" (xi), in *Jazz* she uses her intrusive *Jazz* narrator to, in effect, work on or correct this potential authorial fault. The *Jazz* narrator, although initially exposing Golden Gray's racist attitudes and calling attention to his unheroic selfishness and self-involvement, comes to sympathize with him. At first the *Jazz* narrator finds it difficult to get past the fact that Golden Gray thinks of his clothes first and not the unconscious woman, and when Golden Gray rehearses the story he will tell his father about how he rescued Wild, the narrator calls him a liar and a hypocrite. But then the *Jazz* narrator recognizes that the young Golden Gray "is hurting," and so forgives him "his self-deception and his grand, fake gestures," which the narrator comes to see as shame-based behavior (155). Made aware that he has a father, Golden Gray feels his father's absence—"the place where he should have been and was not"—which he compares to the loss of an arm (158). "Who will take my part? Soap away the shame? . . . Will he?" Golden Gray wonders. "What do I care what the color of his skin is, or his contact with my mother? When I see him, or what is left of him, I will tell him all about the missing part of me and listen for his crying shame. I will exchange then; let him have mine and take his as my own and we will both be free, arm-tangled and whole" (159). By professing Golden Gray's desire to take ownership of his projected shame and to embrace his own "blackness," *Jazz* acts out a reparative fantasy. "What was I thinking of?" asks the *Jazz* narrator. "How could I have imagined him so poorly? Not noticed the hurt that was not linked to the color of his skin . . ." (160). The *Jazz* narrator, who admits to being an "unreliable" storyteller, wants to "alter things," to "dream a nice dream" for Golden Gray and "be the language that wishes him well" (160, 161).

Despite the *Jazz* narrator's healing gesture, the shame issues that impel the Golden Gray story resurface when the story resumes. On first seeing his father, Golden Gray stares at him through the shaming eyes of a white man, his gaze "like a tongue" (169). "I know what you came for. To see how black I was. You thought you was white, didn't you?" remarks Hunters Hunter, who is suggestively named Henry Lestory: that is, "the story," or "the (real or black) story" (172). Even as the narrative subverts the notion of rigid racial categories in its depiction of Golden Gray's mixed racial origins, it also insists on the importance of a black-identified cultural affiliation. "Be what you want—white or black. Choose," Hunter tells an enraged Golden Gray who, in response, thinks about taking a gun and blowing off his father's head (173). If *Jazz* acts out a reparative fantasy by depicting the love relation between Golden Gray and Wild—which is suggested in the mutual attraction of the two and in the fact that Joe later finds Golden Gray's clothes in Wild's cave—it also subsequently undermines this healing gesture by describing Joe's killing of Dorcas-Wild-Beloved.

That Morrison, while she was writing *Beloved*, was also consciously planning the continuation of Beloved's story in *Jazz* is indicated in some comments she made in an interview in the mid-1980s. Recalling her obsession with "two or three little fragments of stories" that she had heard from different sources, Morrison explained how the "book idea" of *Beloved* took shape when she connected the story of Margaret Garner to another story she had read in *The Harlem Book of the Dead*—a collection of photographs of "beloved, departed people" in their coffins or in the arms of their parents (Naylor 206, 207). Morrison was particularly struck by the story accompanying a photograph of an eighteen-year-old girl who was killed while dancing at a party, apparently by a jealous ex-lover. When the dying girl was asked what had happened to her, she repeatedly said, "I'll tell you tomorrow," because she wanted the man who shot her to get away (Naylor 207). Even as Morrison was working on *Beloved*, she was thinking about the love story from *The Harlem Book of the Dead* and about extending Beloved's story into a 1920s Harlem setting "where it switches to this other girl" and yet Beloved is "there also" (Naylor 208; see also Van Der Zee 52–53, 84).

If Morrison, in her original conception of the novel, imagined the death of Dorcas as an example of self-sacrificial love, in *Jazz* she depicts Dorcas's death as sacrificial but she also constructs the Beloved-like Dorcas as more selfish than selfless and as both aggressor and victim. When Joe first sees Dorcas, she is "buying candy and ruining her skin" (29)—a detail that recalls Beloved's greedy appetite for sweet things—and as she takes the gifts Joe showers on her, her behavior recalls Beloved's demandingness. Moreover, she too sleeps with a man old enough to be her father, driving a wedge between Joe and Violet. Pointing to the text's ambivalences and uncertainties in presenting this character, *Jazz* seemingly sympathizes with Dorcas's bluesy sexuality, but it also preassigns the sexually transgressive Dorcas the cultural—and literary—role of murder victim.

Although Alice Manfred tries to raise Dorcas to follow a black middle-class code of conduct, Dorcas, who enjoys doing the forbidden thing, is attracted to the black Harlem jazz culture, and thus she secretly rebels against her middle-class aunt. Alice Manfred wants to protect Dorcas from what she sees as the nasty, lowdown jazz culture of black Harlem and "to keep the heart ignorant of the hips and the head in charge of both" (60). But while Alice works hard to "privatize" Dorcas and ensure that her niece remains socially and sexually insulated and innocent, she is "no match for a City seeping music that begged and challenged each and every day. 'Come,' it said. 'Come and do wrong'" (67).

Dorcas resists Alice Manfred's "protection and restraining hands," for she is attracted to the newly found freedom and sensuality of the black migrant urban culture, and she also, the narrative insists, is in part seduced by the jazz music and the culture it expresses. To Dorcas the "life-below-the-sash" is "all the life" there is. Dorcas's burgeoning sexuality is conveyed in a description that, blueslike, is full of sexual innuendo.⁵ As Dorcas lies on a chenille bedspread, she is "tickled and happy knowing that there was no place to be where somewhere, close by, somebody was not licking his licorice stick, tickling the ivories, beating his skins, blowing off his horn while a knowing woman sang ain't nobody going to keep me down you got the right key baby but the wrong keyhole you got to get it bring it and put it right here, or else" (60). Not unlike Sula, Dorcas is a bold and sexually assertive woman—an embodiment of black female "wildness." And like the shameless Sula, Dorcas dies young: she too is punished, and then, in a classic contempt-disappear scenario, is ushered prematurely out of the text.

"I *chose* you. Nobody gave you to me. Nobody said that's the one for you," Joe thinks of Dorcas. "I picked you out. Wrong time, yep, and doing wrong by my wife. But the picking out, the choosing. Don't ever think I fell for you, or fell over you. I didn't fall in love, I rose in it. I saw you and made up my mind. My mind" (135). Despite this description of the freedom to exercise choice in love, which, as we have seen, Morrison considers to be an important feature of the black migrant experience, Joe's love affair is presented as following a predetermined shame-pride—and blueslike—script. "[Y]ou make me sick. . . . Sick of myself and sick of you," Dorcas says to Joe when she ends their affair (189). Dorcas's contemptuous words hurt Joe, who, becoming caught up in the classic rejection-humiliation-revenge sequence described by shame theorists (see, e.g., Scheff and Retzinger 103–21) tracks Dorcas for five days and ultimately shoots her. In his affair with and murder of Dorcas, the middle-aged Joe Trace, who wants to be "free to do something wild," is described as "bound to the track" (120), not only as he acts out a bluesy script but, more significantly, as he repeats his past.

"Something else takes over when the track begins to talk to you, gives out its signs so strong you hardly have to look," Joe remarks, describing how he once tracked his mother in Virginia and how he similarly tracks Dorcas in the city. The drivenness of traumatic reenactments is conveyed in the description of how Joe first tracks and then shoots Dorcas. "[I]f the trail speaks, no matter what's in the way, you can find yourself in a crowded room aiming a bullet at her heart, never mind it's the heart you can't live without" (130). By alternating descriptions of Joe's earlier search for Wild with those of his search for Dorcas, *Jazz* evokes the experience not only of being haunted by the past but also of having the past return in the present in the form of intrusive thoughts and images. As Joe tracks Dorcas, he imagines that when he finds her she will walk toward him, holding out her hand, thus undoing his earlier rejection by Wild, who refused to give him the sign of recognition he sought by holding out her hand to him. Joe, who asserts that he would never mistreat a woman or make her live the way Wild did, "like a dog in a cave," believes that when he finds Dorcas, she will not "be holed up" with a young man (as Wild was with Golden Gray) and that there will not be any lover's clothes "mixed up with hers" (as Golden Gray's clothes were with Wild's). "She'll be alone. Hardheaded. Wild, even. But alone," he thinks (182). But when, instead, Joe finds Dorcas with the "[h]awk-eyed" Acton at an adult party where "people play for keeps," he shoots her (188, 191). To Joe the gun is not a gun; instead, it is the hand he wants to touch Dorcas with, and when he shoots her, he wants to catch her before she falls and hurts herself. Like Sethe's murder of Beloved or Eva's killing of Plum, Joe's murder of Dorcas is described as an act that combines, in a disturbing way, both protective and brutal behavior.

Joe shoots Dorcas in a moment of blind jealousy and shame-rage, his act a response not only to Dorcas's shaming rejection of him but also to his lifelong feelings of maternal rejection. But by representing Joe's act as non-volitional and insisting on his detached state of mind when he shoots Dorcas—indeed, the shooting is presented as occurring during an episode of depersonalization—*Jazz* engages in a form of textual denial as it distances readers from the crime of violence and silences Dorcas, the sacrificial trauma victim. Even though Joe's murder of Dorcas is announced in the opening passage of the novel and even though the narrative repeatedly and obsessively returns to and circulates around this act of violence as it attempts to explain why it happened, it also de-emphasizes the fact that Dorcas is the victim of a violent physical trauma. Not only does *Jazz* side with the victimizer and discount Dorcas's point of view, it also describes the shooting as an act of love. But Joe's act can also be read as an act of shame-revenge and as his attempt to terrorize, humiliate, and punish Dorcas for her shaming rejection of him. By romanticizing Joe's shooting of Dorcas and portraying Dorcas as a willing victim, *Jazz* counteracts the shame and trauma of the murder scene it stages and thus avoids confronting some of the very troubling aspects of the crime that it represents, including the politically charged gender and racial politics of this scene, which depicts Joe as a black male oppressor of a black woman.[6]

"Am I falling? Why am I falling?" asks Dorcas after she has been shot. "It's dark and now it's light. . . . I see mouths moving; they are all saying something to me I can't hear" (192). While those gathered around the dying Dorcas urge her to tell them the name of the man who shot her, she, seemingly taking on the identity of Wild, thinks to herself, "Mama won't tell" (193). As Dorcas bleeds to death, she hears a woman singing, perhaps a jazz singer or perhaps Beloved or Wild. Aestheticizing the violence of Dorcas's death, the narrative subsequently describes the rooftop jazz musicians of the city who play a tune "high and fine like a young girl singing by the side of a creek, passing the time, her ankles cold in the water. The young men with brass probably never saw such a girl, or such a creek, but they made her up that day" (196). In suggesting that the haunting dead girl—Beloved-Wild-Dorcas, who is everywhere and nowhere—is the inspiration of art, *Jazz* points to its own transformation of violent death into beautiful art.

If *Jazz* presents and yet denies the act of murder at its core, it also invites reader sympathy for the murderer by insisting on Joe's own victimization. "Joe is never arrested, though everyone knows he's guilty. Or is he?" asks one commentator who, in a common response to the novel, refers to Joe's own "past misfortunes" in explaining his behavior (Bawer 11). Joe, writes another, is not branded as "an immoral man" but rather he is a good person whose "bizarre behavior" is shaped by his circumstances, and Joe does not "*intentionally* or with deliberation hurt Dorcas"; instead, when Dorcas rejects Joe, her rejection is a repetition of the maternal rejection he experienced in the past, and thus perhaps in shooting Dorcas, he "discharges the pent-up misery and humiliation of his past" (Furman 86, 87, 88). Focusing on the involuntary nature of the murder, some critics characterize Joe as "driven at a deep level by a primitive instinct" or as "driven by his hunter self"—descriptions that are potentially shaming in their repetition of the notion of black primitivity (Peach 126, Rodrigues, "Experiencing *Jazz*" 746). But if such readings of the murder come close to describing Joe's act as a shame drama, other interpreters act out the antishaming agenda of the text in their readings of the murder. "Clearly, Joe never intended to use the gun . . . ," writes one critic-reader, who describes the "ambiguity" of Joe's act, the coexistence of "[m]urder and love . . . in his criminality" (Otten, "Horrific Love" 663).

While some commentators exonerate Joe, others say that the novel "never convincingly accounts for the horror that Joe . . . feel[s] compelled to wreak" (Gray). And still others are bothered by the victimization of Dorcas. "It is almost as if Dorcas' murder is a fitting end for one who courted danger and flaunted the errant ways of youth. It is almost as if her sacrifice enables Joe and Violet to get back the love they'd lost . . . ," writes a commentator who voices concern not only about the sacrificial nature of Dorcas's death but also the reader's removal from the murder. "[W]hy am I so detached from something that should make me cringe: the unpunished murder of a woman who dares to desire?" Because the horror of Dorcas's murder is apprehended "mainly at the level of the intellect," it is "fascinating to ponder but difficult to feel" (McDowell, "Harlem" 254). If yet another critic-reader has expressed fascination with the novel's "indecipherable explosion of violence," still another has commented that the "almost redemptive and surprisingly venial nature" of violence in *Jazz* makes it a "disturbing" book (Weinstein 129, Hardack 162–63).

While *Jazz* constructs Dorcas as the self-sacrificing and sacrificed female victim and thus represents the black woman as the passive victim of male violence, it also provides a competing vision of black womanhood in its recurrent descriptions of female wildness and women's desire for revenge against men. The split between woman as the passive victim and the wild aggressor finds its textual source in the Wild/Beloved character, who becomes "wild" as the result of being traumatized. As the narrative unfolds, other characters are shown to have an affinity to Wild—who is given her name by Hunters Hunter after she bites him—when they display their own potentially dangerous wildness. Dorcas, who likes to "push people," including men (205), and who enjoys doing risky and scary things, exhibits Wild's aggressiveness, as does Violet, "a brutal woman black as soot known to carry a knife," who is called "Violent" after she attempts to "kill what lay in a coffin" (75, 79). And if *Jazz* presents African-American women as victims of male violence, it also gives voice to the female desire for revenge in deliberately staged encounters between the middle-class Alice and the lower-class Violet. Thus, what the text denies in its account of the murder of Dorcas, it acts out through its descriptions of female revenge fantasies.

Violet, an unlicensed beautician who includes prostitutes among her clients, initially represents the nasty, lowdown jazzy life that Alice shuns, and yet over time Alice looks forward to Violet's visits and her impolite, but frank, conversation. With Violet, "No apology or courtesy seemed required or necessary. . . . But something else was—clarity, perhaps. The kind of clarity crazy people demand from the not-crazy" (83). In the course of her developing friendship with Violet, Alice, who initially feels unprotected and unsafe in the city, comes to see black women as anything but "[n]atural prey" or "easy pickings" (79). When Alice thinks of Violet-Violent, she recalls stories of the dangerous women who have "folded blades, packets of lye, shards of glass taped to their hands" (78). "Men ran through the streets of Springfield, East St. Louis and the City holding one red wet hand in the other, a flap of skin on the face. Sometimes they got to a hospital safely alive only because they left the razor where it lodged" (77). When Alice asks Violet why she "picked up a knife to insult a dead girl," Violet's bluesy response—"Wouldn't you? You wouldn't fight for your man?" (85)—prompts Alice to recall how, years before, she indulged in her own elaborate revenge fantasies after her husband left her for another woman. Alice, who had been shamed—treated like dirt—imagined herself galloping on a horse over the "twitching, pulpy body" of her husband's lover, running over her again and again until there was nothing left of the "hussy" but dirt in the road. Remembering her own shame-anger after her husband left her, Alice comes to think that, if her husband had not died, she might have ended up doing "something wild" (86). Under Violet's influence, Alice imagines that black women are armed and dangerous, and she also secretly identifies with Violet's anger and violence, which reveals her own potential aggressive and dangerous wildness.

"Risky, I'd say, trying to figure out anybody's state of mind. But worth the trouble if you're like me—curious, inventive and well-informed," remarks the *Jazz* narrator at one point in the novel (137). In initially predicting a bad outcome for Joe and Violet's story, the narrator prepares readers for another enactment of the rejection-humiliation-revenge scenario, presumably one in which Violet-Violent kills Joe. The narrator imagines that one day Violet will set fire to Joe's hair with a matchstick and predicts a violent end when, in the spring, Violet invites Felice, the friend of the dead Dorcas, into the Trace household and the "scandalizing threesome" of Joe, Violet, and Felice begins. "What turned out different was who shot whom," the *Jazz* narrator remarks, warning of yet another murder (6). But instead Morrison, in the concluding sections of the novel, defuses the lethal emotions that fuel the narrative. She does this not only by replacing the dangerous and unrestrained—"wild"— Dorcas with the conventional and restrained Felice and the rivalrous love triangle with the wholesome family triad but also by identifying the *Jazz* narrator as the originating and projective source of the destructive feelings that permeate the narrative.

"Pain. I seem to have an affection, a kind of sweettooth for it," the *Jazz* narrator comes to confess, making its presence felt as the percipient and emotional center of the narrative. "Bolts of lightning, little rivulets of thunder. And I the eye of the storm. . . . Figuring out what can be done to save them since they cannot save themselves without me because—well, it's my storm, isn't it?" (219). If the description of the *Jazz* narrator as the I/eye of the storm seems designed to recall the novel's epigraph from the "Thunder, Perfect Mind" passage of *The Nag Hammadi*—which gnostic scholar Elaine Pagels has described as "a revelation spoken by a feminine power" (55)—it does not function to identify the goddesslike power of the narrator, as some commentators have suggested. Instead, Morrison's narrating voice begins to confess its limitations at this point in the narrative. Morrison, in her account of the problem she had figuring out the "voice" of the novel during the writing process, recalls how she "decided that the voice would be one of assumed knowledge, the voice that says 'I know everything.' . . . Because the voice has to actually imagine the story it's telling . . . it's in trouble, because if it's really involved in the process of telling the story and letting the other voices speak, the story that it thought it knew turns out to be entirely different from what it predicted because the characters will be evolving within the story, within the book" (Carabi 41). Remarking on her desire "to re-represent two contradictory things—artifice and improvisation"—in her novel, Morrison explains that her controlling image in *Jazz* was that of a book "writing itself. Imagining itself. Talking. Aware of what it is doing. . . . *Jazz* predicts its own story. Sometimes it is wrong because of faulty vision. It simply did not imagine those characters well enough, admits it was wrong, and the characters talk back the way jazz musicians do. It has to listen to the characters it has invented, and then learn something from them" (Schappell 116–17). In part because Morrison's novel provides self-conscious reflections on its own narrative process and also "emphasizes the irreducible provisionality—the fictionality—of narrative knowledge," it sometimes has been referred to as the "most 'postmodern'" of Morrison's novels (Rubenstein 158, 153). Yet if one of the functions of Morrison's intrusive *Jazz* narrator is to emphasize the provisional, constructed nature of the stories it narrates, the narrating voice of the novel also recalls Morrison's long-term authorial interest in evoking the back-fence world of gossip through her meandering oral style.

"I break lives to prove I can mend them back again . . . ," Morrison's gossipy *Jazz* narrator comes to admit. "[W]hat would I be without a few brilliant spots of blood to ponder? Without aching words that set, then miss, the mark?" (219). If Morrison's intention was to keep the *Jazz* narrator anonymous, she nevertheless comes to identify the narrator not only as a site of shame but also as the originating source of shame-rage in the narrative. And in an interesting turn of events, the voyeuristic *Jazz* narrator, who passes shaming judgments on the characters—calling Violet "mean," Joe a "[r]at," and Dorcas "a pack of lies" (4, 121, 72)—is shamefully exposed. "[W]hen I was feeling most invisible . . . they were whispering about me to each other. They knew how little I could be counted on; how poorly, how shabbily my know-it-all self covered helplessness." The narrator, who felt well "hidden" from the gaze of others, ends up deeply mortified. "[A]ll the while they were watching me. Sometimes they even felt sorry for me and just thinking about their pity I want to die" (220).

In part by projecting the shame and shame-rage of the characters onto the narrator—who thus serves as a kind of textual scapegoat—Morrison is able to redeem her characters. Certain that the end result of the scandalizing threesome of Joe, Violet, and Felice will be another murder, the *Jazz* narrator misses the obvious. "I was so sure it would happen. That the past was an abused record with no choice but to repeat itself at the crack and no power on earth could lift the arm that held the needle. I was so sure, and they danced and walked all over me. Busy, they were, busy being original, complicated, changeable—human, I guess you'd say, while I was the predictable one, confused in my solitude into arrogance, thinking my space, my view was the only one that was or that mattered" (220). Despite the *Jazz* narrator's initial nervousness at the sight of Felice climbing the steps to Violet-Violent's house, Felice ultimately acts as a healing agent. To Violet, Felice represents not only the lost daughter but also the lost and original self. For the dark-skinned Felice is contrasted to the light-skinned Dorcas, who represents the white and light identity that Violet idealized and then symbolically attacked and killed when she violated the corpse of Dorcas. Responding to Violet's story of how she killed first the blond child that lived within her and then the self that killed the blond child, Felice asks, "Who's left?" When Violet answers "Me," she looks as if it is "the first she heard of the word" (209). Violet's newfound me-ness is not a shame- or rage-driven identity, not "some tough somebody, or somebody she had put together for show. But . . . somebody she favored and could count on. A secret somebody you didn't have to feel sorry for or have to fight for" (210).

Felice—whose name, as Joe remarks, means "happy" (212)—also helps the grieving Joe recover from his loss of Dorcas. Not only does she explain that Dorcas "let herself die" (209) by refusing help and thus allowing herself to bleed to death from the gunshot wound to her shoulder, but she also tells Joe that Dorcas's dying thoughts were about him. "There's only one apple. . . . Just one. Tell Joe," the dying Dorcas remarked to Felice, her words echoing Joe's earlier comparison of Dorcas to Eve and himself to Adam who left Eden a "rich man" because he had the taste of the first apple in his mouth for the remainder of his life (213, 133). As the "Blues man. Black and bluesman. Blacktherefore blue man" (119), Joe has spent the winter and spring visibly crying at the window or on the stoop of his Lenox Avenue apartment. But he begins to recover after he learns about Dorcas's dying words, words which provide Joe with the sign of loving affirmation he sought but never received from the elusive Wild.

Recalling how the exorcism of Beloved leads to a potentially hopeful conclusion to the story of Sethe and Paul D, the death of Dorcas similarly brings together Joe and Violet Trace, who suggestively dance together to jazz music in front of Felice as they prepare to make a new beginning. While the *Jazz* narrator originally saw Felice, Joe, and Violet as the "mirror image" of Dorcas, Joe and Violet and thus viewed them as "exotic" and "driven," they were "thinking other thoughts, feeling other feelings, putting their lives together in ways" the *Jazz* narrator "never dreamed of" (221). Felice, who is "nobody's alibi or hammer or toy," represents a happier future, as her name suggests, for though "her speed may be slow . . . her tempo is next year's news" (222). And the middle-aged Joe and Violet share a domestic and loving intimacy, the love of "grown people," in which they "whisper to each other under the covers" and in which "the body is the vehicle, not the point." Joe and Violet are under covers "because they don't have to look at themselves anymore; there is no stud's eye, no chippie glance to undo them. They are inward toward the other . . ." (228). There also is "another part, not so secret" to their loving intimacy: "The part that touches fingers when one passes the cup and saucer to the other. The part that closes her neckline snap while waiting for the trolley; and brushes lint from his blue serge suit when they come out of the movie house into the sunlight" (229). At the outset of the story, the *Jazz* narrator focused attention on human misery, believing that "flesh, pinioned by misery, hangs on to it with pleasure. Hangs on to wells and a boy's golden hair; would just as soon inhale sweet fire caused by a burning girl as hold a maybe-yes maybe-no hand." But as the story of Joe and Violet Trace concludes, the narrator has come to a new recognition of the rogue and jazzlike quality of life and also of the possibility of love, the "[s]omething else" that one must figure in before one can "figure . . . out" human life (228).

In an improvised, jazzy happy ending—as opposed to a predetermined, bluesy, unhappy ending—*Jazz* replaces misery with pleasure, human loss and violence with a rogue love. The closure also continues to aestheticize the violent death of Dorcas by associating her bleeding wound with the natural sign of Wild: the red-winged blackbird. As Joe thinks of Dorcas while looking out a window, "he sees through the glass darkness taking the shape of a shoulder with a thin line of blood. Slowly, slowly it forms itself into a bird with a blade of red on the wing" (224–25). Yet Joe's loud greeting to Violet when he returns home, as if he expects that "a young ghost with bad skin might be there instead" of Violet (223), suggests the continuing ghostly presence of Beloved-Wild-Dorcas, who is at once everywhere and nowhere.

Freed from the belief that the past is "an abused record with no choice but to repeat itself" (220), the *Jazz* narrator, in yet another improvised, happy ending, rewrites the character of Wild. If Wild has served as a literary container for a repertoire of shaming, stereotypical images used to construct African-American female identity, and if Wild's cave was earlier depicted as a site of contamination, the closure actively replaces these associations. Although Wild's sunlit home in the rock is not anything "to be proud of, to show anybody or to want to be in," the *Jazz* narrator nevertheless wants to inhabit Wild's "chamber of gold" and be enclosed "in the peace left by the woman who lived there and scared everybody." A "playful woman who lived in a rock," someone "[u]nseen because she knows better than to be seen," Wild becomes a reflection or double of the *Jazz* narrator and also an embodiment of the Africanist presence in literature, a white projective and shame-ridden image that Morrison redeems by associating it with the deeper unconscious sources of African-American art. Reconfigured as the African-American muse, Wild is the maternal inspiration for the *Jazz* narrator's art. "She has seen me and is not afraid of me. She hugs me. Understands me. Has given me her hand. I am touched by her. Released in secret" (221).

In the novel's closure, in which Morrison imagines the personified book—*Jazz*—talking to the reader, she similarly dramatizes the reader-text transaction as a kind of lover's embrace. *"I love the way you hold me, how close you let me be to you. I like your fingers on and on, lifting, turning. I have watched your face for a long time now, and missed your eyes when you went away from me. Talking to you and hearing you answer—that's the kick."* This passage, as it dramatizes what Morrison has long described as her desire to engage her audience in a form of participatory reading, also points to the intersubjective—and personal-emotional—dimensions of the reading experience. "Say make me, remake me. You are free to do it and I am free to let you . . ." (229). In her remarks on *Jazz,* Morrison has commented on how "the whole act of reading, holding, surrendering to a book, is part of that beautiful intimacy of reading." Describing the "voice" of the talking book, she remarks, "It sounds like a very erotic, sensual love song of a person who loves you. This is a love song of a book talking to the reader" (Carabi 42). Not unlike the adult bedtime lovers' relationship between Violet and Joe (228), the reader-text transaction is envisioned as a kind of "whispering, old-time love" as the reader, in bed, cozies up to the book and enjoys its "undercover whispers."

A work that has prompted a public display of affection for its undercover pleasures of the text, *Jazz* has been described as a "supple, sophisticated love story," a "sensuous and haunting" work, and a "brilliant, daring" novel (Mendelsohn 25, Bernikow, Dorris 241). "The words soar and dip, weave and bop, like some crazy impromptu syncopation, or reverberate like a low-down blues riff," remarks one commentator in a characteristic response to the work (Stuart 39). Yet while commentators praise the jazzlike style of the work, they also sometimes comment that the work lacks the "eviscerating pull" of *Beloved* (Stuart 39). "Do I miss something?" writes one commentator. "Yes. I miss the emotional nexus, the moment shorn of all artifice that brings us headlong into the deepest recesses of feeling . . ." (O'Brien 30). *Jazz* has been variously described as a "[t]echnically adventurous" work that has a "cooler tone" than Morrison's earlier novels; as a work in which the "pain is less intense" than *Beloved*'s, perhaps "because it is absorbed into the poetry, in a way that the blues reverberations make possible"; or as a work in which Morrison's narrator "finds it easier to aestheticize" the characters than to "feel their pain" (Turbide, J. Miller 247, McDowell, "Harlem" 254).

While some commentators miss the "emotional nexus" in *Jazz,* many others look away from the troubling emotional content of the novel and focus instead on the narrative's technical virtuosity and the puzzles surrounding the *Jazz* narrator's identity. Following the text's invitation, critic-readers have speculated on the role and identity of the *Jazz* narrator, who has been interpreted in a variety of ways: as a "personification of the impersonal authorial voice"; as a "multiplicity of voices, both garrulous and censorious, fascinated and penetrating"; and as "jazz" itself, which "speaks in a most human voice but has no human form" (Furman 100, Harding 168, Eckhard 13). "[W]here is the narrative voice located? In a real character? The author? The living pages? Morrison's apparent answer is that the narrator is to be found in all three, plus in the imaginative mind of the reader" (Carmean 103). If, in following the text's promptings, critic-readers try to solve the mystery of the *Jazz* narrator's identity or focus on the cognitive puzzles and aesthetic pleasures of Morrison's *Jazz*, they also tend to de-emphasize or even bypass altogether the troubling emotional drama at the center of the novel, or they collaborate with the text as they, in effect, aestheticize the act of murder that lies at the heart of the narrative. This type of response points to Morrison's ability to defuse the shame-rage feelings—the "mewing hurt" and "overboard rage"— that drive the narrative and to transform black shame and rage into a complicated and cool jazzy-bluesy music.

And yet despite the novel's happy ending and its insistence on the pleasures of mature love, the fact that the central trauma of the narrative—the murder of Dorcas—is talked about but not really confronted as an act of violence has troubled some readers of Morrison's novel. Trying to explain the reader's detachment from the murder of Dorcas, one critic claims that "in the process of 'enlarging' herself, Morrison's narrator has reduced Dorcas to the dimensions of a snapshot—a motionless image, fixed, aestheticized, frozen" (McDowell, "Harlem" 254). Evidence that the closure of *Jazz*, like other closures in Morrison's novels, sends out mixed signals is found in the critical commentary that surrounds the novel. Following the text's directives, some critic-readers argue that love acts as a "redemptive force" in the closure; or that the novel's final improvisation on mature love acts as a "counterpoint" to the Joe-Dorcas relationship; or that *Jazz* is a work in which the "re-visioning of family . . . is finally apocalyptic" (Mayer 258, Peach 126, Heinze 98). But if some critic-readers respond to the conscious optimism of the closure, others argue that *Jazz*'s ending is imposed, that it is a "heavy-handed device" used by the author "to liberate her characters from predictability" by staging a "manipulative about-face in the plot" and having the narrative voice assume "blame for failing to foresee the unexpectedly anticlimactic turn of events" (Hulbert 47). Or they feel that the "optimism" at the end "remains faint" and that the "hard-won equilibrium" between Violet and Joe "seems tentative and fragile" (Harding 84).

In *Jazz*, Morrison creates an elegant, jazzlike narrative as she aestheticizes the violent act she represents. Even as the murder of Dorcas is played and replayed in the novel, it also remains, in essence, an unspeakable act unspoken as the narrative denies the violence of what it describes, turning Dorcas's death into a kind of jazzy-bluesy performance. In describing the mature love of Violet and Joe Trace, the narrative acts out a healing gesture. But the bleeding wound of Dorcas remains as a kind of textual sign of the deep and abiding racial wounds the novel exposes and can only aesthetically repair. In *Jazz*, Morrison focuses on the painful race matters that have long occupied her and that will continue to preoccupy her in her next novel, *Paradise*, where she will again illuminate the impact of shame and trauma on the African-American experience.

8

"He's Bringing Along the Dung
We Leaving Behind"

THE INTERGENERATIONAL TRANSMISSION OF
RACIAL SHAME AND TRAUMA IN *PARADISE*

After Morrison was awarded the Nobel Prize in Literature in 1993, she felt a surge of pride in this confirmation of her gifts as a writer. To her, winning the Nobel Prize was "fabulous." "I felt representational. I felt American. I felt Ohioan. I felt blacker than ever. I felt more woman than ever. I felt all of that, and put all of that together and went out and had a good time" (*USA Today* 2). "When I heard I'd won," Morrison has remarked, "you heard no 'Aw, shucks' from me. The prize didn't change my inner assessment of what I'm capable of doing, but I welcomed it as a public, representational affirmation of my work. I was surprised at how patriotic I felt, being the first native-born American winner since Steinbeck in 1962. I felt pride that a black and a woman had been recognized in such an international forum" (Gray, "Paradise" 64). But Morrison's life also became complicated after she won the Nobel Prize, for she was besieged by the outside world, which made inordinate demands on her time. "I was so happy that I had a real book idea in progress," Morrison recalls. "If I hadn't, I would have thought, 'Uh-oh, can I ever write a novel again?'" (Gray, "Paradise" 63). Being a Nobel laureate, Morrison also must have felt under pressure, as one commentator has observed, to write a book considered "worthy" of someone who had achieved such a rare international distinction. "Already lionized as one of America's best wordsmiths, becoming the first African-American woman to win the Nobel Prize placed her on a singular plateau of achievement. It is one that could have led to artistic paralysis, or worse, a numbing complacency. Faced with the inevitable scrutiny—much of it aimed at proving she really didn't deserve such supreme recognition—she could have decided to play it safe" (Kane 2, 1).[1]

In *Paradise*, Morrison does anything but play it safe as she creates a novel that has been aptly described as "vintage" Morrison, a work in which Morrison's "eloquence," "originality," and "searing vision of the world are as uncompromising . . . as in any of her previous works"; as a "memorable work of epic range and monumental ambition"; and as "the strangest and most original book that Morrison has written" (Turner 1, 4, Prose, Menand 78). A "great sprawl of a narrative" and a work in which Morrison pulls her readers "this way and that" as she "balances rumor, tale, legend, history, and memory, and manages to bring it all home" (Shields 2, Cliff 85), *Paradise* marks the completion of Morrison's long-range project, begun in the 1980s, to write a trilogy about the African-American experience.

Part of Morrison's literary and cultural agenda in *Paradise* is to complete the historical survey of African-American life that she began in *Beloved*'s depiction of slavery and its aftermath, and in *Jazz*'s focus on the post–Civil War era and the black migration to northern cities. In *Paradise* Morrison looks back to slavery, Reconstruction and the post-Reconstruction years and to the black exodus from the South and settlement of Oklahoma, and she also extends the story of black life in America into the mid-1970s, bringing into the novel historical references to World War II and the Vietnam War, and to the civil rights and the black power movements. "The book coalesced around the idea of where paradise is, who belongs in it," Morrison has remarked of the novel (D. Smith B2), which is based, in part, on her readings about the migration of ex-slaves into Oklahoma in the post–Civil War period. During her research on the black settlement of Oklahoma, Morrison learned of a newspaper column that ran from 1891 to 1892 entitled "Come Prepared or Not at All," these words warning the ex-slaves planning to emigrate to bring with them enough resources to last them for two years (Gray 63, McKinney-Whetstone 2). After reading an account describing how two hundred freedmen and their families were turned away from an all-black town by other ex-slaves because they lacked such resources, Morrison became "interested in what on earth that must have felt like, to have come all that way and look at some other Black people who said you couldn't come in" (McKinney-Whetstone 3).[2]

As she worked on *Paradise*, Morrison addressed an issue that she says had always intrigued her: "Why paradise necessitates exclusion" (Mulrine). The "question" she started with in working on her "interrogation of the idea of paradise" is how "fierce, revolutionary, moral people . . . become destructive, static, preformed—exactly what they were running from" (Verdelle 78). Continuing the cultural work of her earlier novels in *Paradise*, Morrison investigates the politics of inclusion and exclusion as she grapples with the troubling issue of intraracial strife. "I think the threat for many of our communities is internecine," Morrison has commented on the novel. "By that I mean the enemy is within, as opposed to being on the outside. Quarreling within the family" (Verdelle 80). Creating in *Paradise* a richly layered narrative that interweaves historical and realistic with religious and mythic discourse, Morrison focuses on the historical struggles and conflicts as well as the complex religious heritage of blacks in America. Like other Morrison novels we have investigated, *Paradise* is a shame- and trauma-haunted work, dealing not only with the traumatic legacies of slavery and racial violence but also with the importance of shame and pride in the formation of racial and cultural identity.

As Morrison interrogates the idea of paradise—an African-American utopia that offers a safe haven from white contempt and persecution—she depicts the founding in 1890 of the all-black town of Haven, Oklahoma, and describes how, in 1949, the descendants of Haven's founders, World War II veterans upset at the economic and social decay of their town, move into a secluded area of Oklahoma some two-hundred-and-forty miles west of Haven. In establishing Ruby—a town of three-hundred-and-sixty people located "off the county road, accessible only to the lost and the knowledgeable" (186)—the town fathers are determined to honor their fathers and grandfathers by preserving their dream of living in an all-black Christian town, a safe haven where the people are physically protected and live away from the temptations and moral failings of the larger American society. Focusing on life in Ruby in the late 1960s through the mid-1970s—specifically from 1968 to 1976—Morrison creates a rich and complex narrative tapestry as she describes the founding of the town in 1950 and the slavery and postslavery roots of the town's fifteen families; the troubled relationships between Ruby's warring families, the Morgans and the Fleetwoods; the religious battle between the conservative Reverend Senior Pulliam and the liberal Reverend Richard Misner; and the generational and community debate over the community symbol, the Oven. As Morrison weaves together the fragmented stories and differing, conflicting voices of a large cast of characters—describing in the process births and deaths, weddings and funerals—she, as in her other novels, looks back to the formative trauma of slavery and also the pain of intraracial shaming, showing the intergenerational transmission of racial wounds and the damaging impact of the color-caste hierarchy on the collective black identity. But unlike her earlier novels, which depict the prejudice lighter-skinned blacks feel toward those with darker skin, in *Paradise* Morrison explores the troubling issue of internalized racism by describing how the dark-skinned families of Ruby construct light skin as a stain and view light-skinned blacks as impure and corrupted, as the "dung" (201) they want to exclude from their black utopia.[3]

"All paradises are described as male enclaves, while the interloper is a woman, defenseless and threatening," Morrison has remarked of the novel. "When we get ourselves together and get powerful is when we are assaulted" (D. Smith B2). Morrison's depiction of the raid by nine Ruby men on the Convent is inspired, in part, by a story she heard during a trip to Brazil in the 1980s about a convent of black nuns who were killed by a group of men for their practice of Candomblé, an African-Brazilian religion. "I've since learned it never happened," Morrison has remarked. "But for me it was irrelevant" (D. Smith B2). As Morrison in *Paradise* brings to light the destructive mechanisms by which the powerful patriarchs of Ruby pathologize the women of the Convent—who thus become community scapegoats—she, as in her other works, illustrates the causes and consequences of racial and social shaming: that is, the dismissive and inherently dangerous othering and demonizing of those people considered different.

By beginning her novel with the abrupt and jarring statement—"They shoot the white girl first" (3)—and then deliberately suppressing information about which character is white as she describes the Convent women, Morrison's intent is to compel her readers to look beyond the category of race in responding to her characters: Consolata and the four castaway women who join her—Mavis, Gigi, Seneca, and Pallas. But Morrison also shows the deadly impact of race matters on the lives of these characters: stigmatized outsiders who are marked as different by the people of Ruby and viewed through the distorting lens of culturally inherited racist and sexist stereotypes. As Morrison tells the stories of the Convent women during the slow unfolding of the novel, she relies on the discourse of social realism as she focuses reader attention on the complex social lives of her characters. The Convent women also become a kind of collective mythic presence in the novel. Like their literary predecessors, Beloved and the Beloved-like Wild and Dorcas in Morrison's *Beloved* and *Jazz*, they become by the end of the novel at once real and unreal—everywhere and nowhere—as they, in Morrison's description, both die in the assault on the Convent and yet escape (Rose). Morrison, in effect, takes on the role of the black artist conjure woman as she uses a kind of authorial magic to rescue and resurrect her characters and as she provides a redemptive transracial vision in the novel's closure. Yet she still is unable to realistically resolve the cultural fears and anxieties that fuel her narrative as she explores the terrible legacy of intraracial shaming and conflict within the African-American community.

Following the narrative technique she uses in *Jazz*, Morrison opens *Paradise* with a dramatic description of a horrific crime—the violent attack on the Convent women by nine Ruby men—and then the narrative slowly and circuitously spirals around this central act of violence in an attempt to make sense of the present by looking at the past lives of the characters. To explain the scapegoating and, as readers learn at the end of the novel, the massacre of the Convent women, the narrative tells the stories of the five marginalized women who make up the all-female society of the Convent side by side with the stories of a wide cast of interrelated characters from Ruby's fifteen families. When an interviewer asked Morrison whether she felt that her readers would need "to keep track of" the names of her Ruby characters, she remarked, "I thought at first that I would put a genealogy in [the front of the book]. But then I thought no, in that little town, you could imagine everybody was married to one another, and they had children by each other, and they go back so long." For Morrison the connections of the Ruby people—their family and personal relations—are "paramount," and in the novel she focuses on "All their secrets. All their confrontations. All their reconciliations. The hierarchy within" (Verdelle 78, 80). Even as Morrison depicts the intense pride of the dark-skinned people of Ruby, she also, as is characteristic of her fiction, divulges the shameful family secrets that haunt the proud community leaders: secrets about the formative hardships and humiliations that Ruby's ancestors suffered during slavery and the postslavery years.

In weaving together the complex and interconnected stories of the people of Ruby, Morrison forces her readers to take on the role of historian and genealogist and to piece together the fragmented stories and conflicting versions of the past represented in the novel's repeated and accretive accounts of the struggles of the original founders of Haven—the Old Fathers—in 1890. Like other Morrison novels we have investigated, *Paradise* calls attention to the formative impact of humiliated and traumatic memory on collective group identity and on the individual and family. The story of the Old Fathers is, at once, a proud tale of group survival and an account of the trauma and humiliations suffered by Ruby's ancestors. "[E]xtraordinary" people whose names were legendary—Blackhorse, Morgan, Poole, Fleetwood, Beauchamp, Cato, Flood, DuPres—they had "served, picked, plowed and traded" in Louisiana beginning in 1755, when Louisiana included Mississippi, and then helped to govern in Mississippi and Louisiana during Reconstruction, from 1868 to 1875, only to be subsequently reduced to working as field laborers (99). The story of the difficult journey of the Old Fathers to Oklahoma is passed down to the New Fathers who establish Ruby and whose fifteen families include nine large intact families who made the original journey to Haven. The twins, Deacon and Steward Morgan—Ruby's bankers and its leading, and wealthiest, citizens—have strong memories. Born in 1924, they have vivid recall of the authorized account told by their grandfather, Zechariah Morgan, which is cast as a biblical story of the hardships and struggles endured by God's chosen people in their exodus from their ungodly persecutors and disallowers.

Zechariah's official and "controlling" (13) account of community history tells of the difficult and humiliating journey on foot from Mississippi and Louisiana to Oklahoma by one hundred and fifty-eight freedmen: seventy-nine ex-slaves from nine large families plus those who join them. During their journey, they are "unwelcome on each grain of soil from Yazoo to Fort Smith. Turned away by rich Choctaw and poor whites, chased by yard dogs, jeered at by camp prostitutes and their children, they were nevertheless unprepared for the aggressive discouragement they received from Negro towns already being built. The headline of a feature in the *Herald*, 'Come Prepared or Not at All,' could not mean them, could it? Smart, strong, and eager to work their own land, they believed they were more than prepared—they were destined." The travelers are "stung . . . into confusion" when they discover that they are "too poor, too bedraggled-looking to enter, let alone reside in, the communities that were soliciting Negro homesteaders" (13–14). In a classic shame defense, Ruby's ancestors respond to their "contemptuous dismissal by the lucky" with reactive pride, becoming "stiffer, prouder with each misfortune, the details of which were engraved into the twins' powerful memories" (14).

"Everything anybody wanted to know about the citizens of Haven or Ruby lay in the ramifications of that one rebuff out of many," the narrative remarks of the "Disallowing" of the original wayfarers by the people of the all-black town of Fairly, Oklahoma (189), a humiliating event that becomes seared in the memories of the Old Fathers and has a formative influence on the collective Ruby memory and group identity. Providing evidence of Morrison's persisting interest in the issues of intraracial shaming, the color-caste hierarchy, and the significance of shame and pride and the deference-emotion system in the construction of group identity, the story of the wayfarers' contemptuous dismissal by the people of Fairly—a "rejection" that the founders of Haven "carried . . . like a bullet in the brain" (109)—is told in bits and pieces and, as is characteristic of Morrison's fiction, there is a prolonged narrative delay before readers learn of the underlying cause and significance of this central scene of shame. When the band of travelers, who are on foot and are lost, are refused entry into Fairly, they become both ashamed and angry. "It was the shame of seeing one's pregnant wife or sister or daughter refused shelter that had rocked them, and changed them for all time. The humiliation did more than rankle; it threatened to crack open their bones. Steward remembered every detail of the story his father and grandfather told, and had no trouble imagining the shame for himself" (95). Even in 1973 in the protected world of Ruby, Steward remains bound in a feeling trap of shame-rage as he recalls how some "highfalutin" black people disallowed his ancestors, telling them to "Get away" from Fairly, Oklahoma. "[T]he thought of that level of helplessness made him want to shoot somebody. . . . All their belongings strapped to their backs or riding on their heads. Young ones time-sharing shoes. Stopping only to relieve themselves, sleep and eat trash. Trash and boiled meal, trash and meal cake, trash and game, trash and dandelion greens" (96).

The "Disallowing"—which refers to the "disbelievable words formed in the mouths of men to other men"—occurs when the light-skinned blacks of Fairly insult the dark-skinned travelers "in ways too confounding for language" (189). The root cause of this contemptuous dismissal, as the reader eventually learns, is the color prejudice of the people of the all-black town of Fairly. Ruby's ancestors, the Old Fathers, have dark "8-rock" skin: 8-rock referring to a type of coal found deep in the coal mines. They are a "Blueblack people, tall and graceful, whose clear, wide eyes gave no sign of what they really felt about those who weren't 8-rock like them." Descendants of a people whose "worthiness was so endemic" that three of their children held elected seats in state legislatures and county offices during Reconstruction, they are a proud people who, after five "glorious years remaking a country," were reduced to poverty because of their 8-rock skin color, and thus they spent fifteen years—from 1875 to 1890—"begging for sweatwork in cotton, lumber or rice" (193). They undertake their difficult journey to Oklahoma to escape their shameful situation, but instead they are "shooed away" from Fairly by light-skinned blacks: "Blue-eyed, gray-eyed yellowmen in good suits" (194, 195).

The light-skinned people of Fairly communicate the classic contempt message—"Get out of my sight: Disappear!" (Wurmser, "Shame" 67)—and reveal their inscription into racist thinking when they contemptuously reject and chase away the 8-rock people. In consolidating their own sense of racial superiority by devaluing the dark-skinned 8-rock people, the Fairly people reproduce the rigid racial and economic demarcations and the polarizing binarisms of white/black and us/them found in the dominant culture. In *Paradise* Morrison exposes how color prejudice functions as a social construction, and she also has an affective and cultural investment in exploring the terrible history and legacy of racist discourse and practices within the African-American community. To the people of Haven, the Disallowing is a formative experience as they forge their own group identity. "[F]or ten generations they had believed the division they fought to close was free against slave and rich against poor. Usually, but not always, white against black. Now they saw a new separation: light-skinned against black. Oh, they knew there was a difference in the minds of whites, but it had not struck them before that it was of consequence, serious consequence, to Negroes themselves. Serious enough that their daughters would be shunned as brides; their sons chosen last; that colored men would be embarrassed to be seen socially with their sisters." In being "disvalued by the impure," the 8-rock people discover that their dark skin, which they view as a sign of "racial purity," has become instead a racial "stain" (194): that is, a sign of a stigmatized and impure racial identity.

Turning shame into pride, Zechariah Morgan's master narrative of what happens after the Disallowing seeks to define the essential nature and collective destiny of the 8-rock people. Countering the racist ideology of the light-skinned people of Fairly, Zechariah's controlling story represents the 8-rocks as God's chosen people. Like a biblical prophet, Zechariah guides the original wayfarers to Haven during their journey, which is presented in the official Ruby history as an amalgam of the Old Testament exodus and search for the promised land[4] and the New Testament story of the journey of Joseph and Mary to Bethlehem. In a recasting of the shaming image of the helpless, rejected, and lost wayfarers, Zechariah's story tells of the walking man with a satchel—the supernatural angelic apparition or ancestral spirit announced by thundering footsteps that Zechariah summons with his humming prayer and that guides him for twenty-nine days, leading the way to Haven. Yet while Zechariah's story depicts the 8-rocks as God's favored people, the Old Fathers, in effect, make a shamefaced retreat from Fairly, and thus in their biblical and "purposeful" (97) journey to Haven, they are also acting out the contempt-disappear scenario of the Disallowing.

During the founding of Haven, Zechariah corrals some of the men into building a brick oven, which functions as a community kitchen and becomes a symbol of communal nurturing and group solidarity. The Oven also recalls the slavery past of the Old Fathers, serving as a visible reminder of their pride in the fact that none of their 8-rock women had worked in white kitchens as slaves, work that carried with it the likelihood of the rape of the slave kitchen workers and thus the tainting of pure African 8-rock blood. The words that Zechariah places on the five-foot-two-inch iron plaque he forges and cements to the base of the Oven's mouth—"Beware the Furrow of His Brow"—carries yet another reminder of the past. Because the first word on the iron plate is lost when the Oven is moved, brick-by-brick, to Ruby where it is reassembled, the people of Ruby end up in a dispute about the wording and meaning of the Oven's famous command or motto. In an interpretation of the Oven's inscription that is given textual authority because it explains the hidden connection between the inscription and the pivotal experience of the Disallowing, Zechariah's words are said to memorialize the deep and enduring "burn" of shame-rage felt by the Old Fathers, for the inscription was meant as a "threat to those who had disallowed" the 8-rock people of Haven (194, 195). The fact that Zechariah's sons take secret pleasure in the subsequent failure of some of the all-black towns founded by ex-slaves, which they view as a sign of God's favor on their town and judgment against their rejectors and enemies, points to their reactive desire to turn the tables on and witness the humiliation of their black humiliators.

Intent on showing the damaging impact of culturally transmitted shame, *Paradise* describes how the people of Ruby, like the Morgans, tell stories of the past heroism of their ancestors but remain quiet about their own lives. In preserving the official and controlling versions of the past, they also suppress shameful family and community secrets. Pat Best, who is working on a genealogy of Ruby's fifteen families, uncovers the shameful community secret of couplings outside of marriage or "takeovers" in which, for example, a widower might ask a distant relative of his if he could "take over" a young girl in the family without marriage prospects (196). And the twins, Steward and Deacon Morgan, actively suppress the family story that depicts the formative shaming of their grandfather, Zechariah Morgan, who was once known as Coffee and had a twin named Tea, and who, in the sanctioned version of Ruby history, ended up shot through the foot—"by whom or why nobody knew or admitted" (189)—during the original journey of the 8-rock families who founded Haven.

Represented in the authorized Ruby history as the proud and righteous patriarch, Coffee-Zechariah, in fact, was a man who was accused of malfeasance in office during Reconstruction, and he was "an embarrassment to Negroes and both a threat and a joke to whites." When he was forced, at gunpoint, to "dance" for some drunken white men with his twin brother, Tea, Coffee refused, and thus took a bullet in the foot (302). Re-creating his identity, Coffee renamed himself after the biblical hero, Zechariah: "the witness to whom God and angels spoke on a regular basis about things Coffee knew something about," such as how those who refused to show compassion would be punished by a scattering of the people and how such a scattering would lead to the loss of pure blood lines (192). Pointing explicitly to the inherent shame of the proud ancestor, *Paradise* describes how Coffee, in the process of renaming and thus refashioning himself as the dignified prophet, viewed his twin brother as an object of contempt not compassion since Tea, unlike Coffee-Zechariah, had accommodated the white men by dancing. Because Zechariah saw in his brother "something that shamed him"—that is, the shame that was "in himself" (303)—he broke all ties with his twin brother in yet another act of disallowing, and indeed in a classic expression of the contempt-disappear scenario, Tea's name was inked out of the Morgan family Bible. Consolidating his identity as the proud and masterful patriarch by externalizing his own status anxiety, Zechariah projected his socially induced feelings of shame and self-contempt onto his twin brother, Tea, who became the humiliated and excluded Other. Thus as the secret Morgan family history reveals, the 8-rock separatist politics of inclusion and exclusion is a direct result of and reaction to the self-loathing that grows out of internalized racism.

In its exploration of the impasse of intraracial tensions, *Paradise* shows how the deep-seated shame-rage and reactive pride of the Old Fathers of Haven become a lethal inheritance passed down to following generations of 8-rock people, who in turn reject and shame light-skinned people: that is, they humiliate the humiliators of their forefathers. Internalizing the racist ideology that divides people into the categories of pure/impure and us/them, the 8-rock people construct those who are non-8-rock as the inferior, degraded, impure Other, and they establish a blood rule to maintain the racial purity of their group and to solidify 8-rock identity. When the New Fathers decide to found a new town to revive the dream of their ancestors, Roger Best breaks the 8-rock blood rule by marrying Delia, a woman he met when he was stationed at an army base in Tennessee and who bore him a daughter out of wedlock during the war. To the 8-rock people, Delia—"a wife of sunlight skin, a wife of racial tampering" (197)—is an object of contempt. Remarking on Roger Best's plan to bring Delia and his illegitimate, light-skinned daughter, Pat, to the new town of Ruby, Steward Morgan, intoning the racist discourse of dirt and defilement, cruelly comments, "He's bringing along the dung we leaving behind" (201).

As Morrison is intent on showing in *Paradise*, when the Old Fathers found the city of Haven in 1890, they remove themselves from the larger society with its shaming categories of difference only to forge their own system of inclusion and exclusion which they pass down to their Ruby descendants. Yet the 8-rock politics of separatism also creates a strong sense of group identity, cultural belonging, and moral purpose in the people of Haven so that their town survives—indeed by 1932, it is thriving—while other all-black towns disappear or come to resemble slave quarters or become obsessed with wealth or hoard money and deeds while falling into disrepair. Maintaining a sense of communal togetherness, the people of Haven share everything and are vigilant to each other's needs. They also create a separatist community where they are safe from "the violence of whites, random and organized, that swirled around them" (108). Just as Zechariah Morgan—also known as Big Papa—had predicted, by staying and working and praying and defending together, the 8-rock people are kept from the fate of black people in places like Downs, Lexington, Sapulpa, and Gans, where people are run out of town, or the fate of those who end up dead or maimed in Tulsa, Norman, and Oklahoma City, or of those who become "victims of spontaneous whippings, murders and depopulation by arson" (112).

Yet over time Haven, "a dreamtown in Oklahoma Territory," becomes "Haven, a ghosttown in Oklahoma State" (5) as people are forced to move elsewhere to survive. Determined to "repeat what the Old Fathers had done," fifteen families move out of Haven in 1949 and found Ruby in 1950 (16). Veterans of World War II, the founders of Ruby return home, see what has happened to Haven, and recognize that they are living through the Disallowing, Part Two, as they hear stories about the missing testicles of black soldiers and about black veterans having their medals ripped off them by rednecks and Sons of the Confederacy. Going deep into Oklahoma, "as far as they could climb from the grovel contaminating the town their grandfathers had made," they determine that it will never happen again, that "nothing inside or out rots the one all-black town worth the pain" (16, 5). In choosing to name the town after Ruby, the sister of the Morgan twins, they memorialize the potentially lethal consequences of being viewed as an object of contempt—indeed, as animallike—in a white-dominated society, for Ruby dies in a nearby town on a waiting room bench in a hospital where the white doctors refuse to offer her medical assistance and a hospital nurse tries to find a veterinarian to treat her.

Except for Ruby and for Delia and her infant, no one dies *in* Ruby, and the townspeople are "real proud about that believing they are blessed" (199). Like the original Haven founded by the Old Fathers, Ruby provides protection from the dangers lurking Out There. "Ten generations had known what lay Out There: space, once beckoning and free, became unmonitored and seething; became a void where random and organized evil erupted when and where it chose. . . . Out There where your children were sport, your women quarry, and where your very person could be annulled. . . . Out There where every cluster of whitemen looked like a posse, being alone was being dead" (16). In Ruby, where people are "free and protected," a sleepless woman can safely walk down the road at night since "[n]othing for ninety miles around" Ruby views her as "prey" (8). Living in a safe but also a circumscribed community suspicious of outsiders, the people of Ruby are "protective, God-loving, thrifty but not miserly" (160). To Deacon, one of the town fathers, Ruby—with its Central Avenue and its gospel-named St. Matthew, St. Mark, St. Luke, and St. John streets—is a black utopia, a place of "Quiet white and yellow houses full of industry; and in them were elegant black women at useful tasks; orderly cupboards minus surfeit or miserliness; linen laundered and ironed to perfection; good meat seasoned and ready for roasting" (111). Yet behind this ideal facade of industry and order, Richard Misner, who is a recent arrival in the town, detects evidence of the town's "unraveling" in the "glacial wariness" between the townspeople, in the community discord over the Oven, and in the troubled behavior of some of Ruby's young people, like Menus, who has become the town drunk, and Billie Delia, who runs away (161).

"[Y]ou in long trouble if you think you can disrespect a row you never hoed," Deacon Morgan says to members of Ruby's younger generation who want to clarify the meaning of Zechariah's inscription on the Oven's iron plaque, which reads ". . . the Furrow of His Brow" because the first word was lost when the Oven was moved from Haven to Ruby (86). The impact of respect and disrespect on intergenerational relations is reflected in the community conflict over the Oven's inscription. To the older generation, the message found on the Oven's plate is a clear command: "Beware the Furrow of His Brow" orders the people to be obedient to God's will and to sustain the dream of the Old Fathers. But the young people of Ruby, who anger their elders with their disrespectful backtalk, argue that "[n]o ex-slave would tell us to be scared all the time. To 'beware' God. To always be ducking and diving, trying to look out every minute in case He's getting ready to throw something at us, keep us down" (84). Under the sway of Reverend Richard Misner—the new Baptist minister who is considered militant by some people in Ruby because of his active support of the Civil Rights movement—the younger generation wants to change the wording of the Oven's inscription. In their view, it should read "Be the Furrow of His Brow": that is, the people, as a race, should *be* God's instrument for social justice, and *be* "the power," an idea that is blasphemous to the older generation (87). To Steward Morgan, who is disgusted with the attitudes of the town's young people, "Cut me some slack" is the slogan Ruby's youth really want to paint on the Oven. Young and naive, they have no idea of what it took to build Ruby: the things they were "protected from" and the "humiliations they did not have to face" (93). Steward scoffs at their black power backtalk and desire for Africanized name changes, "as if word magic had anything to do with the courage it took to be a man" (95). In the view of Deacon, the Oven, which was once a vital community meeting place where the baptized entered "sanctified life," has been "reduced" to a gathering place for Ruby's lazy young people (111). Once a symbol of 8-rock solidarity, the Oven comes to signify community dissension and the loss of group consensus about what to respect and value.

In describing the unraveling of Ruby, Morrison, as is her wont, slowly divulges the shameful secrets that haunt the proud and respectable 8-rock people, including the secrets of the women who have walked the road between Ruby and the Convent in times of trouble. For over twenty years Lone DuPres has observed Ruby's walking women. "Only women. Never men. . . . Back and forth, back and forth: crying women, staring women, scowling, lip-biting women or women just plain lost" (270). The pregnant and deeply shamed Arnette, who went to the Convent in 1970 and, after giving birth, abandoned her baby, is one of Ruby's walking women. In 1974, when K.D. and Arnette get married, Ruby's townspeople look forward to "the union" of the two warring families—the Morgans and the Fleetwoods—and an "end to the animus" that has soaked the friends and members of these families for the past four years, animus that centers on "the maybe-baby the bride had not acknowledged, announced or delivered" (144). As is typical of Morrison's fiction, the narrative, in a piecemeal and delayed fashion, discloses the shameful facts surrounding Arnette's "maybe-baby," explaining how Arnette, who viewed her pregnancy with revulsion, relentlessly hit her stomach and repeatedly inserted a mop handle between her legs in an attempt to "bash the life out of her life" (250). After giving birth to an infant boy, who was born premature, Arnette did not touch, look at, or inquire after the child, who died within several days. Rather than taking ownership of her shameful past, Arnette returns to the Convent four years later on her wedding night and asks for—indeed, screams for—her missing child. In accusing the Convent women of killing her child, she transfers onto them her own disavowed guilt and shame.

Like Arnette, Sweetie Fleetwood walks the road between Ruby and the Convent in a time of difficulty. Sweetie, who enacts the socially prescribed role of the all-giving, self-sacrificing mother, is a young woman who has not been out of the house during the six years she has cared for her damaged children. When Sweetie, in a driven way, strides purposefully through Ruby and then walks out of town toward the Convent, she is joined by a hitchhiker, Seneca, who becomes one of the Convent women. Instead of acknowledging her desire to abandon—to walk out on—her children and thus find relief from the exhausting burden of caring for them, Sweetie projects her own "sinful" desire onto her companion, imagining that she is "walking next to sin" (129). Similarly, when Sweetie is taken in at the Convent, she views the non-8-rock Convent women who care for her as demons and prays for deliverance from them. During her stay at the Convent, Sweetie, who has never heard her own children cry, suggestively hears the "clear yearning call" of a crying child, a potentially healing sound that is like "an anthem, a lullaby" (129–30). Rather than confronting and attempting to work through her own unexpressed grief, Sweetie blocks out "every sound except the admonitions of her Lord." Subsequently, when she is reunited with her husband who asks her what happened, she says of the Convent women, "They made me, snatched me" (130). In placing blame on the Convent women by insisting that they "snatched" her, Sweetie refuses to take ownership of her own wish to walk away from her damaged and silent children.

If some of Ruby's women, like Arnette and Sweetie, have walked the seventeen-mile road between Ruby and the Convent in times of trouble, they nevertheless retain their sense of 8-rock purity and respectability by, in effect, depositing their shame at the Convent. Even though the 8-rock people once saw their Convent neighbors as strange but harmless—indeed, even as helpful on occasion since the women took in people who were lost or needed a rest—over time, as the Convent becomes the repository of the scandalous secrets of the respectable 8-rocks, the people of Ruby come to perceive the Convent women as objects of shame and as potentially dangerous. For Menus, the town drunk who spent some weeks at the Convent drying out, the Convent women—who cleaned up Menus's shit and vomit when he had the d.t.'s and listened to his sobs and curses—serve as a painful reminder of his own shame and dirtiness. K.D., who suffers from his memory of the humiliating love he had for Gigi, projects his own sense of shame onto the Convent women. Like K.D., Deacon Morgan, one of the New Fathers who views the Convent as the entrance to hell, once had a passionate affair with a Convent woman: the green-eyed, golden-skinned Consolata. When Consolata bit Deacon's lip and licked the blood from it, he became revolted and turned against her, seeing her as the sexually savage and primitive female Other. To the proud and respectable Deacon, Consolata stands as a visible reminder of his personal shame. A "Salomé from whom he had escaped just in time," she is an "uncontrollable, gnawing woman who had bitten his lip just to lap the blood it shed" (280, 279). And to Steward Morgan, who knew of his married twin's sexual affair, Consolata is the "hussy" who might have gotten pregnant and had "a mixed-up child." Years later Steward seethes at the thought of his twin brother's "barely averted betrayal of all they owed and promised the Old Fathers" (279).

"Did they really think they could keep this up? The numbers, the bloodlines, the who fucks who?" Pat Best comes to wonder. In Ruby, where skin color determines how people are chosen and ranked, women hold the key to the racial purity of the 8-rocks. "The generations had to be not only racially untampered with but free of adultery too. 'God bless the pure and holy' indeed. That was their purity. That was their holiness. That was the deal Zechariah had made during his humming prayer. It wasn't God's brow to be feared. It was his own, their own." Given the desire of Ruby men for "[u]nadulterated and unadulteried 8-rock blood," everything that troubles the New Fathers "must come from women" (217). In an exposé of the contempt-disgust scripts that fuel intraracial prejudice and the dismissive othering of those deemed to be different, *Paradise* views the Convent women, who are "impure" because they are not 8-rock (297), through the contemptuous gaze of the Ruby men who raid the Convent. In the essentialist racist discourse of the 8-rock people, the Convent women are represented as the impure, uncivilized, degenerate Other. Intoning the shaming discourse of defilement and pathology, the Ruby men construct the Convent women as "slack" and "sloven" women and as "detritus: throwaway people," and the Convent, itself, as the site of community impurity and shame: as "diseased," a place of "filth" (8, 4, 8, 3). "Bodacious black Eves unredeemed by Mary," the Convent women are sexually unrestrained "whores" and racially impure "slime" (18, 288). They are "nasty" women who draw Ruby people to the Convent "like flies to shit," and, in a classic description of shame contagion, everyone who has contact with them is "maimed somehow" and the "mess" ends up seeping back into Ruby's homes and families (275, 276).

In telling the story of the Convent women side by side with the story of how the Ruby men come to pathologize and scapegoat the women, *Paradise* focuses attention on the blocked thinking of racial assumptions and stereotypes. While the opening sentence of the novel indicates that the Ruby men, in their attack on the Convent, shoot the white girl first, Morrison never openly identifies which character is white, an authorial strategy that has prompted some commentators to attempt to solve the racial puzzle posed by the narrative. Describing her intention, Morrison explains that she deliberately withheld racial markers in depicting her characters so that her readers would know "everything, or almost everything, about the characters, their interior lives, their past, their faults, their strengths, except that one small piece of information which was their race" (Timehost 8). "I wanted the readers to wonder about the race of those girls," Morrison comments, "until those readers understood that their race didn't matter. I want to dissuade people from reading literature in that way. . . . Race is the least reliable information you can have about someone. It's real information, but it tells you next to nothing" (Gray, "Paradise" 67). By adamantly refusing to name which character is white, Morrison also urges those readers who try to solve the text's racial puzzle to become aware of their own participation in the blocked thinking of racial stereotypes. Yet while Morrison's aim in her depiction of the Convent women, as she has remarked, is "to write race and to unwrite it at the same time" (Oprah), she also deliberately invokes inherited shaming stereotypes and images in her representation of these characters as marginalized outsiders and female victims. Unable to resolve the intraracial conflict she dramatizes in describing the horrible outcome of the Disallowing of the non-8-rock Convent women, Morrison, as we shall see, instead provides a magical, aesthetic denouement to the deadly contempt-disappear scenario enacted in the text.

Recalling other Morrison mother figures, Mavis Albright—the first Convent woman introduced in the novel—is constructed as a victim but also as a negligent and abandoning mother. Mavis's story begins in Maryland in 1968 after the death of her newborn twins, Merle and Pearl. The twenty-seven-year-old Mavis, who is terrified of her sexually and physically abusive husband, Frank, causes the suffocation death of her twins by leaving them in the backseat of her husband's 1965 mint green Cadillac on a hot day with the windows closed when she rushes out to buy him something for dinner. Believing that Frank is plotting to have her own children, including her eleven-year-old daughter, Sal, kill her, the panic-stricken Mavis drives off in Frank's Cadillac, ultimately ending up at the Convent. If at first glance Mavis appears to be a recognizable social type—a victimized woman with a shameful past—she, like the other Convent women, is shown to transcend easy social formulations. Before leaving town, Mavis, in a framed moment of contemplation that prepares for her later ecstatic dance with the other Convent women, sees a tall rose of Sharon that looks wild as it, stirred by the exhaust fan of an air conditioner, appears to dance. The fact that Mavis senses that the Convent is crowded with the ghosts or spirits of "laughing? singing?" children (41), including her dead twins, Merle and Pearl, and that she sees the dying Mother Superior—Mary Magna—ringed by a blinding white light in a house without electricity suggests that the Convent exists in a liminal space between the material and the ghostly or spiritual worlds, an idea that Morrison repeats and elaborates on as the narrative unfolds.

Just as Morrison invokes culturally powerful and shaming images—those of the battered wife and the neglectful, abandoning mother—in her construction of Mavis, so she initially presents the sexually enticing Gigi as another disreputable type. When Gigi first gets off the bus in Ruby in 1970, K.D. is sexually attracted to her. "K.D., who had never seen a woman mince or switch like that, believed it was the walk that caused all the trouble. . . . [T]here she was . . . in pants so tight, heels so high, earrings so large. . . . She crossed Central Avenue . . . taking tiny steps on towering block heels not seen since 1949" (53). Gigi, who enjoys the "waves of raw horniness slapping her back" as she walks down Ruby's central street (67), is drawn to Ruby by her wish to see the rock formation of Wish, Arizona, described by her jailed boyfriend: that of a black man and woman "fucking forever" (63). Once a part of the Black Power movement, Gigi remains haunted by her memory of how, during a Black Panther demonstration in Oakland that turned into a clash with the police, she saw a well-dressed boy, who had been shot, spit blood into his hands to keep from ruining his glossy shoes the way he had ruined his blood-soaked white shirt. Demoralized by her experiences, Gigi holds on to the story of the eternal desert coupling "for dear and precious life. Underneath gripping dreams of social justice, of an honest people's guard—more powerful than her memory of the boy spitting blood into his hands—the desert lovers broke her heart" (64). What attracts Gigi to Ruby is a story she hears about a magical place in Ruby near a lake where two fig trees grow together, entwined like lovers, a liminal space where the sacred-ecstatic and physical-sexual are conjoined. "[I]f you squeezed in between them in just the right way, well, you would feel an ecstasy no human could invent or duplicate. 'They say after that can't nobody turn you down,'" Gigi is told (66). A study in contrasts, Gigi is a shameful woman, an "[e]xhibitionist bitch" (167) in the view of Mavis, and yet she is also suggestively called "Grace" by Consolata.

The twenty-year-old Seneca, who finds her way to the Convent in 1973, is yet another socially shamed type. Abandoned when she is five years old by Jean, whom Seneca believes is her sister but who, in fact, is her mother, Seneca spends four nights and five days knocking on every door in her public housing building during her search for Jean, who leaves a letter for her daughter next to a box of Lorna Doones. On the fourth day of Seneca's search, a tall crying woman walks past the window, and this crying, walking woman becomes permanently associated in Seneca's mind with the loss of Jean as a kind of "heartbreaking dream" (128). Raised in foster homes, Seneca takes reprimands quietly and never cries. When she is sexually abused by a foster brother in one of the homes, Seneca discovers the secret and shameful habit of self-cutting through the accident of being scratched by her abuser with the safety pin holding together the waistband of her jeans. Becoming involved as a young adult in exploitive relationships—with a boyfriend who ends up imprisoned and a rich woman who uses her as a sex toy—Seneca stows away on trucks, eventually finding herself at the Convent. A sweet girl who takes on the role of peacemaker between the warring Mavis and Gigi, Seneca secretly continues her acts of self-cutting at the Convent. "It thrilled her. It steadied her. Access to this under garment life kept her own eyes dry, inducing a serenity rocked only by crying women, the sight of which touched off a pain so wildly triumphant she would do anything to kill it" (261).

Like Seneca, Pallas Truelove, who is sixteen years old when she arrives at the Convent in 1974, is a sexual victim, and she too is a mother-abandoned girl. When Pallas, who lives with her rich lawyer father, falls in love with Carlos—the maintenance man at her high school and a would-be sculptor— the two travel to New Mexico where they stay at an artist's colony with Pallas's painter mother, Dee Dee. After Pallas discovers her mother and Carlos in the act of having sex, she blindly drives off, is chased by some boys in a truck, forced off the road, and then raped. In order to escape her attackers, she hides in the black water of a nearby lake. Brought to the Convent by Billie Delia, the traumatized Pallas, who remains mute at first, is finally able to tell her "backward and punctured and incomplete story" to Consolata (173). To Pallas—who is renamed "Divine" after her mother, Dee Dee, which is short for Divine—the Convent is a place that feels "permeated with a blessed male-lessness, like a protected domain, free of hunters" (177). And yet at night the sniffling of the traumatized and pregnant Pallas-Divine Truelove—"the sad little rich girl with the hurt but pretty face" (259)—can be heard all over the Convent.

In telling the stories of the social misfits who come to live at the Convent—Mavis, Gigi, Seneca, and Pallas—*Paradise* focuses on their pain and shame while it also provides mysterious hints and guesses of the liminality of the Convent world they inhabit with Connie-Consolata. Also one of life's unfortunate people, Connie-Consolata spends many years as the devoted servant of Mary Magna, who rescued Consolata when she was a nine-year-old girl, refusing to leave the green-eyed girl with "tea-colored hair" and "smoky, sundown skin" in the "shit-strewn" Brazilian city where she found her (223). Consolata, who was molested when she was nine, remains celibate for thirty years until she meets Deacon, a man who reminds her of the black people from her home. During their affair, they meet in the magical place where the two fig trees grow entwined like lovers. After their affair ends and a "sunshot" sears Consolata's right eye, "announcing the beginning of her bat vision," Consolata, like a half-blind seer, begins to see "best in the dark" (241). And she also discovers that she has the power to raise the dead. Deliberately intoning the nonrealistic discourse of occultism and religious miracle, *Paradise* describes how Consolata uses her gift—her ability to step inside other people—to prolong the life of Mary Magna. "Stepping in to find the pinpoint of light. Manipulating it, widening it, strengthening it. Reviving, even raising, her from time to time. And so intense were the steppings in, Mary Magna glowed like a lamp till her very last breath in Consolata's arms" (247).

A contradictory character, Consolata is endowed with magical-spiritual powers and yet the aging Consolata, who feels orphaned after Mary Magna dies, becomes a helpless and hopeless alcoholic full of self-loathing: "a drunken, ignorant, penniless woman living in darkness unable to rise from a cot to do something useful or die on it and rid the world of her stench. Grayhaired, her eyes drained of what eyes were made for, she imagined how she must appear. Her colorless eyes saw nothing clearly except what took place in the minds of others" (248). Consolata, who becomes "repelled by her sluglike existence" and craves "oblivion" (221), eventually turns against the women she has harbored, viewing them as the people of Ruby do, with contempt not compassion. When in 1976 the sixty-year-old Consolata looks at the women who have come to live at the Convent over an eight-year period, she sees "broken girls, frightened girls, weak and lying" (222). Finding it increasingly difficult to tell one from another, Consolata has mostly forgotten what she knew about them, "and it seemed less and less important to remember any of it, because the timbre of each of their voices told the same tale: disorder, deception and . . . drift. The three *d*'s that paved the road to perdition, and the greatest of these was drift" (221–22). On her worst days, Consolata wants to kill them, to snap their necks: "Anything to stop the badly cooked indigestible food, the greedy hammering music, the fights, the raucous empty laughter, the claims. But especially the drift" (222).

That the alcoholic Consolata—a woman tormented by feelings of debilitating self-contempt—is destined by the narrative to become the spiritual leader of the women she contemptuously disallows when she condemns them for their "drift" points to Morrison's conscious determination to counteract shame in her dramatization of the rehabilitation and redemption of the throwaway women who inhabit the Convent. Morrison, in describing *Paradise* as the final work of the trilogy that she began with *Beloved*, explains how she once planned to write a single novel about the nature of "the beloved," which she describes as the part of us "that is reliable, that never betrays us, that is cherished by us, that we tend to cover up and hide and make into a personality" (Straits Times 2). Morrison also remarks that in *Paradise* she explores a special kind of love—"the love of God and love for fellow human beings"—and that as she investigates religious belief in the novel she juxtaposes "organized religion and unorganized magic as two systems" (Donahue 1). Even though the African-American Christianity of Ruby includes glimpses of the mysterious world of dreams and portents and walking men—that is, spiritual or ancestral guides—there is an inevitable clash between Ruby's organized religion and the unorganized magic practiced by the Convent women. Consolata, who comes to practice the African-Brazilian religion Candomblé—a hybrid mixture of Catholicism and African spirit worship[5]— initiates the Convent women into the occult knowledge of the ancestors, thus helping them discover "the beloved": the authentic and divine part of the self hidden behind the socially constructed layers of the personality.

The process of recovering the beloved part of the self begins with Consolata's encounter with the walking man who wears a hat and glittering, mirrored sunglasses. Consolata's stranger recalls Dovey's "Friend," a walking man who, talking without moving his lips, tells Dovey that he lives close by and to whom Dovey freely discusses things she did not know were on her mind. When Consolata's walking stranger approaches her and she asks him who he is, he replies, "Come on, girl. You know me." Suddenly beside her without having moved, looking at her "full of secret fun," he removes his hat. "Fresh, tea-colored hair came tumbling down, cascading over his shoulders and down his back. He took off his glasses then and winked, a slow seductive movement of a lid. His eyes, she saw, were as round and green as new apples" (252). Her guardian deity or ancestral guide, the young and seductive man, who like Consolata has green eyes and tea-colored hair, represents the core part of Consolata's identity—the deity within or beloved part of the self.

Consolata, as she pays heed to her inner guardian, is revitalized over time as she experiences a melding of opposites—that is, of young/old and male/female—into a single identity. "I call myself Consolata Sosa," a transformed Consolata says to the other women at the Convent. "If you want to be here you do what I say. Eat how I say. Sleep when I say. And I will teach you what you are hungry for." When the women look at Consolata, they do not recognize her. "She has the features of dear Connie, but they are sculpted somehow—higher cheekbones, stronger chin. Had her eyebrows always been that thick, her teeth that pearly white? Her hair shows no gray. Her skin is smooth as a peach. Why is she talking that way? And what is she talking about? they wonder." Consolata's promise to the women—"Someone could want to meet you" (262)—prepares for the women's recovery of the deity within and also for Consolata's merging and expanding identities as she assumes the identity not only of the Mother Superior, Mary Magna—indeed Consolata, nunlike, comes to wear a blue dress with a white collar as well as the nun's black shoes—but also of the ancestral or spiritual guide.

Instructing the women to lie naked on the stone floor of the Convent basement in chosen poses, Consolata paints a silhouette around each woman's body and tells each to remain silent within the chosen mold. As a "new and revised Reverend Mother" (265), Consolata teaches a very different lesson from the one taught to her by the nuns who, after purchasing the Convent from an embezzler, attempted to remove all signs of the original owner's fascination with erotica, leaving behind "traces" of their "failed industry" in such details as the female-torso candleholders in the hallway candelabra, the nipple-tipped doorknobs, and the alabaster vagina ashtrays in the game room (72). "Eve is Mary's mother. Mary is the daughter of Eve," Consolata says to the women as she schools them in the ancestral wisdom that conjoins the opposites of body and spirit. "Never break them in two. Never put one over the other," she asserts (263).

When the "loud dreaming" stage of the women's initiation begins, each woman, in spite of or because of her aching body, can "step easily into the dreamer's tale" told by the other women. In describing the "loud dreaming" of the women, Morrison dramatizes her long-held view of the ideal reader-text transaction as one in which the reader-participant is open and receptive to the text. As the women become receptive to and imaginatively enter each other's stories, they undergo a collective and painful process as they experience Mavis's discovery that her twins are dead; Pallas's frightening escape from her attackers; Gigi's experience in the Oakland demonstration; and Seneca's search for the missing Jean. "In loud dreaming, monologue is no different from a shriek; accusations directed to the dead and long gone are undone by murmurs of love. So, exhausted and enraged, they rise and go to their beds vowing never to submit to that again but knowing full well they will. And they do" (264). A collective sharing of trauma, the "loud dreaming" has the potential to heal. For as the women draw pictures of what haunts them—"Rose of Sharon petals, Lorna Doones. A bright orange couple making steady love under a childish sun" (265)—they talk to each other about what they have dreamed or drawn.

Under Consolata's guidance, the Convent women come to meet the beloved part of the self—the "unbridled, authentic self" (177) presaged in their names: Albright, Grace, Seneca, and Divine Truelove. Over time, they alter, having "to be reminded of the moving bodies they wore, so seductive were the alive ones below" (265). Becoming "calmly themselves," they are "no longer haunted" (266). When the longed-for purifying rain comes, they dance in the rain, entering a state of religious ecstasy that heals them of their sorrow and pain, allowing Seneca to let go of the terrible day she was abandoned, Gigi to witness the cleansing of the bloodied shirt of the boy, Mavis to move in the shuddering dance of the rose of Sharon, and Pallas to hold close her son while the rain rinses away her fear of the black water. Afterward, the women, tired but happy from their night dance, listen to Consolata's soothing stories about the mystical, poetical Piedade, "a singing woman who never spoke" (285).

Deliberately, *Paradise* juxtaposes rhapsodic descriptions of the Convent women's discovery of the beloved or divine part of the self—depicting them as "holy women dancing in hot sweet rain" (283)—with grim accounts of the Ruby men honing their evidence against the women and carrying out the assault. To the Ruby men, the Convent women represent a danger to the community. The men see them as "Bitches. More like witches. . . . Before those heifers came to town this was a peaceable kingdom. . . . These here sluts out there by themselves never step foot in church. . . . They don't need men and they don't need God" (276). Each of the men, as the narrative explains, is looking for someone else to blame for personal or family troubles or for problems in the town: Sargeant, for the backtalk of Ruby's youth; Wisdom Poole, for the shooting between his brothers, Brood and Apollo, over Billie Delia; Arnold and Jefferson Fleetwood, for Sweetie's defective children; Menus, for his loss of the redbone woman; Harper, for his failed first marriage; K.D., for his lasting grudge against Gigi; and Steward and Deacon, for the threat Consolata's affair with Deacon represents to their family pride and Ruby dream.

"I wanted to open with somebody's finger on the trigger," Morrison has remarked, "to close when it was pulled, and to have the whole novel exist in that moment of the decision to kill or not" (Mulrine). Showing the deadly consequences of the shame-and-blame drama presented in the text and circling back to the novel's beginning as the men, with their "clean, handsome guns" (3), take aim to save Ruby, Morrison describes the massacre of the Convent women as the men first shoot the white girl, and then, at their leisure, shoot Consolata in the forehead and gun down the rest of the women as they run through the backyard. Immediately after the assault on the Convent, the people of Ruby are disheartened about what has happened. "How hard they had worked for this place; how far away they once were from the terribleness they have just witnessed. How could so clean and blessed a mission devour itself and become the world they had escaped?" (292).

But *Paradise*, even as it represents a horrific crime, refuses to punish the attackers and even erases the physical evidence that a massacre has occurred. In a scene that calls to mind the strange disappearances of the literary predecessors of the Convent women—Beloved and Wild—the bodies of the Convent women mysteriously disappear without a trace. Afterward, there are conflicting versions of what happened: that when the nine Ruby men went to the Convent to persuade the women to either leave or change their ways, there was a fight and the women assumed other shapes and vanished; or that when five of the nine men went to the Convent to evict the women and four to restrain them, some of the five unfortunately killed the old woman while the other four men successfully drove out the rest of the women, who went off in Mavis's Cadillac; or that the women were swept up by God before the very eyes of the people of Ruby to give the townspeople a second chance. Relieved that there are no dead to report, the people of Ruby over time change the story of the assault "to make themselves look good," and the families of the nine men support them by "enhancing, recasting, inventing misinformation." Pat Best believes that the nine men murdered five harmless, non-8-rock women, who were perceived as impure and unholy, because "they *could*—which was what being an 8-rock meant to them and was also what the '8-rock meant to them and was also what the 'deal' required" (297). To Billie Delia, similarly, the men "had seen in lively, free, unarmed females the mutiny of the mares and so got rid of them" (308).

Most of the Ruby men involved in the massacre remain unchanged: for example, Sargeant Person appears "as smug as ever"; an uncontrite Harper Jury assumes the role of the "bloodied but unbowed warrior against evil"; Menus's alcoholism worsens; and Steward Morgan remains "insolent and unapologetic" (299). Deacon Morgan, however, does change. Before the assault, Deacon and Steward had "performed as one man," had "agreed on almost everything," and were "in eternal if silent conversation" (62, 155). But afterward, Deacon's "inside difference" from his twin, Steward, becomes apparent (299). "It was as though he had looked in his brother's face and did not like himself anymore" (300). A remorseful Deacon publicly walks barefoot to Richard Misner's house where he confesses that he has become "the kind of man who set himself up to judge, rout and even destroy the needy, the defenseless, the different" (302).

"The overwhelming question for me," Morrison has remarked in her discussion of *Paradise*, "was how does it happen that people who have a very rich, survivalist, flourishing revolutionary impetus end up either like their oppressor, or self-destructive in a way that represents the very thing they were running from" (McKinney-Whetstone 2). In a passage that openly thematizes the novel, Richard Misner reflects on how the error of the Ruby men has grown out of racial shame. "They think they have outfoxed the whiteman when in fact they imitate him. They think they are protecting their wives and children, when in fact they are maiming them. And when the maimed children ask for help, they look elsewhere for the cause. Born out of an old hatred, one that began when one kind of black man scorned another kind and that kind took the hatred to another level, their selfishness had trashed two hundred years of suffering and triumph in a moment of such pomposity and error and callousness it froze the mind." Questioning the separatist, exclusionary politics of the 8-rock people, Richard Misner wonders how the people of Ruby can hold together their "hard-won heaven defined only by the absence of the unsaved, the unworthy and the strange" (306). When the Oven—once a symbol of community solidarity—shifts slightly on one side and the young people change the graffiti on the Oven's hood to read "We Are the Furrow of His Brow" (298), Lone sees these as signs that the people of Ruby have deviated from God's ways. In its depiction of the lethal consequences of the Disallowing, *Paradise*, like Morrison's other novels, reveals that shame-rage feeling traps can be transmitted from one generation to another in the form of intraracial prejudice and can lead not only to bitter hatred against those who are different but also to black-on-black violence.

Morrison, in describing her struggles with the closure of *Paradise*, remarks that she had to "really work the novel" before she figured out how "the totality of the ending would play out. Would the assault be successful?" (McKinney-Whetstone 3). She recalls how she pondered whether her characters would be killed or would escape until she recognized that they could both be killed and escape (Rose). If part of Morrison's conscious agenda in the closure is to counteract the contemptuous dismissal and othering of the Convent women by describing their spiritual redemption, the narrative also repeats a pattern common in Morrison's fiction as it acts out a contempt-disappear scenario in its depiction of the murder-disappearance of the women. Ending where the narrative began—with an account of the assault on the Convent—*Paradise* presents two competing visions in the concluding scenes: a despairing vision of the intergenerational perpetuation of shame and violence in the horrible scapegoating of the Convent women and a hopeful vision of the healing power of the ancestral imagination to solve the issue of difference. Unable to realistically resolve the conflict between the contradictory value systems embodied in the opposing worlds of Ruby and the Convent, Morrison instead offers an artistic solution to the narrative impasse of *Paradise* in the closure, which turns the contempt-disappear script enacted in the murder of the Convent women into a magical scene of escape and resurrection. In their differing responses to *Paradise*'s problematic closure, commentators reflect the narrative's divided perceptions. Whereas some commentators are troubled by the "slaughter of innocents" that begins and ends the novel or feel that the closure makes "a too easy retreat into the supernatural, escaping the details of everyday struggle" (Bemrose, Bold), others claim that *Paradise* is a novel in which "terrible things happen, but not in a way that stifles joy and hope" or feel that there is "little sense of defeat" at the book's end, which provides a "clear-eyed reckoning" that comes close to "authentic redemption" (Tompkins 3, Shields 3).

Despite Morrison's intention in presenting the Convent women to write a race-free discourse, *Paradise*, like Morrison's other works, shows just how much race matters by pointing to the pervasive and destructive impact of racial prejudice on the lives of the characters. In focusing on the unorganized magic of the Convent women, who learn that "Mary is the daughter of Eve," Morrison also envisions the potentially liberating force of an ancestral belief system premised on the coexistence of contradictory elements within the individual and collective identity. If the Western belief system, with its binary oppositions of male/female, black/white, body/spirit, pure/impure, leads to the demonizing and scapegoating of those designated as Other, the ancestral belief system, which conceives the individual as an embodiment of these opposing elements, has the potential to undo the projective and divisive split between self and other, Morrison suggests in the closure of *Paradise*.

Billie Delia's—and the reader's—hope that the women are "out there," that is, her hope "for a miracle" (308), is answered by Morrison who enacts an authorial rescue of her characters as she depicts the "miracle" of the dead women's survival in a kind of parallel universe. The threshold or passageway between the material and spiritual worlds is the closed door to be opened or the already opened window sensed by Anna Flood and Richard Misner when they visit the deserted Convent. "What would be on the other side? What on earth would it be? What on earth?" (305). What is found on the other side is another place that is "neither life nor death" and is "just yonder" (307). Existing in this liminal state and able to travel between the material and spiritual worlds, Gigi talks to her imprisoned father in the magical place where two trees grow near a lake and Mavis comforts and makes peace with her grown daughter, Sal, while both Pallas and Seneca appear before but do not acknowledge their mothers. Through the stylized description of the goddesslike, sword-bearing Pallas—who appears as the Greek goddess Pallas Athena—and the depiction of Gigi dressed in the military attire of the people's army, *Paradise* replaces the novel's earlier image of the (earthly) woman victim with that of the (spiritual) woman warrior.

In *Paradise*'s final scene, Morrison blurs and transcends racial categories as she represents the mystical union of Consolata and Piedade. In a complex and dynamic way, this scene draws not only on the novel's earlier depictions of the relationship between Mary Magna, the white Mother Superior, and her black servant-daughter-initiate, Consolata, but also on Consolata's identity as a "new and revised" Mother Superior as well as her association with the soothing maternal images "of arms, a lap, a singing voice" (265, 177). *Paradise*'s representation of Consolata also seems designed to evoke the famous Black Madonna image of Our Lady of Guadalupe, the Consoler of the Afflicted who is depicted as having greenish eyes, black hair, and brown skin (see, e.g., Rodriguez 19). In *Paradise*'s final scene, the white Mary Magna, the woman with whom Consolata has had a deep spiritual and daughterly bond, morphs into the Black Madonna, Piedade, which in Portuguese means "piety, pity, compassion, mercy." In a similar way, the brown-skinned Consolata takes on a complex multiracial identity in a description which, perhaps, is also meant to draw on common artistic depictions of the *Pietà* that show Mary holding the dead Christ in her lap: "In ocean hush a woman black as firewood is singing. Next to her is a younger woman whose head rests on the singing woman's lap. Ruined fingers troll the tea brown hair. All the colors of seashells—wheat, roses, pearl—fuse in the younger woman's face. Her emerald eyes adore the black face framed in cerulean blue" (318).

Countering the earlier troubling representations of abandoned and traumatized, or even dead, children, *Paradise* ends with a consoling image of divine maternal love in its depiction of the Black Madonna. A healing figure, the Black Madonna, as Lucia Birnbaum has remarked, "counters racism and sexism and connotes nurturance of the 'other' in contrast to the violence toward the 'other' that has historically characterized established religious and political doctrines" (12).[6] In the text's merging of racial identities—as the white Mother Superior becomes the Black Madonna and the black daughter becomes the racial hybrid with the colors of wheat, rose, and pearl fused in her face—Morrison also evokes the idea of cross-racial mutability and mutuality. Susan Gubar, in her discussion of "racechanges," remarks on how the image of the interdependent—and interracial—mother-child pair can pose "an antidote to racism in a fostering of the Other within the self" (229). Because "[t]he 'intersubjective mode where two subjects meet'— mother and child . . . black and white—negotiates between separateness and relatedness, bounded and unbounded possibilities," explains Gubar, it holds out "some future solution to past conflictual . . . racial Othering" (230).[7] For Gubar, the mixed-race individual is an image of the transgression of racial boundaries that captures the redemptive possibility of a postracist society or transracial consciousness. Even as *Paradise* focuses on the horrific consequences of racial shaming as it describes the scapegoating of the Convent women, the closure also presents the healing and redemptive gesture foreshadowed in the novel's epigraph, which, like the epigraph to *Jazz*, is taken from the gnostic writing "Thunder, Perfect Mind": *"And they will find me there,/ and they will live,/ and they will not die again."*

The Convent women, having packed their knapsacks and said their goodbyes, head to port in the ship that carries the "lost and saved" to a distinctly earthly paradise—a place where Consolata adoringly gazes at the singing Piedade while "[a]round them on the beach, sea trash gleams. Discarded bottle caps sparkle near a broken sandal. A small dead radio plays the quiet surf" (318). Describing her intentions in the closure, Morrison remarks that the reference to ships and passengers is meant to suggest that "an earthly Paradise is the only one we know" (Marcus 1). Moreover, the final word of the novel—"Paradise"—should be corrected to read "paradise," Morrison has insisted, for her desire in her novelistic interrogation of the idea of paradise is to "move" paradise "from its pedestal of exclusion and to make it more accessible to everybody" (Timehost 6). In Morrison's earthly paradise—a liminal world that conjoins the material and spiritual—the Convent women will be reunited with Consolata, their spiritual guide. And there they will meet the singing Piedade, a complex figure who represents not only the Black Madonna and ancestor figure but also the goddesslike muse and the supreme singer-storyteller, for "There is nothing to beat this solace which is what Piedade's song is about. . ." (318). "There is a certain kind of peace," Morrison states, "that is not merely the absence of war. It is larger than that. . . . The peace I am thinking of is the dance of an open mind when it engages another equally open one—an activity that occurs most naturally, most often in the reading/writing world we live in" ("Dancing Mind" 7). In describing Consolata's receptive listening to Piedade's solacing song in the closure of *Paradise*, Morrison dramatizes her view of the reading process as an empathic and interactive connection between the author-storyteller and her readers as she celebrates the deep pleasure of literature found in the peace of the dancing mind.

An author whose works have gained a permanent and honored place in the American literary canon, Morrison herself has come to be regarded as a national treasure. John Leonard, recalling his "Travels with Toni" to Stockholm, Sweden, in 1993 for the Nobel Prize Award ceremony, writes about the glory of Morrison's "enNobeling." "There's never been such majesty," Leonard writes of the magical moment when Morrison descended the marble staircase on the arm of the King of Sweden ("Travels" 62). When Morrison published a novel after being "enNobeled," she faced the possible shame risk of having critics compare *Paradise* unfavorably to her earlier works. "I've been holding my breath since December 1993. After such levitation, weren't all of us in for a fall?" writes Leonard. "I was holding my breath, and she took it away" ("Shooting Women" 25, 29). Retaining her pride of place in American—and, indeed, in world—literature, Morrison, in *Paradise*, provides a hopeful vision of redemption as she gestures toward the utopian possibility of a transracial consciousness in her novel's closure. But she also reminds us that race and the dismissive, contemptuous othering of people still matter and that, indeed, we must attend to race matters for they are, as *Paradise* shows us, a matter of life and death.

Notes

1. "Speaking the Unspeakable"

1. In *Psychoanalysis and Black Novels*, Claudia Tate explains why psychoanalytic theory has been largely shunned by black intellectuals. "Instead of regarding individuals and their stories as products of a dialectic of material circumstances *and* their internalization of them, psychoanalysis, as it generally operates, centers the individual's primary nurturing environment, not the external circumstances that precondition that environment." The psychoanalytic model "relegates the bleak material circumstances of real lives to the background," and thus scholars who study African-American literature "shun" psychoanalysis since it effectively "effaces racism and recasts its effects as a personality disorder caused by familial rather than social pathology" (16). Because of the continuation of racial oppression and "the demand for black literature to identify and militate against it," remarks Tate, "black literature evolves so as to prove that racism exists in the real world and is not a figment of the black imagination" (17).

In the course of this study, I show that the application of shame and trauma theory to the works of Morrison does not efface but instead illuminates the impact of pernicious racist practices on the black American cultural experience. Describing how shame "attends the process of subjection," Joseph Adamson and Hilary Clark write, "Whenever a person is disempowered on the basis of gender, sexual orientation, race, physical disability, whenever a person is devalued and internalizes the negative judgment of an other, shame flourishes" (3, 2–3).

2. In her discussion of the "forgotten history" of trauma, Judith Herman shows how "[p]eriods of active investigation have alternated with periods of oblivion" (*Trauma* 7). Although Freud, in his investigations of hysteria, grasped the truth of the actual sexual trauma suffered by his female

patients, he "retreated . . . into the most rigid denial." Rather than acknowl-edging "the exploitive nature of women's real experiences," Freud "insisted that women imagined and longed for the abusive sexual encounters of which they complained" (19). But when soldiers fighting in the First World War "began to break down in shocking numbers" and behave like hysterical women—"They screamed and wept uncontrollably. They froze and could not move. They became mute and unresponsive. They lost their memory and their capacity to feel"—the "reality of psychological trauma was forced upon public consciousness once again" (20).

Yet interest in trauma waned after the end of the First World War only to be revived again during the Second World War and later the Vietnam War. But it was not until 1980 that the American Psychiatric Association finally gave "formal recognition within the diagnostic canon" to a new category of mental disorder—the post-traumatic stress disorder (28). Only after 1980 did it finally become clear that the post-traumatic stress syndrome is seen in women survivors of rape, domestic battery, and incest (32). It has also been argued that women suffer from the "traumatic stresses" of "everyday" violence against and oppression of women (see Brown).

3. An insightful discussion of the similar neglect of the study of shame in literary scholarship is found in Joseph Adamson and Hilary Clark's intro-duction to *Scenes of Shame*—a collection of essays by literary critics and psychoanalysts who investigate the shame dynamics of works by authors such as Hawthorne, George Eliot, Faulkner, Anne Sexton, Nietzsche, and Kierkegaard. Adamson and Clark also provide an excellent overview of shame theory in their introduction. See also Joseph Adamson's application of shame theory to the analysis of Melville's works in *Melville, Shame, and the Evil Eye*.

4. African-American historian Nell Painter describes the psychic damage caused by slavery in her essay, "Soul Murder and Slavery: Toward a Fully Loaded Cost Accounting." Painter explains that there has been a "reluc-tance to deal with black people's psychology" following the 1960s debate on Stanley Elkins's book, *Slavery: A Problem in American Institutional and Intellectual Life* (1959). Elkins, who compared the trauma of Nazi concen-tration camps to that of slavery, claimed that African-American slaves, like concentration camp inmates, *"internalized"* the attitudes of their masters and that slavery produced "psychologically crippled adults who were docile, irre-sponsible, loyal, lazy, humble, and deceitful, in short, who were Sambos" (130–31).

Elkins was criticized for ignoring not only the importance of slave families and communities but also the fact of slave resistance and revolt. Yet Painter is troubled by the fact that "since the thunder and lightning of the Elkins controversy—even after the appearance of extensive revisionist writing—

scholars and lay people have avoided, and sometimes positively resisted, the whole calculation of slavery's psychological costs. The Sambo problem was solved through the pretense that black people do not have psyches." Arguing that it is "imperative" to reject those claims that deny the "psychological personhood" of slaves (131), Painter discusses the psychological damage resulting from both child abuse and the sexual abuse of women in slavery. But she also argues that both slave families and religious belief offered crucial means of support that helped slaves "resist being damaged permanently." Moreover, Painter claims that the white slave owners "inflicted the psychic damage of slavery upon themselves, their white families, and, ultimately, on their whole society" (139).

5. Like other "demonized" enemies described by Rafael Moses in his discussion of projection and the political process, black Americans have served as the "embodiment" of the "unconscious wishes" and "split-off affects" of the white culture (see 140–41). Moreover, as a scapegoated group in white America, African Americans have been players in the blaming drama that is part of the shame scenario. When shame is projected, "it can be a source of shame in the person receiving the projection," who is now blamed for the negative attributes of the projector. The scapegoating ritual acts out this process, for the designated scapegoat, who is unable to resist the projected shame, carries "all of the blame" and thus those who are freed from blame "become the shamers rather than the shamed" (Nancy Morrison 56).

Black psychiatrist James Comer describes how in the "white mind" the African American became a "receptacle" for the projection of white guilt and anxiety about "'bad' impulses," that is, sexual and aggressive feelings (131). "The conduct of the whites who participated in murdering and lynching blacks suggests that these grisly events served as a catharsis by purging the evil the whites feared in themselves and 'projected' onto the blacks. Black victims were castrated, tortured, burned and mutilated by white men, women and children in drunken, orgy-like atmospheres" (134).

Joel Kovel's analysis of white racism, with its polarizing binarisms of black/white and polluted/pure, also describes the projective—and shaming—mechanisms that have led to the scapegoating of black Americans. The "nuclear experience" of "aversive" white racism, writes Kovel, "is a sense of disgust about the body of the black person based upon a very primitive fantasy: that it contains an essence—dirt—that smells and may rub off onto the body of the racist" (84). Kovel roots racist aversion in a "bodily fantasy about dirt, which rests in turn upon the equation of dirt with excrement: the inside of the body turned out and threatening to return within. And within this nuclear fantasy, black people have come to be represented as the personification of dirt . . ." (89–90). Treating the black as Other, the white racist assigns hated or impure aspects of the self onto the black. "It is precisely this process of purification that creates the need to see another as the exemplar of impurity and to treat him as if he were exactly that" (91). Thus, "The fantasy of dirt and purification is the central theme of white racism from a subjective standpoint," according to Kovel. "It is a quintessential fantasy of Otherness—for the black body from which the white ego flees is his own body, lost in the Cartesian split of the cogito, and projected into the dark Otherness of the black" (xlv).

For an interesting analysis of the role played by the "discourse of dirt and defilement" in the Clarence Thomas Supreme Court confirmation hearings see Kendall Thomas, "Strange Fruit," 376–85.

6. Adrian Piper explains the difficulty inherent in this struggle with terminology. Remarking on the various terms used to designate African Americans—such as "blacks," "Negroes," "colored people," "Afro-Americans," "people of color," and "African Americans"—Piper comments that it "doesn't really matter" which classifying term is used "to designate those who have inferior and disadvantaged status, because whatever term is used will eventually turn into a term of derision and disparagement by virtue of its reference to those who are derided and disparaged, and so will need to be discarded for an unsullied one" (30).

7. Bell is arguing against the optimistic belief that racism was "a terrible and inexplicable anomaly stuck in the middle of our liberal democratic ethos," or the hopeful claim about the "declining significance of race" in American life—the view that "class has become more important than race in determining black life-chances in the modern industrial period" (Hochschild 3, W. J. Wilson 150). Because much of the work studying racial prejudice "assumes that racism derives largely from ignorance and false consciousness," observes Christopher Lane, the belief is that knowledge will enhance "cultural understanding" and diminish "inter- and intragroup hostility" (4, 5). In Lane's view, such assumptions ignore underlying issues that can be illuminated by psychoanalysis and that shed invaluable light on the psychic forces that drive racial resentments and hatreds.

8. In a speech that Morrison gave at Howard University on March 3, 1995 (which has not been published but has been quoted in several news reports), she remarks that "the genius of racism is that any political structure can host that virus. Any developed country can become a suitable home for fascism" (Morgan 35). Presenting a chilling "little scenario," Morrison draws a comparison between the rise of fascism in Nazi Germany and the current plight of African Americans. "Before there was a Final Solution, there was a first one. And after the first, there was a second, and after the second, there was a third. Who knows how many more? Because the descent into a final solution is not a jump. It's one step and then another and then another." The

initial step is to "construct an inferior enemy and use that enemy as both focus and diversion." This step is followed by "overt and coded name-calling, verbal abuse." After gathering "from among the enemy collaborators who agree with and sanitize the process of dispossession," the next step is to "pathologize the enemy" by, for example, recycling "'scientific racism' and the myth of racial superiority." The resultant criminalization of the "enemy" serves to "rationalize the building of holding arenas . . . especially for the males and absolutely [for] the children. Last, maintain at all costs silence" ("Holocaust in D.C.").

9. As postmodern theories of racial formation have observed, writes Epifano San Juan, race is "'an unstable and "decentered" complex of social meanings constantly being transformed by political struggle.' . . . Race can no longer be considered a fixed, ontological essence or a unitary, transcendental category predicated on the epistemological reasoning supplied by anthropology, biology, and other physical sciences. Rather it is a framework for articulating identity and difference, a process that governs the political and ideological constitution of subjects/agents in history" (7). The term "race" denotes a "social construct, a historical conceptualization of how the U.S. social formation was structured in dominance by the construction of every inhabitant as a racialized subject" (6). While "[p]ostmodern critiques of racism have decisively shifted attention away from empirical methodologies to scrutiny of the foundational assumptions of Western rationality," racism "as an ideological and political phenomenon has to be grounded first 'in the material conditions of existence,' the network of modes of production and interacting ideological and political levels" (12, 13).

Responding to the antiessentialist strain of contemporary race theory, Henry Louis Gates remarks on the "treacherous non sequitur that moves us from 'socially constructed' to essentially unreal. We typically go from 'constructed' to 'unstable,' which is one non sequitur, or to 'changeable by will' (which is a bigger problem still, given that 'will' is yet another construction)" (324). On the level of theory, Gates finds the attempt to "dismantle the scheme of differences" important: "it is important to remember that 'race' is *only* a sociopolitical category, nothing more: but it is also important to question the force of that 'only.' In its performative aspect, the proclamation of nonexistence of the Negro usually sounds like the old darky joke about the nigger in the chicken coop, denying his existence on the poultry's behalf. Spivak poses the question: can the subaltern speak? Possibly she can—but a chicken, never. We are, of course, accustomed to other tensions and disjunctions between theory and praxis. What a leading deconstructive theorist describes as 'the sense of loss of historical agency that accompanies the fragmentation of the self characteristic of social abstraction' has bred its own resistance, manifest in the claims of—indeed, in the authority of—experience. Thus Barbara Christian forcefully defends the specificity of the black woman's cultural work as a preserve both discursive and experiential . . ." (325).

See also Joyce Ann Joyce's "'Who the Cap Fit'" and Diana Fuss's "'Race' Under Erasure? Poststructuralist Afro-American Literary Theory" in *Essentially Speaking* 73–96. If Morrison refers to herself as an "African-American" writer despite the claims of some that such a label is essentializing, it is also the case that a "strategic essentialism becomes an almost indispensable tool" for a writer like Morrison who wants "to speak to and about a people whose individual lives may be markedly different, but who nonetheless suffer from a common form of racial hegemony" (McBride 774).

10. "Very few African Americans of a certain generation," writes Morrison, can "forget" the description of blacks found in the Encyclopaedia Britannica's infamous eleventh edition: "'[T]he mental condition of the negro is very similar to that of a child, normally good-natured and cheerful, but subject to sudden fits of emotion . . . capable of performing acts of singular atrocity . . . but often exhibiting in the capacity of servant a dog-like fidelity.'" Because illogic and contradiction are understood as basic characteristics of blacks, "when race is at play the leap from one judgment (faithful dog) to its complete opposite (treacherous snake) is a trained reflex" ("Official Story" xi). In her analysis of the "block and blocked thinking of racial stereotype," Morrison similarly remarks on the opposing fictions and interchangeable racial tropes used to depict African Americans. "Without individuation, without nonracial perception, black people, as a group, are used to signify the polar opposites of love and repulsion. On the one hand, they signify benevolence, harmless and servile guardianship, and endless love. On the other hand, they have come to represent insanity, illicit sexuality, and chaos." Since these are "interchangeable fictions from a utilitarian menu," they can be "mixed and matched to suit any racial palette. Furthermore, they do not need logical transition from one set of associations to another" ("Introduction" xv).

Morrison illustrates the exchange of racial tropes that occurs in racist thinking in her discussion of the shaming public spectacle of the Senate's investigation of Anita Hill's charges against Clarence Thomas, which provided "unprecedented opportunity to hover over and to cluck at, to meditate and ponder the limits and excesses of black bodies" ("Introduction" xvii). Anita Hill's testimony that Thomas sexually harassed her, rather than initiating a search for the truth on the part of the Senate investigators, "simply produced an exchange of racial tropes." As Thomas seemed in danger of "moving from 'natural servant' to 'savage demon,'. . . the force of the balance of the confirmation process was to reorder these signifying fictions. Is he lying or is she? Is he the benevolent one and she the insane one? Or is he the date raper, sexual assaulter, and illegal sexual signal, and she the docile, loyal servant?" ("Introduction" xvi). The accusation of sexual misconduct would have probably disqualified a white candidate, whose suitability would have been tainted by such accusations. "[B]ut with a black candidate, already stained by the figurations of blackness as sexual aggressiveness or rapaciousness or impotence, the stain need only be proved reasonably doubted, which is to say, if he is black, how can you tell if that really is a stain? Which is also to say, blackness is itself a stain, and therefore unstainable." If, to keep the Supreme Court "stain-free," Thomas had to be "bleached, race-free," Anita Hill's allegations of sexual misconduct "re-raced" Thomas: that is, "re-stained him, dirtied him," and thus the "'dirt' that clung to him following those allegations, 'dirt' he spoke of repeatedly, must be shown to have originated elsewhere. In this case the search for the racial stain turned on Anita Hill. Her character. Her motives. Not his" ("Introduction" xviii–xix).

11. If Morrison sees her role as a writer to bear witness, the reader's role in reconstructing Morrison's narratives is not unlike that of listeners of real-life shame and trauma stories who must uncover the shameful secret and reconstruct the fragmented narrative of the trauma sufferer. Because Morrison is aware that she risks hurting—that is, vicariously shaming and traumatizing—her readers, she, not unlike the therapist-listener, must create a safe-holding environment (see Goldberg 169 and Wilson and Lindy 6, 27, 38) for her readers, enabling them to both experience and process the shame- and trauma-driven stories of her characters. While Morrison protects her readers, she also wants her readers to feel something visceral and, indeed, readers of Morrison's fiction may experience intense emotional responses through the interaffective process that psychoanalysts refer to as the "contagion of affect."

Because both shame and trauma are contagious, therapists who deal with real-life shame or trauma sufferers often report experiencing discomforting, if not painful, affects in their role as witness-listeners. They may feel vicarious shame at another's vulnerability. Listening to the story of the shame sufferer may provoke their own sense of "failure" or "self-deficiency," or they may experience a sense of "helplessness," or they may want to "turn away" from another's shame (Andrew Morrison, *Shame* 6, Nathanson, *Shame and Pride* 319, Lewis, *Shame and Guilt* 15–17). In a similar way, those who listen to the trauma story may "experience degrees of hyperarousal" proportionate to the hyperarousal manifested by the traumatized individual; or they may experience "vicarious traumatization" in which imagery associated with the trauma story intrudes into their waking fantasies or dreams; or their "sense of personal vulnerability" may be heightened and they may share the victim's "experience of helplessness" (Wilson and Lindy 17, Herman, *Trauma* 140, 141). Identifying not only with the victim's helplessness but also with his or her rage, listeners may "experience the extremes of anger, from inarticulate fury through the intermediate ranges of frustration and irritability to abstract, righteous indignation" (Herman, *Trauma* 143). And listeners may also suffer "witness" or "bystander guilt" or may identify with the victim "through the experience of profound grief" (Herman, *Trauma* 145, 144). Adding to the complexity of the witness role, the listeners may also enter into shame- and trauma-specific role enactments. Shifting and dynamic, these roles range from positive roles—those of the fellow survivor, the helpful supporter, the rescuer or comforter, the advocate—to negative ones in which listeners are positioned as collaborators or hostile judges or contemptuous shamers or even as perpetrators (see, e.g., Wilson and Lindy 62–82).

2. "The Devastation That Even Casual Racial Contempt Can Cause"

1. Judith Herman's description, in *Father-Daughter Incest*, of the repeated recovery and suppression of the incest secret beginning with Freud reveals the power of such defensive denials (see 7–21).

2. Described by James Berger as marking "a pivotal moment in American racial discourse" (408), Daniel Moynihan's *The Negro Family: The Case for National Action* argues that the breakdown in the structure of the black family is a central cause of the persistence of black poverty. According to the report, "at the center of the tangle of pathology" of black culture is "the weakness of the family structure." The weakened family is "the principal source of most of the aberrant, inadequate, or anti-social behavior that did not establish, but now serves to perpetuate the cycle of poverty and deprivation" (Rainwater 76). A central focus of the Moynihan Report is the damaging impact of being raised in "a disorganized home without a father" (Rainwater 85). The fact that the black community "has been forced into a matriarchal structure . . . out of line with the rest of American society," according to the report, "seriously retards the progress of the group as a whole, and imposes a crushing burden on the Negro male and, in consequence, on a great many Negro women as well" (Rainwater 75).

In the controversy that followed the publication of the Moynihan Report, as Patricia Morton explains, "[c]ritics charged that the report wrongly and damagingly presented black Americans as the cause of their own problems," and they also characterized it as "a damaging and dangerous policy document stamped with government approval, which, in effect, 'blamed the victim'" by faulting African-American culture, particularly the pathology of the black family, for the continuation of African-American inequality (3, 125). Critics of the Moynihan Report also argued that "the Negro pathology thesis was out of step with the times," for the black movement had "challenged the crippled, 'crushed people' portrayal associated with that timeworn thesis by testifying to the resources and strengths of black Americans." Although the "pathology thesis was not quickly or easily dismissed," the black family was reinterpreted in a more positive way in the 1970s (125). "In contrast to the old equation of black deviance from white middle-class norms as pathological and dysfunctional," writes Morton, "the new black family studies increasingly emphasized Afro-American diversity—including familial and sexual departures from white norms—as a positive thing" (126). As the "strength-resiliency" emphasis came to displace the "pathology-disorganization" view of the black family, the family came to be seen not as "a problem" but as the preserver of the "health of black Americans in a racist, classist, and sick society" (Morton 128, 126). This change in perspective also led to the rejection of "the premise that African American culture was merely a shattered distortion of a homogeneous white American culture" (Berger 413).

If in *The Bluest Eye* Morrison represents a dysfunctional family in her portrayal of the Breedloves, in her next novel, *Sula*, as we shall see, she presents a black matriarch in her representation of Eva Peace.

3. It is possible that when Morrison wrote this scene she was remembering and responding to media reports on the response of African-American children to white and black baby dolls. "During the early fifties," recalls Susan Bordo, "when *Brown v. the Board of Education* was wending its way through the courts, as a demonstration of the destructive psychological effects of segregation black children were asked to look at two baby dolls, identical in all respects except color. The children were asked a series of questions: which is the nice doll? which is the bad doll? which doll would you like to play with? The majority of black children, Kenneth Clark reports, attributed the positive characteristics to the white doll, the negative characteristics to the black. When Clark asked one final question, 'Which doll is like you?' they looked at him, he says, 'as though he were the devil himself' for putting them in that predicament, for forcing them to face the inexorable and hideous logical implications of their situation. Northern children often ran out of the room; southern children tended to answer the question in shamed embarrassment [note that both of these are shame responses]. Clark recalls one little boy who laughed, 'Who am I like? That doll! It's a nigger and I'm a nigger!'" (262–63).

3. "I Like My Own Dirt"

1. As Sander Gilman explains this stereotype in his book *Difference and Pathology*, a "common feature of the nexus of blackness and madness" is the "fear of the Other's wildness and potential destructiveness" (136). Drawing on the long-held associations between skin color and pathology, the

myth of black madness projects onto African Americans white fears about the potential violence caused by white oppression.

    2. For some discussions of the mammy stereotype, see hooks, *Ain't I a Woman* 83–85, Jewell 37–44, D. Roberts 1–2, 157, and passim, Christian 7–12.

    3. For an insightful discussion of the representation of the "envious-fascinating-shaming gaze" of the evil eye in Melville's works, see Joseph Adamson's *Melville, Shame, and the Evil Eye* (especially 257–93).

4. "Can't Nobody Fly with All That Shit"

    1. Because group inclusion "is necessary for human survival, showing and detecting shame have survival value," according to Scheff. People need to feel connected, and shame "automatically signals a threat to the safety of [the] *social self*" (*Bloody Revenge* 51). The emotions of shame and pride, which "have a unique status relative to social relationships," are not infrequent but, instead, are "an almost continuous part of human existence not only in crises but also in the slightest of social contacts" (*Bloody Revenge* 3, 51).

    2. In *The Color Complex: The Politics of Skin Color Among African Americans* (1992), Kathy Russell, Midge Wilson, and Ronald Hall provide a detailed history of color prejudice in the United States and they also discuss its persistence into the 1990s. They point out that "the desire for lighter skin is nearly universal. Throughout Central and South America, Asia, and even Africa, society is prejudiced against those with dark skin, especially young dark women. Various theories for this have been advanced, but in a race-stratified society like America the consequences have long been clear. Before the Civil War, the degree of pigmentation could mean the difference between living free and enslavement, and since then variations in skin color and features have divided the educated from the ignorant, the well-off from the poor, the 'attractive' from the 'plain' "(41).

    Charles Parrish, in a 1940s study of skin-color stereotyping in African-American teenagers, discovered that junior high students employed "as many as 145 different terms to describe skin color, including 'half-white,' 'yaller,' 'high yellow,' 'fair,' 'bright,' 'light,' 'red-bone,' 'light brown,' 'medium brown,' 'brown,' 'brownskin,' 'dark brown,' 'chocolate,' 'dark,' 'black,' 'ink spot,' 'blue black,' and 'tar baby.' Each term was associated with a particular personality type: in general, light to medium skin tones were linked to intelligence and refinement, while dark skin tones suggested toughness, meanness, and physical strength." Even though Parrish's study is some fifty years old, "similar attitudes about skin color prevail among today's Black youth. Many believe that light skin is feminine and dark skin is masculine, and very light skinned boys and very dark skinned girls often suffer from being at odds with this cultural stereotype" (66).

3. For some essays focusing on names and naming in the novel see Lucinda MacKethan, Paula Rabinowitz, and Ruth Rosenberg, "And the Children." For some representative discussions of Morrison's use of the monomyth of the hero see Patrick Bjork, Gerry Brenner, Charles De Arman, Jacqueline de Weever, A. Leslie Harris, Trudier Harris, *Fiction*, Dorothy Lee, Marilyn Mobley, *Folk Roots*, Wilfrid Samuels. Discussions of the novel's flight motif and its use of the folktale of the flying Africans (see, e.g., Susan Blake) are standard in the conversation surrounding the novel. For some recent discussions of the novel's representation of black oral culture and communal voices see Joyce Middleton and Marilyn Mobley, "Call and Response."

4. "The politics of hair parallels the politics of skin color" among African-American women, write the authors of *The Color Complex*, Kathy Russell, Midge Wilson, and Ronald Hall. "Among Black women," they explain, "straight hair and European hairstyles not only have been considered more feminine but have sent a message about one's standing in the social hierarchy. 'Good hair' has long been associated with the light-skinned middle class, 'bad hair' with Blacks who are less fortunate." Although the Afro hairstyle was popular in the 1960s, "the old attitudes about hair quickly resurfaced" after the sixties ended. "The tradition of calling hair that was straight and wavy 'good' and hair that was tightly curled and nappy 'bad' had never really gone away." And in the post-1960s world, "hair remains a politically charged subject. To some, how an African American chooses to style his or her hair says everything there is to be said about that individual's Black consciousness, socioeconomic class, and probable life-style, particularly when the individual is a woman" (82). See also Noliwe Rooks's *Hair Raising: Beauty, Culture, and African American Women*.

5. Remarking on the link between excretory epithets and shame, Donald Nathanson explains that shame expressions—such as, "piss on you," "pisser," "shit," "you little shit"—capture the moment of embarrassment when the shamed individual feels "infantile, weak, and dirty, unable to control . . . bodily functions." Although shame "is much more than just excretion," excretory epithets "are about shame" ("Shame/Pride Axis" 198).

6. As Utelinde Wedertz-Furtado points out, it is significant that Guitar remarks that the Seven Days organization originated after the blinding of a black veteran of World War I (see *Song of Solomon* 155). By linking 1920s black militancy to that of the 1960s, "Morrison suggests the cyclical rising of black militant groups after non-violent means have failed to guarantee justice and civil rights" (227). Ralph Story links the Seven Days to black

secret societies of the nineteenth century, such as the Knights of Liberty, an organization that was formed in 1846 to free slaves (152). Guitar's advocacy of violence also recalls the militant rhetoric of the 1920s inspired by the black nationalism of Marcus Garvey. For example, one of Garvey's "chief lieutenants," Hubert Harrison, asserted, "If white men are to kill unoffending Negroes, Negroes must kill white men in defense of their lives and property." In the 1960s, black nationalist Malcolm X remarked, "Revolutions are never fought by turning the other cheek. . . . Revolutions are based upon bloodshed." And Vincent Harding, a radical voice in the 1960s Black Power movement, commented, "If we must fight, let it be on the streets where we have been humiliated. If we must burn down houses, let them be the homes and stores of our exploiters. If we must kill, let it be the fat, pious white Christians who guard their lawns and their daughters while engineering slow death for us. If we must die, let it be for a real cause, a cause of black men's freedom as black men define it" (Berry and Blassingame 410, 417, 419–20).

In the essay "The Psychopathic Racial Personality," the rhetoric of Garveyite Bobby Wright echoes Guitar's words about the depravity of whites. "[I]n their relationship with the Black race, Europeans (Whites) are psychopaths and their behavior reflects an underlying biologically transmitted proclivity with roots deep in their evolutionary history" (2). Since there is no evidence that Whites and Blacks can live together in peace—"without Whites attempting to oppress and exterminate the Blacks"—and since "Blacks are at war with psychopaths, *violence is the only way*" (13).

7. In his description of the "defending scripts" used to protect against shame, Gershen Kaufman explains that rage—"[w]hether in the form of generalized hostility, fomenting bitterness, chronic hatred, or explosive eruptions"—functions to protect the self against exposure and thus defends against shame. Like rage scripts, contempt scripts protect the self, for "[t]o the degree that others are looked down upon, found lacking or seen as lesser or inferior beings, a once-wounded self becomes more securely insulated against further shame" (*Psychology of Shame* 100). Moreover, power scripts, which aim at gaining power over others, also protect the self against shame. "When power scripts combine with rage and/or contempt scripts, the seeking of revenge is a likely outcome. . . . Now the humiliated one, at long last, will humiliate the other" (*The Psychology of Shame* 101).

8. In the dozens game, write Richard Majors and Janet Billson in *Cool Pose*, the players typically attack their opponents' families, especially mothers, in rhyme, and as the exchange becomes "progressively nasty and pornographic, virtually every family member and every sexual act is woven into the verbal assault" (93). In the verbal game, "humiliations are squeezed

into rhyming couplets that testify to the player's ability to keep cool under mounting pressure" (92). For the African-American adolescent male, the dozens game "might be defined as a rite of passage because of the way it tests his control, character, and courage. In the final analysis, if he can handle the insults peers direct at his mother in the dozens, then it is likely he can take whatever insults society might hurl at him" (96).

5. "Defecating Over a Whole People"

1. The Tar Baby story, from Joel Chandler Harris's *Uncle Remus: His Songs and His Sayings* (1880), is included in J. Mason Brewer's *American Negro Folklore* (Chicago: Quadrangle Books, 1968) and B. A. Botkin's *A Treasury of American Folklore: Stories, Ballads, and Traditions of the People* (New York: Crown Publishers, 1944). In the Tar Baby story, Brer Fox, in an attempt to trap Brer Rabbit, makes a tar baby figure. When Brer Rabbit tries to exchange polite greetings with the figure, he is angered by the tar baby's silence. He retaliates by first hitting the figure with his fists, then kicking it, and thus ultimately he finds himself completely stuck to the figure. In the sequel to the tale, Brer Fox looks for a way to kill the trapped rabbit. The rabbit begs the fox to burn, or hang, or drown, or skin him to death, claiming that any method of death is preferable to being thrown into the briar patch. When the fox consequently throws the rabbit into the briar patch, where the rabbit was bred and born, the rabbit escapes.

Remarking on the rabbit's angry response to the tar baby's silence, Robert Bone writes that Brer Rabbit, in his bullying behavior, takes on "the white man's ways of arrogance and willfulness" as he intimidates "the tarry representative of blackness" (143). In escaping, the rabbit "borrows his defense from his environment; a hostile universe is thus converted to a sanctuary and a home" (144). To Bernard Wolfe, the rabbit's bullying speech to the tar baby—"Ef you don't take off dat hat en tell me howdy, I'm gwineter bus' you wide open"—is also telling. Reading "like a parody of the white man's demand for the proper bowing-and-scraping etiquette from the Negro," it reflects "the satiric mimicry of the whites which the slaves often indulged in among themselves." Wolfe reads the tar-baby trap as a complex symbol of black yieldingness. "[T]ar, blackness, by its very yielding, traps. Interesting symbol, in a land where the mere possession of a black skin requires you, under penalty of death, to yield, to *give*, everywhere. The mark of supreme impotence suddenly acquires the power to render impotent, merely by its flaccidity, its inertness. . . . There is a puzzle here: it is the Rabbit who is trapped. But in a later story . . . the Rabbit . . . gets the

Fox to set him free from the tar-trap and thus avoids being eaten by his enemy. The Negro, in other words, is wily enough to escape from the engulfing pit of blackness, although his opponents, who set the trap, do their level best to keep him imprisoned in it. But it is not at all sure that anyone else who fell victim to this treacherous black yieldingness—the Fox, say—would be able to wriggle out so easily" (80).

For some representative discussions of Morrison's use of the Tar Baby story see Trudier Harris, *Fiction and Folklore* 116–27, Angelita Reyes, "Ancient Properties" 22–23, and Craig Werner, 154–56.

2. Daryl Dance, in *Shuckin' and Jivin': Folklore from Contemporary Black Americans* (pub. 1978), includes a chapter entitled, "A Nigger Ain't Shit: Self-Degrading Tales." Commenting on the "self-abasing jokes" found in the "Black folk repertoire" in his introduction to this chapter, Dance writes that "a large number of popular Black folktales seem to fall into the category of self-abasement. . . . Many jokes are intended solely for Black ears and contain severe criticism of alleged character defects in Blacks. Other tales ridicule the Black person's color and hair, apparently indicating an acceptance of them as badges of inferiority, or deal with the Black person's preference for things white" (77–78). Dance also claims that the rejection of white values and affirmation of blackness coming out of the black pride movement have "undoubtedly caused a decline (though certainly not a demise) in the popularity of this type of humor," which he links to the self-degrading tales of other ethnic groups (78).

3. See W. E. B. Du Bois, *The Philadelphia Negro: A Social Study.* 1899. New York: Schocken Books, 1967. See also Gatewood 96–97.

4. "That the term *Bad Nigger* from its beginning has had positive connotations to certain Black people and negative connotations to white people suggests its early meaning as a Black man who fought against the system," writes Daryl Dance. "The Bad Nigger is and always has been *bad* (that is, villainous) to whites because he violates their laws and he violates their moral codes. He is *ba-ad* (that is, heroic) to the Black people who relish his exploits for exactly the same reasons. The Bad Nigger of folklore is tough and violent. He kills without blinking an eye. He courts death constantly and doesn't fear dying. . . . He asserts his manhood through his physical destruction of men and through his sexual victimization of women" (224–25). Dance's chapter, "I'm a Bad Motherfucker: Tales of the Bad Nigger," includes the tales of "John Henry" (227–28) and "Stag" (228–29).

For some analysis of the historical links between the "bad nigger" and the "badman" folk hero and a discussion of the ambivalent response of a diverse African-American community to the "bad nigger" figure, see John Roberts's *From Trickster to Badman.*

6. "Whites Might Dirty Her All Right, but Not Her Best Thing"

1. *The Black Book*, edited by Middleton Harris, quotes from P. S. Bassett's description of his visit to Margaret Garner, published in the *American Baptist*. Bassett reports on Garner's "detailed account" of the infanticide:

> She said, that when the officers and slave-hunters came to the house in which they were concealed, she caught a shovel and struck two of her children on the head, and then took a knife and cut the throat of the third, and tried to kill the other,—that if they had given her time, she would have killed them all—that with regard to herself, she cared but little; but she was unwilling to have her children suffer as she had done.
>
> I inquired if she was not excited almost to madness when she committed the act. No, she replied, I was as cool as I now am; and would much rather kill them at once, and thus end their sufferings, than have them taken back to slavery, and be murdered by piecemeal. (10)

Black Women in White America: A Documentary History, edited by Gerda Lerner, quotes some passages from Levi Coffin's *Reminiscences* (pub. 1876) on the Garner case and also quotes from local newspaper accounts of the Garner story. Coffin writes that

> Margaret Garner, the chief actor in the tragedy which had occurred, naturally excited much attention. She was a mulatto, about five feet high. . . . On the left side of her forehead was an old scar, and on the cheek-bone, on the same side, another one. When asked what caused them, she said: "White man struck me." . . .
>
> She appeared to be twenty-two or twenty-three years old. . . . The babe she held in her arms was a little girl, about nine months old, and was much lighter in color than herself. . . . The little boys, four and six years old, respectively . . . sat on the floor near their mother during the trial, playing together in happy innocence . . . . The murdered child was almost white, a little girl of rare beauty.
>
> The case seemed to stir every heart that was alive to the emotions of humanity. . . . (61)

According to local newspaper accounts, Garner said that "she had killed one and would like to kill the three others, rather than see them again reduced to slavery" (62). While the federal authorities worked to enforce the Fugitive Slave Act, the state authorities attempted to save Garner by trying her for murder. But her owner returned her to the South and to slavery. According to newspaper accounts, the ship returning Garner to slavery, the

Henry Lewis, had an accident. While one report said that Garner was thrown into the river with her child, another report said that Garner "threw her child into the river and jumped after it. . . . It is only certain that she was in the river with her child, and that it was drowned, while she was saved. . . . The last that was seen of Peggy, she was on the *Hungarian* [the rescue ship], crouching like a wild animal near the stove, with a blanket wrapped around her" (62–63). For discussions of the Margaret Garner case, see Julius Yanuck's "The Garner Fugitive Slave Case" and Steven Weisenburger's *Modern Medea: A Family Story of Slavery and Child-Murder from the Old South*. For an important psychoanalytic study of women's slave narratives, see Jennifer Fleischner's *Mastering Slavery: Memory, Family, and Identity in Women's Slave Narratives*.

2. As Maggie Sale has observed, "[B]ecause pro-slavery writers figured slavery as an uplifting institution for heathen Africans, where a divinely sanctioned aristocracy gently rested on the labor of contented slaves, in their discourse an act such as Garner's is marked as barbaric, bloodthirsty, and deviant, and calls for a shocked, condescending, even angry response." In contrast, the abolitionist press represented the infanticide "in the heroic tradition of the American fight for Liberty" (44). See also Weisenburger 5–11, 263–75.

3. Darlene Hine discusses three methods used by female slaves to resist their economic and sexual oppression: sexual abstinence, abortion, and infanticide. While there are only a "small number of documented cases" of infanticide, the fact that it happened at all is "significant" in Hine's view. Responding to Eugene Genovese's remark that "for the most part . . . the slaves recognized infanticide as murder" and thus "courageously" attempted to raise their children "as best they could," Hine faults Genovese for not "acknowledging the motivations for infanticide offered repeatedly by the slave parents themselves. Far from viewing such actions as murder, and therefore indicating these as lack of love, slave parents who took their children's lives may have done so out of a higher form of love and a clearer understanding of the living death that awaited their children under slavery" (125). Infanticide may also have resulted as a response to rape or forced pregnancy and sometimes slave children were used "as pawns in a power struggle between plantation owners and their slaves" (126). Steven Weisenburger comments that "when the infanticidal mother acts out the system's violent logic in the master's face, thus displaying anger and revenge against his class, she mirrors his violent politics in profoundly disruptive ways. . . . In such moments the dispossessed mother represents unutterable contradictions that the dominant culture must repress or mask" (263).

4. In *Degeneration, Culture, and the Novel*, William Greenslade remarks, "By the mid-nineteenth century racial biology had mapped out a

'science of boundaries between groups and the degenerations that threatened them when those boundaries were transgressed.' . . . In contrast to industrious 'historic races' of northern Europe, certain races were cast as degenerate types. The biologist Cuvier identified the negro race as 'the most degraded human race whose form approaches that of the beast.' . . . For the major race theorist of the nineteenth century, Comte de Gobineau (1816–1882), such was the necessity of keeping the races apart, that miscegenation and race-mingling would inevitably lead to degeneration and the extinction of civilisation. For many race theorists, including Robert Knox and Charles Kingsley in Britain, the degenerate races were best off dead" (21–22).

Nancy Stepan, in "Biological Degeneration: Races and Proper Places," discusses the interest of racial biologists in the idea of racial types and their "proper places." "On the basis of analogies between human races and animal species, it was argued that races, like animal types, tended to be confined to definite localities of the earth." Not only did races have ties to particular geographical places, but movement out of their designated places "caused a 'degeneration.'" A common theme "sounded in the typological theory of racial degeneration" was "the degenerations caused by the movement of freed blacks into the geographical and social spaces occupied by whites and into the political condition of freedom" (99).

A "major concern" of American racial biologists was the "proper place" of blacks in the Americas, observes Stepan. "Most racial theorists in the United States shared, by the 1840s and 1850s, the typological orientation of the European scientists" (99–100). It was argued, for example, that "though Negroes fared well in the hotter, southern latitudes of the United States, north of forty degrees latitude they steadily deteriorated." After the Civil War and the freeing of the slaves, the "old belief that freed blacks were, of all blacks, the 'most corrupt, depraved, and abandoned element in the population,' was . . . given a biological rationale" (101). "Freedom was an unnatural environment which removed constraints and plunged the Negro into 'natural' and innate excesses and indulgence of the racial appetites." Given freedom, blacks returned "to their primitive state of savagery and sexuality, revealing the ancient features of the race by a process of reversion" (102).

5. Angela Davis, in her discussion of the treatment of slave women as breeders and field workers, quotes from Moses Grandy's description of the floggings pregnant workers received for failing to complete the day's quota of work or for protesting their treatment:

> A woman who gives offense in the field, and is large in a family way, is compelled to lie down over a hole made to receive her corpulency, and is flogged with the whip or beat with a paddle, which has holes

in it; at every stroke comes a blister. One of my sisters was so
severely punished in this way, that labor was brought on, and the
child was born in the field. This very overseer, Mr. Brooks, killed
in this manner a girl named Mary. Her father and mother were in
the field at that time. (Davis 9; quoted from the *Narrative of the
Life of Moses Grandy: Late a Slave in the United States of America*
[Boston: 1844])

When pregnant women were treated with more leniency, writes Davis, "it
was seldom on humanitarian grounds. It was simply that slaveholders appre-
ciated the value of a slave child born alive in the same way that they appre-
ciated the value of a newborn calf or colt" (9–10).

6. A. Leon Higginbotham, Jr., in his detailed historical and legal
analysis of the precept of racial inferiority, remarks on the racial contempt of
the abolitionists. "The abolitionists' perception of African Americans as
saintly savages, however benign, was but a mirror image of the slaveholders'
perception of African Americans as demonic workhorses," he writes. Both
representations were "rooted in the precept of inferiority," which assumed
and defended the racist ideology that defined whites as superior and blacks
as inferior (60).

7. "The Dirty, Get-on-Down Music"

1. In an essay published in 1925 in *The New Negro*—which attempted
to "offer a definition" of the Harlem Renaissance movement (Rampersad ix)—
James Weldon Johnson describes 1920s Harlem. A place where "175,000
Negroes live closely together . . . in the heart of New York—75,000 more
than live in any Southern city—" Harlem is a "great Mecca" for ambitious
and talented blacks, according to Johnson (310, 301). "In the make-up of
New York, Harlem is not merely a Negro colony or community, it is a city
within a city, the greatest Negro city in the world. It is not a slum or a fringe,
it is located in the heart of Manhattan and occupies one of the most beautiful
and healthful sections of the city. It is not a 'quarter' of dilapidated tenements,
but is made up of new-law apartments and handsome dwellings, with well-
paved and well-lighted streets. It has its own churches, social and civic
centers, shops, theaters and other places of amusement. And it contains more
Negroes to the square mile than any other spot on earth" (301).

2. Alice's negative assessment of jazz recalls an essay by J. A. Rogers,
which was published in 1925 in the Harlem Renaissance anthology, *The
New Negro*. "[C]ondemned in certain quarters, enthusiastically welcomed in
others," jazz "isn't music merely, it is a spirit that can express itself in
almost anything. The true spirit of jazz is a joyous revolt from convention,

custom, authority, boredom, even sorrow—from everything that would confine the soul of man and hinder its riding free on the air. . . . It is the revolt of the emotions against repression" (216–17). And yet while "serious modernist music and musicians, most notably and avowedly in the work of the French modernists Auric, Satie, and Darius Milhaud, have become the confessed debtors of American Negro jazz," the true home of jazz is "the none too respectable cabaret. And here we have the seamy side to the story. Here we have some of the charm of Bohemia, but much more of the demoralization of vice" (222). Tracing the appeal of jazz to the desire to forget the "horrors and strain of war," Rogers also writes that, while people found a "temporary forgetfulness" in the "fresh joyousness" of jazz, people cannot "sensibly condone its excesses or minimize its social danger if uncontrolled; all culture is built upon inhibitions and control. But it is doubtful whether the 'jazz-hounds' of high and low estate would use their time to better advantage. In all probability their tastes would find some equally morbid, mischievous vent. Jazz, it is needless to say, will remain a recreation for the industrious and a dissipater of energy for the frivolous, a tonic for the strong and a poison for the weak. For the Negro himself, jazz is both more and less dangerous than for the white—less, in that he is nervously more in tune with it; more, in that at his average level of economic development his amusement life is more open to the forces of social vice" (222–23).

3. During the Harlem Renaissance, the term "New Negro," remarks Arnold Rampersad, which "had been used from time to time in the late 1890s . . . quickly became the term of choice to describe the spirit of the 1920s among many black Americans" (xi).

4. Noliwe Rooks, in the course of her study of the politics of hair in the African-American community, makes mention of the significance of hair-dressing as a career choice for African-American women in the early twentieth century, showing how black women were urged in advertisements to become hairdressers as a way of making money. See, for example, 45, 58–59, 87.

5. Lawrence Levine remarks that while the "physical side of love . . . was largely missing from popular music," it was "strongly felt in the blues" (279). One of the examples Levine provides to illustrate how the blues records of the 1920s and 1930s were filled with "rich sexual imagery," are these lines of Bo Carter: "I come over here, sweet baby, just to get my ashes hauled, / . . . . / Won't you draw on my cigaret, smoke it there all night long, / Just draw on my cigaret, baby, until you make my good ashes come" (242).

6. For some discussions of the claim by some black male critics that authors like Toni Morrison, Gayl Jones, Alice Walker, and Gloria Naylor have publicly slandered black men by depicting the black male oppression of

black women in their fiction, see Ann duCille's *Skin Trade* (60–80) and Deborah McDowell's "Reading Family Matters." McDowell reports that, as a result of this public controversy, "certain black women writers have expressed their fear and concern about how their depictions of black men would be received, and, more sobering, others might even be said to have adjusted their aesthetic vision because of the pressures of negative publicity" (94). See also Morrison's interview with Cecil Brown, 456–58.

8. "He's Bringing Along the Dung We Leaving Behind"

1. Winning the Nobel Prize, as Morrison has remarked, "doesn't help you write better and if you let it, it will intimidate you about future projects" (Timehost 3). One can speculate that the publication of and intense public scrutiny by reviewers of her first novel after winning the Nobel Prize was a potentially risky business for Morrison. Despite some negative assessments of *Paradise*—one reviewer, for example, compared *Paradise* unfavorably to Morrison's *Beloved* and called it a "contrived, formulaic book" (Kakutani)—most commentators have been favorable in their appraisals of the novel.

2. From 1891–1892, Edward McCabe's newspaper, the *Langston City Herald*, printed a column with the headline "Come Prepared or Not at All" in its promotion of the settlement of the all-black community of Langston City, Oklahoma. (Note that in *Paradise* Morrison quotes this newspaper feature headline on page 13). In 1890, Edward McCabe and William Eagleson joined Charles Robbins, a white real estate speculator, in founding the all-black town of Langston City, and McCabe's newspaper boosted settlement of the town. "Langston City is a Negro City, and we are proud of that fact," McCabe asserted in the *Herald*. "Her city officials are all colored. Her teachers are colored. Her public schools furnish thorough educational advantages to nearly two hundred colored children." The *Herald* urged prosperous blacks to come to Langston City, calling for "active, energetic men and women with some money," those who could "support themselves and families until they could raise a crop" (Taylor 146). Not only did the *Langston City Herald* promote the town to those blacks with capital to invest, it also openly discouraged poor blacks from settling in the town. On learning that three hundred poor blacks had arrived in Fort Smith, Arkansas, the *Herald* tried to deter their entry into Oklahoma, stating that "common labor is not in demand, the supply is already too great." In 1891, the *Herald* opposed the acting governor's proposal to assist five hundred poor blacks settling in Oklahoma, remarking that it was "a mistake for any but self-supporting people" to migrate to Oklahoma (Hamilton 104). The *Herald* also appealed to blacks with middle-class values in promoting the town, telling its readers that Langston was not "a town of saloons, bummers, and crap-

shooters" but instead was a town of "homes, churches and schools" where settlers could raise their families "in good and respectable society." Insisting that Oklahoma needed virtuous, hard-working, and intelligent inhabitants, the *Herald* urged its readers to "use every effort in their power to keep the ignorant and worthless class" from attempting to settle in the Oklahoma territory. "If we can't get the best class of our people, we don't want any," the *Herald* asserted (Hamilton 105).

In Oklahoma, there were thirty-two black towns, including Bailey, Boley, Bookertee, Clearview, Langston City, Rentiesville, Tullahassee, and Vernon (for a complete list see Hamilton 153). The "most celebrated" black town was Boley, which was founded in 1903 (Franklin 17). In 1908, Booker T. Washington visited Boley and had this to say about the town: "Boley, like the other negro towns that have sprung up . . . represents a dawning race consciousness, a wholesome desire to do something to make the race respected; something which shall demonstrate the right of the negro, not merely as an individual, but as a race, to have a worthy and permanent place in the civilization that the American people are creating. In short, Boley is another chapter in the long struggle of the negro for moral, industrial, and political freedom" (cited by Franklin 17).

By 1907, Boley had a population of a thousand, with another two thousand farmers living in the surrounding countryside. But by 1910, Boley's "spectacular growth" had ended. In 1907, when the Twin Territories (Indian and Oklahoma) became the state of Oklahoma, the state legislature "quickly disenfranchised black voters and segregated public schools and accommodations," and thus "Oklahoma was no longer a place where African Americans could escape Jim Crow." While black men could vote in town elections, local political control "could not compensate for powerlessness at the courthouse or the state capital controlled by unsympathetic officials." Moreover, because of crop failures and the decline in agricultural prices, places like Boley soon confronted a new threat—the attractions of the city—as the "dreams of autonomy and prosperity that propelled an earlier generation to create Boley now encouraged the second generation to leave the town" (Taylor 151).

3. In the all-black town of Boley, Oklahoma, not only was light skin rejected as a status symbol but light-skinned blacks "sometimes suffered" in the community. One man describes how he was treated in Boley as a child because of his light skin color. "I happened to be light skinned and, boy, did I have a time. Those 'darkies' in Boley don't like light-skinned Negroes and they show it. I was a victim of their prejudice. . . . All the boys would refer to each other as 'nigger' . . . but I could never use that word." When he eventually got married, he chose a dark-skinned wife so that his children "wouldn't have to go through all that mess. . . . It was hell!" (cited by Crockett 69).

4. As Albert Raboteau has remarked, "No single symbol captures more clearly the distinctiveness of Afro-American Christianity than the symbol of Exodus" (9). Used primarily to foster internal resistance among the slaves, the Exodus story contradicted the white Christian claim that Africans were intended by God to be slaves and, indeed, appeared to prove that slavery was "against God's will." Functioning as an "archetypal myth" for slaves, Exodus symbolized the "common history and common destiny" of black Christians (13). "Identification with Israel . . . gave the slaves a communal identity as a special, divinely favored people. This identity stood in stark contrast with racist propaganda, which depicted them as inferior to whites, as destined by nature and providence to the status of slaves. Exodus, the Promised Land, and Canaan were inextricably linked in the slaves' minds with the idea of freedom. Canaan referred not only to the condition of freedom but also to the territory of freedom—the North or Canada" (14). Emancipation validated the slaves' belief that God would free them just as he had once freed Israel. Yet after slavery ended only to be replaced with other types of racial oppression, black Americans, "as decade succeeded decade . . . repeated the story of Exodus, which for so many years had kept their hopes alive. It was, then, a very old and evocative tradition that Martin Luther King, Jr., echoed in his last sermon: '. . . And I've seen the Promised Land. And I may not get there with you. But I want you to know . . . that we as a people will get to the Promised Land'" (14–15).

5. The fact that Morrison traveled to Brazil to learn about Candomblé (see Leonard, "Shooting Women" 25) suggests the link between the occult practices of the Convent women and the African-Brazilian religion of Candomblé. Established in Brazil in the nineteenth century, Candomblé "has been continually nourished by contacts with Africa, and its priests and priestesses have been dedicated to maintaining the purity of its African roots" (Murphy 44). When Morrison was in Brazil, she heard a story, which turned out to be false, about a convent of black nuns who were murdered by a group of men because they were rumored to practice Candomblé (D. Smith B2, Rose). Similarly, in *Paradise*, the Convent women are accused by the men who storm the Convent and massacre the women of being part of a cult or a coven. Lone reminds the Catholic Consolata—who is originally from Brazil—of the African-Brazilian belief in the *orixás* when she remarks to Consolata, "You need what we all need: earth, air, water. Don't separate God from His elements. He created it all. You stuck on dividing Him from His works. Don't unbalance His world" (244).

Nature gods, the *orixás* "are associated with distinct provinces of the natural world—water, air, forest, and earth—and it is from these primary sources that they gather and impart their *axé*, or vital energy. Each physical domain, in turn, corresponds to an array of perceived personality traits. The *orixás* are archetypes for the range of behaviors exhibited by their mortal followers. They embody the strength and foresight of their adherents as well as their weaknesses." For example, whereas the female deity Yemanjá—the goddess of the sea—is "cool and calm," in contrast Iansã—the goddess of winds and storms—is impatient and short-tempered (Voeks 56). In the Candomblé system, *orixás* correspond to figures in the Catholic religion: thus, Oxalá is syncretized to Jesus; Iansã to Saint Barbara; Yemanjá to the Virgin Mary (Voeks 61). (For comparisons of the *orixás* to ancient Greek gods, see Hess, *Samba* 42).

In the female-directed Candomblé *terreiro* or temple, the *mãe-de-santo*, or mother-of-saints, "represents the principal line of communication between the material world of mortals and the spiritual world of the deities" (Voeks 63). The main objective of the *mãe-de-santo* is "the maintenance and cultivation of *axé*, the vital force of existence. . . . Nurtured and properly tended, *axé* grows like a sacred flame, imparting spiritual strength, prosperity, and health to its mortal attendants" (Voeks 65). In the temple, the *filhas-de-santo*, or daughters-of-the-saints, manifest the *orixás* during possession trance and thus help accumulate for the temple the magical energy of *axé*—the "life-giving nutrient of the material and spiritual realms," which is especially present in blood (Voeks 73).

During the Candomblé ceremony, as the dancers become possessed by the *orixás*, they take on the physical characteristics and personality of their particular deities. "Ogun dances with hard thrusts of his sword alluding to his battles. Oxossi picks healing leaves from the forest floor and draws his bow on his quarry. Omulu sweeps away disease. . . . Iemanjá brings the rolling ocean waves from her breasts. Xangô brings down lightning and justice. Iansá whirls in the storm winds. Oxun dances in luxury and refinement. With each dance the community participates in another phase of its history. Each dancer recalls the great dances of the past and the royal ancestors of Africa who now can emerge in this sacred space and time" (Murphy 73). In the "dance of the gods," as the dancers incarnate the *orixás*, the people watching the ceremony believe that they are in the presence of the powerful spirit saints.

Paradise, in its depiction of the Convent as a refuge, recalls how the Brazilian Candomblé serves not only as "a mutual aid society, [and] a residence" but also as "a family" into which the initiates are "reborn" and which is presided over by the senior female initiate—the mother-of-the-saints or mother-of-the-spirits—who is usually addressed as "mother" (Murphy 51, 52, 55). In *Paradise*, Consolata, as a "new and revised Reverend Mother" (265), takes on the role of the mother-of-the-saints when she begins her initiation of the Convent women. Just as Morrison's Convent women are all represented as victims of some trauma, so the individual who becomes a Candomblé medium "must be called by the spirit through a direct disturbance in her or his life. The more dramatic and obvious the disturbance, the more likely that one is being called. Often a serious illness, a direct confrontation with the reality of death, will constitute the first evidence of a call" (Murphy 59).

The initiation of the Convent women by Consolata also recalls the initiation rites of Candomblé. During the Candomblé initiation, the initiates are isolated for months; their hair is cut and their heads are shaved; their clothes are destroyed and they are given new clothes; they are given new names; they learn the songs and dances of their particular *orixás*; and when they are prepared to receive the god, they dance to induce a trancelike state of possession in which they are overtaken by the *orixá*, the spirit or keeper of the head who directs the lives of adherents. Consolata's words to the women as she prepares for their recovery of the deity within—"Someone could want to meet you," she says (262)—can also be linked to Candomblé. The individual who is called by the *orixá* is "under 'obligation' to 'seat' or 'make'" the *orixá*, that is, to "bring the presence" of the *orixá* into his or her life and self (Murphy 59). The *orixá* becomes "a part of the person, 'seated' or 'mounted' upon their *ori*, the 'soul' that precedes the birth of the body and survives its death" (Murphy 78). The *orixás* can be understood as "external forces"—as ancestors or as the forces of nature—and as "interior dimensions" of the individual, as part of the human soul and self (Murphy 78–79).

There are other possible links to Candomblé in *Paradise*. In its depiction of the light that Consolata learns to manipulate, *Paradise* may be referring to the magical energy of the *axé*. And the closure of the novel, with its depiction of the "escape" of the dead characters into a parallel universe, seems designed to evoke the Candomblé notion that "the material and spiritual worlds are exact duplicates, parallel expressions of the same reality" so that "[a]ll material objects and beings—plant, animal, mineral, and human—find their copy in *orun*, the spiritual universe" (Voeks 71).

Morrison's remark that Consolata's ritual "has echoes of New Age and spiritual regeneration" (Marcus 3) also points to another possible Brazilian source or influence in the novel: Brazilian spiritism. In the words of David Hess, the "Brazilian New Age . . . makes that of California seem bland in comparison" (*Spirits* 2). Brazilian spiritism, a movement founded by Allan Kardec in the nineteenth century, includes a belief in the existence of a spiritual or astral body and the use of spiritual energies in healing. See David Hess, *Spirits and Scientists: Ideology, Spiritism, and Brazilian Culture* and *Samba in the Night: Spiritism in Brazil*.

For an interesting discussion of the connections between the various ceremonies of the African diasporan tradition—including Brazil's Candomblé, Haiti's Vodou, Cuba's Santería, and the Black Church of the United States— see Joseph Murphy's *Working the Spirit*.

6. See also Ean Begg, *The Cult of the Black Virgin*, which includes a discussion of the Gnostic-Christian origins of the Black Madonna and the cult of Mary Magdalene. According to Begg, "It is . . . undeniable that a remarkably high proportion of Madonnas over 200 years old, that are credited with miraculous powers, are black, as are the traditional patronesses of nations, provinces and cities" (130).

It is interesting to note that in Brazilian Catholicism, "The Catholic church's patron saint for Brazil—at least in terms of the physical icon—is a black, female Virgin Mary. . ." (Hess, *Samba* 145). Piedade, as the Black Madonna, can also be associated with the Candomblé *orixá* Yemanjá, who is associated with the Virgin Mary and is a symbol of motherhood. The goddess of the sea, Yemanjá is "[w]arm, maternal, and stable" (Voeks 56).

7. In this scene, Morrison may also be invoking the African-Brazilian notion of cultural "mesticismo," the gradual fusion of the Amerindian, European, and African races in Brazil to create a new race. But according to David Brookshaw, mesticismo "is a cultural stance, a type of nationalism aimed against the complete cultural hegemony of Europe and North America, while at the same time regarding itself as superior to pure Afro-Amerindian cultural influences because of the 'purifying' action which the white heritage exercises on these . . . '[M]esticismo' is the diluting of Afro-Amerindian culture" (277).

Gilberto Freyre's idea of *metarraça* in Brazil—that is, "metarace" or "beyond race"—"still permits the bleaching out of what, for whites, are traditionally negative racial features," writes Brookshaw (280). Whereas "white Brazil's defense against the inevitable tide of fusion and integration with Afro-Brazil has lain traditionally in the heralding of a Latin-Portuguese identity," so black Brazil has defended itself "against its enforced suicide by stressing the dignity of being black." Moreover, "In Salvador, the most African of Brazilian cities, this defense of blackness is represented in cultural terms by the 'candomblé' sects, many of which are traditionally closed to white participation, and which maintain close contact with West Africa, to where initiates are sent in order to become fully acquainted with religious ritual in its purest form" (282).

According to Brookshaw, "The social integration of blacks in a spirit in which they do not lose their identity or self-respect, and the formation of a mestizo nation in which all ethnic elements can take pride in their roots, are the principal concerns of Afro-Brazilians in literature. . . . The black poets of today seem to be saying that only by a common acceptance of their country's pluri-cultural identity, will Brazilians achieve the real harmony that so many of them have claimed really exists in their multiracial nation" (306).

Works Cited

Primary Sources

Morrison's Fiction

Beloved. 1987. New York: Plume/Penguin, 1988.
The Bluest Eye. 1970. New York: Plume/Penguin, 1994.
Jazz. 1992. New York: Plume/Penguin, 1993.
Paradise. New York: Knopf, 1998.
Song of Solomon. 1977. New York: Plume/Penguin, 1987.
Sula. 1973. New York: Plume/New American Library, 1982.
Tar Baby. 1981. New York: Plume/Penguin, 1982.

Morrison's Nonfiction

"Afterword." 1993. *The Bluest Eye* 209–16.
"City Limits, Village Values: Concepts of the Neighborhood in Black Fiction." *Literature and the Urban Experience: Essays on the City and Literature.* Ed. Michael Jaye and Ann Watts. New Brunswick: Rutgers UP, 1981. 35–43.
"The Dancing Mind, 6 November, 1996." Speech upon Acceptance of the National Book Foundation Medal for Distinguished Contribution to American Letters. New York: Knopf, 1996.
"Introduction: Friday on the Potomac." *Race-ing Justice, En-gendering Power: Essays on Anita Hill, Clarence Thomas, and the Construction of Social Reality.* Ed. Toni Morrison. New York: Pantheon, 1992. vii–xxx.
"The Official Story: Dead Man Golfing." *Birth of a Nation'hood: Gaze, Script, and Spectacle in the O. J. Simpson Case.* Ed. Toni Morrison and Claudia Lacour. New York: Pantheon/Random House, 1997. vii–xxviii.

"On the Backs of Blacks." *Arguing Immigration: The Debate Over the Changing Face of America.* Ed. Nicolaus Mills. New York: Touchstone/ Simon and Schuster, 1994. 97–100. (Rpt. *Time* [Fall 1993].)

Playing in the Dark: Whiteness and the Literary Imagination. 1992. New York: Vintage/Random, 1993.

"Rootedness: The Ancestor as Foundation." *Black Women Writers (1950–1980): A Critical Evaluation.* Ed. Mari Evans. Garden City, NY: Anchor/Doubleday, 1983. 339–45.

"The Site of Memory." *Inventing the Truth: The Art and Craft of Memoir.* Ed. William Zinsser. Boston: Houghton Mifflin, 1987. 103–24.

"Unspeakable Things Unspoken: The Afro-American Presence in American Literature." *Michigan Quarterly Review* 28. 1 (Winter 1989): 1–34.

Interviews with Morrison

Angelo, Bonnie. "The Pain of Being Black: An Interview with Toni Morrison." Taylor-Guthrie, *Conversations* 255–61. (Rpt. *Time* 133. 21 [22 May 1989]: 120–23.)

Bakerman, Jane. "The Seams Can't Show: An Interview with Toni Morrison." Taylor-Guthrie, *Conversations* 30–42. (Rpt. *Black American Literature Forum* 12. 2 [Summer 1978]: 56–60.)

Black Creation Annual. "Conversation with Alice Childress and Toni Morrison." Taylor-Guthrie, *Conversations* 3–9. (Rpt. *Black Creation Annual* 1974–1975: 90–92.)

Brown, Cecil. "Interview with Toni Morrison." *The Massachusetts Review* 36. 3 (Autumn 1995): 455–73.

Caldwell, Gail. "Author Toni Morrison Discusses Her Latest Novel *Beloved.*" Taylor-Guthrie, *Conversations* 239–45. (Rpt. *Boston Globe* [6 October 1987]: 67–68.)

Carabi, Angels. "Toni Morrison." (Interview) *Belles Lettres: A Review of Books by Women* 10.2 (Spring 1995): 40–43.

Darling, Marsha. "In the Realm of Responsibility: A Conversation with Toni Morrison." Taylor-Guthrie, *Conversations* 246–54. (Rpt. *Women's Review of Books 5* [March 1978]: 5–6.)

Donahue, Deirdre. "Morrison's Slice of Paradise." *USA Today Books* 8 January 1998. <http://www.usatoday.com/life/enter/books/b128.htm> (30 January 1998).

Dreifus, Claudia. "Chloe Wofford Talks About Toni Morrison." *New York Times Magazine* 11 September 1994. 72–75.

Fussell, Betty. "All That Jazz." Taylor-Guthrie, *Conversations* 280–87. (Rpt. *Lear's* 5.8 [1 Oct. 1992]: 68.)

Jones, Bessie and Audrey Vinson. "An Interview with Toni Morrison." Taylor-Guthrie, *Conversations* 171–87. (Rpt. Bessie Jones and Audrey Vinson, *The World of Toni Morrison: Explorations in Literary Criticism*. Dubuque: Kendall Hunt, 1985. 127–51.)

Koenen, Anne. "The One Out of Sequence." Taylor–Guthrie, *Conversations* 67–83. (Rpt. *History and Tradition in Afro-American Culture*. Ed. Gunther Lenz. Frankfurt: Campus, 1984: 207–21.)

LeClair, Thomas. "The Language Must Not Sweat: A Conversation with Toni Morrison." Taylor-Guthrie, *Conversations* 119–28. (Rpt. *New Republic* 184 [21 March 1981]: 25–29.)

Marcus, James. "This Side of Paradise." <http://www.amazon.com/exec/obidos/...ison-interview/002-1129687-7452244> (29 April 1998).

McKay, Nellie. "An Interview with Toni Morrison." Taylor-Guthrie, *Conversations* 138–55. (Rpt. *Contemporary Literature* 24.4 [1983]: 413–29.)

McKinney-Whetstone, Diane. "A Conversation with Toni Morrison." *B.E.T. Weekend* February 1998. <http://www.betnetworks.com/weekend/current/wk_cover.html> (19 February 1998).

Moyers, Bill. "A Conversation with Toni Morrison." Taylor-Guthrie, *Conversations* 262–74. (Rpt. *A World of Ideas* II. Ed. Andie Tucher. Garden City: Doubleday, 1990.)

Mulrine, Anna. "This Side of 'Paradise.'" *U.S. News and World Report* 124. 2 (19 January 1998): 71.

Naylor, Gloria. "A Conversation: Gloria Naylor and Toni Morrison." Taylor-Guthrie, *Conversations* 188–217. (Rpt. *Southern Review* 21 [1985]: 567–93.)

Neustadt, Kathy. "The Visits of the Writers Toni Morrison and Eudora Welty." Taylor-Guthrie, *Conversations* 84–92. (Rpt. *Bryn Mawr Alumnae Bulletin* [Spring 1980]: 2–5.)

Oprah Winfrey Show. "The Oprah Book Club." 6 March 1998.

Parker, Betty Jean. "Complexity: Toni Morrison's Women." Taylor-Guthrie, *Conversations* 60–66. (Rpt. *Sturdy Black Bridges*. Ed. Roseann Bell. Garden City: Doubleday, 1979: 251–57.)

Rose, Charlie. "Toni Morrison Suggests 'Paradise' Defined by Inclusion." Show # 2077. 19 January 1998.

Ruas, Charles. "Toni Morrison." Taylor-Guthrie, *Conversations* 93–118. (Rpt. *Conversations with American Writers*. New York: McGraw Hill, 1984: 215–43.)

Russell, Sandi. "It's OK to Say OK." McKay, *Critical Essays on Toni Morrison* 43–47. (Rpt. *Women's Review* [London] 5 [March 1986]: 22–24.)

Schappell, Elissa and Claudia Lacour. "Toni Morrison: The Art of Fiction." *Paris Review* 35.128 (Fall 1993): 82–125.

Stepto, Robert. "Intimate Things in Place: A Conversation with Toni Morrison." Taylor-Guthrie, *Conversations* 10–29. (Rpt. *Massachusetts Review* 18 [1977]: 473–89.)

Straits Times. "Why Did the Women Get Shot?" *The Straits Times Interactive* 17 January 1998. <http://web3.asia1.com.sg/archive/st/1/pages/b011702.html> (28 January 1998).

Tate, Claudia. "Toni Morrison." Taylor-Guthrie, *Conversations* 156–170. (Rpt. *Black Women Writers at Work*. Ed. Claudia Tate. New York: Continuum, 1983. 117–31.)

Taylor-Guthrie, Danille, ed. *Conversations with Toni Morrison*. Jackson: UP of Mississippi, 1994.

Timehost. "Toni Morrison." Transcript from Jan. 21, 1998. <http://www.pathfinder.com/time/community/transcripts/chattr012198.html> (6 March 1998).

USA Today. "Morrison Enjoys Spotlight of Latest Tour." <http://www.usatoday.com/life/enter/books/b227.htm> (19 February 1998).

Verdelle, A. J. "Paradise Found: A Talk with Toni Morrison About Her New Novel." *Essence* 28.10 (February 1998): 78, 80.

Washington, Elsie. "Talk with Toni Morrison." Taylor-Guthrie, *Conversations* 234–38. (Rpt. *Essence* [October 1987]: 58, 136–37.)

Watkins, Mel. "Talk with Toni Morrison." Taylor-Guthrie, *Conversations* 43–47. (Rpt. *New York Times Book Review* 7 [11 September 1977]: 48–50.)

Wilson, Judith. "A Conversation with Toni Morrison." Taylor-Guthrie, *Conversations* 129–37. (Rpt. *Essence* [July 1981]: 84–86, 128.)

Secondary Sources

Adamson, Joseph. *Melville, Shame, and the Evil Eye: A Psychoanalytic Reading*. Albany: State U of New York P, 1997.

Adamson, Joseph and Hilary Clark, eds. *Scenes of Shame: Psychoanalysis, Shame, and Writing*. Albany: State U of New York P, 1999.

Askeland, Lori. "Remodeling the Model Home in *Uncle Tom's Cabin* and *Beloved*." *American Literature* 64. 4 (December 1992): 785–805.

Atlas, Marilyn. "The Darker Side of Toni Morrison's *Song of Solomon*." *Society for the Study of Midwestern Literature Newsletter* 10.2 (1980): 1–13.

———. "Toni Morrison's *Beloved* and the Reviewers." *Midwestern Miscellany* 18 (1990): 45–57.

Atwood, Margaret. "Haunted by Their Nightmares." Rev. of *Beloved*. *Toni Morrison: Modern Critical Views*. Ed. Harold Bloom. New York:

Chelsea, 1990. 143–47. (Rpt. *New York Times Book Review* [13 Sept. 1987]: 1, 49–50.)

Baker, Houston. "When Lindbergh Sleeps with Bessie Smith: The Writing of Place in *Sula.*" *Toni Morrison: Critical Perspectives Past and Present.* Ed. Henry Louis Gates, Jr., and K. A. Appiah. New York: Amistad, 1993. 236–60.

Banyiwa-Horne, Naana. "The Scary Face of the Self: An Analysis of the Character of Sula in Toni Morrison's *Sula.*" *SAGE* 2.1 (Spring 1985): 28–31.

Barnett, Pamela. "Figurations of Rape and the Supernatural in *Beloved.*" *PMLA* 112.3 (May 1997): 418–27.

Bassin, Donna, Margaret Honey and Meryle Kaplan. "Introduction." *Representations of Motherhood.* Ed. Donna Bassin, Margaret Honey, Meryle Kaplan. New Haven: Yale UP, 1994. 1–25.

Bawer, Bruce. "All That Jazz." *The New Criterion* 10.9 (May 1992): 10–17.

Begg, Ean. *The Cult of the Black Virgin.* London: Arkana/Routledge, 1985.

Begley, Adam. "Toni Morrison's Public Persona." *Mirabella* 6.1 (June 1994): 50–54.

Bell, Bernard. "*Beloved*: A Womanist Neo-Slave Narrative; or Multivocal Remembrances of Things Past." *African American Review* 26.1 (1992): 7–15.

Bell, Derrick. *Faces at the Bottom of the Well: The Permanence of Racism.* New York: BasicBooks/HarperCollins, 1992.

Bell, Roseann. "Review of *Sula.*" McKay, *Critical Essays on Toni Morrison* 24–27. (Rpt. *Obsidian* 2 [Winter 1976]: 93–95.)

Bemrose, John. "Trouble in Utopia." Rev. of *Paradise. Macleans* 111.13 (March 30, 1998): 65.

Berger, James. "Ghosts of Liberalism: Morrison's *Beloved* and the Moynihan Report." *PMLA* 111.3 (May 1996): 408–20.

Bernikow, Louise. "Jazz." Rev. of *Jazz. Cosmopolitan* 212.4 (April 1992): 32.

Berry, Mary Frances and John Blassingame. *Long Memory: The Black Experience in America.* New York: Oxford UP, 1982.

Birnbaum, Lucia. *Black Madonnas: Feminism, Religion, and Politics in Italy.* Boston: Northeastern UP, 1993.

Bjork, Patrick. *The Novels of Toni Morrison: The Search for Self and Place Within the Community.* New York: Lang, 1992.

Blake, Susan. "Folklore and Community in *Song of Solomon.*" *MELUS* 7.3 (Fall 1980): 77–82.

Bold, Christine. "An Enclave in the Wilderness." Rev. of *Paradise. Times Literary Supplement* (27 March 1998): 22.

Bone, Robert. "The Oral Tradition." *Critical Essays on Joel Chandler Harris.* Ed. R. Bruce Bickley, Jr. Boston: G. K. Hall, 1981. 130–45.

Booker, M. Keith. "Approaches to *Beloved* by Toni Morrison." *A Practical Introduction to Literary Theory and Criticism.* White Plains: Longman, 1996. 285–315.

Bordo, Susan. *Unbearable Weight: Feminism, Western Culture, and the Body.* Berkeley: U of California P, 1993.

Botkin, B. A. *A Treasury of American Folklore: Stories, Ballads, and Traditions of the People.* New York: Crown, 1944.

Bowers, Susan. "*Beloved* and the New Apocalypse." *The Journal of Ethnic Studies* 18.1 (Spring 1990): 59–77.

Bowman, Diane. "Flying High: The American Icarus in Morrison, Roth, and Updike." *Perspectives on Contemporary Literature* 8 (1982): 10–17.

Brenkman, John. "Politics and Form in *Song of Solomon.*" *Social Text* 39 (Summer 1994): 57–82.

Brenner, Gerry. "*Song of Solomon*: Rejecting Rank's Monomyth and Feminism." McKay, *Critical Essays on Toni Morrison* 114–25. (Rpt. *Studies in American Fiction* 15 [1987]: 13–24).

Brewer, J. Mason. *American Negro Folklore.* Chicago: Quadrangle, 1968.

Broad, Robert. "Giving Blood to the Scraps: Haints, History, and Hosea in *Beloved.*" *African American Review* 28.2 (1994): 189–96.

Brookshaw, David. *Race and Color in Brazilian Literature.* Metuchen, NJ: Scarecrow, 1986.

Brown, Laura. "Not Outside the Range: One Feminist Perspective on Psychic Trauma." *American Imago* 48.1 (Spring 1991): 119–33.

Byerman, Keith. "Beyond Realism: The Fictions of Toni Morrison." *Toni Morrison: Modern Critical Views.* Ed. Harold Bloom. New York: Chelsea, 1990. 55–84. (Rpt. *Fingering the Jagged Grain: Tradition and Form in Recent Black Fiction.* Athens: U of Georgia P, 1985. 184–216).

———. "Intense Behaviors: The Use of the Grotesque in *The Bluest Eye* and *Eva's Man.*" *CLA Journal* 25.4 (June 1982): 447–57.

Carmean, Karen. *Toni Morrison's World of Fiction.* Troy: Whitston, 1993.

Caruth, Cathy. "Introduction." *Psychoanalysis, Culture and Trauma.* Ed. Cathy Caruth. Spec. issues of *American Imago* 48.1 (Spring 1991): 1–12; 48.4 (Winter 1991): 417–24.

Christian, Barbara. *Black Women Novelists: The Development of a Tradition, 1892–1976.* Westport: Greenwood, 1980.

Cliff, Michelle. "Great Migrations." Rev. of *Paradise. The Village Voice* 43. 4 (27 January 1998): 85–86.

Coleman, James. "Beyond the Reach of Love and Caring: Black Life in Toni Morrison's *Song of Solomon.*" *Obsidian II: Black Literature in Review* 1.3 (Winter 1986): 151–61.

———. "The Quest for Wholeness in Toni Morrison's *Tar Baby.*" *Black American Literature Forum* 20.1–2 (Spring-Summer 1986): 63–73.

Collins, Patricia. *Black Feminist Thought: Knowledge, Consciousness, and the Politics of Empowerment*. 1990. New York: Routledge, 1991.

Comer, James. *Beyond Black and White*. New York: Quadrangle Books, 1972.

Crockett, Norman. *The Black Towns*. Lawrence: Regents Press of Kansas, 1979.

Dance, Daryl. *Shuckin' and Jivin': Folklore from Contemporary Black Americans*. Bloomington: Indiana UP, 1978.

Danieli, Yael. "The Treatment and Prevention of Long–term Effects and Intergenerational Transmission of Victimization: A Lesson from Holocaust Survivors and Their Children." *Trauma and Its Wake: The Study and Treatment of Post-Traumatic Stress Disorder*. Ed. Charles Figley. New York: Brunner/Mazel, 1985. 295–313.

Davis, Angela. *Women, Race and Class*. New York: Random House, 1981.

Davis, Cynthia. "Self, Society, and Myth in Toni Morrison's Fiction." *Toni Morrison: Modern Critical Views*. Ed. Harold Bloom. New York: Chelsea, 1990. 7–25. (Rpt. *Contemporary Literature* 23.3 [Summer 1982]: 323–42.)

Dean, Jodi. *Solidarity of Strangers: Feminism After Identity Politics*. Berkeley: U of California P, 1996.

De Arman, Charles. "Milkman as the Archetypal Hero." *Obsidian: Black Literature in Review* 6.3 (Winter 1980): 56–59.

Dee, Ruby. "Black Family Search for Identity." *Critical Essays on Toni Morrison*. Ed. Nellie McKay. Boston: G. K. Hall, 1988. 19–20. (Rpt. *Freedomways* 11 [1971]: 319–20.)

Demetrakopoulos, Stephanie. "Bleak Beginnings: *The Bluest Eye*." Holloway and Demetrakopoulos 31–36.

———. "Maternal Bonds as Devourers of Women's Individuation in Toni Morrison's *Beloved*." *African American Review* 26.1 (1992): 51–59.

———. "Morrison's Creation of a White World: *Tar Baby* and Irreconcilable Polarities." Holloway and Demetrakopoulos 131–42.

———. "*Sula* and the Primacy of Woman-to-Woman Bonds." Holloway and Demetrakopoulos 51–66.

de Weever, Jacqueline. "Toni Morrison's Use of Fairy Tale, Folk Tale and Myth in *The Song of Solomon*." *Southern Folklore Quarterly* 44 (1980): 131–44.

Dittmar, Linda. "'Will the Circle Be Unbroken?': The Politics of Form in *The Bluest Eye*." *Novel* 23.2 (Winter 1990): 137–55.

Domini, John. "Toni Morrison's *Sula*: An Inverted Inferno." *High Plains Literary Review* 3.1 (Spring 1988): 75–90.

Dorris, Michael. "Singing the Big City Blues." Rev. of *Jazz*. *Chicago Tribune—Books* (April 19, 1992): 1, 5. Rpt. Draper, *Contemporary Literary Criticism Yearbook 1993*, 241–42.

Draper, James, ed. *Contemporary Literary Criticism Yearbook 1993*. Detroit: Gale, 1994.

Du Bois, W. E. B. *The Philadelphia Negro: A Social Study*. 1899. New York: Schocken, 1967.

———. *The Souls of Black Folk*. 1903. New York: Everyman's Library/Knopf, 1993.

duCille, Ann. *Skin Trade*. Cambridge: Harvard UP, 1996.

Duvall, John. "Authentic Ghost Stories: *Uncle Tom's Cabin*, *Absalom, Absalom!*, and *Beloved*." *Faulkner Journal* 4.1–2 (Fall 1988–Spring 1989): 83–97.

———. "Descent in the 'House of Chloe': Race, Rape, and Identity in Toni Morrison's *Tar Baby*." *Contemporary Literature* 38.2 (Summer 1997): 325–49.

———. "Doe Hunting and Masculinity: *Song of Solomon* and *Go Down, Moses*." *Arizona Quarterly* 47.1 (Spring 1991): 95–115.

Eckard, Paula. "The Interplay of Music, Language, and Narrative in Toni Morrison's *Jazz*." *CLA Journal* 38.1 (September 1994): 11–19.

Erickson, Peter. "Images of Nurturance in Toni Morrison's *Tar Baby*." *CLA Journal* 28.1 (September 1984): 11–32.

Erikson, Kai. "Notes on Trauma and Community." *American Imago* 48.4 (Winter 1991): 455–72.

Everson, Susan. "Toni Morrison's *Tar Baby*: A Resource for Feminist Theology." *Journal of Feminist Studies in Religion* 5.2 (Fall 1989): 65–78.

Fabi, M. Giulia. "On Nobel Prizes and the 'Robinson Crusoe Syndrome': The Case of Toni Morrison." *Journal of Gender Studies* 2.2 (November 1993): 253–58.

Fanon, Frantz. *Black Skin, White Masks*. Trans. Charles Markmann. New York: Grove, 1967.

Ferguson, Rebecca. "History, Memory and Language in Toni Morrison's *Beloved*." *Feminist Criticism: Theory and Practice*. Ed. Susan Sellers. Toronto: U of Toronto P, 1991. 109–27.

Fields, Karen. "To Embrace Dead Strangers: Toni Morrison's *Beloved*." *Mother Puzzles: Daughters and Mothers in Contemporary American Literature*. Ed. Mickey Pearlman. Westport: Greenwood, 1989. 159–69.

Finney, Brian. "Temporal Defamiliarization in Toni Morrison's *Beloved*." *Obsidian II: Black Literature in Review* 5.1 (Spring 1990): 20–36.

FitzGerald, Jennifer. "Selfhood and Community: Psychoanalysis and Discourse in *Beloved*." *Modern Fiction Studies* 39.3–4 (Fall/Winter 1993): 669–87.

Fleishner, Jennifer. *Mastering Slavery: Memory, Family, and Identity in Women's Slave Narratives*. New York: New York UP, 1996.

Franklin, Jimmie Lewis. *Journey Toward Hope: A History of Blacks in Oklahoma.* Norman: U of Oklahoma P, 1982.

Furman, Jan. *Toni Morrison's Fiction.* Columbia: U of South Carolina P, 1996.

Fuss, Diana. *Essentially Speaking: Feminism, Nature, and Difference.* New York: Routledge, 1989.

Gates, Henry Louis. "Critical Remarks." *Anatomy of Racism.* Ed. David Goldberg. Minneapolis: U of Minnesota P, 1990. 319–29.

Gatewood, Willard. *Aristocrats of Color: The Black Elite, 1880–1920.* Bloomington: Indiana UP, 1990.

Gibson, Donald. "Text and Countertext in Toni Morrison's *The Bluest Eye.*" *LIT* 1 (1989): 19–32.

Gillespie, Diane and Missy Kubitschek. "Who Cares? Women-Centered Psychology in *Sula.*" *Black American Literature Forum* 24.1 (Spring 1990): 21–48.

Gilman, Sander. *Difference and Pathology: Stereotypes of Sexuality, Race, and Madness.* Ithaca: Cornell UP, 1985.

———. *Inscribing the Other.* Lincoln: U of Nebraska P, 1991.

———. *Jewish Self-Hatred: Anti-Semitism and the Hidden Language of the Jews.* Baltimore: Johns Hopkins UP, 1986.

Göbel, Walter. "Canonizing Toni Morrison." *AAA: Arbeiten aus Anglistik und Amerikanistik* 15.2 (1990): 127–37.

Goldberg, Carl. *Understanding Shame.* Northvale, NJ: Jason Aronson, 1991.

Gordon, Lewis. *Bad Faith and Antiblack Racism.* Atlantic Highlands, NJ: Humanities Press International, 1995.

Grant, Robert. "Absence into Presence: The Thematics of Memory and 'Missing' Subjects in Toni Morrison's *Sula.*" McKay, *Critical Essays on Toni Morrison* 90–103.

Gray, Paul. "Paradise Found." Rev. of *Paradise. Time* 151. 2 (19 January 1998): 62–68.

———. "Riffs on Violence." Rev. of *Jazz. Time* 139.17 (April 27, 1992): 70.

Greenslade, William. *Degeneration, Culture and the Novel: 1880–1940.* Cambridge: Cambridge UP, 1994.

Grier, William H. and Price M. Cobbs. *Black Rage.* 1968. New York: BasicBooks/HarperCollins, 1992.

Gubar, Susan. *Racechanges: White Skin, Black Face in American Culture.* New York: Oxford UP, 1997.

Hacker, Andrew. *Two Nations: Black and White, Separate, Hostile, Unequal.* 1992. New York: Ballantine/Random House, 1995.

Hamilton, Kenneth. *Black Towns and Profit: Promotion and Development in the Trans-Appalachian West, 1877–1915.* Urbana: U of Illinois P, 1991.

Hardack, Richard. "'A Music Seeking Its Words': Double-Timing and Double-Consciousness in Toni Morrison's *Jazz*." *Black Warrior Review* 19.2 (Spring/Summer 1993): 151–71.

Harding, Wendy and Jacky Martin. *A World of Difference: An Inter-Cultural Study of Toni Morrison's Novels*. Westport: Greenwood, 1994.

Harris, A. Leslie. "Myth as Structure in Toni Morrison's *Song of Solomon*." *MELUS* 7.3 (Fall 1980): 69–76.

Harris, Middleton, ed. *The Black Book*. New York: Random House, 1974.

Harris, Trudier. *Exorcising Blackness: Historical and Literary Lynching and Burning Rituals*. Bloomington: Indiana UP, 1984.

———. *Fiction and Folklore: The Novels of Toni Morrison*. Knoxville: U of Tennessee P, 1991.

Hawthorne, Evelyn. "On Gaining the Double-Vision: *Tar Baby* as Diasporean Novel." *Black American Literature Forum* 22.1 (Spring 1988): 97–107.

Hedin, Raymond. "The Structuring of Emotion in Black American Fiction." *Novel* 16.1 (Fall 1982): 35–54.

Heinze, Denise. *The Dilemma of "Double-Consciousness": Toni Morrison's Novels*. Athens: U of Georgia P, 1993.

Henderson, Mae. "Toni Morrison's *Beloved*: Re-Membering the Body as Historical Text." *Comparative American Identities: Race, Sex, and Nationality in the Modern Text*. Ed. Hortense Spillers. New York: Routledge, 1991. 62–86.

Herman, Judith Lewis. *Father-Daughter Incest*. Cambridge: Harvard UP, 1981.

———. "Father-Daughter Incest." *Post-Traumatic Therapy and Victims of Violence*. Ed. Frank Ochberg. New York: Brunner/Mazel, 1988. 175–95.

———. *Trauma and Recovery*. New York: HarperCollins/BasicBooks, 1992.

Hernton, Calvin. *Sex and Racism in America*. 1965. New York: Anchor/Doubleday, 1992.

Hess, David. *Samba in the Night: Spiritism in Brazil*. New York: Columbia UP, 1994.

———. *Spirits and Scientists: Ideology, Spiritism, and Brazilian Culture*. University Park: Pennsylvania State UP, 1991.

Higginbotham, A. Leon. *Shades of Freedom: Racial Politics and Presumptions of the American Legal Process*. New York: Oxford UP, 1996.

Hine, Darlene. "Female Slave Resistance: The Economics of Sex." *Western Journal of Black Studies* 3 (Summer 1979): 123–27.

Hirsch, Marianne. "Knowing Their Names: Toni Morrison's *Song of Solomon*." *New Essays on Song of Solomon*. Ed. Valerie Smith. Cambridge: Cambridge UP, 1995. 69–92.

―――. "Maternity and Rememory: Toni Morrison's *Beloved*." *Representations of Motherhood*. Ed. Donna Bassin, Margaret Honey, and Meryle Kaplan. New Haven: Yale UP, 1994. 92–110.

―――. *The Mother/Daughter Plot: Narrative, Psychoanalysis, Feminism*. Bloomington: Indiana UP, 1989.

Hochschild, Jennifer. *The New American Dilemma: Liberal Democracy and School Desegregation*. New Haven: Yale UP, 1984.

Hoffarth-Zelloe, Monika. "Resolving the Paradox?: An Interlinear Reading of Toni Morrison's *Sula*." *Journal of Narrative Technique* 22.2 (Spring 1992): 114–27.

Holloway, Karla. "African Values and Western Chaos." Holloway and Demetrakopoulos 117–29.

―――. "*Beloved*: A Spiritual." *Callaloo* 13 (1990): 516–25.

―――. "The Language and Music of Survival." Holloway and Demetrakopoulos 37–47.

―――. "Response to *Sula*: Acknowledgment of Womanself." Holloway and Demetrakopoulos 67–81.

Holloway, Karla and Stephanie Demetrakopoulos. *New Dimensions of Spirituality: A Biracial and Bicultural Reading of the Novels of Toni Morrison*. Westport: Greenwood, 1987.

"Holocaust in D.C." *New Republic* 212.13 (27 March 1995): 9.

hooks, bell. *Ain't I a Woman: Black Women and Feminism*. Boston: South End, 1981.

―――. *Black Looks: Race and Representation*. Boston: South End, 1992.

―――. *Killing Rage: Ending Racism*. 1995. New York: Owl/Holt, 1996.

―――. *Outlaw Culture: Resisting Representations*. New York: Routledge, 1994.

Horvitz, Deborah. "Nameless Ghosts: Possession and Dispossession in *Beloved*." *Studies in American Fiction* 17.2 (Autumn 1989): 157–67.

Hulbert, Ann. "Romance and Race." Rev. of *Jazz*. *New Republic* 206.20 (May 18, 1992): 43–48.

Janoff-Bulman, Ronnie. *Shattered Assumptions: Towards a New Psychology of Trauma*. New York: Free/Macmillan, 1992.

Jessee, Sharon. " 'Tell me your earrings': Time and the Marvelous in Toni Morrison's *Beloved*." *Memory, Narrative, and Identity: New Essays in Ethnic American Literatures*. Ed. Amritjit Singh, Joseph Skerrett, Jr., Robert Hogan. Boston: Northeastern UP, 1994. 198–211.

Jewell, K. Sue. *From Mammy to Miss America and Beyond: Cultural Images and the Shaping of US Social Policy*. New York: Routledge, 1993.

Johnson, Diane. "The Oppressor in the Next Room." *New York Review of Books* (10 Nov. 1977): 6, 8.

Johnson, James Weldon. "Harlem: The Culture Capital." Locke, *New Negro* 301–11.

Jones, Bessie and Audrey Vinson. *The World of Toni Morrison: Explorations in Literary Criticism*. Dubuque: Kendall/Hunt, 1985.

Jones, Carolyn. "*Sula* and *Beloved*: Images of Cain in the Novels of Toni Morrison." *African American Review* 27.4 (1993): 615–26.

Joyce, Joyce Ann. "'Who the Cap Fit': Unconsciousness and Unconscionableness in the Criticism of Houston A. Baker, Jr., and Henry Louis Gates, Jr." *New Literary History* 18. 2 (Winter 1987): 371–84.

Kakutani, Michiko. "Wary Town, Worthy Women, Unredeemable Men." Rev. of *Paradise. New York Times* 6 January 1998: B8.

Kane, Eugene. "With New Novel, Toni Morrison Proves She's up to Nobel Challenge." Rev. of *Paradise. Milwaukee Journal Sentinel* 25 January 1998. <http://www.onwis.com/news/sunday/books/0125bkpar.stm> (11 February 1998).

Kaufman, Gershen. *Shame: The Power of Caring*. 1980. 3rd ed., revised and expanded. Rochester, VT: Schenkman, 1992.

———. *The Psychology of Shame: Theory and Treatment of Shame-Based Syndromes*. New York: Springer, 1989.

Keenan, Sally. "'Four Hundred Years of Silence': Myth, History, and Motherhood in Toni Morrison's *Beloved*." *Recasting the World: Writing after Colonialism*. Ed. Jonathan White. Baltimore: Johns Hopkins UP, 1993. 45–81.

Kovel, Joel. *White Racism: A Psychohistory*. 1970. New York: Columbia UP, 1984.

Kowalewski, Michael. *Deadly Musings: Violence and Verbal Form in American Fiction*. Princeton: Princeton UP, 1993.

Krumholz, Linda. "The Ghosts of Slavery: Historical Recovery in Toni Morrison's *Beloved*." *African American Review* 26.3 (Fall 1992): 395–408.

Kuenz, Jane. "*The Bluest Eye*: Notes on History, Community, and Black Female Subjectivity." *African American Review* 27.3 (1993): 421–31.

LaCapra, Dominick. "Introduction." *The Bounds of Race: Perspectives on Hegemony and Resistance*. Ed. Dominick LaCapra. Ithaca: Cornell UP, 1991. 1–16.

Lane, Christopher. "The Psychoanalysis of Race: An Introduction." *The Psychoanalysis of Race*. Ed. Christopher Lane. New York: Columbia UP, 1998. 1–37.

Langer, Lawrence. *Holocaust Testimonies: The Ruins of Memory*. New Haven: Yale UP, 1991.

Laub, Dori. "Bearing Witness, or the Vicissitudes of Listening." *Testimony: Crises of Witnessing in Literature, Psychoanalysis, and History*. By Shoshana Felman and Dori Laub. New York: Routledge, 1992. 57–74.

Lee, Dorothy. "*Song of Solomon*: To Ride the Air." *Black American Literature Forum* 16.2 (Summer 1982): 64–70.

Leonard, John. "Shooting Women." Rev. of *Paradise*. *Nation* 266.3 (26 January 1998): 25–29.

———. "Travels with Toni." *Nation* 258.2 (January 17, 1994): 59–62.

Lepow, Lauren. "Paradise Lost and Found: Dualism and Edenic Myth in Toni Morrison's *Tar Baby*." *Contemporary Literature* 28.3 (Fall 1987): 363–77.

Lerner, Gerda, ed. *Black Women in White America: A Documentary History*. 1972. New York: Vintage/Random House, 1973.

Levine, Lawrence. *Black Culture and Black Consciousness: Afro-American Folk Thought from Slavery to Freedom*. New York: Oxford UP, 1977.

Levy, Andrew. "Telling *Beloved*." *Texas Studies in Literature and Language* 33.1 (Spring 1991): 114–23.

Lewis, Helen Block. "Introduction: Shame—the 'Sleeper' in Psychopathology." Helen Lewis, *Role of Shame* 1–28.

———. "Preface." Helen Lewis, *Role of Shame* xi–xii.

———. "The Role of Shame in Depression Over the Life Span." Helen Lewis, *Role of Shame* 29–50.

——— (ed). *The Role of Shame in Symptom Formation*. Hillsdale, NJ: Lawrence Erlbaum, 1987.

———. *Shame and Guilt in Neurosis*. New York: International Universities, 1971.

———. "Shame and the Narcissistic Personality." Nathanson, *Many Faces of Shame* 93–132.

Lewis, Michael. *Shame: The Exposed Self*. 1992. New York: Free Press/Simon and Schuster, 1995.

Liscio, Lorraine. "*Beloved's* Narrative: Writing Mother's Milk." *Tulsa Studies in Women's Literature* 11.1 (Spring 1992): 31–46.

Locke, Alain, ed. *The New Negro: Voices of the Harlem Renaissance*. 1925. New York: Atheneum/Macmillan, 1992.

Lounsberry, Barbara and Grace Ann Hovet. "Principles of Perception in Toni Morrison's *Sula*." *Black American Literature Forum* 13.4 (Winter 1979): 126–33.

MacKethan, Lucinda. "Names to Bear Witness: The Theme and Tradition of Naming in Toni Morrison's *Song of Solomon*." *CEA Critic* 49.2–4 (Winter 1986–Summer 1987): 199–207.

Majors, Richard and Janet Billson. *Cool Pose: The Dilemmas of Black Manhood in America*. New York: Lexington/Macmillan, 1992.

Mason, Marilyn. "Shame: Reservoir for Family Secrets." *Secrets in Families and Family Therapy*. Ed. Evan Imber-Black. New York: Norton, 1993. 29–43.

Matza, Diane. "Zora Neale Hurston's *Their Eyes Were Watching God* and Toni Morrison's *Sula*: A Comparison." *MELUS* 12.3 (Fall 1985): 43–54.

Mayer, Elsie. "Recent Fiction—*Jazz* by Toni Morrison." *America* 167.10 (October 10, 1992): 257–58.

Mbalia, Doreatha. *Toni Morrison's Developing Class Consciousness*. Selinsgrove: Susquehanna UP, 1991.

McBride, Dwight. "Speaking the Unspeakable: On Toni Morrison, African American Intellectuals and the Uses of Essentialist Rhetoric." *Modern Fiction Studies* 39.3–4 (Fall-Winter 1993): 755–76.

McDowell, Deborah. "Harlem Nocturne." *Women's Review of Books* 9.9 (June 1992): 1, 3–5. Rpt. Draper, *Contemporary Literary Criticism Yearbook 1993*, 252–55.

———. "Reading Family Matters." *Changing Our Own Words: Essays on Criticism, Theory, and Writing by Black Women*. Ed. Cheryl Wall. New Brunswick: Rutgers UP, 1989. 75–97.

———. "'The Self and the Other': Reading Toni Morrison's *Sula* and the Black Female Text." McKay, *Critical Essays on Toni Morrison* 77–90.

McKay, Nellie, ed. *Critical Essays on Toni Morrison*. Boston: G. K. Hall, 1988.

McKinstry, Susan. "A Ghost of An/Other Chance: The Spinster-Mother in Toni Morrison's *Beloved*." *Old Maids to Radical Spinsters: Unmarried Women in the Twentieth-Century Novel*. Ed. Laura Doan. Urbana: U of Illinois P, 1991. 259–74.

Menand, Louis. "The War Between Men and Women." Rev. of *Paradise*. *The New Yorker* 73.42 (12 January 1998): 78–82.

Mendelsohn, Jane. "Harlem on Her Mind: Toni Morrison's Language of Love." Rev. of *Jazz*. *Village Voice—Literary Supplement* 37.19 (May 12,1992): S25–S26.

Middleton, Joyce. "From Orality to Literacy: Oral Memory in Toni Morrison's *Song of Solomon*." *New Essays on Song of Solomon*. Ed. Valerie Smith. Cambridge: Cambridge UP, 1995. 19–39.

Middleton, Victoria. "*Sula*: An Experimental Life." *CLA Journal* 28.4 (June 1985): 367–81.

Miller, Jane. "New Romance." Rev. of *Jazz*. *London Review of Books* 14.9 (May 14, 1992): 6. Rpt. Draper, *Contemporary Literary Criticism Yearbook 1993*, 246–48.

Miller, Susan. *The Shame Experience*. Hillsdale, NJ: Analytic, 1993.

Miner, Madonne. "Lady No Longer Sings the Blues: Rape, Madness, and Silence in *The Bluest Eye*." *Toni Morrison: Modern Critical Views*. Ed. Harold Bloom. New York: Chelsea, 1990. 85–99. (Rpt. *Conjuring*:

Black Women, Fiction, and Literary Tradition. Ed. Marjorie Pryse and Hortense Spillers. Bloomington: Indiana UP, 1985. 176–91.)

Mobley, Marilyn. "Call and Response: Voice, Community, and Dialogic Structures in Toni Morrison's *Song of Solomon*." *New Essays on Song of Solomon*. Ed. Valerie Smith. Cambridge: Cambridge UP, 1995. 41–68.

——. *Folk Roots and Mythic Wings in Sarah Orne Jewett and Toni Morrison: The Cultural Function of Narrative*. Baton Rouge: Louisiana State UP, 1991.

Montgomery, Maxine. "A Pilgrimage to the Origins: The Apocalypse as Structure and Theme in Toni Morrison's *Sula*." *Black American Literature Forum* 23.1 (Spring 1989): 127–37.

Morgan, Joan. "Toni Morrison Warns of Lurking Fascism." *Black Issues in Higher Education* 12.2 (23 March 1995): 34–35.

Morrison, Andrew. *The Culture of Shame*. New York: Ballantine/Random House, 1996.

——. *Shame: The Underside of Narcissism*. Hillsdale, NJ: Analytic, 1989.

Morrison, Nancy. "The Role of Shame in Schizophrenia." Helen Lewis, *Role of Shame* 51–87.

Morton, Patricia. *Disfigured Images: The Historical Assault on Afro-American Women*. Westport, CT: Praeger, 1991.

Moses, Rafael. "Projection, Identification, and Projective Identification: Their Relation to Political Process." *Projection, Identification, Projective Identification*. Ed. Joseph Sandler. Madison, CT: International Universities, 1987. 133–50.

Murphy, Joseph. *Working the Spirit: Ceremonies of the African Diaspora*. Boston: Beacon, 1994.

The Nag Hammadi Library in English. Ed. James Robinson. San Francisco: Harper and Row, 1988.

Nathanson, Donald (ed). *The Many Faces of Shame*. New York: Guilford, 1987.

——. *Shame and Pride: Affect, Sex, and The Birth of the Self*. 1992. New York: Norton, 1994.

——. "The Shame/Pride Axis." Helen Lewis, *Role of Shame in Symptom Formation* 183–205.

——. "A Timetable For Shame." Nathanson, *Many Faces of Shame* 1–63.

Nichols, Michael. *No Place to Hide: Facing Shame So We Can Find Self-Respect*. New York: Simon and Schuster, 1991.

Novak, Phillip. "Signifying Silences: Morrison's Soundings in the Faulknerian Void." *Unflinching Gaze: Morrison and Faulkner Re-Envisioned*. Ed. Carol Kolmerten, Stephen Ross, and Judith Wittenberg. Jackson: UP of Mississippi, 1997. 199–216.

O'Brien, Edna. "Jazz." Rev. of *Jazz*. *New York Times Book Review* 97 (April 5, 1992): 1, 29–30.

Ogunyemi, Chikwenye. "*Sula*: 'A Nigger Joke.'" *Black American Literature Forum* 13.4 (Winter 1979): 130–33.

Omolade, Barbara. "Hearts of Darkness." *Powers of Desire: The Politics of Sexuality*. Ed. Ann Snitow, Christine Stansell, and Sharon Thompson. New York: Monthly Review, 1983. 350–67.

Osagie, Iyunolu. "Is Morrison Also Among the Prophets?: 'Psychoanalytic' Strategies in *Beloved*." *African American Review* 28.3 (1994): 423–40.

O'Shaughnessy, Kathleen. "'Life life life life': The Community as Chorus in *Song of Solomon*." McKay, *Critical Essays on Toni Morrison* 125–33.

Otten, Terry. *The Crime of Innocence in the Fiction of Toni Morrison*. Columbia: U of Missouri P, 1989.

———. "Horrific Love in Toni Morrison's Fiction." *Modern Fiction Studies* 39.3–4 (Fall/Winter 1993): 651–67.

Pagels, Elaine. *The Gnostic Gospels*. New York: Random House, 1979.

Painter, Nell. "Hill, Thomas, and the Use of Racial Stereotype." *Race-ing Justice, En-gendering Power: Essays on Anita Hill, Clarence Thomas, and the Construction of Social Reality*. Ed. Toni Morrison. New York: Pantheon, 1992. 200–14.

———. "Soul Murder and Slavery: Toward a Fully Loaded Cost Accounting." *U.S. History as Women's History: New Feminist Essays*. Ed. Linda Kerber, Alice Kessler-Harris, and Kathryn Kish Sklar. Chapel Hill: U of North Carolina P, 1995. 125–46.

Paquet, Sandra. "The Ancestor as Foundation in *Their Eyes Were Watching God* and *Tar Baby*." *Callaloo* 13 (1990): 499–515.

Patterson, Orlando. *Slavery and Social Death: A Comparative Study*. Cambridge: Harvard UP, 1982.

Peach, Linden. *Toni Morrison*. New York: St. Martin's Press, 1995.

Pesch, Josef. "*Beloved*: Toni Morrison's Post-Apocalyptic Novel." *Canadian Review of Comparative Literature* 20.3–4 (September-December 1993): 395–408.

Peterson, Nancy. "Introduction: Canonizing Toni Morrison." *Modern Fiction Studies* 39.3–4 (Fall/Winter 1993): 461–79.

Phelan, James. "Toward a Rhetorical Reader–Response Criticism: The Difficult, The Stubborn, and the Ending of *Beloved*." *Modern Fiction Studies* 39.3–4 (Fall/Winter 1993): 709–28.

Piper, Adrian. "Passing for White, Passing for Black." *Transition* 58 (1992): 4–32.

Portales, Marco. "Toni Morrison's *The Bluest Eye*: Shirley Temple and Cholly." *Centennial Review* 30.4 (Fall 1986): 496–506.

Prose, Francine. "Paradise" by Toni Morrison." Rev. of *Paradise. People Magazine*. <http://www. pathfinder. com/people/980119/picksnpans/pages/pages1.html> (22 January 1998).

Rabinowitz, Paula. "Naming, Magic and Documentary: The Subversion of the Narrative in *Song of Solomon, Ceremony* and *China Men*." *Feminist Re-Visions: What Has Been and Might Be*. Ed. Vivian Patraka and Louise Tilly. Ann Arbor: U of Michigan Women's Studies Program, 1983. 26–42.

Raboteau, Albert. "African-Americans, Exodus, and the American Israel." *African-American Christianity: Essays in History*. Ed. Paul Johnson. Berkeley: U of California P, 1994. 1–17.

Rainwater, Lee and William Yancey, eds. *The Moynihan Report and the Politics of Controversy*. Cambridge, MA: MIT P, 1967.

Rampersad, Arnold. "Introduction." Locke, *The New Negro* ix–xxiii.

Reckley, Ralph. "On Looking into Morrison's *Tar Baby*." *Amid Visions and Revisions: Poetry and Criticism on Literature and the Arts*. Ed. Burney Hollis. Baltimore: Morgan State UP, 1985. 132–38.

Reddy, Maureen. "The Tripled Plot and Center of *Sula*." *Black American Literature Forum* 22. 1 (Spring 1988): 29–45.

Reilly, Joseph. "Under the White Gaze: Jim Crow, the Nobel, and the Assault on Toni Morrison." *Monthly Review* 45.11 (April 1994): 41–46.

Reyes, Angelita. "Ancient Properties in the New World: The Paradox of the 'Other' in Toni Morrison's *Tar Baby*." *Black Scholar* 17.2 (March-April 1986): 19–25.

———. "Politics and Metaphors of Materialism in Paule Marshall's *Praisesong for the Widow* and Toni Morrison's *Tar Baby*." *Politics and the Muse: Studies in the Politics of Recent American Literature*. Ed. Adam Sorkin. Bowling Green: Bowling Green State University Popular P, 1989. 179–205.

Rhodes, Jewell. "Toni Morrison's *Beloved*: Ironies of a 'Sweet Home' Utopia in a Dystopian Slave Society." *Utopian Studies* 1.1 (1990): 77–92.

Roberts, Diane. *The Myth of Aunt Jemima: Representations of Race and Region*. New York: Routledge, 1994.

Roberts, John. *From Trickster to Badman: The Black Folk Hero in Slavery and Freedom*. Philadelphia: U of Pennsylvania P, 1989.

Rodrigues, Eusebio. "Experiencing *Jazz*." *Modern Fiction Studies* 39.3–4 (Fall/Winter 1993): 733–54.

———. "The Telling of *Beloved*." *The Journal of Narrative Technique* 21.2 (Spring 1991): 153–69.

Rodriguez, Jeanette. *Our Lady of Guadalupe: Faith and Empowerment Among Mexican-American Women*. Austin: U of Texas P, 1994.

Rogers, J. A. "Jazz at Home." Locke, *The New Negro* 216–24.

Rooks, Noliwe. *Hair Raising: Beauty, Culture, and African American Women.* New Brunswick: Rutgers UP, 1996.

Rosenberg, Ruth. "'And the Children May Know Their Names': Toni Morrison's *Song of Solomon.*" *Literary Onomastics Studies* 8 (1981): 195–219.

———. "Seeds in Hard Ground: Black Girlhood in *The Bluest Eye.*" *Black American Literature Forum* 21.4 (Winter 1987): 435–45.

Rozin, Paul, Jonathan Haidt, Clark McCauley. "Disgust." *Handbook of Emotions.* Ed. Michael Lewis and Jeannette Haviland. New York: Guilford, 1993. 575–94.

Rubenstein, Roberta. "History and Story, Sign and Design: Faulknerian and Postmodern Voices in *Jazz.*" *Unflinching Gaze: Morrison and Faulkner Re-Envisioned.* Ed. Carol Kolmerten, Stephen Ross, and Judith Wittenberg. UP of Mississippi, 1997. 152–64.

Rushdy, Ashraf. "Daughters Signifyin(g) History: The Example of Toni Morrison's *Beloved.*" *American Literature* 64.3 (September 1992): 567–97.

Russell, Kathy, Midge Wilson, and Ronald Hall. *The Color Complex: The Politics of Skin Color Among African Americans.* New York: Harcourt Brace, 1992.

Sale, Maggie. "Call and Response as Critical Method: African-American Oral Traditions and *Beloved.*" *African American Review* 26.1 (1992): 41–50.

Samuels, Wilfrid. "Liminality and the Search for Self in Toni Morrison's *Song of Solomon.*" *Minority Voices* 5.1–2 (Spring-Fall 1981): 59–68.

Samuels, Wilfred and Clenora Hudson-Weems. *Toni Morrison.* Boston: Twayne, 1990.

San Juan, Epifanio. *Racial Formations/Critical Transformations: Articulations of Power in Ethnic and Racial Studies in the United States.* Atlantic Highlands, NJ: Humanities, 1992.

Scheff, Thomas. *Bloody Revenge: Emotions, Nationalism, and War.* Boulder: Westview, 1994.

———. "The Shame-Rage Spiral: A Case Study of an Interminable Quarrel." Helen Lewis, *Role of Shame* 109–49.

Scheff, Thomas, and Suzanne Retzinger. *Emotions and Violence: Shame and Rage in Destructive Conflicts.* Lexington, MA: Lexington/Heath, 1991.

Scheff, Thomas, Suzanne Retzinger, and Michael Ryan. "Crime, Violence, and Self-Esteem: Review and Proposals." *The Social Importance of Self-Esteem.* Ed. Andrew Mecca, Neil Smelser, and John Vasconcellos. Berkeley: U of California P, 1989. 165–99.

Schmudde, Carol. "Knowing When to Stop: A Reading of Toni Morrison's *Beloved.*" *CLA Journal* 37.2 (December 1993): 121–35.

Schneider, Carl. *Shame, Exposure, and Privacy.* 1977. New York: Norton, 1992.

Schneiderman, Stuart. *Saving Face: America and the Politics of Shame.* New York: Knopf, 1995.

Scruggs, Charles. "The Invisible City in Toni Morrison's *Beloved.*" *Arizona Quarterly* 48.3 (Autumn 1992): 95–132.

Shannon, Anna. "'We Was Girls Together': A Study of Toni Morrison's *Sula.*" *Midwestern Miscellany* 10 (1982): 9–22.

Shields, Carol. "Heaven on Earth." Rev. of *Paradise. Washington Post* 11 January 1998: X01. <http://wp4.washingtonpost.com/wp-s...te/ 1998-01/11/0261-011198-idx.html> (30 January 1998).

Skolnick, Neil and Jody Davies. "Secrets in Clinical Work: A Relational Point of View." *Relational Perspectives in Psychoanalysis.* Ed. Neil Skolnick and Susan Warshaw. Hillsdale, NJ: Analytic, 1992. 217–38.

Smith, Dinitia. "Mixing Tragedy and Folklore." Rev. of *Paradise. New York Times* 8 January 1998: B1–B2.

Smith, Valerie. "Reading the Intersection of Race and Gender in Narratives of Passing." *Diacritics* 24.2–3 (Summer–Fall 1994): 43–57.

Spallino, Chiara. "*Song of Solomon*: An Adventure in Structure." *Callaloo* 8.3 (Fall 1985): 510–24.

Spillers, Hortense. "A Hateful Passion, a Lost Love." *Toni Morrison: Modern Critical Views.* Ed. Harold Bloom. New York, Chelsea, 1990. 27–54. (Rpt. *Feminist Studies* 9.2 [Summer 1983]: 293–323).

Stave, Shirley. "Toni Morrison's *Beloved* and the Vindication of Lilith." *South Atlantic Review* 58.1 (January 1993): 49–66.

Stein, Karen. "Toni Morrison's *Sula*: A Black Woman's Epic." *Black American Literature Forum* 18.4 (Winter 1984): 146–50.

Steinberg, Marlene. "Systematizing Dissociation: Symptomatology and Diagnostic Assessment." *Dissociation: Culture, Mind, and Body.* Ed. David Spiegel. Washington: American Psychiatric, 1994. 59–88.

Stepan, Nancy. "Biological Degeneration: Races and Proper Places." *Degeneration: The Dark Side of Progress.* Ed. J. Edward Chamberlin and Sander Gilman. New York: Columbia UP, 1985. 97–120.

———. "Race and Gender: The Role of Analogy in Science." *Anatomy of Racism.* Ed. David Goldberg. Minneapolis: U of Minnesota P, 1990. 38–57.

Stepan, Nancy, and Sander Gilman. "Appropriating the Idioms of Science: The Rejection of Scientific Racism." *The Bounds of Race: Perspectives on Hegemony and Resistance.* Ed. Dominick LaCapra. Ithaca: Cornell UP, 1991. 72–103.

Story, Ralph. "An Excursion into the Black World: The 'Seven Days' in Toni Morrison's *Song of Solomon.*" *Black American Literature Forum* 23.1 (Spring 1989): 149–58.

Stuart, Andrea. "Blue Notes." Rev. of *Jazz*. *New Statesman and Society* 5.200 (May 1, 1992): 39–40.

Tanner, Laura. *Intimate Violence: Reading Rape and Torture in Twentieth-Century Fiction*. Bloomington: Indiana UP, 1994.

Tate, Claudia. *Psychoanalysis and Black Novels: Desire and the Protocols of Race*. New York: Oxford UP, 1998.

Taylor, Quintard. *In Search of the Racial Frontier: African Americans in the American West: 1528–1990*. New York: Norton, 1998.

Thomas, Kendall. "Strange Fruit." *Race-ing Justice, En-gendering Power: Essays on Anita Hill, Clarence Thomas, and the Construction of Social Reality*. Ed. Toni Morrison. New York: Pantheon, 1992. 364–89.

Todd, Richard. "Toni Morrison and Canonicity: Acceptance or Appropriation?" *Rewriting the Dream: Reflections on the Changing American Literary Canon*. Ed. W. M. Verhoeven. Amsterdam-Atlanta: Rodopi, 1992. 43–59.

Tomkins, Silvan. *Affect Imagery Consciousness. Vol. 2. The Negative Affects*. New York: Springer, 1963.

Tompkins, Jane. "Mysteries of the Flesh." Rev. of *Paradise*. *Brightleaf: A Southern Review of Books* March/April 1998. <http://www.brightleaf-review.com/Mar98/tompkins.html> (23 June 1998).

Travis, Molly. "*Beloved* and *Middle Passage*: Race, Narrative, and the Critic's Essentialism." *Narrative* 2.3 (October 1994): 179–200.

Traylor, Eleanor. "The Fabulous World of Toni Morrison: *Tar Baby*." McKay, *Critical Essays on Toni Morrison* 135–50. (Rpt. *Confirmation: An Anthology of African American Women*. Ed. Amiri Baraka and Amina Baraka [New York: Quill, 1983]: 333–52.)

Turbide, Diane. "Taking the A Train: Toni Morrison Re-creates Harlem at its Peak." Rev. of *Jazz*. *Maclean's* 105.22 (June 1, 1992): 51.

Turner, Patricia. "Paradise Lost." Rev. of *Paradise*. *San Francisco Chronicle* 11 January 1998. <http://www.sfgate.com/cgi-bin/chro...tory=/chronicle/archive/1998/01/11> (14 January 1998).

Ulman, Richard and Doris Brothers. *The Shattered Self: A Psychoanalytic Study of Trauma*. Hillsdale, NJ: Analytic, 1988.

van der Kolk, Bessel. "Foreword." *Countertransference in the Treatment of PTSD*. Ed. John Wilson and Jacob Lindy. New York: Guilford, 1994. vii–xii.

van der Kolk, Bessel, and Onno van der Hart. "The Intrusive Past: The Flexibility of Memory and the Engraving of Trauma." *American Imago* 48.4 (Winter 1991): 425–54.

Van Der Zee, James, Owen Dodson, Camille Billops. *The Harlem Book of the Dead*. Dobbs Ferry: Morgan and Morgan, 1978.

Voeks, Robert. *Sacred Leaves of Candomblé: African Magic, Medicine, and Religion in Brazil.* Austin: U of Texas P, 1997.

Wagner, Linda. "Toni Morrison: Mastery of Narrative." *Contemporary American Women Writers: Narrative Strategies.* Ed. Catherine Rainwater and William Scheick. Lexington: UP of Kentucky, 1985. 191–205.

Waites, Elizabeth. *Trauma and Survival: Post-Traumatic and Dissociative Disorders in Women.* New York: Norton, 1993.

Walton, Anthony. "Patriots." *Lure and Loathing: Essays on Race, Identity, and the Ambivalence of Assimilation.* Ed. Gerald Early. New York: Allen Lane/Penguin, 1993. 245–63.

Wedertz-Furtado, Utelinde. "Historical Dimensions in Toni Morrison's *Song of Solomon.*" *History and Tradition in Afro-American Culture.* Ed. Günter Lenz. Frankfurt: Campus Verlag, 1984. 222–41.

Weinstein, Philip. *What Else But Love? The Ordeal of Race in Faulkner and Morrison.* New York: Columbia UP, 1996.

Weisenburger, Steven. *Modern Medea: A Family Story of Slavery and Child-Murder From the Old South.* New York: Hillard Wang/Farrar, Straus, and Giroux, 1998.

Werner, Craig. "The Briar Patch as Modernist Myth: Morrison, Barthes and Tar Baby As-Is." McKay, *Critical Essays on Toni Morrison* 150–67.

West, Cornel. *Race Matters.* 1993. New York: Vintage/Random House, 1994.

Wiegman, Robyn. *American Anatomies: Theorizing Race and Gender.* Durham: Duke UP, 1995.

Wilson, John and Jacob Lindy. *Countertransference in the Treatment of PTSD.* New York: Guilford, 1994.

Wilson, William Julius. *The Declining Significance of Race: Blacks and Changing American Institutions.* Chicago: U of Chicago P, 1978.

Woidat, Caroline. "Talking Back to Schoolteacher: Morrison's Confrontation with Hawthorne in *Beloved.*" *Modern Fiction Studies* 39.3–4 (Fall/Winter 1993): 527–46.

Wolfe, Bernard. "Uncle Remus and the Malevolent Rabbit: 'Takes a Limber-Toe Gemmun fer ter Jump Jim Crow.'" *Critical Essays on Joel Chandler Harris.* Ed. R. Bruce Bickley, Jr. Boston: G. K. Hall, 1981. 70–84.

Wolff, Cynthia. "'Margaret Garner': A Cinncinnati Story." *Discovering Difference: Contemporary Essays in American Culture.* Ed. Christoph Lohmann. Bloomington: Indiana UP, 1993. 105–22. (Rpt. *Massachusetts Review* 32 [1991]: 417–40.)

Wright, Bobby. *The Psychopathic Racial Personality and Other Essays.* Chicago: Third World, 1984.

Wurmser, Léon. *The Mask of Shame.* 1981. Northvale, NJ: Jason Aronson, 1994.

————. "Shame: The Veiled Companion of Narcissism." *The Many Faces of Shame*. Ed. Donald Nathanson. New York: Guilford, 1987. 64–92.

Wyatt, Jean. "Giving Body to the Word: The Maternal Symbolic in Toni Morrison's *Beloved*." *PMLA* 108.3 (May 1993): 474–88.

Yanuck, Julius. "The Garner Fugitive Slave Case." *The Mississippi Valley Historical Review* 40 (June 1953-March 1954): 47–66.

Index

savage and dangerous primitive, 105, 112–13, 114–15, 116, 121–22; stigmatized racial identity of, 105, 112–14, 116, 117; Tar Baby story, retelling of, 125

—Valerian Street: culpability of, 111–12; as a father, 111–12; marriage of, 110; physical decline of, 112, 116; plantation world of, 109; as a white capitalist and colonizer, 109–10; and white master, dethroning of, 109–10, 112, 116

—Margaret Street: as child abuser, 109, 110–11; marriage of, 110; Son, response to, 113, 121–22; as an unnatural woman, 110–11

—Sydney and Ondine: contempt for black islanders, expression of, 108; middle-class identity of, 108, 113–14; as Philadelphia Negroes, 108, 114, 230n.3; pride of, 108; Son, shaming of, 113–14

—Thérèse: Americans, story about, 109; contempt for black Americans, 108–09; Jadine, indictment of, 109, 128; as a maternal figure, 107, 128; Son, response to, 109

Tate, Claudia, 217n.1
Taylor, Quintard, 236–37n.2
Thomas, Kendall, 220n.5
Todd, Richard, 162
Tomkins, Silvan, 9, 15, 36, 58, 64, 96
Tompkins, Jane, 213–14
Trauma: and the African-American experience, 3, 13; and children, 8; and classical psychoanalytic theory, 6–7, 217–18n.2; cultural denial of, 6, 12–13, 217–18n.2, 224n.1; and dissociation, 7; forgotten history of, 6, 217–18n.2; and the individual, 6–8; intergenerational transmission of, 8; as link between cultures, 3–4; and slavery, 13, 218–19n.4; trauma sur-

vivors, diminished life of, 8; trauma victim's story, therapists' responses to, 223–24n.11 traumatic events, definition of, 3, 7; traumatic events, victim's responses to, 7, 218n.2; traumatic memory, description of, 7. *See also* individual novels

Travis, Molly, 162
Traylor, Eleanor, 126
Turbide, Diane, 188
Turner, Patricia, 192

Ulman, Richard, 6

van der Hart, Onno. *See* van der Kolk, Bessel
van der Kolk, Bessel, 6, 7, 8, 100, 134
Van Der Zee, James, 179
Vinson, Audrey. *See* Jones, Bessie
Voeks, Robert, 238–39, 240 n. 5, 241n.6

Wagner, Linda, 70
Waites, Elizabeth, 6, 8, 59, 173
Walton, Anthony, 17–18
Wedertz-Furtado, Utelinde, 227n.6
Weinstein, Philip, 182–83
Weisenburger, Steven, 232n.1, n.2, n.3
Werner, Craig, 230n. 1
West, Cornel, 13, 15–16
Wiegman, Robyn, 114, 116, 133
Wilson, John, 223–24n.11
Wilson, Midge. *See* Russell, Kathy
Wilson, William Julius, 220n.7
Woidat, Caroline, 161
Wolfe, Bernard, 229–30n.1
Wolff, Cynthia, 133
Wright, Bobby, 228n.6
Wurmser, Léon, 9, 10, 11, 15, 35, 36, 40–41, 43, 45, 48, 59, 140, 150, 197
Wyatt, Jean, 147

Yanuck, Julius, 232n.1